THE LIFE OF BENJAMIN DISRAELI
EARL OF BEACONSFIELD

Benjamin D'Israeli the Elder
From a picture at Hughenden

THE LIFE OF
BENJAMIN DISRAELI
EARL OF BEACONSFIELD.

BY WILLIAM FLAVELLE MONYPENNY

VOLUME I.

1804—1837.

WITH PORTRAITS AND ILLUSTRATIONS

Read no history, nothing but biography, for that is life without theory.—CONTARINI FLEMING.

LONDON:
JOHN MURRAY, ALBEMARLE STREET, W.
1910.

CONTENTS OF VOL. I.

LIST OF ILLUSTRATIONS TO VOL. I.

PREFACE

The main source of the biography of which this is the first volume is the great mass of papers bequeathed by Lord Beaconsfield to the late Lord Rowton and now in the keeping of the trustees of the Beaconsfield estate; and my first duty is a grateful recognition of the unfailing kindness and confidence which Lord Rothschild and the other trustees have bestowed upon me since I began my long and arduous enterprise. For this volume, the most difficult and laborious portion of the whole work, it has not been possible to derive much assistance from extraneous sources other than those which are accessible to all: my principal obligations are to Lady Layard for Disraeli's correspondence with the Austens; to Sir Herbert Thompson for the letters to William Pyne; and to Captain C. L. Lindsay for some of the original material which formed the basis of the published volume *Lord Beaconsfield's Letters*.

To the King I owe my dutiful acknowledgment of the permission which his Majesty has been graciously pleased to accord me to print the letter to Queen Victoria in Appendix A; and I have to thank Lord Grey, Lord Tennyson, and Constance Lady Haldon for access to, or permission to publish, other single documents. I have also to thank Mr. Coningsby Disraeli for much assistance with the illustrations, in particular for allowing the reproduction of pictures at Hughenden;

and Mr. Moberly Bell and Mr. G. W. Prothero for their kindness in reading the proof sheets and for many valuable criticisms and suggestions.

While still in his youth Disraeli adopted the practice, which he followed scrupulously and consistently to the end of his life, of spelling words such as 'honor,' 'favor,' and so forth, according to their Latin origin; and in passages where his own language is reproduced this spelling has been allowed to stand, though elsewhere the ordinary English usage has been followed.

W. F. M.

OCTOBER, 1910.

CHAPTER I.

Ancestry.

What a famous man believes as to his remote ancestral origins is often of more import than the dry, literal truth, and it will be best, therefore, to begin with the story of the Disraelis as it shaped itself in the mind of the subject of these memoirs.

There have been two great colonies of the Jewish race in Europe—in Spain and in Sarmatia. The origin of the Jews in Spain is lost in the night of time. That it was of great antiquity we have proof. The tradition, never derided, that the Iberian Jews were a Phœnician colony has been favoured by the researches of modern antiquaries, who have traced the Hebrew language in the ancient names of the localities. . . . We know that in the time of Cicero the Jews had been settled immemorially in Spain. When the Romans, converted to Christianity and acted on by the priesthood, began to trouble the Spanish Jews, it appears by a decree of Constantine that they were owners and cultivators of the soil, a circumstance which alone proves the antiquity and the nobility of their settlement, for the possession of the land is never conceded to a degraded race. The conquest of Spain by the Goths in the fifth and sixth centuries threatened the Spanish Jews, however, with more serious adversaries than the Romans. The Gothic tribes, very recently converted to their Syrian faith, were full of barbaric zeal against those whom they looked upon as the enemies of Jesus. But the Spanish Jews sought assistance from their kinsmen the Saracens on the opposite coast; Spain was invaded and subdued by the Moors, and for several centuries the Jew and the Saracen lived under the same benignant laws and shared the same brilliant prosperity. In the history of Spain during the Saracenic supremacy any distinction of religion or race is no longer traced. And so it came to pass that when at the end of the fourteenth century, after the fell triumph of the Dominicans over the Albigenses, the Holy Inquisition was introduced into Spain, it was reported to Torquemada that two-thirds of the nobility of Arragon—that is to say, of the proprietors of the land—were Jews.

All that these men knew of Christianity was that it was a religion of fire and sword, and that one of its first duties was to revenge some mysterious and inexplicable crime which had been committed ages ago by some unheard-of ancestors of theirs in an unknown land. The inquisitors addressed themselves to the Spanish Jews in the same abrupt and ferocious manner in which the monks saluted the Mexicans and the Peruvians. All those of the Spanish Jews who did not conform after the fall of the Mahomedan kingdoms were expatriated by the victorious Goths, and these refugees were the main source of the Italian Jews, and of the most respectable portion of the Jews of Holland. These exiles found refuge in two republics—Venice and the United Provinces.[1]

After this historic preamble we enter the more dubious region of family tradition and genealogical legend.

My grandfather, who became an English denizen in 1748, was an Italian descendant of one of those Hebrew families whom the Inquisition forced to emigrate from the Spanish Peninsula at the end of the fifteenth century, and who found a refuge in the more tolerant territories of the Venetian Republic. His ancestors had dropped their Gothic surname on their settlement on the terra firma, and, grateful to the God of Jacob who had sustained them through unprecedented trials and guarded them through unheard-of perils, they assumed the name of Disraeli, a name never borne before or since by any other family, in order that their race

[1] *Life of Lord George Bentinck*, ch. 24.

might be for ever recognised. Undisturbed and unmolested they flourished as merchants for more than two centuries under the protection of the lion of St. Mark, which was but just, as the patron Saint of the Republic was himself a child of Israel. But towards the middle of the eighteenth century the altered circumstances of England, favorable, as it was then supposed, to commerce and religious liberty, attracted the attention of my great-grandfather to this island, and he resolved that the youngest of his two sons, Benjamin, the son of his right hand, should settle in a country where the dynasty seemed at length established through the recent failure of Prince Charles Edward, and where public opinion appeared definitively adverse to persecution of creed and conscience.

The Jewish families who were then settled in England were few, though, from their wealth and other circumstances, they were far from unimportant. They were all of them Sephardim—that is to say, Children of Israel, who had never quitted the shores of the Midland Ocean until Torquemada had driven them from their pleasant residences and rich estates in Arragon, and Andalusia, and Portugal, to seek greater blessings even than a clear atmosphere and a glowing sun, amid the marshes of Holland and the fogs of Britain. Most of these families, who held themselves aloof from the Hebrews of Northern Europe, then only occasionally stealing into England, as from an inferior caste, and whose synagogue was reserved only for the Sephardim, are now extinct; while the branch of the great family, which, notwithstanding their own sufferings from prejudice, they had the hardihood to look down upon, have achieved an amount of wealth and consideration which the Sephardim, even with the patronage of Mr. Pelham, never could have contemplated. Nevertheless, at the time when my grandfather settled in England, and when Mr. Pelham, who was very favourable to the Jews, was Prime Minister, there might be found, among other Jewish families settled in this country, the Villa Reals, who brought wealth to these shores almost as great as their name, though that is the second in Portugal, and who have twice allied themselves with the English aristocracy, the Medinas, the Laras—who were our kinsmen—and the Mendez da Costas, who, I believe, still exist.

Whether it were that my grandfather, on his arrival, was not encouraged by those to whom he had a right to look up—which is often our hard case in the outset of life—or whether he was alarmed at the unexpected consequences of Mr.

Pelham's favorable disposition to his countrymen in the disgraceful repeal of the Jew Bill which occurred a very few years after his arrival in this country, I know not; but certainly he appears never to have cordially or intimately mixed with his community. This tendency to alienation was, no doubt, subsequently encouraged by his marriage, which took place in 1765. My grandmother, the beautiful daughter of a family who had suffered from persecution, had imbibed that dislike for her race which the vain are too apt to adopt when they find that they are born to public contempt. The indignant feeling that should be reserved for the persecutor, in the mortification of their disturbed sensibility, is too often visited on the victim; and the cause of annoyance is recognised not in the ignorant malevolence of the powerful, but in the conscientious conviction of the innocent sufferer. Seventeen years, however, elapsed before my grandfather entered into this union, and during that interval he had not been idle. He was only eighteen when he commenced his career and when a great responsibility devolved upon him. He was not unequal to it. He was a man of ardent character; sanguine, courageous, speculative, and fortunate; with a temper which no disappointment could disturb, and a brain, amid reverses, full of resource. He made his fortune in the midway of life, and settled near Enfield, where he formed an Italian garden, entertained his friends, played whist with Sir Horace Mann, who was his great acquaintance, and who had known his brother at Venice as a banker, ate macaroni which was dressed by the Venetian Consul, sang canzonettas, and, notwithstanding a wife who never pardoned him for his name, and a son who disappointed all his plans, and who to the last hour of his life was an enigma to him, lived till he was nearly ninety, and then died in 1817[1] in the full enjoyment of prolonged existence.

My grandfather retired from active business on the eve of that great financial epoch, to grapple with which his talents were well adapted; and when the wars and loans of the Revolution were about to create those families of millionaires, in which he might probably have enrolled his own. That, however, was not our destiny.[2]

Such is Benjamin Disraeli's story of the vicissitudes of his family, such the background of historic truth

[1] He really died in Nov., 1816, at the age of 86.

[2] Memoir of Isaac D'Israeli prefaced to the collected edition of his works published in 1849.

and genealogical legend in which he sought his connexion with the larger vicissitudes of his race. In these ancestral matters we are most of us prone to mistake possibilities for probabilities, and to rear grandiose theories on a very slender foundation of fact. Disraeli was no exception to the rule : indeed, all his days he was haunted, more than most men, by a longing to escape from the sordid details of commonplace life into spacious historical atmospheres. In the present instance he had probably very little precise knowledge to cool his ardent imagination. His father, in spite of his multifarious curiosity, appears never to have troubled himself about his own family antecedents, and Benjamin D'Israeli the elder died before his grandson was of an age to have his curiosity awakened. It need not then surprise us to find that criticism has been busy with the narrative which has just been given. The tradition of an ancestor who took part in the great Jewish exodus from Spain in the time of Ferdinand and Isabella may or may not be well founded, but it is not supported by any independent evidence. The story of the long sojourn in Venice is even more open to suspicion ; no trace of the family having been discovered in Venetian archives till a period subsequent to the migration to England. What we know for certain is that the grandfather Benjamin D'Israeli, who 'became an English denizen in 1748,' had his Italian home not in Venice but at Cento in Ferrara[1] : we know also that a Jewish colony, no doubt mainly of Levantine origin, existed in Ferrara before the Spanish exodus, but that it was largely reinforced by the exiles who fled from Torquemada. The name,[2]

1 In his formal deed of denization in England, dated 1801, he described himself as 'of Cento in Italy.' Cento is best known as the birthplace of the painter Guercino, and it is worthy of note that among the possessions of the D'Israeli family were a couple of pictures by that master which Lord Beaconsfield used to say had been a wedding present to his grandfather from an Italian friend.

2 The whole question of Disraeli origins has been examined with much learning and industry by Mr. Lucien Wolf in two articles contributed to *The Times* on the occasion of the Disraeli centenary in 1904, to which I am indebted for several of the facts here given.

for which we have to be content with a less picturesque derivation than was claimed for it by the man who has made it so famous, is equally consistent either with a Spanish or a Levantine origin. It was only after his arrival in England that Benjamin D'Israeli, the grandfather, began to write it with the D'. His father was one Isaac Israeli, of whom we know nothing besides, and Israeli, it would appear, is an Arabic word meaning Israelite, which from its constant application to individual Jews by the non-Jewish population in Moorish Spain and in the Levant frequently developed into a permanent surname. Thus all that our positive knowledge amounts to is that the D'Israelis were of the seed of Abraham, and that they came proximately from Italy—a land which has produced so many more than its due allotment of the world's great statesmen and rulers.

The circumstances of the young immigrant who came to London to seek his fortune were in all likelihood humble enough, and we need not suppose that when he set out for England the security of the Hanoverian dynasty figured very largely in his calculations. He was content to begin as a clerk in an Anglo-Italian house, and though he presently established himself in a business of his own as an Italian merchant, it was long before real prosperity came to him. To vary the monotony of his business as a merchant he tried experiments in the stock market; but these at first were unfortunate, and though eventually he won a good position as a stockbroker, and even became a member of the Stock Exchange Committee, he was for a time involved in serious difficulties. In 1765, however, he married, as his second[1] wife, one Sarah Siprut de Gabay, who, through her paternal grandmother, inherited the blood

[1] He had previously married in 1756 Rebecca Mendez Furtado, and the offspring of this union was a daughter Rachel, who in her turn became the mother of four daughters by a second marriage with one Angelo Todosto (or Tedesco). Rachel Todosto eventually migrated with her children to Italy, where their descendants are living at the present day.

of the Villa Reals, a fact which her grandson in later days loved to recall. What is more to the point, she seems to have brought her husband both capital and credit, and from this time onward he made steady progress and ultimately attained to substantial prosperity. It is only, however, in the imagination of his grandson that he was ever even a possible rival of the Rothschilds. At his death he left estate real and personal which was sworn under £35,000. In his will he sums up his vicissitudes of residence by describing himself as 'formerly of Enfield in the County of Middlesex, and then of Woodford in the County of Essex and of Old Broad Street, London, but late of Church Street, Stoke Newington,' where he died. His tomb, restored by his grandson when in the plenitude of his fame and greatness, may still be seen in the Portuguese Jews' Cemetery at Mile End, in the East of London.

Benjamin D'Israeli the elder remained to the end of his life a member of the Sephardi congregation of Bevis Marks, and though, as we are told,[1] he was somewhat lax in his observances and took no great interest in the affairs of the Synagogue, he contributed liberally to its support and increased his donations as the growth of his fortune gave him warrant. On one occasion he even served in the minor office of Inspector of the Charity School, though apparently his zeal in the performance of the duties was not remarkable. From the few glimpses we get of him, he seems to have been a man of winning and kindly disposition. His son Isaac, writing after his death, dwells on his 'sweetness of temper and generosity of feeling'; and more than half a century later his grandson still affectionately remembered the 'kind good-natured man who was in the habit of giving me presents when his wife was away.' Far different were Lord Beaconsfield's recollections of his grandmother: 'a demon,' as he described her to Lord Rowton in

[1] Picciotto's *Sketches of Anglo-Jewish History*, p. 295.

his grandiose way, 'only equalled by Sarah Duchess of Marlborough, Frances Anne [Marchioness of Londonderry], and perhaps Catherine of Russia.'

She lived till 1825, when she died, aged 82, and was buried in Willesden Church, where her monument is. She was informally a Protestant at the time of her death. She came to stay with my father and mother at Hyde House near Chesham in the year 1825, and was kind and suave to all: upon seeing which I recollect that my mother remarked 'Depend upon it she is going to die.' I remember with horror the journeys on Sundays from Bloomsbury Square to Kensington when I was a boy. No public conveyances, no kindness, no tea, no tips—nothing.

Sarah, Wife of Benjamin D'Israeli 1796.
From a picture by Ferrière
at Hughenden

CHAPTER II.

ISAAC D'ISRAELI.

To Benjamin and Sarah D'Israeli a son Isaac, their only child, was born in 1766.

Nature [proceeds the Memoir from which we have already drawn] had disqualified him, from his cradle, for the busy pursuits of men. A pale, pensive child, with large dark brown eyes, and flowing hair, had grown up beneath this roof of worldly energy and enjoyment, indicating even in his infancy, by the whole carriage of his life, that he was of a different order from those among whom he lived. Timid, susceptible, lost in reverie, fond of solitude, or seeking no better company than a book, the years had stolen on, till he arrived at that mournful period of boyhood when eccentricities excite attention and command no sympathy. Then commenced the age of domestic criticism. His mother, not incapable of deep affections, but so mortified by her social position that she lived until eighty without indulging in a tender expression, foresaw for her child only a future of degradation. Having a strong, clear mind, without any imagination, she believed that she beheld an inevitable doom. The tart remark and the contemptuous comment on her part, elicited, on the other, all the irritability of the poetic idiosyncrasy. After frantic ebullitions, for which, when the circumstances were analysed by an ordinary mind, there seemed no sufficient cause, my grandfather always interfered to soothe with good-tempered commonplaces, and promote peace. He was a man who thought that the only way to make people happy was to make them a present. He took it for granted that a boy in a passion wanted a toy or a guinea. At a later date when my father ran away from home, and after some wanderings was brought back, found lying on a tombstone in Hackney Churchyard, he embraced him, and gave him a pony.

Soon however these remedies ceased to avail.

The crisis arrived, when, after months of abstraction and irritability, my father produced a poem. For the first time my grandfather was seriously alarmed. The loss of one of his argosies, uninsured, could not have filled him with more blank dismay. His idea of a poet was formed from one of the prints of Hogarth hanging in his room, where an unfortunate wight in a garret was inditing an ode to riches, while dunned for his milk-score.

Decisive measures were at once adopted and the young poet was sent to Amsterdam, 'consigned like a bale of goods to my grandfather's correspondent, who had instructions to place him at some collegium of repute in that city.' Here he lived for the next three or four years in the charge of a tutor who gave the intelligent boy the run of an excellent library, but made no attempt to impart the mental discipline that might have been so salutary. 'Before his pupil was fifteen, he had read the works of Voltaire and had dipped into Bayle,' authors, it may be remarked, whose influence can be seen in all his subsequent work and may be detected even in the mind of his more famous son. 'When he was eighteen he returned to England a disciple of Rousseau,' and no better equipped than when he left for taking the place which the commercial ambition of his father or the social aspirations of his mother would have assigned to him. The father proposed to place his son in a mercantile establishment at Bordeaux. Isaac replied that 'he had written a poem of considerable length, which he wished to publish, against commerce which was the corruption of man.' Finally a compromise was discovered.

He was sent abroad, to travel in France, which the peace then permitted, visit some friends, see Paris, and then proceed to Bordeaux if he felt inclined. My father travelled in France, and then proceeded to Paris, where he remained till the eve of great events in that capital. This was a visit recollected with satisfaction. He lived with learned men and moved in vast libraries, and returned in the earlier part of 1788, with some little knowledge of life, and with a considerable quantity of books.

As early as 1786 D'Israeli had appeared in print in the *Gentleman's Magazine*, and the year after his return from Paris he published in the same serial an anonymous satire in verse which is now forgotten but was fortunate enough to attract some attention at the time and to win for its author, when his identity was revealed, the acquaintance of some of the minor literary celebrities of the day. Poetry, however, was not his field, and he presently struck a more productive vein. In his twenty-fifth year he published, again anonymously, a volume of anecdotes, sketches, and observations which under the happy title of "Curiosities of Literature" soon became popular. A second volume followed a couple of years later, and the success of this work gave a bias to its author's mental development and eventually determined his whole literary career. Many years indeed of undecided purpose, of 'hesitating and imperfect effort' and of vague aspirations after fame in the creative fields of literature were still to come; for, with ample means to supply his immediate wants provided under the will of his maternal grandmother and ample prospects secured in the succession to his father's fortune, Isaac D'Israeli missed the salutary compulsion which the necessity of earning his daily bread would have imposed. But at the age of thirty-five he renounced his dreams and, according to his son, 'resolved to devote himself for the rest of his life to the acquisition of knowledge.'

This crisis in his mental development coincided with an important change in the external ordering of his life. In 1802 he married Maria Basevi, the youngest daughter of an Italian Jew who had settled in England later than Benjamin D'Israeli. In the case of most great men the mother's influence is perhaps more potent than the father's in the shaping of character and career; but the subject of this biography seems to have been an exception.

The Basevi family were then and later not devoid of intellectual distinction, but no portion of it seems to have fallen to the lot of Maria D'Israeli. She lived till 1847—long enough to see her son one of the foremost men in Parliament; yet in the family correspondence we seldom hear of her, or if she is mentioned it is usually in connexion with some passing illness or some domestic detail. In the Memoir of Isaac D'Israeli, which his son contributed to a collected edition of his works published after his death, and which forms the basis of this and the preceding chapter, she finds no place at all. Her daughter, writing on its appearance to congratulate her brother on 'the success of his labour of love' and writing with a sister's admiring partiality, was nevertheless quick to notice the omission.

> Your essay must ever rank among the most delightful biographic sketches in our language, if not the most so, and I can at this moment remember nothing like it. Never was there a character at once so skilfully, tenderly, and truthfully delineated. Every line told in my heart as I eagerly ran over them. As for the whole, no one but ourselves can know how true it is, but everybody will feel how charming. Only your magic pen could have so grouped materials which seemed so scant into a picture full of interest for all the world. If it be short, it is full of matter. Every thing is in it,—everything at least but one. I do wish that one felicitous stroke, one tender word had brought our dear Mother into the picture. You will think me ungrateful not to be quite satisfied. It is easy for one who can do nothing else to make remarks.

Maria D'Israeli in fact appears to have been an excellent wife and mother, who kept the affection of her husband and won the affection of her children, but never counted for much in the intellectual life of either.

For Isaac D'Israeli the ten years that followed his marriage were years mainly of accumulation. 'His pen was never idle, but it was to note and to register, not to compose. His researches were prosecuted every morning among the MSS. of the British Museum, while his own ample collections permitted him to pursue his investigation in his own library into the night.' Boxes of his papers still survive which bear testimony to this untiring if somewhat desultory industry—a chaos of fragmentary notes in small and crowded penmanship, no scrap of paper that came to hand and had an unused corner being either too high or too low to serve his need. Eventually the desire of composition again came over him. 'From 1812 to 1822 the press abounded with his works. His *Calamities of Authors*, his *Memoirs of Literary Controversy*, in the manner of Bayle ; his *Essay on the Literary Character*, the most perfect of his compositions, were all chapters in that History of English Literature which he then commenced to meditate, and which it was fated should never be completed.' There is evidence that even before his marriage the idea of this monumental work had occurred to him : it became no doubt the leading inspiration of his studies and gave to them whatever unity of purpose they possessed ; and it hovered before his eyes for forty years till blindness overtook him. But his activity was by no means confined within the bounds of this great design. His early work, the *Curiosities of Literature*, was cosmopolitan rather than exclusively English in its range, and as the public continued to buy and read it, the author was eventually induced to begin a process of revision and enrichment under which it grew in time to its final ample dimensions. In its enlarged form it more than retained the favour it had already won, and remains to this day the most popular of his writings. Even more deserving of notice in a biography of his son are his excursions into the realm of political history. His literary studies had led him on to an *Inquiry into the Literary and Political Character of James the First*, in which he strove to vindicate the reputation of that monarch against the strictures of historians dominated by the Whig tradition ; and, pursuing the same line of study, he gave five years of his life to an elaborate and ambitious treatise intended to perform a similar office for James's successor. The

Commentaries on the Life and Reign of Charles I. have long been superseded by the works of later historians; but they won for their author an honorary degree at Oxford to which he was presented as the 'optimi regis vindex optimus'; and they have won for him also lasting credit as one of the first of English historians to recognise the value and attempt the exploration of the masses of manuscript material lodged in the British Museum and elsewhere.

Among his contemporaries, and not least among those whose praise was best worth having, Isaac D'Israeli's reputation stood high. Byron, Scott, Southey, Rogers, were all among his admirers. 'There's a man,' said Rogers to Southey, 'with only half an intellect who writes books that must live.' Byron was less caustic in his appreciation. 'I don't know a living man's books,' he wrote to his publisher, 'I take up so often—or lay down more reluctantly—as Israeli's;'[1] 'If there is anything new of Israeli's send it me. . . . He is the Bayle of literary speculation and puts together more amusing information than anybody.'[2]

Shortly after the publication of the first two cantos of *Childe Harold* Byron and D'Israeli met, apparently not for the first time, and a scrap in Benjamin Disraeli's hand has preserved his father's recollection of his intercourse with the poet.

I never knew a man with a more modest, gentlemanly, and perfectly unaffected manner. He was now in full fame, and until he left England I often met him. He treated me with so much respect—I had almost said reverence—that I, being a somewhat modest and retired man, thought at first that he was quizzing me, but I soon found that I did him injustice.

[1] Byron's *Letters and Journals* (Ed.: R. E. Prothero), IV., p. 274. The letter reproaches Murray for his indiscretion in showing D'Israeli Byron's copy of the original issue of the *Literary Character* full of marginal notes and emendations. This copy was the proximate cause of a revised and enlarged edition of that work, which appeared in 1818. Byron read the book in its new form and added notes which were embodied in the edition of 1822. In a note to the preface of the 1818 edition Byron declared that he had read D'Israeli's works 'oftener than perhaps those of any English writer whatever, except such as treat of Turkey.'

[2] *Ibid.*, V., p. 390.

The fact is my works being all about the feelings of literary men were exceedingly interesting to him. They contained knowledge which he could get nowhere else. It was all new to him. He told me that he had read my works over and over again. I thought this, of course, a compliment, but some years afterwards found it to be true.

D'Israeli in his turn was of course not behindhand in appreciation of the poet, and his son grew to manhood in a household where the name of Byron was always held in reverence. Yet in spite of this it is hard to believe that the father was really in sympathy with the romantic movement of the day. His true idol was Pope, and in the whole complexion of his mind we find an affinity with the eighteenth century rather than with the nineteenth. The son was more deeply penetrated with the spirit of the later time; and he had the dæmonic force which his father lacked and which that spirit calls for or inspires in its votaries. Yet we shall find, as we proceed, in subtle combination with very different matter, a certain eighteenth century element in the intellect of the son which, unless we are to explain it by direct inheritance from his father, was doubtless the result of early education and of constant intercourse during the impressionable age with a mind originally cast in the eighteenth century mould.

Isaac D'Israeli's works, especially the *Curiosities*, still have their readers, but his reputation has hardly rested at the level to which it rose during his life. It is as the father of his son that he now mainly interests us, and as a capital influence in the formation of that son's mind and character. Superficially the resemblance is slight between the student recluse buried in his books and the statesman who through the turmoil of public life forced his way to fame and honour, and the son was well aware that his father never fully understood him; yet he assigned to his father a foremost place among the few from whose wisdom he had himself drawn profit, and to the end of his days he retained the most unquestioning admiration for his works and was never weary of paying affectionate homage to his genius and attainments. If we bear in memory the lineaments of the father as drawn by the son, we shall catch in the son himself many a suggestion of heredity even where the contrast between the two seems sharpest and where resemblance is least to be expected. Take, for instance, the following :—

> He was a complete literary character, a man who really passed his life in his library. Even marriage produced no change : he rose to enter the chamber where he lived alone with his books, and at night his lamp was ever lit within the same walls. Nothing, indeed, was more remarkable than the isolation of this prolonged existence. . . . He disliked business, and he never required relaxation ; he was absorbed in his pursuits. In London his only amusement was to ramble among booksellers ; if he entered a club, it was only to go into the library. In the country, he scarcely ever left his room but to saunter in abstraction upon a terrace ; muse over a chapter, or coin a sentence. He had not a single passion or prejudice : all his convictions were the result of his own studies, and were often opposed to the impressions which he had early imbibed. He not only never entered into the politics of the day, but he could never understand them. He never was connected with any particular body or set of men ; comrades of school or college, or confederates in that public life which, in England, is, perhaps, the only foundation of real friendship.

D'Israeli the elder lived through one of the most stirring periods in the history of the world, yet in all his correspondence there is hardly an allusion to passing events. Not the sort of man, one would say, whose son was likely to become Prime Minister of England ; but we shall find as we proceed in the son himself something of the same tendency to aloofness and isolation, and many of the habits of the student recluse not eradicated though held in subordination by what was strenuous and enterprising in his character and genius.

Though at this stage it is in part an anticipation, one

last extract from the Memoir by his son will complete the picture of Isaac D'Israeli :—

On his moral character I shall scarcely presume to dwell. The philosophic sweetness of his disposition, the serenity of his lot, and the elevating nature of his pursuits, combined to enable him to pass through life without an evil act, almost without an evil thought. As the world has always been fond of personal details respecting men who have been celebrated, I will mention that he was fair, with a Bourbon nose, and brown eyes of extraordinary beauty and lustre. He wore a small black velvet cap, but his white hair latterly touched his shoulders in curls almost as flowing as in his boyhood. His extremities were delicate and well-formed, and his leg, at his last hour, as shapely as in his youth, which showed the vigour of his frame. Latterly he had become corpulent. He did not excel in conversation, though in his family circle he was garrulous. Everything interested him, and blind and eighty-two he was still as susceptible as a child. One of his last acts was to compose some verses of gay gratitude to his daughter-in-law, who was his London correspondent, and to whose lively pen he was indebted for constant amusement. He had by nature a singular volatility which never deserted him. His feelings, though always amiable, were not painfully deep, and amid joy or sorrow the philosophic vein was ever evident. He more resembled Goldsmith than any man that I can compare him to ; in his conversation, his apparent confusion of ideas ending with some felicitous phrase of genius, his naïveté, his simplicity not untouched with a dash of sarcasm affecting innocence—one was often reminded of the gifted friend of Burke and Johnson. There was however one trait in which my father did not resemble Goldsmith ; he had no vanity. Indeed, one of his few infirmities was rather a deficiency of self-esteem.

CHAPTER III.

EARLY YEARS.

1804—1821.

On his marriage early in 1802, Isaac D'Israeli, who had been living in chambers in James Street, Adelphi, moved to 6, King's Road, Bedford Row,[1] and there at half-past five in the morning of Friday, December 21, 1804, or according to the Jewish reckoning the 19th of Tebet, 5565, his eldest son Benjamin was born. On the eighth day the boy was duly initiated into the covenant of Abraham, the rite of circumcision being performed by a relative of his mother's, David Lindo. Benjamin was not the eldest child, for a daughter Sarah had preceded him on December 29, 1802; and three sons were to follow —Naphtali (who died in infancy) in 1807, Raphael (Ralph) in 1809, and Jacobus (James) in 1813.

The glimpses we are able to catch at this distance of time of the future statesman's childhood are few and of slight significance. 'My son Ben assures me you are in Brighton. He saw you! Now, he never lies,' wrote Isaac D'Israeli from Brighton, where he was a frequent visitor, to his friend John Murray when the boy was

[1] Now 22, Theobald's Road. The house, though in what is now a noisy thoroughfare, has a pleasant outlook over Gray's Inn Garden, and is marked by a memorial tablet affixed by the London County Council. Oddly enough, Lord Beaconsfield seems never to have been certain either of the place of his birth or of the year in which it occurred.

Benjamin Disraeli as a Child
From a miniature by R. Cosway R.A.
in the possession of Mr. Coningsby Disraeli

between four and five. Perhaps not only truthfulness, but a certain precocious alertness, is to be deduced from this. At the age of six, or earlier,[1] Benjamin was sent to a school at Islington which was kept by a Miss Roper, and which is described by one who knew it as 'for those days a very high-class establishment.' Miss Roper had a Bucks connexion, so that by an odd coincidence Benjamin's schoolmates included a number of boys belonging to families among whom the Disraelis afterwards settled in that county. From Islington in process of time he passed to a school of higher grade kept by the Rev. John Potticany, an Independent minister, it is said,[2] in Elliott Place, Blackheath. Here the atmosphere, we are told, was liberal 'as to both politics and religion,' though most of the boys appear to have attended the services of the Established Church. Probably it was only in a school of a certain latitude in religious matters that room could be found in those days for a professing Jew; and we learn that Ben was not only allowed to stand back at prayer time, but in common with a schoolfellow who was also a Jew received instruction in Hebrew from a Rabbi who visited them on Saturdays. Among his contemporaries at Blackheath was Milner Gibson, the well-known Radical politician, who in later days was to sit opposite him in the House of Commons. From another contemporary we get a pleasant picture of Mr. Potticany's most distinguished pupil:—

When my father took me to school he handed me over to Ben, as he always called him. I looked up to him as a big boy, and very kind he was to me, making me sit next to him in play hours, and amusing me with stories of robbers and caves, illustrating them with rough pencil sketches, which he continually rubbed out to make way for fresh ones. He was a very rapid reader, was fond of romances, and would often let me sit by him and read the same book, good-naturedly waiting before turning a leaf till he knew I had reached the bottom of the page. He was very fond of playing at horses,

[1] So early that he used afterwards to say he believed he was sent there to learn to speak.

[2] *Jewish Chronicle*, May 29, 1868.

and would often drive me and another boy as a pair with string reins. He was always full of fun ; and at Midsummer, when he went home for the holidays in the basket of the Blackheath coach, fired away at the passers-by with his pea-shooter.[1]

Another and less friendly account, which appears to be based on the recollections of his Jewish schoolfellow, describes Disraeli as

> a lazy boy who excelled in none of the school exercises. However, he would amuse his companions on a wet half-holiday with a little extemporised drama. Being able to draw he would also construct a castle in paper as the scene of the adventures which he described. He had a taste not uncommon among schoolboys for little acts of bargaining and merchandise. . . . Mr. Potticany forbade newspapers, but a clique, of which the two Jew boys were members, were allowed to take in *Bell's Weekly Messenger*. So far as politics, the talk of the embryo Premier was pronounced Toryish.

According to this writer the youthful Benjamin was not only dramatist but actor ; in a school performance of *The Merchant of Venice* he took the part of Gratiano, but failed to win applause.[2]

Meagre indeed, in other respects, is our knowledge of those schooldays at Blackheath, though they extended into a good many years. In both the reminiscences that have been cited we find touches that remind us of Disraeli's own pictures of the boyhood of his heroes in *Vivian Grey* and *Contarini Fleming* ; and these two novels in their turn, which have an autobiographic significance above that of all the others, may help us to imagine what manner of boy their author must have been. Like both his heroes, we may surmise that he was daring and impetuous, sometimes perhaps mutinous and pugnacious ;

1 Rev. E. Jones in the *Standard* of April 28, 1887. Mr. Jones was only six months younger than his protector, who had no doubt, however, both physically and mentally, the precocious development of his race.

2 *Jewish Chronicle*, May 29, 1868. Published soon after Disraeli had become Prime Minister for the first time, these recollections are open to the suspicion of having taken a colour from the political animus of later years.

keenly sensitive and warmly affectionate ; a leader when he chose to lead, but somewhat isolated and much given to reverie and castle-building. According to a recollection of his brother Ralph's, he was fond of 'playing at Parliament' in the holidays, and always reserved for himself the part of leader and spokesman of the Government, keeping the others, somewhat to their annoyance, in the cold shades of opposition. Of Benjamin's studies at Blackheath we know nothing at all. The only letter of his early years that has come down to us is severely laconic and gives us no assistance. It owes its preservation to the fact that the reverse of the paper on which it is written afforded space for one of his father's multifarious notes, and it runs : 'Dear Mama,—I have arrived safe. B. D'Israeli.' From a letter by his grandfather which has also floated down, and which incidentally gives us a pleasant taste of the kind-hearted old man who wrote it, we hear of a serious illness by which the child was stricken in a summer vacation of this period. In August, 1816, Benjamin D'Israeli the elder writes to a relation :— 'We are now in great anxiety for poor little Ben, who has been very ill. . . . I am very much alarmed by the account I have from Isaac, and very much afeard. God preserve him and grant that he may get the better and recover!' 'Little Ben' recovered, but three months later the grandfather died.

His death proved in its indirect consequences an important event in the life of the child. In the first place, Isaac D'Israeli, grown more affluent now by the accession of his father's fortune, moved in the course of the following year from King's Road to 6, Bloomsbury Square,[1] a better house, with the further advantage of closer neighbourhood to the British Museum. Here he resided till twelve years later he left London for the country, and here his eldest son grew up to manhood. In the religious history of the family the removal of the

[1] This house also is marked by a tablet affixed by the London County Council in accordance with their excellent practice.

grandfather from the scene was quickly followed by serious developments which his presence had delayed. By temperament and training Isaac D'Israeli was ultra-liberal or Laodicean in his attitude towards the traditional faith; his mother, we know, had little affection for it; and some of the Basevi family into which he had married shared his dislike for the narrow orthodoxy which was still supreme in the Synagogue. Nevertheless his children were until their grandfather's death brought up in the Jewish faith, special provision being made, as we have seen, for the religious instruction of his eldest son in Mr. Potticany's establishment; and though Isaac himself neither attended the Synagogue nor took any interest in its affairs, he paid his dues regularly and would no doubt have been content to retain his nominal connexion with it if only he had been left in peace. But in 1813 he was for some pedantic reason elected Parnass or Warden of the Congregation of Bevis Marks; and on his writing to the Mahamad or Chamber of Elders to point out the 'singular impropriety' of the choice, and to decline the office, he was fined £40, and told that his election was in strict accordance with the laws of the Congregation. The quarrel was pursued with curious obstinacy on the part of the Elders and growing irritation on the part of their rebellious colleague. A long letter of remonstrance which D'Israeli wrote in December, 1813, defines his attitude:—

> A person who has always lived out of the sphere of your observation; of retired habits of life; who can never unite in your public worship, because, as now conducted, it disturbs, instead of exciting, religious emotions, a circumstance of general acknowledgment; who has only tolerated some part of your ritual, willing to concede all he can in those matters which he holds to be indifferent; —such a man, with but a moderate portion of honour and understanding, never can accept the solemn functions of an Elder in your congregation, and involve his life, and distract his pursuits, not in temporary but in permanent duties always repulsive to his feelings.

Though in this letter he threatened to withdraw from

their society, the dispute did not as yet come to any definite head. Without rescinding their decrees the Elders were content for the present not to enforce them; but three years later they renewed their demands and D'Israeli, no longer under the restraint of his father's influence, responded by insisting that his name should be erased from the list of their members. His resignation was not formally accepted till several years had elapsed, but the connexion of the D'Israeli family with the Synagogue was now at an end.

Isaac D'Israeli though he ceased to be a Jew never became a Christian; and apparently he saw no reason at first why his children should not remain in the same amphibious condition. 'It was Mr. Sharon Turner[1] who persuaded my father—after much trouble—to allow his children to be baptized. He, one day, half consented, upon which Mr. Turner called on the day following and took us off to St. Andrew's, Holborn.' This was Lord Beaconsfield's account of the matter in his later days, and no doubt it fairly represents the general situation; but like many of his autobiographic recollections it is inaccurate in detail, for the children were not all baptized on one day. Benjamin himself was received into the Church on July 31, 1817, the two younger boys, Ralph and James, having preceded him earlier in the month, and his sister following after a short interval. No one could have foreseen how fruitful in great consequences this event was to be—neither the Elders of the Synagogue who forced the rupture, nor the Voltairian father, nor the zealous family friend, nor Mr. Thimbleby, who in Benjamin's case performed the ceremony of baptism. If the gentlemen of the Mahamad had shown less obstinacy or more worldly wisdom—and it was only, we are told, a question of two or three votes—that strange political career which was to fascinate a later generation might well have been impossible.

[1] The well-known historian of Anglo-Saxon England.

Whether it was that the change of religion made a change of school seem desirable, or that, as there is some reason to suspect, the establishment at Blackheath was closed, Benjamin about this time entered on a new stage of his education. He was transferred to 'a school in Epping Forest where there were about 50 or 60 boys, and where,' as he once told Lord Rowton after reading in some hostile article a sneer at his un-English Education,' 'the whole drama of public school life was acted in a smaller theatre.' The head of the school was a Unitarian Minister, the Rev. Eli Cogan.

There were two brothers Cogan, the eldest a physician and a man of mark in his day. He was the founder of the Humane Society, having brought the idea from Holland. Dr. Cogan had travelled much and was a member of foreign Universities. He published his travels in Germany and Holland and other works. His brother was not a public character, but Dr. Parr said of him that he was the only Nonconformist who was a Greek scholar.[1] He was a complete one; of the Porson school, and was really intended by Nature for a College Don. My father made his acquaintance at a bookseller's shop, where Cogan purchased always the finest editions in the finest condition. My father assumed for a long time that he was a clergyman. When he discovered that he was a schoolmaster, he thought I should be his pupil. I was thirteen, or about to be thirteen, when I went to him, at Higham Hall, an old manor house, about two miles from Walthamstow. Nothing was thought of there but the two dead languages, but he was an admirable instructor in them as well as a first rate scholar.

I remained there four years, and was quite fit to have gone to a University when I left Cogan—I mean, I did not require any preliminary cramming at a private tutor's. Not that I was more advanced than other boys of my age: not so advanced, and never could reach the first class, which consisted once of only one boy, Stratton, afterwards at Trinity College, Cambridge, and who, it was supposed, was to have carried everything before him there, and everywhere else,

[1] 'I am almost entirely, and in Greek altogether, self-taught,' says Mr. Cogan himself in a letter to Isaac D'Israeli, 'and have been obliged to acquire without assistance when a man what ought to have been communicated to me when a boy.'

but I have never heard of him since. The first class dealt with Æschylus, Aristophanes, Aristotle, Plato, and the Greek Orators. I never could reach this stage, though I listened to many of the interpretations and expositions of the master with interest and admiration Though a very reserved, shy, calm man, his whole being became animated when he was interpreting a great classic writer. This I fully experienced when I went before him with my Terence. After our dull construing, he would himself interpret the scene. It was acting—full of humor.

However, though I never reached the first class, and was not eminent even in the second, I learnt, or rather read a great deal in those years. In Greek, all Herodotus ; much of Thucydides ; the greater part of the *Iliad* ; something of the *Odyssey* ; the *Ajax*, *Œdipus Rex* and *Antigone* of Sophocles ; the *Medea*, *Hippolytus* and *Alcestis* of Euripides ; Theocritus, the *Idylls* (my copy is now in the Library, with notes)[1] ; and Xenophon, the *Retreat* and part of the *Cyropædia*. In Latin he bathed us in Cicero, and always impressed on us that, so far as style was concerned, in lucid arrangement of subject, and power of expression the *Pro Milone* was an education in itself ; Cæsar ; much of Livy ; something of Tacitus ; all Virgil and Horace ; some of the best things in Catullus and the elegiac poets ; the first book of Lucretius ; and all Terence.[2]

The accounts which Disraeli gives of his early years, in such fragments of autobiography, letters, notes, and conversations as have come down to us, are not easy to harmonise. Mr. Potticany's school he nowhere mentions, and in later years the memory of Higham Hill seems to have absorbed many of the recollections both of what preceded and what followed in his education. It is probable that his stay at Cogan's was a good deal shorter than he makes it in the account just cited. In another narrative he himself reduces the period to two or three years ; and the best conjecture would appear to be that

[1] Perhaps Disraeli had this copy in mind when in a somewhat imaginative piece of autobiography which he once addressed to a correspondent he wrote :—'In the pride of boyish erudition I edited the Adonisian Eclogue of Theocritus, which was privately printed. This was my first production : puerile pedantry.'

[2] Autobiographic note written for Lord Rowton.

he left about the end of his fifteenth year, and during the couple of years that followed continued his education at home, probably, as the same narrative informs us, under the guidance of a private tutor. With this version a diary of studies for the year 1820 that has come down to us in a mutilated form would appear best to harmonise ; it certainly bears out a further statement that his education was at this time 'severely classical.' Readers of *Vivian Grey* will recollect how the boy when he went to Burnsley Vicarage, 'although more deficient than most of his own age in accurate classical knowledge, found himself in talents, and various acquirements, immeasurably their superior' ; and how afterwards when he 'sat down to read' at home, 'twelve hours a day, and self-banishment from society, overcame in twelve months the ill effects of his imperfect education.' The same tale is told in almost the same words of Contarini Fleming, and though we may doubt whether young Disraeli was equally successful in overcoming the defects of early training, it is clear that he made an heroic attempt. In the list of authors which he claims to have read while at Higham Hill there is probably a good deal of anticipation of subsequent study, but the testimony of the diary is all in favour of its virtual accuracy. Questions have been sometimes raised as to the extent of Disraeli's classical acquirements, and he has been accused in this connexion of pretending to knowledge which he did not really possess. The truth would seem to be that he contrived at this time to make himself a fair Latin scholar and retained in after life a moderate familiarity with the great Roman authors ; but that his Greek was scanty in the beginning, and, in spite of his efforts after leaving school, remained scanty to the end. A thorough training in the Greek language and a better acquaintance with Greek literature might have been wholesome discipline for a mind that was too apt to be slipshod and a taste that was too apt to be artificial. But the Disraeli that we know would not have been himself if he had received the stamp that a public school education places upon intellect and character. The diary reveals the lack of that severe grounding in the elements which smooths the approach to the classical authors for the clever public school boy; but they show also a precocity of mind, a readiness to appraise and criticise, and a confidence in passing judgment that would be no less alien to the public school boy of fifteen than the frequent blunders in Greek accidence by which its pages are disfigured. A few extracts will bring us closer to the mind of the youthful student :—

Monday [May ?].—Lucian—his *Timon* increases in interest. Terence, the *Eunuch*. French—read the sensible preface of M. Marmontel to the *Henriade*. Livy—finished the Speech of Camillus. Writing, ciphering, &c.; prepared my Greek; made Latin verses; grammar.

Friday, June 2nd.—Lucian. Terence—the *Adelphi*, which promises to be an interesting play. *Henriade*. Writing, ciphering. Virgil—2nd book of the *Georgics*, which begins with a splendid invocation to Bacchus; it, however, all vanishes in a sleepy lecture on grafting boughs and lopping trees. Prepared Greek. Read Webb on the Greek metres; the author is not very profound, yet it is an useful work for a Tyro. Grammar, &c.

Lucian, as various entries show, he read with no small relish, and to the impression then produced we are no doubt in part indebted for *Ixion* and *The Infernal Marriage*. The future leader of the agricultural party was at first at all events disappointed with the *Georgics*. He admired indeed the 'extraordinary elegance of the versification,' but thought 'the celebration of ploughshares, of fallow land, and rainy days' but a poor subject for the genius of a great poet. In course of time, however, appreciation grew, and Lucretius from the first filled him with enthusiasm :—

Wednesday.—Demosthenes, *Philipp.* 1. I find it difficult. Lucretius—most beautiful : his invocation to Venus is very elegant and his description of Religion with her head among the clouds is sublime. Apollonius Rhodius. Gibbon, Vol. 12.

Friday.—*Georgics*, Bk. 2nd, 430 line; this glorious passage is evidently imitated from Lucretius; but it is the finest specimen of versification that any language has ever produced. Horace—read six odes, 1st Bk. with myself.

Saturday.—This evening I again with increased admiration compared the passages of Lucretius and Virgil. I wonder extremely that Lucretius is not a greater favourite. . . .

Friday.—Lucretius—on Death: a sublime chapter, full of original and grand ideas, but the versification is rugged and wants the harmonious flow of Virgil.

An independent attack upon the *Iliad* leads to a curious outburst against his unlucky editor:—

Tuesday.—Euripides—*Alcestis*, to 98 line. Verses. Cicero—the *Oration for Milo*. Latin Exercise. Drawing. Began with myself the *Iliad*, Valpy's Edition; the notes are prolix and numerous, but little information is to be gleaned from them. Valpy rejects the digamma and supports the ridiculous theory of the self-sufficient Professor of Edinburgh. The Doctor and the Professor are equally contemptible. They mistake incapacity for originality, and endeavour to compensate for their moderate talents by rejecting every established rule and advocating every ridiculous system. One libels Heyne and the other criticizes Hermann. Illumined by such stars as these, surely the horizon of classical literature can never be clouded!

Greek metres, 'a dry but, I am afraid, necessary study,' were a sore affliction: but the young student was not easily discouraged.

Friday.—Again at the Greek Metres—bewildered! lost! miserable work, indeed. Writing. Prepared Greek. Read Gibbon, Vol. 9. Homer—the *Iliad*, Bk. 1st by myself.

Saturday.—Read *Literary Character* [his father's essay], three first chapters.

Monday.—Lucian, Εκκλησια θηων [sic]. Tibullus, Lib. 3, Eleg. 6. *Henriade*. Gibbon — Vol. 9. Livy. The Speech of Minutius and Fa. Maximus. Greek metres—a ray of light. Latin verses. Homer with myself.

Wednesday.—Greek metres—tolerable success.

Demosthenes, as we have seen, was not found easy, nor at first did he inspire much admiration.

Whether it is to be ascribed to my difficulty in understanding him or to my deficiency of taste, I know not, but I must own I rather prefer the elegant and musical Orations of Cicero. I have a prejudice against Demosthenes, and, though his speeches are replete with Virtue, Patriotism and Courage, history tells me he was a Villain, a Partisan, and a Poltroon!

Presently, however, we find the entry, 'Demosthenes, *παρα* [sic] *του στεφανου* a most eloquent and irresistible passage'; and a complacent repetition of the blunder makes us suspect that deficiency of Greek as much as deficiency of taste determined the initial want of appreciation. Finally, in spite of every obstacle, the *Crown Oration* arouses real enthusiasm :—

Friday.—Demosth. *Orat. de Corona.* In my lesson of to-day is included that magnificent passage in which the Athenian Orator swears by the warriors of Marathon and the day of Salamis, and a more eloquent and enchanting passage mortal hand never penned, mortal ear never heard. The eloquence of Demosthenes is indeed irresistible, and while we peruse the pages of his genius, we lose our prejudices against the man in our admiration of the orator. At length I must own that Cicero is his inferior. . . . We admire in Cicero the well-turned sentence and the cadenced period, the subtile argument, and the acute remark. But in reading Demosthenes we think not of these, our imagination is fired, our enthusiasm awakened, and even I, I who have been obliged to wade through his beauties, with a hateful lexicon at my side, have often wished to have lived in the olden time, when Philip was King of Macedon and Demosthenes demagogue of Athens.

Pericles, of course, was his favourite among Athenian statesmen, 'the greatest and most accomplished of the characters of antiquity, his policy sound, his judgment unequalled.'

Tuesday.—Read Gibbon—the factions of the Theatre are described with his usual felicity, but I think he has not made the most of the character of Belisarius. He speaks, I think, too slightingly of Justinian, a monarch who, with all his faults and weaknesses, was infinitely superior to the rest of the later Roman Emperors.

Saturday, Sept. 9.—Apollonius Rhodius ['this weak gentleman,' as he elsewhere calls him] . . . . Cicero's

Oration for Milo ['impressive eloquence, well-timed irony, and subtle reasoning'] . . . . Gibbon, his chapter on the Doctrine of the Incarnation—as usual

Sapping a solemn creed with solemn sneer.[1]

Tuesday.— . . . . Read Mitford: he is deeply versed in Greek literature, but his style is wretched, nay, scarcely English, a striking contrast to the cadenced periods of the *Decline and Fall.*

Thursday.—Voltaire—Critique on the *Œdipus* of Sophocles. Some just criticism mixed with much frivolity and bad taste. . . .

He then reads the *Œdipe,* but with little satisfaction; and 'a furious denunciation against Oracles and Superstition, brazen pipes and flagitious priests,' which he finds in it moves him to the following reflection: 'This is a speech worthy of a French *Illuminé*; but in the heroic age *Philosophers* did not exist, and the good men were contented to obey and consult those institutions which from their youth upward they were taught to respect and reverence.' An intimate friend of Disraeli's once, in a moment of pique, described him as a Voltairian in religion. The description was not very happy, for, as these boyish jottings alone would show, the Voltairian spirit aroused an instinctive antagonism in a mind cast from the beginning in the Semitic mould. And yet even thus early the subtle contradictions of a most complex character reveal themselves. In a note-book, which is probably not later than the period we have reached, we find this pencil entry in Disraeli's hand: 'Resolution.—To be always sincere and open with Mrs. E. Never to say but what I mean—*point de moquerie,* in which she thinks I excel.' Who 'Mrs. E.' may have been does not appear, but an anecdote that has floated down from the school-days at Cogan's bears witness to her discernment. The boys at Higham Hill who were members of the Church of England had to walk some distance on Sundays to attend morning service; and it resulted from this that they fared rather badly at the

[1] *Childe Harold,* III., 107.

midday dinner, which was usually half over by the time they got back. Disraeli was himself among the victims, and his new religion had as yet aroused in him none of the zeal of a martyr ; so he solemnly threw out the suggestion to his Anglican companions that it might be as well if they all became Unitarians for the term of their life at school.

CHAPTER IV.

Law and Travel.

1821-1824.

At seventeen, Disraeli tells us, a great change took place in his life. In November, 1821, he was articled to a firm of solicitors in the City—Messrs. Swain, Stevens, Maples, Pearse, and Hunt, of Frederick's Place, Old Jewry.

My father had a great friend, the head of the most eminent solicitors' firm in the City, except Freshfield's, of whom they were the honored rivals. He was very rich (the firm of five partners divided, though in unequal portions, fifteen thousand per annum), a man of considerable taste, with a fine library and collections of art, and one daughter, by no means without charm, either personally or intellectually. This gentleman wished that I should enter into his profession, and, in due course, his firm, and the parents wished and meant something else, also in due course. . . . My father was very warm about this business: the only time in his life in which he exerted authority, always, however, exerted with affection. I had some scruples, for even then I dreamed of Parliament. My father's refrain always was Philip Carteret Webb, who was the most eminent solicitor of his boyhood and who was an M.P.

It would be a mistake to suppose that the two years and more that I was in the office of our friend were wasted. I have often thought, though I have often regretted the University, that it was much the reverse. My business was to be the private secretary of the busiest partner of our friend. He dictated to me every day his correspondence, which was as extensive as a Minister's, and when the clients arrived I did not leave the room, but remained not only to learn my business but to become acquainted with my future clients. They were in general men of great importance—bank directors, East India directors, merchants, bankers. Often extraordinary scenes when firms in the highest credit came to announce and prepare for their impending suspension; questions, too, where great amounts were at stake; the formation, too, of companies, &c., &c. It gave me great facility with my pen and no inconsiderable knowledge of human nature.

Unfortunately, if indeed I ought to use the word, the rest of my life was not in harmony with this practice and business. I passed my evenings at home, alone, and always in deep study. This developed at last different feelings and views to those which I had willingly but too quickly adopted when I was little more than seventeen. I became pensive and restless, and before I was twenty I was obliged to terminate the dream of my father and his friend. Nothing would satisfy me but travel. My father then made a feeble effort for Oxford, but the hour of adventure had arrived. I was unmanageable. Let me say one word about the lady. She said to me one day, and before I had shown any indication of my waywardness, 'You have too much genius for Frederick's Place: it will never do.'

We were good friends. She married a Devonshire gentleman and was the mother of two general officers, of whom we have heard a good deal of late [Zulu War, 1879], and whom I employed as a Minister! Such is life!

The 'two years and more' in Frederick's Place really stretched out to three. 'Most assiduous in his attention to business and showing great ability in the transaction of it'[1] was the impression he left on the mind of one of the partners; though all the evidence is not equally favourable, and Mr. Maples's recollections may have taken a colour from Disraeli's subsequent fame. In the formal sense his education no doubt had suffered, and we may be inclined to echo his own regret that he missed what Oxford could have given him—not merely the scholastic training, but the other gifts of even higher value which she bestows upon the aspirant to a public career. But 'nature is more powerful than education'; and this maxim, which was given to Contarini Fleming for his guidance, was signally verified in the case of Benjamin Disraeli. Nor in those evenings of deep

[1] Froude's *Lord Beaconsfield*, p. 22.

study at home was the learning of the Universities neglected. He pursued his heroic attacks on the Greek and Latin classics, and presently, like Vivian Grey, he made the discovery 'that there were classics in other languages besides Greek and Latin,' and in his father's library 'was introduced to that band of noble spirits, the great poets and legislators and philosophers of modern Europe.' In the eager pursuit of knowledge he had his father's example to draw him on and his father's experience, no doubt, to guide him; and it was at this time that he acquired the wide, though possibly superficial, acquaintance with books which we find even in his earliest writings, and that he laid the foundations of that really remarkable and highly unconventional knowledge of history, English and other, which he shows in all his works, and upon which he justly prided himself throughout his career. From his multifarious reading even law books were not wholly excluded, or so at least some scraps in the litter of early remains appear to indicate; though more often we find the law profaned by the use of fragments of legal documents for literary notes and verses.

In his enthusiasm for knowledge Vivian Grey narrowly escaped 'being all his life a dreaming scholar,' and a similar danger may have seemed at this time to threaten the young Disraeli. Inherited instinct and his father's example alike pointed in this direction. But though the thirst for knowledge was present in the son as in the father, and the habit of dreaming was there also, and remained there till the end, there was that in the son besides which made it impossible that his father's fate should overtake him. 'Destiny bears us to our lot and destiny is our own will.'[1]

Neither *Vivian Grey* nor *Contarini Fleming* can be used without discrimination as an authority for biographical details. In both, and especially in *Contarini*, which was written five years later than the other, the events of the

[1] *Contarini Fleming*, Pt. III. ch. 11.

author's childhood and youth are viewed through the refracting medium of his subsequent experience; and in both the story takes a colour from his mood at the time of writing. When Disraeli wrote *Vivian Grey* his ambition was turned towards the world of action; and when he wrote *Contarini* he was dreaming of winning fame by literary creation. It is the supreme interest of his character that he combined in such high degree the qualities that make for greatness in either sphere, the brooding temperament and glowing imagination of the poet with the practical energy, compelling will, and daring initiative of the man of action; and the two novels reveal as competing tendencies in the youth powers which were harmonised in the complex character of the man. Judiciously interpreted they supplement each other and abound in touches and incidents that help us to complete the picture of these years of adolescence. But it is to *Contarini* that we must look for the most vivid representation of the internal struggles by which Disraeli's youth, no less than his hero's, must have been torn. In Contarini ambition awakes at a very early age. While still a child he is consumed with desire to be 'something great and glorious and dazzling,' and 'entertains a deep conviction that life must be intolerable unless he be the greatest of men.' Yet he hovers perpetually between the two ideals of the life of glorious action on the one hand and the life of contemplation and literary achievement on the other, and hardly even at the end of the novel has he succeeded in finding rest. At one moment he 'longs to wave his inspiring sword at the head of armies or dash into the very heat and blaze of eloquent faction': at another he feels the delight of composition and grows 'intoxicated with his own eloquence'; he 'begins to ponder over the music of language; he studies the collocation of sweet words and constructs elaborate sentences in lonely walks': and then again, losing confidence in his powers, he falls into 'the agony of doubt and despair which is the doom of youthful genius.' Affected by the spectacle of 'greatness achieved, moving before him in its quick and proud reality,' he turns with disgust from his 'weak meditations of unexecuted purposes and dreamy visions of imaginary grandeur' and becomes a worldling; or he writes a romance or tragedy and throws it aside dissatisfied. Now he plunges into action; again he finds 'a substitute for the excitement of action in the excitement of thought.' To-day 'in reverie he is an Alberoni, a Ripperda, a Richelieu'; to-morrow he has 'resolved to be a great historical writer,' and expound 'the nature of man and the origin of nations in glowing sentences of oracular majesty.'

Through all these phases or something like them the young Disraeli no doubt passed. Over Vivian Grey and Contarini Fleming indeed he had one great advantage. Amid his wildest day-dreams the constant attendance at Frederick's Place must have been a steadying influence, and have introduced an element of discipline into his life that was lacking to both his heroes. When he was most a bookworm it helped to keep the active instincts within him alive; which was the more fortunate as in his father's house and the society that frequented it he can have found little to feed them or to point the way to his subsequent career. 'Neither the fortune nor the family of Mr. Grey entitled him to mix in any other society than that of what is, in common parlance, termed the middling classes; but from his distinguished literary abilities he had always found himself an honoured guest among the powerful and the great.'[1] If the former part of the sentence is true of Benjamin Disraeli's father, no less than of Vivian Grey's, the latter is not. Isaac D'Israeli was a recluse, and while there is no reason to suppose that he was sought by the powerful and the great, it is certain that he never sought them. The pictures that have been drawn of the young Disraeli's securing early initiation into the world of fashion and politics through the guests whom he met at his father's table are devoid of truth.

[1] *Vivian Grey*, Bk. I. ch. 8.

His father's chosen companions were those with whom his attendance at the British Museum brought him into contact or his studies into sympathy, men like Francis Douce and Sharon Turner, Crofton Croker and Francis Cohen; and, above all, John Murray, his publisher. Murray, indeed, has a place of some importance in our story. Being on terms of closest intimacy with the D'Israeli family, he had seen the eldest son grow up from childhood, and was among the first to note his unusual capacity; so much so that before the youth had completed his eighteenth year we find the shrewd publisher seeking his opinion as to the merits of a tragedy which there was some thought of producing. In recognition of his precocity Benjamin was early admitted to the privilege of accompanying his father to Murray's dinner parties, where he listened with rapt attention to the discourse of Murray's guests, usually literary celebrities, small or great. Of one of these feasts of wit and learning we have a record from his own pen which helps us to realise the character of them all.

November 27th, 1822. Wednesday.—Dined at Murray's. Present Tom Moore, Stuart Newton, John Murray, Walter Hamilton, my father and self. Moore very entertaining. . . .

Moore.—This is excellent wine, Murray.

D'Israeli.—You'll miss the French wines.[1]

M.—Yes; the return to port is awful.

D.—I am not fond of port, but really there is a great deal of good port in England, and you'll soon get used to it.

M.—Oh! I have no doubt of it. I used to be very fond of port—but French wines spoil one for a while. The transition is too sudden from the wines of France to the port of Dover. . . .

D.—Pray is Lord Byron much altered?

M.—Yes, his facing has swelled out and he is getting fat; his hair is gray and his countenance has lost that 'spiritual expression' which he so eminently had. His teeth are getting bad, and when I saw him he said that if ever he came to England it would be to consult Wayte about them.

[1] Moore had recently returned from his long residence abroad.

B. D.—Who is since dead, and therefore he certainly won't come.

M.—I certainly was very much struck with an alteration for the worse. Besides he dresses very extraordinarily.

D.—Slovenly ?

M.—Oh, no ! no ! He's very dandified, and yet not an English dandy. When I saw him he was dressed in a curious foreign cap, a frogged great coat, and had a gold chain round his neck and pushed into his waistcoat pocket. I asked him if he wore a glass and took it out, when I found fixed to it a set of trinkets. He had also another gold chain tight round his neck, something like a collar. He had then a plan of buying a tract of land and living in South America. When I saw Scrope Davies and told him that Byron was growing fat he instantly said, 'Then he'll never come to England.'[1] . . .

M.—Rogers is the most wonderful man in conversation that I know. If he could write as well as he speaks he would be matchless, but his faculties desert him as soon as he touches a pen.

D.—It is wonderful how many men of talent have been so circumstanced.

M.—Yes ! Curran, I remember, began a letter to a friend thus : 'It seems that directly I take a pen into my hand it remembers and acknowledges its allegiance to its mother goose.' . . .

D.—Have you read the *Confessions of an Opium Eater* ?

M.—Yes.

D.— It is an extraordinary piece of writing.

M.—I thought it an ambitious style and full of bad taste.

D.—You should allow for the opium. You know it is a genuine work.

M.—Indeed.

D.—Certainly. The author's name is De Quincey. He lives at the lakes. I know a gentleman who has seen him.

Murray.—I have seen him myself. He came to me on business once. He was the man whom the Lowthers procured to edit a paper against Brougham's party. He read me the prospectus, and the first thing he said was

[1] See *Vivian Grey*, Bk. IV. ch. 1, where the foregoing conversation about Byron is reproduced almost verbatim.

to tell the reader the whole story of his being hired by Lord Lonsdale.

M.—Ha! ha! ha!

Murray.—From this you may judge what kind of man he is, and I need not tell you that there never was a being so ignorant of the world's ways.

M.—I read the confessions in the *London Magazine*, and I had no idea that it was a genuine production. . . .

To the young law clerk these dinners were evidently something of an event; they gave him his earliest glimpses into a greater world; and when in *Vivian Grey* he wanted to reproduce the conversation of men of fashion of the more serious type it was to his recollections of John Murray's dinner parties that he turned for his model, and in part for his material.

As the years rolled by, however, and the boy outgrew his bookworm habits, the social side of his nature must have found room for expansion elsewhere; certainly he developed tastes and manners which neither his father's library nor Murray's dining-room could have suggested. Vivian Grey, we are told, when at the age of nineteen he emerged from the seclusion of his study and began to mingle in society, was 'an elegant lively lad with just enough of dandyism to preserve him from committing gaucheries and with the devil of a tongue'; and at a similar stage of his career the young Disraeli, we may suppose, was much the same. The dandyism at all events was already visible. From the wife of one of the partners of Frederick's Place testimony has come down that even thus early Benjamin Disraeli dressed very differently from other young men: he used to come to her house in 'a black velvet suit with ruffles, and black stockings with red clocks—which in those days was rather conspicuous attire.' Both *Vivian Grey* and *Contarini Fleming* indicate that the love of feminine society, and the susceptibility to feminine influence, which were abiding features of his character, made their appearance early; though beyond his mother and his sister, to whom he was then, as always, devoted, we know nothing of the women who were at this time of his circle. Vivian Grey's 'devil of a tongue' made him popular with the ladies of his acquaintance, and he in his turn discovered that 'there is no fascination so irresistible to a boy as the smile of a married woman.' The men trembled at Contarini's sarcasms, but 'the women repeated with wonderment his fantastic raillery.' Clever, spirited, and handsome, and with as much assurance and as sharp a tongue as either of his heroes, the young Disraeli no doubt had much the same success.

Meanwhile, as he shed the habits and manners of the scholar, his taste for the profession to which his father had devoted him did not increase. There is a story of a friendly solicitor endeavouring to quicken his flagging interest in the law by installing him for a time in his own office; but when he found the youth reading Chaucer during business hours he came to the conclusion that nature had not intended him to be a lawyer, and advised that he should be allowed to follow his own inclinations and devote himself to literature.[1] To literature at all events he about this time seriously applied himself. The first attempt of which we have any record is curiously indicative of the trend of his subsequent genius. Encouraged by the kindness of John Murray, he submitted for publication in May, 1824, a short manuscript which under the guise of a tale was intended to be a satire on 'the present state of society.' Of society outside Bloomsbury the youthful satirist can have known nothing, except what he had picked up at Murray's dinner parties or a vivid imagination could teach him; and Murray showed so little eagerness to publish that a month later the author asked him to forget the 'indiscretion' and consign the manuscript to the flames.[2] A couple of chapters which had been mislaid when the manuscript was first sent to Albemarle Street have by that accident

[1] Sir Henry Layard's *Autobiography*, I., p. 47.
[2] Smiles's *Life of Murray*, II., p. 182.

survived, and they seem to show that the work was a crude anticipation of *Popanilla*, its theme being the adventures of one Aylmer Papillon in a visit to Vraibleusia. It was characteristic of Disraeli that in spite of disappointment at the first the project, though allowed to sleep, should not have been abandoned. Nearly all his successes in life were founded on previous failures.

To Mr. T. F. Maples.

WINDSOR,
Aug. 2, 1823.

MY DEAR SIR,

A letter which begins with congratulations is generally a pleasant thing, and I therefore feel very grateful for the opportunity of thus happily commencing my epistle to the young stranger who

porrigens teneras manus
matris e gremio suae
Dulce rideat ad patrem
semihiante labello.[1]

But to leave Catullus and congratulations for a more matter of fact subject. As no particular time was settled for my return, and as you expressed a wish that I would communicate with you upon it, I am under the necessity of intruding upon you, surrounded of course by crowds of hurrying and eager friends who hail this new accession to the house of Montague, to ask the very uninteresting and business-like question of, when would you wish me to return?

If you can find time to write me half a line upon this subject I shall feel much obliged.

Present my best compliments to Mrs. Maples.

With the wish that every day of your daughter's life may be as sunny as the present and that she may never know the miseries of a wet summer,

I remain, my dear Sir,
Yours sincerely,
B. DISRAELI.[2]

When that letter was written the Disraeli family were spending a summer holiday on the Thames. In their

[1] Catullus, *Carm.* LXI., 210.

[2] It seems to have been about the beginning of this year, when he was eighteen, that Benjamin dropped the apostrophe in his name. His brothers and sister followed his example, though their father retained the old spelling to the end.

annual excursions they rarely went far afield, but in 1824, Benjamin, whose travels had hitherto been confined probably within a hundred miles of London, had a notable extension of his experience. His health was already becoming delicate and his father was also ailing; so father and son set forth for a six weeks' tour on the Continent, accompanied by a young family friend called Meredith, who had just taken his degree at Oxford, and whom we shall meet again hereafter. Leaving London towards the end of July, the travellers went by steamer to Ostend, posted through Belgium to Cologne, and ascended the Rhine valley as far as Mannheim and Heidelberg. We have Benjamin's impressions of the tour partly in an unfinished diary and partly in voluminous letters to his sister, which show in the writer, in addition to some merely boyish pertness and vivacity, a keen eye alike for the picturesque and the ridiculous; a good deal of descriptive power; an interest in the fine arts and a knowledge of them, both surprising in one so young; and a no less surprising interest in gastronomy, regarded also as an art and not merely as ministering to a healthy boy's appetite.

To Sarah Disraeli.

BRUGES,
Thursday, July 29, 1824.

MY DEAR SA,

I add a few lines to my father's letter not only out of my great affection for you, but also that you may not misconceive the meaning of his dubious paragraph respecting our triumph. The truth is that we had a very stiff breeze, and almost every individual was taken down stairs save ourselves, who bore it out in the most manly and magnificent manner, not even inclining to indisposition. We came in with a very fresh sea; the night was most magnificent—indeed, I never witnessed a finer night. The governor was most frisky on his landing, and on the strength of mulled claret, &c., was quite the lion of Ostend. This latter place we found sufficiently disgusting, uninteresting for anything with the exception of its fortifications and harbour. We left it at 8 o'clock same morning as we arrived, and proceeded to Bruges in diligence through a flat but richly wooded country full of *châteaux*, long avenues, and *paysannes* with wooden shoes and rich lace caps. Bruges is the city of cities. Nothing but churches and grand *maisons*—not a hovel in it. The streets the handsomest and widest and the architecture the most varied and picturesque imaginable. I never knew the governor in such fine racy spirits. I see he has hinted at the Hamiltons adventure. Sir John is certainly rather a bore, but

'upon my life
he has two daughters and a ladye wife;'

the first are regular prime girls, both fine women, the youngest devilish pretty, regularly unaffected, full of sketching, and void of sentimentality. He has introduced us with the greatest *sangfroid*, and Meredith and myself intend to run away with them. We have put up at the same inn at Bruges, a capital one by the bye. . . . Meredith and myself talk French with a mixture of sublimity and *sangfroid* perfectly inimitable. We are off to Gand to-morrow by canal after having passed a long and luscious day at Bruges. Give my best love to *ma mère* and the dear young slave drivers.

Yours,
B. Disraeli.

Antwerp,
Monday, Aug. 2.

My dear Sa,

We have been in Antwerp about two hours and a half, and the post goes off to-morrow morning. My father, as usual emulous of saving postage, positively forbids our writing separate letters, and he has been, of course, the whole two hours and a half writing his half page. I myself am extremely tired, and have not room, even if I had time, enough to write you a letter as long as I could desire, but I trust that by next post my father will sicken of his Sévigné fit, and resign the sheet in my favour. We left Bruges excessively delighted on Friday morning in the barque. The vessel was very full. The Hamiltons, &c. There was an Irishman among the passengers who would have made an inimitable hero for Matthews. It was his debut on the Continent, and, with a most plentiful supply of ignorance and an utter want of taste, he was enthusiastically fond of paintings; for many years running he had come up from Dublin on purpose to see the exhibition, and after a discourse with him on Rubens, the Flemish School, &c., on all of which subjects he exhibited the most splendid enthusiasm, he coolly remarked that he should have enjoyed his journey much more had he not missed the Watercolor Exhibition. I met him two or three times afterwards in different places, and his salutations were exceedingly rich; it was always 'How do you do, Sir; wonderful city this, Sir, wonderful! Pray have you seen the crucifixion by Vandyke, wonderful picture, Sir, wonderful, Sir.'

We arrived at Ghent after a pleasant passage of six hours on Friday at 3. I was agreeably surprised by the place, which I had imagined would have been Bruges on a larger scale. Its character, however, is perfectly different; there seems a great deal of business going on, or at least the numerous canals and the river Scheldt, by which it is intersected, and which are tolerably well filled with shipping, give it that appearance. We of course visited Mr. Schamp's collection, the University, Cathedral, &c., and of course we always thought each thing more wonderful than another, were exceedingly delighted, and tired ourselves to death. At St. Nicholas we took it into our heads to dine, perfectly extemporaneous. We ordered of course something cold, not to be detained. The hostess, however, seemed peculiarly desirous to give us a specimen of her cookery, and there was a mysterious delay. Enter the waiter. A *fricandeau*, the finest I ever tasted, perfectly admirable, a small and very delicate roast joint, veal chops dressed with a rich sauce piquant, capital roast pigeons, a large dish of peas most wonderfully fine, cheese, dessert, a salad preeminent even among the salads of Flanders which are unique for their delicate crispness and silvery whiteness, bread and beer *ad lib.* served up in the neatest and purest manner imaginable, silver forks, &c.; cost only six francs, forming one of the finest specimens of exquisite and economic cookery I ever witnessed. We have had a good deal of veal stewed with sorrel, and not bad. The paper in this country is bad, the ink infamous, and the pens wusser. Love to Mere and all.

Your affectionate Brother,

B. DISRAELI.

Sometimes the diary is an interesting supplement to the letters.

BRUGES,
Thursday.

Magnificent city, perpetual palaces, not an ordinary house. The proportions of the town perfect. The Cathedral a very ancient building. The tower a rude shapeless pile, rises like a great leviathan. The bricks of which it is built are of a most diminutive size. This apparently adds to its height,

. . . The city is three times too extensive for its inhabitants, and you may lounge down magnificent parades, bounded on both sides by palaces and churches, without being disturbed by a single sound or meeting a single individual. In its decay, its splendour, its antiquity and its silence, it very much resembles our Winchester.

GHENT,
Sunday.

Cathedral High Mass. Clouds of incense and one of Mozart's sublimest masses by an orchestra before which San Carlo might grow pale. The effect inconceivably grand. The host raised, and I flung myself on the ground.

To Sarah Disraeli.

BRUSSELS,
Friday, *Aug.* 6.

MY DEAR SA,

The *sermones gubernatorii* are this time rather diminished. We have heard that a post has arrived from England this evening; there is therefore some little chance of a letter; if however we do not receive one we shall be off on Saturday morning. We were more delighted with Antwerp than with any place we have yet been at. We put up at the Grand Laboureur, unfortunately no table d'hôte, but capital private feeds; our living for the last week has been the most luxurious possible, and my mother must really reform her table before our return. I have kept a journal of dinners for myself and of doings in general for my father, so I shall leave the account of the churches, cathedrals, and cafés till we come home. We have had a perfect debauch of Rubens, and Meredith and myself have destroyed the reputation of half the cathedrals in Flanders by our mysterious hints of the spuriousness of their Sir Pauls.

On Tuesday morning we set off for Brussels. We dined at Mechlin, and stayed between four and five hours there; dinner good and Cathedral magnificent, oysters as small as shrimps, but delicately sweet; hunted up an old bookseller. The entrance to Brussels is very striking. The part in which we reside, the new town, is a perpetual Waterloo Place, a regular succession of grand places and Rue Royales in a magnificent style of architecture.

The governor is particularly well. He has mounted a black stock, and this, added to his former rather military appearance, very materially aided a very pleasant mistake which occurred a short time ago. Our affectionately slang appellation of governor aided by the aforesaid military appearance has caused him to be lionised over a *maison de force* with regular major-general honors.

We visited the *Comédie* last night; but the performances were meagre and the house ill attended. The King of Holland pays the actors, and, of course, there is no theatrical spirit in Bruxelles. We pass the evenings very agreeably in cafés, where Meredith and myself play dominoes in a most magnificent manner and the governor invents or discovers new ices, lectures on sorbettes and liqueurs, and reads the Flanders papers, which are a copy a week old of the Parisian copies of the English. We then rush home to selzer water and Moselle, sugar and lemon, an invention of a waiter and my father, and which, to use our favorite national phrase, if it is equalled by any cup in Europe, is certainly not excelled. . . .

Brussels is full of English. The Belle Vue crowded. An Irish officer, rather grand, invited me to a picnic party at Waterloo; also told me he thought an Irish gentleman was the completest gentleman in the world when he chose, fancying his brogue did not detect him. We visit the field of Waterloo not so much for the scenery, but, as Mrs. Young says, for the idea. Yours,

B. DISRAELI.

Some notes on pictures and gastronomy may be added from the diary.

ANTWERP,
Monday.

It is impossible without visiting Antwerp to have any idea of the character and genius of Rubens. It is ridiculous to hear the sage critiques on his particular style and manner. No artist seems to have painted so differently. His style in his large pictures is sometimes sketchy and rapid, while in the Museum are many pictures finished with almost a miniature exactness.

Without a pause, the diarist goes on to a subject that interested him as much as pictures.

The dinner was good. The Grand Laboureur is, as the Clerk of the Police well termed it, *un hotel pour les riches.* The *vol au vent* of pigeons was admirable. The peas were singularly fine. The idiots, imagining they could please our English taste, dressed them *au naturel! Peste!*

Tuesday.

Rose at 5,—was at the Museum at 6. The *Déput́é Directeur* a civil fellow. Copied some drolls from an ancient picture of

Hans of Malines. In the midst of my sketching, the D.D. mysteriously beckoned me away and conducted me to a large and curtained picture which when unveiled displayed to my awe-struck vision the Christ between the Thieves, by Rubens. The picture had been lately undergoing an operation and strict orders had been given that it was to be shown to no one. The D., however, with whom we had formed a kind of *mon ami* acquaintance, took advantage of the early morn to display to us the most magnificent painting in the world. This is an additional argument in favour of early rising.

BRUSSELS,
Wednesday.

Table d'hote at Belle Vue—between 30 and 40 persons. Sufficiently amusing. Dinner excellent—frogs—*paté de grenouilles*—magnificent! Sublime!

To Sarah Disraeli.

COLOGNE,
Saturday, Aug. 14.

DEAR SA,

We are in a city in which there are so many churches to lionise that I am afraid we shall never get out of it. We arrived at Cologne last night. I wrote to you last from Brussels. . . . On Saturday we left Brussels for Waterloo, lionised over the field of battle and the adjoining country by old Shorter himself, a jolly antique. He harangued in a mixture of Dutch, Flemish, French, and English—very rich—forming a kind of Belle Alliance lingo, most likely in compliment to the place. We dined at Genappe most admirably; by the bye, we hired a carriage at Brussels. It is a complete travelling carriage left behind by a Hamburg gentleman at the Belle Vue, perhaps for his bill. We got to Namur by 11 o'clock at night. At Genappe the country rises and the road for about seven leagues is through a bold but highly cultivated country. We left Namur, where there is little to see, on Sunday afternoon. Our road lay through the valley of the Meuse, and after proceeding for about 20 miles we arrived at Huy, a small village most romantically situated amidst lofty hills on the banks of the Meuse. The journey to Huy is a succession of scenery which I think the Rhine can scarcely equal. On Monday morning we continued our journey for about 30 miles, as far as Liège, still through the valley. The scenery if possible even more picturesque than before and the valley considerably wider. . . .

At seven in the morning on Tuesday we set off for Spa. We passed over a mountainous country, and for miles continued to ascend. The road to Spa is a perfect debauch of gorgeous scenery. We arrived at the far-famed watering place ; pen and ink, and particularly the miserable material with which I am scratching, can give you no idea of our rich adventures. We rode on the Spa ponies to the distant springs. They are handsome little galloways ; the governor was particularly equestrian. I have become a most exquisite billiard player ; we shewed off to great advantage at the Wells and Aix, to which place we were off on Wednesday. We were asleep when we entered the Prussian frontier, and the governor mistook the officer for an inn-keeper and kindly informed him that he had taken refreshment at Limburg. The rest of this scene, which was exquisite, when we meet.

Aix is close and inelegant, the pictures we saw *magnifique*. We slept on Thursday at Juliers, and had rich adventures at a country inn, and arrived at the Rhine last night. It is flowing in sight of our windows. Excuse false construction and vicious grammar, as I have lost my English. Everything has gone right except hearing from you. I suppose you missed the English post. We did not sufficiently calculate. As for our own journey, if we find a letter at Mayence, saying dear Mother is well, we may perhaps favor you by not returning at all, as really your manners are so barbarous and your dishes so detestable that, &c. Give my love to all. I trust my Mother and yourself are well. I meant to have written to Ralph, but my father approves of concentrated postage. How is Jem ?

Yours ever,

B. DISRAELI.

On the road between Spa and Aix he notes in the diary :—' The Belgians seem extremely hostile against the Dutch. It may be questioned whether, in case of a war, they might not rebel against the present authorities ' —probably his first political observation of which there is record. One of the pictures at Aix which he found so '*magnifique*' leads to a strange rhapsody :—

Head of Christ by Morales, exactly as in the description in the pseudo letter of the Roman Proconsul. Morales well entitled to his surname of Divino. The first painters depicted the Saviour with the common national countenance, always undignified and sometimes vulgar. The great masters, aware of the impropriety, were not bold enough to alter what they

Isaac D'Israeli 1834.
From a drawing by S. P. Denning
in the possession of Mr. Coningsby Disraeli

attempted to improve, and in their attenuated and uninteresting figures they have only spiritualized a sad humanity. In the present picture, the auburn locks seem only prevented from growing over the countenance by the moiety of the star which forms the glory : everything which can even be conceived as necessary to the formation of a face of perfect beauty, but nothing earthly in the appearance. You could not mistake the head for an Apollo or an Adonis. The eyes, beaming with human beauty, are nevertheless bright with the effulgence of celestial light, and fixed upon no particular object. They seem looking on the world. The nose is exquisitely formed, and the flesh tints seem immortal.

To Sarah Disraeli.

MAINZ,
Aug. 19.

MY DEAR SA,

We arrived at Mainz yesterday morning, and immediately rushed to the post-office, though we were all convinced of the utter impossibility of receiving a letter. To our great joy one was immediately handed us. It was very clever in you writing to M. The non-receipt of a letter was the only circumstance which threw a cloud over our enjoyment, and to receive it so unexpectedly was quite delightful. My father recovered his spirits in an instant. . . . Since I last wrote from Cologne our adventures have been grand. So much was to be seen at Cologne that we hired a fiacre, as we thought, from our host, determined to ride all over the city. To our great surprise a most elegant landaulet with the coachmen in military livery stopped at our gate. This, we were informed, was the fiacre, and also nearly the only carriage in Cologne. We were almost stopped in our progress by the stares of the multitude, who imagined we were Archdukes at least. We have always put up at the crack hotels, which we find the most reasonable. We travel, as I wrote to you, in a most elegant equipage, and live perfectly *en prince*. The governor allows us to debauch to the utmost, and Hochheimer, Johannisberg, Rudesheimer, Assmannshausen, and a thousand other varieties are unsealed and floored with equal rapidity.

On Sunday we left Cologne early, dined at Bonn —where we stayed some short time—passed Drachenfels and the seven mountains, reached Coblenz early next morning, left it in the afternoon, visited Ehrenbreitstein —for which our landlord got us a ticket—and left for the present the Rhine to proceed on our tour to the Baths of the Taunus Mountains. We entered the principality of Nassau, and arrived at Ems at five o'clock. The scenery is of a nature baffling all description, the chief feature richly wooded mountains. The baths of Ems are now among the most fashionable of the continent. Spa and those kind of place are now out of date, or visited merely by English. The establishment consists of a mansion which covers nearly an acre of ground and which was formerly a palace of Nassau. It contains upwards of 230 rooms, besides 80 baths, which are similar to those at Aix. The lodgings are a concern of the Prince, and on each door the price of the bed, &c., is affixed. Over this department a *maître d'hôtel* appointed by the Prince presides. The rest of the establishment is perfectly separate, and is constructed by a restaurateur at his own risk. There is a Saloon of an immense length and magnificently furnished, at which there is a *table d'hôte* every day at 1, all other meals and refreshments independent in different parts of the Saloon. Opposite to the mansion are beautiful gardens running by the side of the river Lahn.

Such is a slight sketch of Ems, a most singular, indeed, an unique spot. A watering place without shops and without houses ; the very Castle of Indolence. Above all, its situation is, perhaps, one of the most magical in the world, this in a small valley surrounded by ranges of lofty but wooded mountains. The river Lahn winds through them, and walks and gardens are on its banks. Further on the heights and woods of Nassau, studded with old grey ruins, and without a sign of population. The visitors are perfectly in unison with the genius loci. Lounging and lackadaisical, they bask on sunny banks or doze in acacia arbors. Some creep to the woods of Nassau, others are rowed down the river, music perpetual. The ladies patronise superb donkeys. There seems an utter void of all thought and energy, and positively in this place even the billiard room and the gambling table are deserted. Above all, no English. The Hamiltons, whom we met again, the only ones. After this account you will perhaps rejoice to hear that we left this fatal and delicious paradise next day at 12, a glorious morning, passed to and through Nassau, the country, if possible, increasing in loveliness. . . . We are all exceedingly well. Have made many acquaintances, chiefly among the military, the governor being perpetually mistaken for a *général anglais*. His black stock is grand, and he has long left off powder. . . .

Your affectionate Brother,

B. DISRAELI.

Heidelberg,
Monday, Aug. 23.

My dear Sa,

We arrived at Heidelberg, or, as my father terms it, Heligoland, this morning and received your letter. On Thursday the 19th we left Mainz, crossed again the Rhine, re-entered Nassau, and arrived at Frankfort early. We remained in this city until Sunday morning, and were very much amused. F. is a very populous, busy, and dashing city. The Opera is one of the best in Germany. We went on Thursday night, Cherubini's *Medea.* The house crammed full. The boxes private, as in London, save two in the centre for strangers. We were much amused. We lounged a great deal at Frankfort. Our banker was extremely civil, and gave us a ticket for the Casino, an institution similar to our crack London clubs, and not inferior to them in style or splendor. Here we read all the English newspapers and billiardised. Returning home we discovered at a *confiseur's* something superb beyond conception ; we committed an excess, and have talked of the ambrosia ever since. My father has bought some fine prints at F.—Albrecht Dürers, Max Antonios, and many Rembrandts, very magnificent impressions and very reasonable. On Saturday we visited the collection of Mr. Bethmann ; in it Dannecker's grand Ariadne on the Lion, which you remember described in Dodd. In the evening we rushed to the Opera, the *Zauberflöte.* . . .

On Sunday, after visiting the Museum, we left Frankfort for Darmstadt, a lounging little city full of new and architectural streets. The Opera is celebrated throughout Europe, and justly so. We attended it in the evening—*Otello* ; the scenery is the most exquisite I ever met with, the discipline of the orchestra admirable. The Grand Duke an immense amateur. The Royal Box is a large pavilion of velvet and gold in the midst of the Theatre. The Duke himself, in grand military uniform, gave the word for the commencement of the overture, standing up all the time, beating time with one hand and watching the orchestra through an immense glass with the other.

We left Darmstadt this morning, a very fine day, travelled through a beautiful country at the foot of the Bergstrasse mountains, reached Heidelberg, which is beautifully situated on the Neckar, surrounded and partly built on lofty mountains. We called and delivered our letters to Mrs. Fobin, a cleverish, pleasant woman. She was very civil, pressed us very much to stay at Heidelberg, asked us to meet Lady Davy and Lord Dudley, who are both at H , which we declined, as we set off to-morrow. . . . We rise very early and travel chiefly in the early morning. We shall be back, I dare say, in a fortnight, as there are no great cities to visit on our return. We have been only a month coming to Heidelberg, and have done anything but hurry, spending in Brussels and Frankfort alone upwards of a week. . . . Remember me to all, my best love to my mother. . . . I expect no more letters from you, but shall enquire at Mannheim and Mainz and Coblenz before our excursion into Luxembourg. We are now in the Duchy of Baden; have been much disappointed in not seeing the *Freischütz*. It would have been a great treat to have seen it at Darmstadt.

Your affectionate Brother,

B. Disraeli.

Coblenz,
Sunday, *Aug.* 29.

My dear Sa,

I wrote to you last from Heidelberg, which pretty place we left on Wednesday last. We had the misfortune of having very rainy weather there, but the new moon has brought us at last the most beautiful weather that I ever remember. We reached Mannheim, a beautiful city—a fête on the birthday of the G. Duke of Baden; the Opera, very elegant house and very fully attended; *Don Giovanni*—very bad. From Mannheim we travelled through Worms and arrived again at Mayence on Friday.

Yesterday having made necessary arrangements for the conveyance of our carriage, we commenced our voyage down the Rhine. So much has been read and written about this descent that I will not bore you with descriptions of a country which you know almost as well as myself. I can only say that the most glowing descriptions do but imperfect justice to the magnificent scenery. It answered my highest expectations, which, after passing over the Bergstrasse and the Taunus, is saying a great deal. We set off at 6 o'clock, stopped at Bingen two hours for dinner, but the time not suiting us we had supplied ourselves with prog. We therefore took a boat during these two hours and made an excursion to the ruined castle of Ehrenfels, near Bingen and opposite the famous tower of Archbishop Hatto. . . .

We landed in the evening again at Coblenz after passing through 60 miles of the most beautiful part of the river. Here we are digesting an excursion into Luxembourg. Our host at Coblenz is a most excellent fellow. My love to my mother and all. The weather continues most beautiful. Tell Ralph we had two military bands alternately playing while we dined at Mannheim. Jem I hope is prospering.

Our host at Coblenz has discovered since our last visit that the governor is a great author and has coolly informed him this morning he shall be obliged to him for his works. Our dinners, if possible, improve. Game is rushing in in all directions. Partridges abound. The roebuck is superb beyond imagination. At Mannheim we had sour craut, but this is not the season for it.

Yours ever,

B. Disraeli.

Here Disraeli's own record of his journey comes to an end. From Coblenz the travellers made their way up the valley of the Moselle by Treves to Luxembourg; and thence by Sedan and Valenciennes to Calais. Nine years later, when he had occasion to recall this visit to the Rhine, Disraeli wrote:—'I determined when descending those magical waters that I would not be a lawyer.' His father, forgetful of his own early experience, seems not to have yielded without a struggle: 'a father is, perhaps, the worst judge of his son's capacity; he knows too much—and too little.'[1] But he yielded in the end, and though the connexion with Frederick's Place was not formally severed at once, we soon hear of the son in other fields of activity. 'The hour of adventure had arrived.'

[1] *Vivian Grey*, Bk. II. ch. 3.

CHAPTER V.

FINANCE AND JOURNALISM.

1825.

The law was to be abandoned, but what was to take its place? Conscious of extraordinary powers, and resolved at all hazards to find a field for their exercise, the young Disraeli was not to be bound in the trammels of any of the conventional professions. His first attempt in literature had failed, and his aims, though not yet definitely political, were now clearly directed towards the world of action. We can imagine that, like Vivian Grey—

In the plenitude of his ambition he stopped one day to enquire in what manner he could obtain his magnificent ends:—'The Bar—pooh! law and bad jokes till we are forty; and then with the most brilliant success, the prospect of gout and a coronet. Besides, to succeed as an advocate, I must be a great lawyer, and to be a great lawyer, I must give up my chance of being a great man. The Services in war time are fit only for desperadoes (and that truly am I); but, in peace, are fit only for fools. The Church is more rational. Let me see: I should certainly like to act Wolsey, but the thousand and one chances against me! and truly I feel *my* destiny should not be on a chance. Were I the son of a Millionaire, or a noble, I might have *all*. Curse on my lot! that the want of a few rascal counters, and the possession of a little rascal blood should mar my fortunes!'[1]

[1] *Vivian Grey*, Bk. I. ch. 9.

The rascal blood could not be changed, but the rascal counters might be won, and to win them by some speedy method seemed the easiest solution of the problem. Even before his visit to the Rhine, Disraeli, in partnership with a fellow clerk in Frederick's Place called Evans, had tried his fortune on the Stock Exchange, with what results we do not know, though the stakes were probably small. He now, however, increased them. The English people were at this moment suffering from one of those attacks of speculative mania to which they are subject. Some years of great national prosperity had preceded, and for the capital then accumulated and now seeking investment a new outlet had been found in the revolted colonies of Spain. Canning's foreign policy, of which these colonies were the pivot, helped to give an air of respectability, or even of patriotism, to the schemes of company promoters, and presently all the phenomena of the South Sea Bubble were reproduced. The old stories of the mineral riches of the New World were revived, companies were formed in great numbers to exploit them, and the shares eagerly bought by a credulous public. Disraeli and Evans did not escape the prevalent mania. At the moment when they caught the infection the revolted States were clearly on the eve of receiving formal recognition from England, and the tide of speculation was nearing its height. Having found a confederate in another youth, the son, apparently, of a rich stockbroker, the partners began a series of operations in Spanish American shares, the first recorded transaction being in November, 1824. Their operations were disastrous from the beginning: by the close of the year there was a balance against them of nearly £400; by the end of January, 1825, this adverse balance was nearly £1,000; and by the end of June they had lost about £7,000, of which half had been paid in cash, provided mainly, it would seem, by Evans. It is not clear how the losses were distributed between the partners; the accounts that have been preserved are confused, nor is it worth while to disentangle them. What concerns us is that Disraeli at the age of twenty had incurred a debt of several thousand pounds, a debt which was not finally liquidated till nearly thirty years later, when he had already led the House of Commons and been Chancellor of the Exchequer. The 'rascal counters' were thrown into the scale against him, and his folly or misfortune on this occasion was the beginning of financial embarrassments by which he was tormented through a great portion of his career.

When they began their operations Disraeli and Evans were speculating for the fall; they reversed their tactics and became 'bulls,' most unluckily just at the moment when the market was losing its buoyancy. Their first instinctive judgment of the financial situation had been sound, though their action had been premature, and the change of view and tactics may have been owing to the influence of a man who now for a time plays an important part in the life of Disraeli. Mr. John Diston Powles was the head of a financial house which had been reaping a rich harvest from the boom, and whose credit was deeply involved in its continuance and justification. The firm had promoted several mining companies with large capital, and to two of these, including one, the Anglo-Mexican Mining Association, which had become the focus of great speculative excitement, Messrs. Swain and Stevens were solicitors. In this way, perhaps, it came about that young Disraeli made the acquaintance of Mr. Powles, and, with an extraordinary power which he already possessed of influencing men, even of years and standing far greater than his own, he appears speedily to have won his way into the counsels and confidence of the financier, and the two formed a close alliance. Disraeli possibly thought he had found the road to a great position in the world of finance and to the fortune of which he was in quest; Powles, on the other hand, no doubt saw that his young confederate's glowing imagination, ready pen, and connexion through John Murray with the world of literature and journalism, a connexion which, we may be sure, lost none of its importance in the setting forth, were assets that might be turned to valuable account. The speculative fever had risen to such a height that cool observers were beginning to feel alarm; Lord Eldon, the Chancellor, had drawn a parallel between the present mania and the South Sea Bubble; and the air was full of rumours of interference by the Legislature. To avert the danger of such interference and reassure the public, Disraeli's pupil pen was enlisted, and in March the first result of his labours, a pamphlet of nearly a hundred pages, was published by Murray on commission, under the title of 'An Enquiry into the Plans, Progress, and Policy of the American Mining Companies.'

This pamphlet, which was anonymous, seems to have been Disraeli's first appearance as an author. Its ostensible aim was 'to afford the public accurate data for forming an opinion as to the nature of these undertakings,' and so arriving at a decision as to the expediency of legislative interference. In pursuance of this aim our author discourses learnedly of mining methods, sets forth the main facts as to the principal companies, and arrives at the conclusion that 'their general promise is performed,' that 'the profits which have accrued by managing the American Mines in the market are not of an extraordinary nature,' and that 'the value of the shares of the different companies will be found to be relative to the progress which they have made in mining, and to the former reputation of the mines which belong to them.' On the question of policy the line he takes is high. He compares the mining interest in America to the manufacturing interest in England and dwells on the benefits to both countries that must follow from its development; he deprecates in the approved style of nineteenth century thought attempts to control 'the spirit of commercial enterprise'; and concludes with an appeal to 'our lawgivers to pause before they decide, and to enquire before they legislate, and not to be induced by frivolous tales and unfounded fears to restrain or prevent the agency of undertakings which are not the least conspicuous parts of a system on which mainly depend the wealth, the power, and the glory of our country.' The style becomes more flowing and the tone more declamatory as we proceed, and the dulness of the subject is relieved by occasional passages of picturesque impudence. The pamphlet was dignified with a review in the *Gentleman's Magazine*,[1] and ran through several editions.

Presumably it realised the expectations of the author and his patrons; for it was shortly followed by another. The second was entitled 'Lawyers and Legislators, or Notes on the American Mining Companies' and dedicated 'without permission' to Canning, who is lauded as 'not more eminent for his brilliant wit and classic eloquence than for that sedate sublimity of conception which distinguishes the practical statesman from the political theorist.' In this the note of declamation rises even higher than before, and in the style there is something also of that vituperative quality which the fashion of the day encouraged and which runs through all Disraeli's earlier political writings and speeches till he refined it into the rapier-like manner of his full maturity. In substance the second pamphlet is a development of the argument of the first against restrictive legislation. The attack on Lord Eldon is pressed home with greater vigour than before. The 'perfect fallacy' of his parallel between the present time and that which had generated the South Sea Bubble is demonstrated to the satisfaction of the writer; the law and policy of his observations in a case which had recently come before the Courts are both impugned, the former with no small ostentation of legal learning; and the so-called Bubble Act of 1820, with the terrors of which the Chancellor had menaced the company promoters, is denounced as a 'disgusting

[1] May, 1825.

and disgraceful statute,' a 'miserable medley of royal favour and penal legislation, gracious charters and terrific *praemunires*.'[1] So much for the lawyers. A couple of legislators, Mr. Alexander Baring [2] and Mr. Hobhouse,[3] who had raised their voices in the House of Commons in condemnation of the prevalent mania, are handled with even more severity; and in one sweeping indictment they and all the other assailants of the mining companies are charged with 'supporting their anathemas by statements which are so utterly unfounded that they might make mendacity blush and so awfully ridiculous that they might make folly grave.' Finally, and not without a certain insight and prescience, the Legislature is invited to deal with the subject of joint stock companies, though not in a hostile spirit, but with the purpose of recognising their existence and making them 'amenable to the law of which under the present system they are forced to be independent.'

Whether that policy will be pursued [our pamphleteer concludes with becoming gravity] it is not for us to divine. These sentiments come not from one who sits in Royal Councils, or mingles in the assemblies of legislative wisdom, but they come from one who has had some opportunity of investigation, some patience for inquiry, whose opinions are unbiased by self-interest, and uncontrolled by party influence, who, whatever may be the result will feel some satisfaction, perchance some pride, that at a time when warring and inconsistent councils were occasioning the very ruin which they affected to deprecate, when Ignorance was the ready slave of Interest, and Truth was deserted by those who should have been her stoutest champions, there was at least one attempt to support sounder principles and inculcate a wiser policy.

A third pamphlet in the series was issued by Murray on 'The Present State of Mexico'; but it was in the

[1] The Act, or so much of it as related to joint stock companies, was, on the initiative of the Government, repealed later in the Session of Parliament.

[2] Afterwards the 1st Lord Ashburton.

[3] John Cam Hobhouse, the friend of Byron, afterwards Lord Broughton.

main a translation of a report presented to the Mexican Congress by a Minister in high office who was also a subsidised ally of the mining companies. Disraeli, however, contributed some explanatory notes, and introduced the Minister in question in a memoir which has no appearance of doing less than justice to the merits of its subject or the other Mexican statesmen of the day. 'Inconsiderate ignorance,' it is true, was 'daily stigmatising them as weak and unprincipled adventurers.' But 'if they be not pure and practical patriots,' exclaims the indignant biographer in one of his roundest periods, 'we know not what names should be inscribed on the illustrious scroll of national gratitude.'

The brilliant pen of the young pamphleteer, whatever else it may have accomplished, did not avail, as we have seen, to save his private speculations from disaster. He was still undismayed; but as the fortune which was to serve as a main instrument of his ambition had eluded his grasp, it became necessary to frame some new combination, and the materials were soon discovered. In his preoccupation with finance Disraeli had not forgotten nor been forgotten by his old friend John Murray. He seems even to have persuaded Murray into joining him in a speculation in South American shares; and as the mining pamphlets could hardly be regarded as a contribution to literature, Murray in his turn provided his young ally with another opportunity of making an appearance as an author.[1] Having decided to issue for English readers a Life of Paul Jones, based on the same material as the Life by Sherburne, which was on the eve of publication in the United States, Murray entrusted the manuscript to young Disraeli and requested him to prepare it for the press. Immersed in what he no doubt thought was more important business, the editor seems to have discharged his duty in a rather

[1] Smiles, II., pp. 182-194.

perfunctory manner, but the work [1] in due course appeared with a preface [2] from his pen, which is remarkable only for its flatness and banality. Meanwhile, Murray had formed the habit of consulting the precocious youth in the perplexities of his business, had learnt to place a high value on his judgment,[3] and had taken him into his confidence with ever-diminishing reserve. Encouraged by the success of the *Quarterly Review*, Murray had for some time cherished the ambition of establishing a periodical which should appear at more frequent intervals; and in a fateful moment he confided this ambition to his young adviser.[4] Disraeli's eager imagination at once went to work and discovered possibilities latent in the project that Murray had never dreamt of. *The Times* had already taken a commanding position in daily journalism, but it was too independent of party affiliations to suit an ardent Canningite such as Disraeli, with his new world interests, had now become. Why, asked the audacious youth, should it not be possible to establish a daily paper in the Conservative interest which should equal or even surpass *The Times* in influence? And who more fitted than Benjamin Disraeli, with Murray's resources behind him and assistance from his new friends in the City, to be the triumphant organiser? He was without experience, it is true; but 'If a person have imagination, experience appears to me of little use,' and this heresy of Contarini Fleming's, if heresy it be, was

[1] 'The Life of Paul Jones, from original documents in the possession of John Henry Sherburne, Esq., Register of the Navy of the United States. London, John Murray, 1825.' The exact relationship of the English book to the American is not clear; but the former seems also to have been written by an American, and the original manuscript, which has been preserved, shows that Disraeli's share in it was limited to the introduction here and there of a word or phrase where the excision of a passage rendered such amendment necessary.

[2] Dr. Smiles treats this preface as Disraeli's earliest appearance as an author; but the first of the Mining Pamphlets was published in March, and the *Life of Paul Jones* not till September.

[3] It was to Disraeli's advice, for instance, that the publication of Crofton Croker's *Fairy Legends of Ireland*, one of the successful books of the time, appears to have been due.

[4] For the story of *The Representative* see Smiles's *Life of Murray*, II. ch. 26; Lang's *Life of Lockhart*, I. ch. 12; and Scott's *Familiar Letters*, II., Appendix.

one from which Disraeli was never quite delivered. It was an easy matter to persuade himself of the feasibility of the scheme, and once persuaded he threw himself into it with all the eager enthusiasm of a temperament that was impulsive by nature and, well as the fact was concealed in after years, remained impulsive to the end. The first step was to win Murray's acquiescence, and Murray was pursued, as he afterwards put it, 'with unrelenting excitement and importunity,'[1] till he yielded. Powles was then approached and his support secured. He and Murray were made acquainted by Disraeli's intervention, about the end of July, and on August 3 the three signed an agreement for the establishment of a morning paper under Murray's management, the property in which was to be vested as to one half in Murray and as to the other in equal shares in Powles and Disraeli, the three contributing the capital in like proportions. Where Disraeli's share of the capital was to come from does not appear, and was a subject to which probably that sanguine youth gave little consideration; but Murray, who must have known his want of resources, no doubt regarded Powles as good enough for the share of both.

The paper was to make its first appearance early in the new year, and in the meantime an organisation had to be created and multitudinous details to be arranged. The first problem was to find an editor, and for some reason Murray had fixed on Lockhart, Scott's son-in-law, as the most suitable person for the post. It is not impossible that the suggestion may have come from Canning, with whom Murray was in communication, and to whom apparently he presented, or endeavoured to present, Disraeli.[2] At all events, Murray resolved to consult Sir Walter, who had given him valuable aid in the

[1] Smiles, II., p. 217. It is well to note, however, that this phrase was used when Murray was smarting from the disappointment of recent failure. At an earlier stage of the enterprise he wrote to Jerdan:— 'I have never attempted anything with more considerate circumspection.'—*Ibid.*, p. 205.

[2] *Ibid.*, p. 189.

establishment of the *Quarterly*; and as the matter was too delicate to be settled by correspondence, Disraeli was despatched to the North to try the effect of his persuasive eloquence in the conduct of the negotiations. He was armed with two letters of introduction to Lockhart—one from Murray, in which he is described as 'my most particular and confidential young friend,' and Lockhart is requested to receive his communications 'as if they were given to you in person by myself'; the other from a Mr. Wright, a barrister, who, by Murray's wish, 'suggests the place of superintendent of the new paper,' and adds his belief that Canning wishes Lockhart to accept.[1] Disraeli's own letters to Murray give a graphic account of the mission, and incidentally show that the young plenipotentiary neither underrated its importance nor failed to take himself as seriously as the occasion required.

The first letter, written apparently on September 17,[2] is from Edinburgh, where he had arrived the night before, having 'slept at Stamford, York, and Newcastle, and by so doing felt quite fresh at the end of my journey. I never preconceived a place better than Edinburgh. It is exactly what I fancied it, and certainly is the most beautiful town in the world.' He has already discovered that Lockhart is at Chiefswood, his country cottage near Abbotsford, and has despatched Wright's letter thither; and he has visited a printing and bookbinding establishment, where his eyes are open for suggestions as becomes a practical man of business. 'I intend to examine the whole minutely before I leave, as it may be useful. I never thought of binding. Suppose you were to sew, &c., your own publications.'

I arrived at York in the midst of the Grand Festival. It was late at night when I arrived, but the streets were crowded and continued so for hours. I never witnessed a city in such an extreme bustle and so delightfully gay. It was a perfect carnival. I postponed my journey from five in the morning

[1] Lang, pp. 364, 367. [2] Dr. Smiles's dates are obviously inaccurate.

to eleven, and by so doing got an hour for the Minster, where I witnessed a scene which must have far surpassed, by all accounts, the celebrated commemoration in Westminster Abbey. York Minster baffles all conception. Westminster Abbey is a toy to it. I think it is impossible to conceive of what Gothic architecture is susceptible until you see York. I speak with the cathedrals of the Netherlands and the Rhine fresh in my memory. I witnessed in York another splendid sight—the pouring in of all the nobility and gentry of the neighbourhood and the neighbouring counties. The four-in-hands of the Yorkshire squires, the splendid rivalry in liveries and outriders, and the immense quantity of gorgeous equipages—numbers with four horses—formed a scene which you can only witness in the mighty and aristocratic county of York. It beat a Drawing Room hollow, as much as an oratorio in York Minster does a concert in the Opera House. The delightful stay at York quite refreshed me. . . . I find Froissart a most entertaining companion, just the fellow for a traveller's evening; and just the work, too, for it needs neither books of reference nor accumulation of MS.

Next day he writes from Edinburgh again. Lockhart has invited him to Chiefswood, and he will of course accept the invitation. 'I intend to go to Melrose to-morrow, but as I will not take the chance of meeting him the least tired, I shall sleep at Melrose and call on the following morning.' Then with an impressive air of mystery he gives Murray a code under which, owing to the very delicate nature of the names he will have to mention, he deems it wise to veil them; and, this serious business disposed of, he unbends sufficiently to end his letter with the information 'I revel in the various beauties of a Scotch breakfast; cold grouse and marmalade find me, however, constant.'

The third letter is worth giving at greater length.

To John Murray.

CHIEFSWOOD,
Sept. [21 ?], 1825.

MY DEAR SIR,

I arrived at Chiefswood yesterday. M. [Lockhart] had conceived that it was my father who was coming. He was led to believe this through Wright's letter. In addition, therefore, to his natural reserve there was, of course, an evident disappointment at seeing me. Everything looked as black as possible. I shall not detain you now by informing you of fresh particulars. I leave them for when we meet. Suffice it to say that in a few hours we completely understood each other, and were upon the most intimate terms. M. enters into our views with a facility and readiness which were capital. He thinks that nothing can be more magnificent and excellent; but two points immediately occurred: first, the difficulty of his leaving Edinburgh without any ostensible purpose; and, secondly, the losing caste in society by so doing. He is fully aware that he may end by making his situation as important as any in the empire, but the primary difficulty is insurmountable. . . .

The Chevalier [Sir Walter] breakfasted here to-day, and afterwards we were all three closeted together. The Chevalier entered into it excellently. . . . He agrees with me that M. cannot accept an official situation of any kind, as it would compromise his independence, but he thinks *Parliament for M. indispensable*, and also very much to *our interest*. I dine at Abbotsford to-day, and we shall most probably again discuss matters.

Now, these are the points which occur to me. When M. comes to town, it will be most important that it should be distinctly proved to him that he *will* be supported by the great interests I have mentioned to him. He must see that, through Powles, all America and the Commercial Interest is at our beck; that Wilmot H[orton],[1] &c., not as mere under-secretary, but as our private friend, is most staunch; that the Chevalier is firm; that the West India Interest will pledge themselves; that such men and in such situations as Barrow,[2] &c., &c., are *distinctly in our power*; and, finally, that he is coming to London, not to be an Editor of a Newspaper, but the Director-General of an immense organ, and at the head of a band of high-bred gentlemen and important interests.

The Chevalier and M. have unburthened themselves to me in a manner the *most confidential* that you can possibly conceive. Of M.'s capability, *perfect complete capability*,

1 Under-Secretary for War and the Colonies in Lord Liverpool's Administration.

2 Secretary of the Admiralty, afterwards Sir John Barrow; the well-known founder of the Royal Geographical Society.

there is no manner of doubt. Of his sound principles, and of his real views in life, I could in a moment satisfy you. Rest assured, however, that you are dealing with a *perfect gentleman*. There has been no disguise to me of what has been done, and the Chevalier had a private conversation with me on the subject, of a nature the most satisfactory. With regard to other plans of ours, if we could get him up, we should find him invaluable. I have a most singular and secret history on this subject when we meet.

Now, on the grand point—Parliament. M. cannot be a representative of a Government Borough. It is impossible. He must be free as air. I am sure that if this could be arranged, all would be settled; but it is '*indispensable*,' without you can suggest anything else. M. was two days in company with X. [Canning] this summer, as well as X.'s and our friend, but nothing transpired of our views. This is a most favourable time to make a parliamentary arrangement. What do you think of making a confidant of Wilmot H.? He is the kind of man who would be right pleased by such conduct. There is no harm of Lockhart's coming in for a Tory Borough, because he is a Tory; but a Ministerial Borough is impossible to be managed.

If this point could be arranged, I have no doubt that I shall be able to organise, in the interest with which I am now engaged, a most *immense party*, and a *most serviceable one*. Be so kind as not to leave the vicinity of London, in case M. and myself come up *suddenly*; but I pray you, if you have any real desire to establish a mighty engine, to exert yourself at this present moment, and assist me to your very utmost. Write as soon as possible, to give me some idea of your movements, and direct to me here, as I shall then be sure to obtain your communication. The Chevalier and all here have the highest idea of Wright's *nous*, and think it most important that he should be at the head of the legal department. I write this despatch in the most extreme haste.

Ever yours,

B. D.

Before the end of the month he writes again :—

The Abbotsford and Chiefswood families have placed me on such a friendly and familiar footing, that it is utterly impossible for me to leave them while there exists any chance of M.'s going to England. M. has introduced me to most of the neighbouring gentry, and receives with a loud laugh any mention of my return to Edinburgh. I dined with Dr. Brewster the other day. He has a pretty place near Melrose. It is impossible for me to give you any written idea of the beauty and unique character of Abbotsford.

His father was delighted with these letters from the 'young plenipotentiary.' 'I know nothing against him but his youth,' he wrote to Murray, 'a fault which a few seasons of experience will infallibly correct; but I have observed that the habits and experience he has acquired as a lawyer often greatly serve him on matters of business. His views are vast, but they are based on good sense, and he is most determinedly serious when he sets to work.' Still more interesting is Murray's own opinion of his youthful partner.

John Murray to J. G. Lockhart.

Sept. 25, 1825.

I left my young friend Disraeli to make his own way with you, confident that, if my estimation of him were correct, you would not be long in finding him out. But as you have received him with so much kindness and favour, I think it right to confirm the good opinion which you appear so early to have formed of him, by communicating to you a little of my own. And I may frankly say, that I never met with a young man of greater promise, from the sterling qualifications which he already possesses. He is a good scholar, hard student, a deep thinker, of great energy, equal perseverance, and indefatigable application, and a complete man of business. His knowledge of human nature, and the practical tendency of all his ideas, have often surprised me in a young man who has hardly passed his twentieth year, and above all, his mind and heart are as pure as when they were first formed; a most excellent temper, too, and with young people, by whom he is universally beloved, as playful as a child. I have been acquainted with him from his birth, but it is only within the last twelve months that I have known him. I can pledge my honour, therefore, with the assurance that he is worthy of any degree of confidence that you may be induced to repose in him—discretion being another of his qualifications. If our great plan should take effect I am certain that you will find in him a most invaluable, trustworthy friend, from whose energies you may derive the most valuable assistance. But he is yet very young.[1]

Disraeli's stay at Chiefswood lasted about three weeks. 'Here,' writes Sir Walter immediately after his departure, 'has been a visitor of Lockhart's, a sprig of the root of Aaron, young D'Israeli. In point of talents he reminded me of his father, for what sayeth Mungo's garland ?—

"Crapaud pickanini,
Crapaud himself,"

which means a young coxcomb is like the old one who got him.'[2] It is clear that the 'young coxcomb' made no small impression on both Scott and Lockhart, and succeeded in enlisting the interest of both in the 'great plan' which he had invented. But the obstacle to which he alludes in his first letter from Chiefswood was not easily overcome. In those days it would appear the editorship of a daily newspaper was not supposed to be an office that became 'a scholar and a gentleman,' and neither the title of 'Superintendent' nor Disraeli's still more splendid appellation, 'Director - General of an immense organ' could overcome the fastidiousness of Scott and his son-in-law, or reconcile them to the 'loss of caste' which an undisguised acceptance of Murray's proposal was thought to involve. Lockhart, however, came to London with Disraeli in the second week of October, and there a compromise was arranged. A vacancy was about to occur in the editorship of the *Quarterly Review*, and this apparently was an office that ranked as quite 'respectable'; so two agreements were signed in the presence of Disraeli, by one of which Lockhart became editor of the *Quarterly* at a salary of £1,000 a year, while by the other he undertook 'to the best of his skill and ability to aid and assist' Murray in the production of his newspaper, to write articles for publication therein, and 'by all other means consistent with his rank in life

[1] Scott's *Familiar Letters*, II., p. 405. [2] *Ibid.*, II., p. 355.

to promote the sale and character' of the said newspaper, receiving for these services £1,500 a year.[1]

On his return to town Disraeli flung himself into the work of organisation with headlong energy. Premises had to be taken, offices to be planned, a printing establishment to be fitted up ; reporters and sub-editors had to be interviewed and engaged, contributions to be secured from commercial authorities in the City, and home and foreign correspondents to be appointed and instructed. In all he was indefatigable. He employs his cousin Basevi as architect or arranges for the examination of title when a building has been secured. He writes one day to his host of the previous year at Coblenz, whom he found 'a most excellent fellow,' assures him that the new paper is to be 'the focus of the information of the whole world,' and that 'the most celebrated men in Europe have promised their assistance to Mr. Murray in his great project,' and enlists him as correspondent for the Rhine. 'I have been engaged at the *magnum opus* unceasingly since we parted,' he tells Lockhart on the day following. 'I have received six letters from different correspondents in the Levant and Morea who all appear very intelligent. I have written to them fully.' Or again: 'Much, my dear Lockhart, has happened since we parted, I think of importance. In the first place *Maginn is engaged.* I called upon the Doctor shortly after your departure.' Maginn was a journalist of experience whose services they were anxious to secure, but in this interview with Disraeli he was inclined at first to dismiss the whole project as ridiculous.

As I felt the importance of arguing the question with a man who might fairly be considered a very prosopopoeia of the public press, I thought the experiment might be hazarded

[1] Mr. Lang shows a curious anxiety to minimise the part Lockhart played in connexion with *The Representative*, but there can be no doubt whatever that Lockhart was at first virtually editor, as there can equally be no doubt that he was quite unfitted for the post. It is worth noting that in the agreement between him and Murray, though Disraeli signed as witness, there is nothing to indicate that Murray had partners in his undertaking.

of giving him a slight and indefinite sketch of our intentions. This I did with great caution, and mentioning no names. To give you an idea of the effect I produced is utterly impossible. The Doctor started from his chair like Giovanni in the banquet scene, and seemed as astounded—as *attonitus*—as Porsenna when Scaevola missed him. A new world seemed open to him, and this sneering scribe, this man of vast experience, who had so smiled at our first mentioning of the business, ended by saying that as to the success of the affair doubt could not exist, and that a year could not elapse without our being the very first paper going. . . . In brief, the Doctor goes to Paris.'[1]

In the same letter he transmits to Lockhart 'a sketch of our correspondence at present established.' He has provided for all South America, for the United States and Mexico, for all the Levant, and for every important place in Europe from Constantinople to Paris and from Rome to St. Petersburg. He has been 'very much assisted in this grand coup of Germany by Mrs. Wm. Elliot,[2] who, when devoid of humbug, is very clever.' 'I have no doubt that in a few days I shall get a most excellent correspondent at Cadiz; but I have not yet succeeded in Madrid, which is most important.' 'We have established also at Liverpool, Glasgow, Manchester, Birmingham, &c., &c.:—actually established.'

About the middle of November Disraeli was at Chiefswood again, and an entry in Sir Walter's journal tells us the object of this second visit. A cabal headed apparently by John Wilson Croker, Secretary to the Admiralty, had been formed among the old contributors to the *Quarterly* against Lockhart's appointment as Editor. Murray, 'the most timorous, as Byron called him, of all God's booksellers,' took fright at their opposition, so 'down comes young D'Israeli to Scotland imploring Lockhart to make interest with my friends in London to remove objections and so forth.' Scott wrote to a couple of his friends, and he also wrote to

[1] Scott's *Letters*, II., p. 408.
[2] A lady of German birth who had married Murray's brother-in-law.

Murray himself 'in something of a determined style.' 'My physic,' he remarks, 'has wrought well, for it brought a letter from Murray saying all was right, that D'Israeli was sent to me not to Lockhart . . . and other incoherencies which intimate his fright has got into another quarter.'[1] The result was that when Disraeli returned to London on November 21 he found himself in disgrace.

To J. G. Lockhart.

Nov. 21, *half-past five o'clock.*

I have arrived after a most fatiguing journey. I went immediately to the Emperor [Murray], and my reception was most unfavourable. I would use a harsher word if I remembered one. . . . He swears that he understood I undertook to go to Sir W. *au secret*, and not to you ; that I have ruined and *mêléed* everything, &c. ; that he only wanted Sir W. to write a few letters in consequence of the spirit evinced against you, &c., &c. I was too ill to answer him and I trust to the course of events to settle all things. He swears also that I ought not to have mentioned Barrow's name, &c. All these things, I need not tell you, appear to me very extraordinary, as I am not aware of having violated any confidence or instructions whatever.

By the following morning, however, the wearied traveller has recovered his elasticity, and 'three hours' uninterrupted conversation with Murray' puts everything right again.

To J. G. Lockhart.

Nov. 22, 1825.

My dear Lockhart,

Forget the letter, which, in a moment of great agitation about your business, and utterly exhausted in mind and body I wrote you yesterday evening. I rose this morning, having previously sworn by the God of the Silver Bow to slay the mighty Python of Humbug, whose vigorous and enormous folds were so fast and fatally encircling us. Thank the God, I have succeeded ! You will now come to London in *triumph*.—Yours ever,

B. D.[2]

[1] Scott's *Journal*, I., pp. 21, 22. [2] Scott's *Letters*, II., pp. 410, 411.

That he did not overrate his success Murray himself furnishes testimony in a letter to Lockhart on the following day.

I have yesterday and to-day listened to Mr. Disraeli's admirable details of his conferences with you and Sir Walter, and I can now state with my whole heart that nothing could have proved more completely gratifying; it has put me into complete possession of your views and character, and I can only repeat what I told him to say to you, that after this, Heaven and Earth may pass away, but it cannot shake my opinion.[1]

It was probably at this time that Disraeli first began to feel that dislike of Croker which was to find memorable expression in *Coningsby*. In a letter to Murray he speaks, with obvious reference to Croker and Barrow, of 'the junta of official scamps who have too long enslaved you.' To Lockhart he is even more explicit :—

I have often complained to you of Murray's inconsistency, vacillation, and indecision. I have done more, I have complained of them to himself. I regret it. Had I had any conception of the intriguing, selfish and narrow-minded officials by whom he has been so long surrounded, I certainly would have restrained my sentiments, and have pitied the noble and generous-minded being who was subjected to such disgusting thraldom. . . . It is impossible in a letter to give you any idea of the agitating and curious scenes which have taken place during these last days. The scales, however, have at length fallen from our friend's eyes, and the walls of the Admiralty have resounded to his firm and bold but gentlemanly tones. . . . Thank God I did not postpone my departure to town one other second![2]

With the obscure intrigues to which this and other letters refer we are not much concerned. Lockhart came to London in the first week of December, and a fortnight later, at Disraeli's suggestion and with the approbation of all, the new paper was named *The Representative*. There, as far as Disraeli is involved, the story abruptly ends. In a letter to Lockhart on

[1] Scott's *Letters*, II., p. 414. [2] *Ibid.*, II., p. 413.

November 28 he alludes to 'the terrific agitation in which the city and the whole commercial interest have been thrown during the last three weeks.' About the middle of December the agitation culminated in panic, and the crash which had for some time been inevitable came, spreading disaster far and wide, and burying Disraeli's hopes in the general ruin. Thenceforth, at all events, his name disappears from the records which tell the story of *The Representative*, and it is probably a safe conjecture to seek the explanation in the bursting of the City bubble, though we know nothing definite.[1] Murray went on with his enterprise, and in due course the paper was published; but, badly managed and badly edited, it was a failure from the beginning, and after a flickering life of half a year and a cost to its proprietor of £26,000 it ceased to exist.

So ended this bold attempt by the young Disraeli to storm the heights to which his ambition aspired. In after years, it would seem, his memory dwelt with little pleasure on the episode. He had more than once to deny statements that he had been the editor of *The Representative*, but as to his real connexion with the enterprise he was silent. There is nothing surprising in this; public men do not love to have their names associated with failure, and Disraeli was no exception. But apart from the failure there is nothing discreditable to him in the story as far

[1] Dr. Smiles, indeed, definitely states that, when the time came for Murray's partners to contribute their share of the capital, they both of them failed to fulfil their engagements; but this still leaves something unexplained in the story as it affects Disraeli, for Mr. Powles, as the correspondence shows, retained his position in respect of Murray and the newspaper apparently unquestioned for at least a couple of months after Disraeli had disappeared. As some things in the published accounts of these transactions have given offence to the living representatives of Mr. Powles's family, it is only fair to note that his own version of the story is unfortunately not available. Though the crisis of 1826 involved him in bankruptcy, it would appear that he afterwards recovered his position and paid his creditors in full; and his family state that he maintained friendly relations with Murray down to the latter's death. Certainly Disraeli, as his correspondence proves, even after he had become Chancellor of the Exchequer, remained in confidential communication with Mr. Powles, whom he valued both as a leading City Conservative and an authority on subjects in which the City took a special interest.

as it can be traced to-day. He had shown amazing energy, amazing self-confidence, and amazing power of winning to his views men older and riper in experience than himself. His faults had been the faults of youth, an over-sanguine temperament, and immaturity of judgment. In trusting so implicitly to his alliance with the mining interests in the City, he had built upon foundations of sand, but older heads than his, before and since, have been guilty of a similar error. It is not clear that the conception of the newspaper was in itself unsound. Until the last moment, in spite of its appearance at a time of severe financial stress, the success of *The Representative* was generally anticipated, and it was only the feebleness of the first few numbers that destroyed its chances. For this Disraeli, who had withdrawn a month before, can hardly be held responsible; if he had remained the result might have been the same, but it is not impossible that his dæmonic energy would have imparted to the paper some of the life and vigour which it so conspicuously lacked.

Murray, it ought to be said, seems to have cherished a feeling that, apart from the loss of his money, he had grounds for indignation against one who, in his own touching words, had received from him 'nothing but the most unbounded confidence and parental attachment'; but that feeling appears to have been of later origin. Whatever the circumstances and explanation of the young Disraeli's withdrawal from *The Representative*, the event at first made not the slightest difference to the intimate relations between the Murray and Disraeli families. A few months later, however, *Vivian Grey* was published, and the situation changed at once.[1] Because the Disraelis had expressed, or were supposed to have expressed, their approbation of this performance,

[1] Mr. Murray allows me to cite him in support of the view here taken:—'I believe the real cause of my grandfather's resentment was not *The Representative* affair nor the loss of his money, but the feeling that he had been caricatured and that his confidence had been betrayed by Disraeli in *Vivian Grey*. So my father always told me.'

Maria, Wife of Isaac D'Israeli 1805.
From a picture by J. Downman A.R.A.
at Hughenden

Murray dropped their acquaintance, and his feelings were shown by a letter written later in the year in which he speaks of Benjamin's 'outrageous breach of all confidence and of every tie which binds man to man in social life in the publication' of the novel. *Vivian Grey*, as we shall see, is full of boyish impudence, but there is nothing in it that can be even thought of as giving justification for language such as this. Murray apparently fancied that he had been satirised in the character of the Marquis, though it is not easy to detect the slightest resemblance between them. As Sharon Turner assured him, 'If the author were to swear to me that he meant the Marquis for you, I could not believe him: it is in all points so entirely unlike.' The fact is, Murray's temper, which was naturally far from perfect, was by the time the novel appeared in a state of sore trial. *The Representative* was not succeeding, and Murray found himself committed to a hopeless undertaking and left to bear alone the burden of a heavy weekly loss. It was not consoling to remember that he, a shrewd man of business of no small experience, had been led into the venture by one who was a boy in years; and the boy had made enemies who apparently did not neglect to foster the prejudice against him. Not only did Murray break off relations with the Disraelis, but he seems to have spoken of Benjamin in terms which struck the latter as 'outrageous' and 'inexplicable.' Young Disraeli replied with a menace of legal action, which he conveyed in a letter to Mrs. Murray invoking her interference to avert such a deplorable necessity; and Maria D'Israeli followed with a vigorous and sensible letter of protest addressed to Murray himself. 'I feel your disappointment,' she writes, 'and can forgive your irritability, yet I must resent your late attack on Benjamin'; and she expresses the shrewd opinion that 'the failure of *The Representative* lay much more with the proprietor and his editor than it ever did with my son.' Murray, as she reminds him, had known the boy from his cradle, and knew his want of resources, and how could he have been deceived? Her son, though 'a clever boy,' was 'no prodigy,' but Murray 'had formed in his versatile imagination a perfect being and expected impossibilities, and found him on trial a mere mortal and a very very young man.' 'What can you mean by saying that our son had divulged and made public your secrets? I must beg an explanation of this enigma.' Isaac D'Israeli also was stirred to unwonted vigour.

Eventually it would appear there was a reconciliation between Murray and the parents; but between Murray and the son, though business relations were resumed, friendship was at an end. How deeply this estrangement was regretted by young Disraeli, who beneath all appearance had a truly affectionate heart, is shown by his subsequent efforts to bring it to an end. When he began to make a name as a novelist it became one of his dearest ambitions to have a book published by Murray, and he never rested till this ambition was achieved. More than a year after his retirement from *The Representative*, when he found himself in possession of a little money, the earnings no doubt of *Vivian Grey*, though his debts on the Stock Exchange swallowed up the greater portion, he contrived to send £150 to Murray in payment for the printing of the mining pamphlets. 'I have never been able,' he explains, 'to obtain a settlement of those accounts from the parties originally responsible, and it has hitherto been quite out of my power to exempt myself from the liability, which, I have ever been conscious, on their incompetency, resulted from the peculiar circumstances of the case to myself.'[1] Murray's heart, however, remained unsoftened. Disraeli seems to have thought, and perhaps not without reason, that Lockhart's influence was used against him; at all events, from this time onwards we find him, whenever occasion offers,

[1] Smiles, II., p. 254.

showing a hearty dislike for Lockhart, who appears indeed from his side to have reciprocated the feeling with no less cordiality.[1]

Among Disraeli's papers there is a reminiscence, written nearly forty years later, of his early visits to Scotland and his intercourse with Sir Walter Scott.

When I was quite a youth (1825) I was travelling in Scotland, and my father gave me a letter to Sir Walter Scott. I visited him at Abbotsford. I remember him quite well. A kind, but rather stately, person: with his pile of forehead, sagacious eye, white hair and green shooting coat. He was extremely hospitable; and after dinner, with no lack of claret, the quaighs and whisky were brought in. I have seen him sitting in his armchair, in his beautiful library, which was the chief rendezvous of the house, and in which we met in the evening, with half a dozen terriers about him: in his lap, on his shoulders, at his feet. 'These,' he said to me 'are Dandie Dinmont's breed.' They were all called Mustard and Pepper, according to their color and their age. He would read aloud in the evening, or his daughter, an interesting girl, Anne Scott, would sing some ballad on the harp. He liked to tell a story of some Scotch chief, sometimes of some Scotch lawyer.

I was at Abbotsford again later in the year for a day. The *Edinburgh Review* had just arrived. Mr. Lockhart, then about thirty or so, but a very experienced literary man, I remember saying, 'Well, they may say what they like, but no man can write like Jeffrey on poetry. The article on Milton in the new number is the finest thing we have had for years.' As I came down to dinner, Sir Walter was walking up and down the hall with a very big, stout, florid man, apparently in earnest conversation. I was introduced to him before dinner as Mr. Constable—the famous publisher of the *Edinburgh Review* and the Waverley Novels, the authorship of them not then acknowledged; at least, not formally. It struck me, that I had never met before such an ostentatious man, or one whose conversation was so braggart. One would think that he had written the Waverley Novels himself, and certainly that Abbotsford belonged to him. However, he seemed to worship Scott, and to express his adoration. His carriage was announced, while he was at dinner, and he was obliged to go, as he had to return to Edinburgh to

[1] See for instance Lockhart's remarks on *Coningsby*, Lang, II., p. 199.

transact some business, and then go up to London by the morrow's mail, by which also I was to return.

So we met again, and I sate opposite him. He put a rich velvet cap with a broad gold band on his head, and looked like a great heraldic lion crowned. We had two fellow passengers, I am sure, but I don't recollect anything about them. But I never shall forget Constable's conversation. It was only about Abbotsford and the Waverley Novels. He informed me, that he intended to build a new wing to Abbotsford next year, and you would have supposed from what he said that Sir Walter had only commenced developing a new Eldorado. I never in my life met such a braggart, or a man so full of self-importance. Something had gone wrong on the journey; the guard or the coachman had displeased. He went into an ecstasy of pompous passion. 'Do you know who I am, man? I am Archibald Constable,' &c., &c., &c. This man was on the point of a most fatal and shattering bankruptcy; had gone up to town with some desperate resolve; and in less than a week the crash came.

When he had exhausted Abbotsford and the Waverley Novels, he began bragging about the *Edinburgh Review*: and dilated much on an article on Milton. I, like a youth, repeating at second-hand, ventured to observe, that no one wrote on poetry like Jeffrey. I copied this from Lockhart, but I flatter myself, that if I had read the article, I should not have made the observation; for it always afterwards gave me a very low opinion of Lockhart's literary discrimination. No man with a good nose could have for an instant supposed that Jeffrey had written the article in question. Constable informed me, that it was not by Jeffrey but that it was a secret: but so little was his power of reserve and reticence, or so great the excitement under which he then laboured, that before long I had no difficulty in worming out from him, that it was by a young lawyer of the name of Macaulay, from whom he expected great things. Therefore, I arrived in London with a sort of literary secret.

CHAPTER VI.

Vivian Grey.

1826.

Disraeli was never easily discouraged. His twenty-first birthday, which he celebrated on the 21st of December, a few days after the crash in the City, must have been gloomy enough; but, foiled in his practical ambition, he turned again to literature, and within four months had produced a book which became the talk of London and won for him celebrity or notoriety in a measure that few secure when they have barely crossed the threshold of manhood.

In the previous year a novel called *Tremaine* had appeared which was much read and talked about at the time, though it is now forgotten. It was a 'novel of fashionable life' and its popularity had given a certain vogue to this form of literature. The author,

Robert Ward, better known by his later name of Plumer Ward, was a person of some prominence in Parliament and society; but his book was published anonymously, and owed not a little of its success to the mystery in which its authorship was for some time carefully wrapt. As it happened, the Disraeli family rented Hyde House, Ward's residence near Amersham, for some months in the autumn of 1825, and here Disraeli always said he wrote *Vivian Grey*, taking the idea from *Tremaine* and completing the book before he was twenty-one. The link between the Disraelis and Ward was Ward's solicitor, Austen, who, living close by in Guilford Street, had formed an acquaintance with the family in Bloomsbury Square. It was Austen who, according to the very doubtful story, had found Benjamin reading Chaucer in chambers, and decided that he would never make a lawyer; and it was through Austen that Hyde House was taken by the Disraelis. Austen, as Ward's agent, had made the arrangements for the publication of *Tremaine*, and his young and clever wife was also in Ward's confidence, and had played a part in the negotiations. Aware, no doubt, of her relations with Colburn the publisher, Disraeli, who had no longer John Murray to apply to, turned to her for advice and assistance when his own novel was becoming ripe for publication. Sara Austen was well fitted to be the Egeria of a precocious youth of genius. 'She was a woman,' as her nephew Sir Henry Layard describes her, 'of more than ordinary talent and of more than ordinary beauty, very ambitious of shining in society and fond of flattery and admiration. Her accomplishments were many and various. She was a clever musician, a skilful artist, a good judge and critic of literary merit, and an excellent letter-writer. Had she chosen to be an authoress she would probably have been a successful one.'[1] Disraeli's earlier letters to her have unfortunately

[1] Layard's *Autobiography*, I., p. 46.

perished, but enough remain of Mrs. Austen's to help to elucidate our story.

From Mrs. Austen.

Saturday Morning. 25*th* [*Feb.*,[1] 1826].

My dear Sir,

Patience is not one of my virtues, as I fear you will discover to your cost, and I could just as easily sit without speaking till Tuesday as wait till then to give you my opinion of your MS. I am quite delighted with it, and enter into the spirit of the book entirely. I have now gone through it twice, and the more I read the better I am pleased. I never make any professions, but if you can do no better take me as an ally upon trust: at least I will be faithful to your secret and can undertake to manage it exactly in accordance to your wishes in Burlington Street [Colburn's offices]. *Trouble* is an odious word which shall be henceforth banished our vocabulary. I only long to receive my credentials, for indeed you have no time to lose on account of a very extraordinary coincidence,[2] which I dare not explain on paper, but of which you shall know enough the first time we meet to prove the advantage of its going to press immediately. The moment I have your permission and instructions I will write to C[olburn]. Pray send me the remainder of your MS. as soon as possible, for I am in a state of complete excitation on the subject.——I forget Mr. D'I's christian initial so must direct 'Junior.'[3]

Your sincere friend and ally

S. A.

At Mrs. Austen's instance Colburn accepted the novel for publication, though the secret of the authorship was rigorously withheld from him, as even for a time from Disraeli's own family. That the mystification might be

[1] March 25 was also a Saturday, but as the book was announced for publication at the beginning of April the earlier date must be chosen.

[2] The reference is without doubt to the approaching appearance of Ward's second novel, *De Vere*.

[3] Sir Henry Layard, writing half a century later of events which happened when he was a child, has, as this letter and others show, antedated the intimacy between the Austens and Disraeli, and has perhaps somewhat exaggerated the part they played in his life. The Chaucer story seems to me of doubtful authenticity, and not less so another story which is often quoted on Sir Henry Layard's authority of his accompanying his aunt in a call on the Disraelis and finding 'Ben' in the middle of a boxing lesson.

complete, Mrs. Austen copied the whole of the manuscript in her own hand, and her friends believed that she had helped to write the story; but her letters at the time confirm the statement she made more than half a century later: 'She had given him advice and had occasionally induced him to suppress or modify passages which she considered objectionable in taste, but nothing more.'[1] Why Disraeli should have taken so much trouble to preserve the anonymity of the book, or whether he had any more solid reasons than a native love of mystery and a desire to follow the fashion which Scott had established and to which lesser lights like Plumer Ward had conformed, we cannot be sure; but the publisher was so far from disliking the mystery thus created that he skilfully availed himself of it for purposes of his own. A master of the art of advertising, Colburn controlled, or was in a position to influence, several of the best-known organs of literary opinion; and presently in the daily journals and in weekly and monthly periodicals hints began to be given of the approaching appearance of a new society novel by an author who for obvious reasons desired to remain anonymous and in whose pages all the leading people of the day were to appear under thin disguises. The book was to be 'extremely satirical,' and was to contain 'portraits of living characters, sufficient to constitute a National Gallery'; it was to be 'a sort of Don Juan in prose,' and the hero was 'to become acquainted with every literary and fashionable character in existence.' By arts such as these curiosity was aroused and expectation created, and when towards the end of April *Vivian Grey* appeared in two octavo volumes its success was at once assured. Long reviews were published in many of the leading newspapers and periodicals; society amused itself by endeavouring to identify the originals of the characters; and at the same time speculation,

[1] Layard, I, p. 46.

diligently fomented by the ingenious Colburn, raged as to the identity of the author. From their different points of view both publisher and author had every reason to be satisfied with the success they had achieved.

Though we may safely assume that Disraeli was not averse from the prospect of notoriety, there is nothing to show that he had any real responsibility for the puffing arts of Colburn. He only received £200 for the novel,[1] and he was not even in direct communication with his publisher; but in the end he had to pay the penalty for Colburn's delinquencies as well as for his own. As long as it was supposed that *Vivian Grey* was the work of a man of high position the Press, where it did not praise, was silent; but in spite of Colburn's attempts to connect well-known names with the authorship, or at least to encourage the belief that the author was a 'man of fashion,' some of the critics were from the first suspicious. Jerdan, of the *Literary Gazette*, for instance, was acute enough to observe that 'the class of the author was a little betrayed by his frequent recurrence to topics about which the mere man of fashion knows nothing and cares less,' and that the book 'somewhat smacked of the literary writer'; and presently—it would seem through Jerdan, who had somehow ferreted out the secret, and in spite of the greatest exertions on the part of Mrs. Austen to 'blind' all concerned—the truth leaked out. When it was realised that the author of *Vivian Grey* was only an audacious boy, Colburn's enemies abandoned their reserve. 'Christopher North' in *Blackwood*[2] denounced 'the shameful and shameless puffery' by which the sale of the book had been secured, and dismissed it as 'a paltry catchpenny' by 'an obscure person for whom nobody cares a straw.' Another writer, in an article entitled 'The New Unknown,' revealed the author's identity by name, branded him as

[1] That is to say for the novel as it originally appeared. For the Second Part, published in the following year, he received £500 in addition.

[2] July, 1826, p. 98.

having acquired popularity 'by the meanest and most revolting artifices and the total disregard of all honourable feeling'; ridiculed 'his most ludicrous affectation of good breeding'; and even accused Disraeli and Mrs. Austen of having tricked Colburn into paying a high price for the novel by leading him to believe that it was from the pen of Plumer Ward.[1] With all his assurance Disraeli was by nature sensitive, and this was his first taste of the malignant abuse which was to be showered upon him all through life and against which experience was to make him proof. There is an obvious reminiscence of the effect upon the victim's mind in the well-known passage in which Contarini Fleming describes his sensations after reading the review of his novel *Manstein*:—

> With what horror, with what supreme, appalling astonishment, did I find myself for the first time in my life a subject of the most ruthless, the most malignant, and the most adroit ridicule. I was scarified, I was scalped. . . . The criticism fell from my hand, a film floated over my vision; my knees trembled. I felt that sickness of heart that we experience in our first serious scrape. I was ridiculous, it was time to die.

Yet in spite of the critics, perhaps to some extent because of their violence and acerbity, which revived the interest of the public as it began to flag, *Vivian Grey* survived. 'There was little art in my creation,' says

[1] *Literary Magnet*, Vol. II., pp. 1 and 129. From the same writer the legends took their origin that Disraeli had been the first editor of *The Representative* and responsible for its failure; and that he had also been editor of *The Star Chamber*, a weekly publication which appeared for a couple of months in the spring of 1826, and author of the 'Dunciad of To-day,' a satirical poem which was printed in *The Star Chamber* and provoked much resentment. The statement about *The Representative*, as we have seen, was not true. As for *The Star Chamber*, it was founded by a certain Peter Hall, a friend of Meredith's at Brasenose, who, through Meredith, had become acquainted with Disraeli. Disraeli contributed some fables with a political application under the title of 'The Modern Æsop,' at least one review, and perhaps other matter. But in later life he expressly denied (*The Times*, Nov. 3, 1871; *Leisure Hour*, Nov. 4, 1871) having been editor, if indeed there ever was an editor; and in the second part of *Vivian Grey* (Bk. V. ch. 1) he declared, with obvious reference to the 'Dunciad,' that he never wrote a single line 'of the various satires in verse' that had been attributed to him, and the internal evidence is in complete agreement with this repudiation.

Contarini of an early composition, 'but there was much vitality,' and the description exactly fits the first part of *Vivian Grey*. The novel owed its success no doubt in the first instance to Colburn's ingenious puffing, but it had sufficient merit of its own to reward the attention that had been artificially drawn to it. By the beginning of July a second edition had been called for, and a third, with certain modifications, was issued in the following year. Within three years of its first appearance Disraeli had come to reckon *Vivian Grey* among his 'juvenile indiscretions,'[1] and for a quarter of a century, as he wrote in 1853, he refused to reprint it; but in that year, as the book had 'baffled even the efforts of its creator to suppress it,' he submitted it to a severe expurgation and gave it a place in a collected edition of his works. He was careful, however, in a preface, to disarm the critics by anticipating their harshest censure.

> Books written by boys, which pretend to give a picture of manners and to deal in knowledge of human nature, must necessarily be founded on affectation. They can be, at the best, but the results of imagination, acting upon knowledge not acquired by experience. Of such circumstances exaggeration is a necessary consequence, and false taste accompanies exaggeration. . . . Such productions should be exempt from criticism, and should be looked upon as a kind of literary lusus.

In the face of this frank avowal, it would be absurd to embark on any pedantic inquiry into the worth of the book as a permanent contribution to literature. The question that is really interesting is its biographical value—what light, if any, does it throw on the developing mind and character of the author? The scheme of the novel is very simple. A couple of lines from *The Merry Wives of Windsor*—

> 'Why, then the world's mine oyster,
> Which I with sword will open,'

appear as a motto on the title-page. Vivian Grey, the

[1] *Life of Bulwer Lytton*, II., p. 316.

clever and precocious son of a distinguished man of letters, after a stormy career at school and a period of hard study thereafter looks about at the age of twenty for the means to satisfy his already inordinate ambition. Vivian's sword is his wit, and

> at this moment how many a powerful noble wants only wit to be a Minister, and what wants Vivian Grey to attain the same end? That noble's influence. . . . Supposing I am in contact with this magnifico, am I prepared? Now let me probe my very soul. Does my cheek blanch? I have the mind for the conception; and I can perform right skilfully upon the most splendid of musical instruments—the human voice—to make those conceptions beloved by others. There wants but one thing more—courage, pure, perfect courage;—and does Vivian Grey know fear?

He finds his magnifico in the Marquis of Carabas, a weak but vain and ambitious nobleman whom he meets at his father's table. Vivian fascinates him by his ready wit, plays upon his vanity, is invited to his country house, Château Désir, and there proceeds to organise a Carabas party out of the friends of the Marquis, prominent among whom, strange to say, is a Lord Beaconsfield—'a very worthy gentleman, but between ourselves, a damned fool.' The new party will require a leader in the House of Commons, and as Vivian with calculated modesty declines the task, he is at his own suggestion despatched to Wales to win over by his diplomacy a certain Cleveland, a young and once promising politician who had been betrayed by the Marquis and had retired from politics in disgust. The mission is successful, and Vivian carries Cleveland back with him to Château Désir. Now, however, a woman who has long been on the scene, but whose place in the scheme of the novel has hitherto seemed uncertain, begins to play a more definite part. Either from jealousy or from sheer love of mischief, she poisons the mind of the Marquis against Vivian Grey, and the catastrophe speedily comes. Dissension and treachery invade the ranks of the plotters, the house of cards that has been so laboriously constructed suddenly collapses, Cleveland is killed in a duel by Vivian Grey, and the hero retires to Germany discomfited in his ambition and a prey to bitter remorse.

Now that there is a large element of autobiography in the external setting of this fantastic story is soon apparent. Horace Grey is clearly a picture of Isaac D'Israeli; Vivian Grey's early years are, as has already been seen, described in great part from the author's own experience; the journey to Wales to secure Cleveland's adhesion to the Carabas party is obviously suggested by Disraeli's own mission to Scotland to enlist the services of Lockhart for *The Representative*; and we can trace in the book the influence of nearly every important fact of which we have knowledge in the author's previous history—his father's library, his conversations with literary men at Murray's, his tour in Germany, his intercourse with financial magnates in the City. All this is natural: a man can only write of what he knows, and at twenty-one his experience is so limited that his range of choice is narrow. But a question of greater interest and difficulty remains. Is Vivian Grey's character a reflexion of the author's own? Is his view of life the view which Benjamin Disraeli had deliberately adopted on the threshold of manhood? Are his ideals and ambitions Disraeli's youthful ideals and ambitions, and his adventures in some degree an anticipation of Disraeli's own career? It has generally been assumed that these things are so, and Disraeli's friends, accepting the assumption, have offered the best apology they could, while his enemies have exultantly pointed to the moral. But another theory is possible. A recent critic,[1] while admitting, or rather insisting on, the autobiographic significance of the book, has argued with some plausibility that the story is not an anticipation, but a retrospect; that it embodies not an ideal, but a confession and a warning; that the author is drawing from his own past experience in a very literal sense, and

[1] Mr. Lucien Wolf in his edition of *Vivian Grey*.

is transposing into the form of fiction the story of *The Representative* and the shipwreck of his own precocious ambitions.

As so often happens, Disraeli himself can be quoted in support of either theory. In a reply he made to his critics in the second part of the novel, he anxiously explained that he had been conscious from the beginning of the moral obliquity of his hero.

> I conceived the character of a youth of great talents whose mind had been corrupted, as the minds of many of our youth have been, by the artificial age in which he lived. . . . In his whole career he was to be pitied; but for his whole career he was not to be less punished. When I sketched the feelings of his early boyhood, as the novelist, I had already foreseen the results to which those feelings were to lead; and had in store for the fictitious character the punishment which he endured.[1]

This statement appears explicit enough; but it was written a year later when Disraeli was suffering from ill-health and the depression that attends it, and when for the moment he had lost his native buoyancy and self-confidence; and if that be remembered, the explanation ceases to carry conviction. To no reader of the earlier chapters of *Vivian Grey* would it ever occur that the purpose of the novel is to unfold the moral lesson of the consequences to which ambition uncontrolled by moral principle must inevitably lead. The author's sympathies are obviously with his hero, and the reader's sympathies, whether he will or not, are enlisted on the same side. The author no less than the reader may be intellectually aware of the hero's imperfections, but even when the action is well advanced there are few signs of moral reprobation. The catastrophe when it comes is a mere matter of machinery, and hardly affects the *ethos* of the story; it comes only, one feels, because the story had to be ended somehow, and a satisfactory ending was hardly to

[1] *Vivian Grey*, Bk. V. ch. 1.

be found. But we have testimony from Disraeli himself which is more convincing than an apology framed while he was still smarting from the wounds inflicted by the critics. Seven years later he wrote in a diary which till after his death was probably never seen by any eyes but his own : ' Poetry is the safety valve of my passions—but I wish to *act* what I *write*, My works are the embodification of my feelings. In *Vivian Grey* I have portrayed my active and real ambition.' Here again we might seem to have a final settlement of the matter ; but even this declaration must not be pressed too far. Disraeli, with his infinitely subtle and elusive mind and character, is a perpetual snare to the unwary who place too literal a construction upon his isolated words and actions. If it is ridiculous on the one hand to pretend that *Vivian Grey* is a confession written in a fit of penitence and remorse, it would be no less ridiculous on the other to pretend that Disraeli was unconscious of or indifferent to the moral obliquity of his hero, or that he deliberately set him up as an example which he afterwards meant to follow.

Though neither of the rival theories is wholly satisfactory, neither is wholly false, and it is not impossible to effect a harmony between them. Disraeli, as has been seen, used in later life to declare that he wrote *Vivian Grey* at Plumer Ward's house, where his family spent the autumn of 1825. It is not easy to see how in the whirl of those crowded months he could have found the leisure necessary for the completion of such a task ; and Mrs. Austen's letters seem to imply that a good deal of work was done on *Vivian Grey* after the secret had been confided to her in the following spring. But it is highly probable that a beginning had been made before, either at Hyde House in the month preceding Disraeli's first visit to Abbotsford, or even at an earlier date ; and that the story was picked up again after the catastrophe of *The Representative*. No one reading *Vivian Grey*, especially if he read it in the original edition, can fail to be struck by the contrast between the first volume and the second. All the merit of the book lies in the first volume.[1] In the earlier chapters especially we find the author writing from a genuine artistic impulse and with a joyous interest in his subject; and his story has all the coherence that comes from a strong and living conception of the character of the hero. The subordinate actors duly play their parts, though Mrs. Felix Lorraine is somewhat of an enigma, and is evidently beyond the powers of a boy of twenty-one. The style is light and vivacious, full of sparkle and epigram; and, though faults of taste are numerous, this first volume on the whole is a most amusing blend of cleverness and impudence. Even the flippancy and cynicism are too obviously boyish affectations to cause real offence. If we remember that *Vivian Grey* is only a work of fiction, and a work of fiction with a large element of caricature and exaggeration, and if we make allowance also for that subtle Disraelian irony which pervades all the novels, we may fairly say that in the first volume the hero is Disraeli himself; though just for that reason the work ought to have remained a fragment, as without a further development of the author's personality the story of the hero's adventures could not be carried on in conformity with the original conception.

The second volume opens with the mission to Wales, which bears so close a resemblance in detail to Disraeli's own mission to Scotland that it could hardly have been written except in the light of that experience; but signs of haste and discord at once begin to be apparent, and the remainder of the novel is a continuous descent. Both the narrative and the characters become incoherent, whole chapters of irrelevant padding are introduced, and the author's main preoccupation now appears to be to stretch his story out to a fairly respectable length

[1] Containing the first two books of the ordinary editions.

and then with the least possible trouble in the development of the plot to bring it to some sort of conclusion. Presently we lapse into vulgar and hideous melodrama. Mrs. Felix Lorraine, who before was an enigma, now becomes a monster, and, monster as she is, the hero in his revenge upon her shows himself a fiend. 'As hot and hurried a sketch as ever yet was penned,' is Disraeli's own description of the first part of the novel in his apology a year later, and he probably had in mind the second volume especially and the conditions under which it was written. It is just such work as we might expect from a boy without experience who, in the reaction after a period of unnatural tension ending in great misfortune, is endeavouring in headlong haste to bring an earlier literary sketch to some sort of conclusion. We now instinctively feel that the artistic impulse has spent itself, that the author is no longer inspired by genuine love of his subject, and that we are dealing with a mere piece of crude and hasty book-making. There is no definite artistic motive, not even the motive of contrition, though the treatment has taken a colour from the author's own misfortunes; and certainly the hero now is as far from reflecting Disraeli's ideals and ambitions as this second volume is from exhibiting his literary power.

So much on the question as to the sense in which Vivian Grey is a portrait of Disraeli himself; on the larger question as to whether the novel as a whole is a gallery of portraits from living originals something remains to be said. Elaborate keys were published at the time, one especially, as it appeared in *The Star Chamber*, being supposed to have the author's sanction. But the key-makers were probably just as well able as the author to affix a name to most of the characters. It required no great penetration to translate Lord Past Century into Lord Eldon or the Duke of Waterloo into the Duke of Wellington. By thin disguises such as these and by the frequent introduction of names of living persons the reader is certainly encouraged in the first part of *Vivian Grey* to search for real characters behind the fictitious names. Disraeli admitted as much himself in a letter which he wrote after the publication of the sequel in the following year. Colburn had made a circuitous attempt to extract from him information as to the prototypes of his characters; and Disraeli's answer well defines his position then and later on the whole question of portraiture from living originals in his novels.

To William Jerdan.

[1827.]

I am very much surprised at Mr. Colburn's request. How my knowledge of the characters in *Vivian Grey* can be necessary to, or, indeed, in the slightest degree assist any one in understanding the work, is to me a most inexplicable mystery. Let it be taken for granted that the characters are purely ideal, and the whole affair is settled. If any collateral information be required in order to understand the work, either *Vivian Grey* is unworthy to be read, or, which is, of course, an impossible conclusion, the reader is not sagacious enough to penetrate its meaning.

Of course, I have no intention of denying that these volumes are, in a very great degree, founded on my own observation and experience. Possibly, in some instances, I may have very accurately depicted existing characters. But *Vivian Grey* is not given to the public as a gallery of portraits, nor have I any wish that it should be considered as such. It will give me great pleasure if the public recognise it as a faithful picture of human nature in general. Whether it be anything further, rests with the author and can only interest him. I cannot prevent surmises; but I shall always take care that from me they shall receive neither denial nor confirmation.

In part of the former volumes, a number of names and characters were introduced which were evident portraits or caricatures. I can understand any reader of those pages being naturally desirous to comprehend their full meaning, and seeking auxiliary means to procure the desired knowledge; but to comprehend the full meaning of the present volumes, the public has only to read them; and if there be anything obscure or unsatisfactory, it is the author's fault—he is a blunderer. All the notes and keys in the kingdom will not make him more intelligible.

The Author of *V. G.*[1]

As a matter of fact, Disraeli's knowledge of the world of politics and society when he wrote the first part of *Vivian Grey* was far too slight for genuine portraiture beyond a very limited circle. The characters which have an obvious reference to originals in high places are names and little more ; in the world of letters he was more at home, and the sketch of Theodore Hook in Stanislaus Hoax is a good deal more ambitious ; but most of the *dramatis personæ* were merely conventional types, and in many cases we may believe that the key-makers in their zeal traced them to originals of whom the author had never heard.

[1] Jerdan's *Autobiography*, IV., p. 78.

CHAPTER VII.

A Tour in Italy.

1826.

Twelve months' continual strain and excitement were too much for a constitution that was never really robust. In June we hear of serious illness, and in an opportune hour, when the need of rest and change had become apparent, there came an invitation from the Austens to accompany them in a tour through Switzerland and Northern Italy. The invitation was at once accepted.

To Benjamin Austen.

[*July* (?), 1826.]

Dear Austen,

Having met many women who were too beautiful at the last night's dance, I slept off the memory of their loveliness by an extra three hours of oblivion, and was therefore unable to answer your note immediately; which, however, I am now doing surrounded by a much better breakfast than graced your board this morning.

A devil, though an ugly name, is certainly the wisest style of *déjeuner*—an innocent egg perhaps the silliest: why I say innocent I know not, for certainly if a devilled turkey's leg is the real limb of Satan, the other article may not inaptly be considered the 'yoke of sin.'

According to your advice, I have 'perused your note with attention and considered your offer with care,' and, as the man says who is going to be hired, 'I think the sitiation will suit.' It ill befits any man to dilate on his own excellence, but I may perhaps be allowed to observe that my various, not to say innumerable, accomplishments are not altogether unknown to you; and as for my moral capacities, why, I can have a good character from my last place, which I left on account of the disappearance of the silver spoons. I defy, also, any one to declare that I am not sober and honest, except when I am entrusted with the key of the wine cellar, when I must candidly confess I have an ugly habit of stealing the claret, getting drunk, and kissing the maids. Nevertheless, I've no doubt but that we shall agree very well. You certainly could not come to any person better fitted for ordering a dinner, and as to casting up accounts, if there's anything in the world I excel in that's the very one—and as I've got into the habit of never attending to the shillings and pence because they make my head ache, I generally detect the *aubergiste* in a super-charge. . . . .

B. D.

For this second Continental journey we have the same voluminous material in the shape of letters and journals as for the former. Setting forth in the beginning of August, the travellers crossed from Dover to Boulogne.

To Isaac D'Israeli.

PARIS,
Aug. 9, 1826.

MY DEAR FATHER,

. . . Our journey to Paris was much pleasanter than I expected. We slept the first night at Montreuil, at the inn you mentioned. It was full of English, but the accommodation is as delightful as ever. Being overtaken by a storm in the next day's journey we stopped short at Grandvilliers instead of reaching Beauvais, passing in our way through Abbeville, where we stopped two hours; the next day passing through Beauvais, where we stopped a couple of hours to see the old Cathedral, painted glass, tapestry, &c. We reached Paris Sunday afternoon, and are now in the Rue de Rivoli, the best situation here, having obtained these apartments in a manner which would make an excellent chapter in *Gil Blas*, and beat the adventure of the *Hotel Garni* hollow.

'Paris is delightful.' I never was so much struck with anything in the whole course of my life. I expected another London, but there are no points of resemblance. I did not expect in so short a distance to have met such a contrariety of manners and life. . . . Yesterday I lionised the old

City and the Quais, Notre Dame, &c. I was very much struck with the resemblance of the Old Town of Edinburgh to the ancient parts of Paris; indeed, at some times the resemblance was perfect. I am going to the Louvre this morning and to the Opera this evening, for we do not leave Paris until Friday. . . .

I have not kept my journal, but of course shall. My fellow travellers will, however, make up for all my negligence; Austen's journal commencing at Guilford Street, with the incidents of wheel-greasing and vail-giving not forgotten, and Mrs. A. having already filled her quarto, although having more modestly commenced only at Dover. . . . God bless you.

Yours most affectionately,
B. DISRAELI.

From Paris they posted by the road through Dijon to Geneva. There are some brightly written letters from Mrs. Austen to Sarah Disraeli, which give us here and there an interesting side-glimpse of her young fellow-traveller. 'The real improvement in your brother's health and looks quite surprises me,' she writes from Dijon. 'He seems to enjoy everything, *pour ou contre*, and has just said high mass for a third bottle of burgundy.' Burgundy was always his favourite wine.

To Isaac D'Israeli.

GENEVA,
Aug. 21.

MY DEAR FATHER,

. . . . At the termination of the Jura ridge which bounds one side of the plain of Geneva, did I on Friday morning witness the most magnificent sight in the world—the whole range of the high Alps with Mont Blanc in the centre *without a cloud*[1]; the effect was so miraculous that for a long time I did not perceive the lovely scene under me, the plain and city and lake of Geneva, the latter of ultra-marine blue. Such a view of the Alps has been seen by few persons in this country, and was occasioned by the unparalleled dryness and heat of the season, which, as we are daily informed by travellers, exceeds by much the heat now experienced on the other side of the Alps, in Italy. The heat does not, however, affect me the least. I have not had a

[1] Compare *Contarini Fleming*, Pt. III. ch. 1.

Sarah Disraeli 1828.

From a drawing by D. Maclise R.A.

in the possession of Mr. Coningsby Disraeli

day's, nay an hour's, illness since I left England. . . . . I take a row on the lake every night with Maurice, Lord Byron's celebrated boatman. Maurice is very handsome and very vain, but he has been made so by the English, of whom he is the regular pet. He talks of nothing but Lord Byron, particularly if you shew the least interest in the subject. He told me that in the night of the famous storm described in the third Canto of C[hilde] H[arold], had they been out five minutes more the boat must have been wrecked. He told Lord Byron at first of the danger of such a night voyage, and the only answer which B. made was stripping quite naked and folding round him a great *robe de chambre*, so that in case of wreck he was ready prepared to swim immediately. Lord B., he assures me, was out all night without even stockings, and up most of the night to his knees in water. I asked him if he spoke. He said that he seldom conversed with him or any one at any time, but that this night he (Maurice) was so employed in managing the boat and sail, &c., that conversation would have been quite impossible.

One day Byron sent for him and, sitting down in the boat, he put a pistol on each side (which was his invariable practice) and then gave him 300 napoleons, ordering him to row to Chillon. He then had two torches lighted in the dungeon and wrote for two hours and a half. On coming out, the *gendarme* who guarded the castle humbly asked for *quelque-chose à boire*. 'Give him a napoleon,' said his Lordship. '*De trop, milor;*' said Maurice, who being but recently installed in his stewardship was somewhat mindful of his master's interest. 'Do you know who I am ?' rejoined the master, 'Give it to him and tell him that the donor is Lord Byron !' This wonderful piece of information must have produced a great effect on the poor miserable tippling *gendarme*. But in the slightest things was Byron, by Maurice's account, most ludicrously ostentatious. He gave him one day five napoleons for a swimming race across the lake. At the sight of the club foot Maurice thought he was sure to win, but his Lordship gained by five minutes. Byron, he says, was not a quick swimmer, but he was never exhausted, by which means he generally won when the distance was great. One morning Maurice called for him very early to swim. Byron brought to the boat his breakfast, consisting of cold duck, &c., and three or four bottles of wine. He scarcely eat anything, but drank all the wine, and then amused himself, while they were sailing to the appointed place, by throwing the provisions gradually into the water. Upon this honest

Maurice gently hinted that he had not himself breakfasted, and that he should swim much better if he had some portion of his Lordship's superfluity. 'Friend Maurice,' said B., 'it ill becomes true Christians to think of themselves; I shall give you none. You see I eat no breakfast myself: do you also refrain, for the sake of the fishes.' He then continued his donations to the pikes (which here are beautiful) and would not bestow a single crumb on his companion. 'This is all very well,' says Maurice, 'but his Lordship forgot one little circumstance. He had no appetite; I had.' He says that he never saw a man eat so little as B. in all his life, but that he would drink three or four bottles of the richest wines for his breakfast. I shall perhaps remember more when we meet.

I have been on the lake at all hours, and seen Mt. Blanc by all lights, twice by sunset, when the whole mighty mountain is quite rosy. The effect is beyond all description. The living at Secheron is most excellent; we much wanted it. Except at Dijon I have scarcely had anything to eat since I left Paris. In the Juras we were literally without a meal. The honey of the Alps, wild strawberries, butter, cheese, and eggs are all very well in romance and certainly are not to be despised as collaterals, but with us they were principals for successive days. Travellers require nourishing food. In the Juras we could not even get a bottle of common wine, and the bread was black and not only sour but acid. . . .

Mrs. A. is very well, and speaks French with even greater rapidity than she does English. I hope to God my mother is better. Love to all. Tell Jim and Ralph I'd give anything for an election.

Your most affectionate son,

B. DISRAELI.

An eloquent passage in the diary supplements this letter :—

GENEVA,
Aug. 20.

I was on the lake again this night. It was partially cloudy; the moon finally gained the ascendency. Swift lightning played opposite her at intervals. In valleys of mountains it is very beautiful to watch the effect of sunrise and sunset. The high peaks are first illumined: the soft yellow light then tips the lower elevations, and the bright golden showers soon bathe the whole valley, except a dark streak at the bottom, which is often not visited by sunlight. The effect of sunset is perhaps still more lovely : the highest peaks are those which the sun loves most. One by one mountains relatively to their elevations steal into darkness ; and the rosy tint is often suffused over the peaks and glaciers of Mt. Blanc, while the whole world below is perfectly in the darkest twilight.[1]

To Isaac D'Israeli.

Milan,
Sept. 2.

My dear Father,

. . . . I mentioned that I had been to Ferney in my last letter. . . . Of the situation I had no previous idea, and can give you no present description. It is sublime ! placed between two of the most splendid ranges of Alps in the world, with eternal snows, and a gigantic lake, and forest of pines, it should have inspired a more Homeric epic than the *Henriade*, and chastened a more libidinous effusion than the *Pucelle*.

I had my heart's content before I left Geneva—the night before. My friend Maurice sent for me after a very cloudy day to say that there was every prospect of a fine storm upon the lake. As it was just after dinner, and Austen was with me, I was obliged to take a companion, but, as we had discussed a considerable quantity of Burgundy, I was soon freed from his presence, for he laid down in the boat on my cloak, and ere half an hour was passed was fast asleep, never disturbing us save with an occasional request to participate in our brandy bottle. As for myself, I was soon sobered, not by sleep, but by the scene. It was sublime—lightning almost continuous, and sometimes in four places, but as the evening advanced the lake became quite calm, and we never had a drop of rain. I would willingly have staid out all night, but we were to leave the next morning at five, and nothing was packed up. . . .

After the lake we entered the valley of the Rhone and approached the high Alps. The scenery was really painfully sublime. We gazed till our eyes ached, and yet dared not withdraw them from the passing wonders. . . . The passage of the Simplon is the grand crowning scene. We staid one day at Brieg, where the passage commences, on account of the stormy weather, but as it did not abate we set off the next day. Nothing could be more awful than the

[1] Compare again *Contarini*, Pt. III. ch. 1.

first part of our passage; the sublimity of the scenery was increased by the partial mists and the gusts of rain. Nothing is more terrific than the near roar of a cataract which is covered by a mist. It is horrible. When we arrived at the summit of the road the weather cleared, and we found ourselves surrounded by perpetual snow. The scenery here and for a mile or two before was perfect desolation, cataracts coursing down crumbled avalanches whose horrible surface was only varied by the presence of one or two blasted firs. Here in this dreary and desolate scene burst forth a small streak of blue sky, the harbinger of the Italian heaven. During our whole descent down the Italian side, which is by far the most splendid, we enjoyed the sun. We were for a long time, however, very cold. The contrast on descending into Italy is wonderfully striking . . . the purple mountains, the glittering lakes, the cupola'd convents, the many-windowed villas crowning luxuriant-wooded hills, the undulation of shore, the projecting headland, the receding bay, the roadside uninclosed, yet bounded with walnut and vine and fig and acacia and almond trees bending down under the load of their fruit, the wonderful effect of light and shade, the trunks of every tree looking black as ebony, and their thick foliage, from the excessive light, looking quite thin and transparent in the sunshine, the thousand villages, each with a church with a tall, thin tower, the large melons trailing over walls, and, above all, the extended prospect are so striking after the gloom of Alpine passes, are so different in their sunny light from the reflected unearthly glitter of eternal snows that we are constrained to feel that, in speaking of Italy, romance has omitted for once to exaggerate. But you must remember that we are in the most beautiful parts of northern Italy, and that I have not yet entered the plains of Lombardy. I say the most beautiful part, for I have just quitted the Lago Maggiore, and I am about to introduce you to the Lake of Como.

It is a much smaller lake than Maggiore, and yet quite different—wooded mountains green with vineyards and descending immediately into the water without any shore to the lake. It is literally covered with glittering palaces. It is difficult to make you understand the difference between these two magical lakes, but Maggiore, with the exception of Isola Bella, is of a severer kind of beauty. Lago Maggiore is a precious stone and the Lake of Como is a gem; perhaps you now understand me a little better. We were on the lake six or seven hours. We visited the Villa Pliniana, so called, not because it was the residence of a Pliny, but because of a celebrated intermittent spring, the curiosity of which supplied a chapter to the naturalist and a letter to the nephew. I also saw the Villa d'Este, the residence of the late Queen. The apartments are left in exactly the same state as in her lifetime; there is the theatre in which she acted Columbine, and the celebrated statues of Adam and Eve covered with the yet more celebrated fig-leaves. It is a villa of the first grade, and splendidly adorned, but the ornaments are, without an exception, so universally indelicate that it was painful to view them in the presence of a lady. . . . Here, if they possessed any interest, might you obtain thousands of stories of her late Majesty, but the time is passed, thank God, for them. Our riots in her favor are the laughing stock of Italy. . . .

Dr. Ciceri, to whom Forbes gave me a letter, is of the greatest use to us at Milan. He is a very singular character and of great importance in this city. We find him extremely courteous, and through him see everything here to great advantage. I was yesterday at the refectory of Santa Maria delle Grazie to see the Last Supper. It is in a much better state than I had imagined. The engraving of Morghen is very unlike. I do not think the expression of any of the countenances is correct. . . . The pride of Ciceri is to be considered an Englishman. He lives among the English nobility who travel through and reside here, and is their factotum on every subject. He lodges in a palace, and dines every day on a beefsteak. He is known to everybody in Italy, and manages the business of all Milan. He is a sort of intellectual Paul Pry, the best of cicerones, of course, and with a little management the most courteous of men, but he is a little surly at first, because he conceives that that is keeping up the English character. However, our acquaintance with him is extremely fortunate. My fellow travellers are very kind and very accommodating. Austen is particularly learned in coins and postilions and exchange. We have met lots of people whom the Austens know, and these occasional *rencontres* are very agreeable. I meant to have written a whole letter about La Scala and the ballet here, which ranks almost with tragedy, but my long letter is full. I shall write from here again when I have received yours, or from Venice, where I shall be on Thursday. We travel slowly, which is delightful. Could you but see a few of our countrymen, how much they do and how little they enjoy and understand! The excitement of idiotism I never witnessed before, and it is very ludicrous, but I must introduce you to characters orally. God bless you all.

Your affectionate son,

B. DISRAELI.

It must have been on this journey through the Alps that Disraeli made an excursion to the Great St. Bernard, and the visit rewarded him with an incident which he used to recall in later years.

The Brotherhood on hearing that a young Englishman was in the Hospice expressed an anxious desire to see me, and I waited on the Superior. I found that all the anxiety arose from a desire to hear how the Thames Tunnel had succeeded. I had to confess I had never seen it, and I afterwards reflected that one must travel to learn what really is to be seen in one's country, and resolved at once on my return to supply the omission. But do you know, I have never seen it yet.[1]

In Milan under the guidance of his friend Ciceri Disraeli saw, in addition to Leonardo's great picture, everything notable that there was to be seen: the Cathedral, for which he has only qualified praise; 'it stands alone without a rival, but whether rivalry is desirable is dubious'; the Brera, where strangely enough the two pictures that struck him most were Salvator's 'Souls being delivered from Purgatory' and Guercino's 'Abraham dismissing Hagar'—but those were the days before Ruskin; and the Ambrosian Library, where, more in accordance with modern taste, he notes 'an exquisite Holy Family by Luini—a mannerist who for once is delicious.' Nor had he an eye only for churches and pictures. A visit to the Corso leads to many reflections on the life and manners of the Milanese; and here we come across the original of a sketch in the second part of *Vivian Grey*.

Count Ciconia is the leader of the *ton* at Milan. He is a dandy of genius, worthy of Brummell. He is about 45,

[1] From a note by Lord Rowton.

dresses very plainly, has been frequently in England, and pays constant trips there to study. He is young in figure, but his face is long and old, a bachelor with a loud shrill voice. He is curious in horses, drives four-in-hand in perfect style, and was attended always by English grooms till their idleness forced him to give them up. They will not do for Italy. Ciconia is as rapid in the change of his style and dress as in his conceptions. White hats are at Milan the rage, which Ciconia introduced. He appeared the last day on the Corso in a black one. This formed the subject of the afternoon's conversation at all the cafés and circles. The dandies are numerous and splendid: Italians, Austrians, Hungarians; mustaches of all colours and descriptions.

From Milan the travellers proceeded to Brescia and thence by Desenzano, 'where we breakfasted on delicious trout on the banks of the Lago di Garda and opposite to the villa of Catullus,' to Verona.

To Isaac D'Israeli.[1]

Verona is full of pictures which have never been painted. Every step excites emotion and gives rise to unaffected reflection. In the course of a short stroll, you may pass by a Roman amphitheatre, still used, then the castle of some petty prince of the Middle Ages, and while you are contrasting the sublime elevation of antiquity with the heterogeneous palace of a Scaliger your eyes light on a gate of Oriental appearance and fantastic ornament erected by the Venetians when they were the conquerors of the most fertile district of Northern Italy. Memorials of this wonderful people are constantly before you. In the market place rises a lofty pillar which evidently once bore some sculptured burden. Ask, it was the winged Lion of St. Mark. Stand in the Piazza dei Signori at Verona. There is the palace of the Council of Sansovino—on another hill is a Saracenic palace, once an office of Venetian administration, three or four perspectives are afforded by various arches which open into streets or other piazzas, and a magnificent tower rises from a corner. The illusion is perfect, the eye rests with pain on the passing citizens in their modern costumes; you

[1] The descriptions now begin to lag so much behind the journey that we only reach Venice in a letter written from Florence; and I have omitted the date-lines where they might mislead or confuse.

look for black velvets and gold chains, white feathers and red stockings. . . .

From Verona through a beautiful country, where the vine is married to the mulberry, we travelled to Vicenza. The famous Palladian palaces are in decay. They are built of brick, sometimes plastered, occasionally *whitewashed* ; the red material is constantly appearing and vies in hideous color with the ever offensive roof. It is a miserable thing that a man worthy of Athens or Rome should have worked with such materials. . . .

From Vicenza, with its much-appreciated treasures of Palladian architecture, the travellers drove through Padua and along the banks of the Brenta to Venice.

To Isaac D'Israeli.

I entered [1] Venice with a magnificent setting sun on a grand fête day. As we glided in a gondola up the great Lagune we passed St. Mark's, the Campanile, the Palace of the Doges, the Bridge of Sighs, the Prison, before we reached our hotel, once the proud residence of the Bernadinis, a family which has given more than one Doge to the old Republic ; the floors of our rooms were of marble, the hangings of satin, the ceilings painted by Tintoretto and his scholars full of Turkish triumphs and trophies, the chairs of satin and the gilding though of two hundred years' duration as brightly burnished as the new mosaic invention. After a hasty dinner we rushed to the mighty Place of St. Mark. It was crowded, two Greek and one Turkish ship of war were from accidental circumstances in port, and their crews mingled with the other spectators with high foreheads and higher caps and elevated eyebrows ; then there was the Austrian military band, and the bearded Jew with his black velvet cap was not wanting. Three gorgeous flags waved on the mighty staffs which are opposite the Church in all the old drawings and which once bore the standards of Candia, Crete, and the Morea. Tired with travelling we left the gay scene crowded, but the moon was so bright that a juggler was conjuring in a circle under our window, and an itinerant Italian opera performing by our bridge. Serenades were constant during the whole night ; indeed, music is never silent in Venice. I wish I could give you an idea of the moonlights there, but that is impossible. Venice by moon-

[1] On Sept. 8.

light is an enchanted city; the floods of silver light upon the moresco architecture, the perfect absence of all harsh sounds of carts and carriages, the never-ceasing music on the waters produced an effect on the mind which cannot be experienced, I am sure, in any other city in the world.

Five days in all were spent in Venice, and they were days of intense enjoyment. To one so deeply imbued with historic feeling and with an innate love of the gorgeous East it could not be otherwise.

To Isaac D'Israeli.

Sailing down the Grand Canal the palaces of Foscari, Grimani, Barberigo, and other names which make the coldest heart thrill rise rapidly before you. . . . The Palace of the Doges is still kept up for public offices, library, &c. Its walls are painted by the greatest masters of the miraculous Venetian school, and its roof is gilt and adorned in a manner which leaves far behind all the magnificence of all the palaces in the world. In every room you are reminded of the glory and the triumphs of the Republic: the door of one chamber once closed upon the Mosque of St. Sophia, the pillars of another graced a temple in the Morea, and even Solomon's Temple is not forgotten, and two pillars of fantastic architecture were carved from large columns of granite which were brought in triumph by a noble Venetian from the ruins of Jerusalem. St. Mark's Church is a pile of precious stones, the walls are of all kinds of the rarest marbles and even of jasper, *lapis lazuli*, and the richest porphyry and Oriental agates, the interior is cased with mosaics of gold, and in the front figure five hundred pillars of all kinds of architecture and colors, some of which are of verd antique. The four brazen horses amble, not *prance*, as some have described, on the front, and five cupolas, hooded cupolas, crown this Christian Mosque. . . . It is vain to write anything here of the pictures, the churches, the palaces, with which this city abounds. According to the common opinion I saw all that ought to be seen, but I never felt less inclined to quit a place. It is in these spots that I wish to stay, for it is in such places that the mind receives that degree of wholesome excitation which is one of the great benefits of travel, I mean an excitation which quickens the feelings and the fancy, and which enables the mind to arrive at results with greater facility and rapidity than we do at home, and in our studies.

But in these sage reflections and in all this enthusiasm for the external splendour of Venice, there is still something wanting, as readers of *Contarini* will feel. We find not a trace of the peculiar excitement and exultation with which the hero of that novel approached the home of his fathers. Clearly Disraeli had not yet evolved the theory of his own Venetian origin; and he does not even seem to have been aware that he had near relations living in the City at the time of his visit. Even his appreciation of the art treasures of Venice—of 'the miraculous Venetian school'—seems to have been far from perfect. 'Venice,' he writes later from Florence, 'revealed to me the Venetian school, Titian, Giorgione, Tintoretto, Paul Veronese, Palma, &c.' But alas! without a pause he adds, 'Bologna in its public gallery introduced me to perhaps a still more illustrious band, taken altogether, the finest school in Italy, the three Carracci and their four wonderful scholars, Domenichino, Guido, Albani, Guercino; the latter, perhaps the most wonderful, and who from his miraculous and enchanting use of chiaroscuro was called the *magician of art*, is a native of a little town a few miles from Bologna, *Cento*, which perhaps you remember.' Apparently he had no suspicion of the fact that Cento had a place in his own family history.

On the way from Venice to Bologna a pilgrimage was made to the tomb of Petrarch at Arqua, and in Ferrara of course the cell of Tasso was visited. 'The door posts of this gloomy dungeon are covered with the names of its visitors; here scratched with a great nail on the brick wall I saw sprawled "Byron"; "Sam Rogers" printed in pencil in a neat banker's hand was immediately underneath.' Bologna he 'left on the second day with regret,' and crossed the Apennines to Florence. A long letter to his father retails his impressions and adventures during a fortnight's stay in this 'most delightful city.' He has now, after seeing the pictures of the great Florentine masters and 'many of the finest works of Raphael and other painters of the Roman school' in the

Uffizi and Pitti Palaces, acquired 'a very tolerable idea of the comparative styles and merits of the great Italian schools.' He has 'gazed upon the Venus de Medici without prejudice and left it with veneration.' He has 'seen enough in Italy to know that we are not setting about the right way in England to form a National Gallery.' At a recent sale in Florence 'the finest pictures were sold for a song. Why had not the National Gallery an agent on the spot? What is Lord Burghersh paid for?' and so forth.[1]

To Isaac D'Israeli.

FLORENCE,
Sept. 29, 1826.

There are some clever artists and sculptors at Florence. Among the latter, since the death of Canova, Bertolini is reckoned the most eminent in Italy. He is a man of genius. I had the honor of a very long conversation with him, of course upon his art. He is a friend of Chantrey, but the god of his idolatry, and indeed of all the Italians, is Flaxman. Bertolini said that he considered that Flaxman had revived the taste of Europe, that he was a classic, and that he thought that a young man might study his works with as much advantage as the treasures of the Vatican or the Tribune. He asked me to explain the reason of the indifference of the English to this great man, and expressed his surprise at finding him almost unknown to the great number of our travelling countrymen, and little esteemed even by our great artists. He mentioned Wilkie's opinion of Flaxman with his eyes up to the sky. It seems the English Teniers is no great admirer of one whom Bertolini says is the greatest poet that ever lived, though he never wrote a verse. The studios of all these men are open to all travellers, and form the most agreeable and instructive lounges. . . .

In one of my speculations I have been disappointed. In the Pitti Palace there is a most beautiful portrait of Charles 1st by Vandyke, the most pleasing and noble likeness that I have ever seen. It is a picture highly esteemed.

[1] Disraeli's interest in the Christian Middle Age was never great, and in the letters from Florence there is not a single mention of Dante. Of Michael Angelo, as we may gather from the long tirade in *Vivian Grey* (Bk. V. ch. 2), he was 'no extravagant admirer'; even the great monuments in the Sacristy of San Lorenzo he was not able to look upon 'without disappointment.'

I engaged a miniature painter here (a class of artists much esteemed at Florence) to make me an exquisite copy of this picture with which I intended to surprise you. After a week's work he has brought it to-day, but has missed the likeness! And yet he was the Court painter, Signor Carloni. I have refused to take the work and am embroiled in a row, but in this country firmness is alone necessary and the Italians let you do what you like, so I've no fear as to the result. My mortification and disappointment, however, are extreme.

We have some agreeable acquaintance here. Among them a very extraordinary man of the name of Saunders. He is the descendant of one of those Scotch families who used so often to emigrate on speculation to Russia. He was the intimate friend of the late Emperor Alexander, and is highly esteemed by the present Emperor . . . is still attached to the Court of Russia, is an Aulic Councillor, &c. He is a deep student, full of philosophy, first principles, and the study of the beautiful, but eloquent and profound. Though of a very close temper, he was so delighted to get hold of some one who had a literary turn that we have become tolerably intimate, and I occasionally visit him at his country villa, which, by the bye, is the *Villa Vespucci*, rented by him of a noble family of that name, the lineal descendants of the famous Americus. He is now engraving the most valuable picture in Italy, the masterpiece of Fra Bartolommeo.[1]

Florence is not only one of the most delightful cities to live in, but is also the cheapest in Europe. Here cheapness, *real* cheapness, is to be found, for here luxuries are cheap. An English family of the highest respectability may live in Florence with every convenience and keep a handsome carriage, horses, liveries, &c., for five hundred a year. I speak here of an average sized family, as ours. On this income you might enter into the best society, and the best society here is excellent. You may live in a palace built by Michael Angelo, keep a villa two miles from the city in a most beautiful situation, with vineyards, fruit and pleasure gardens, &c., &c., keep *two* carriages, have your opera box, and live in every way as the first Florentine nobility, go to Court, have your own night for receiving company, &c., &c., on less than a thousand a year, and this with no miserable managing, but with the enjoyment of every comfort and luxury.

[1] The 'Madonna della Misericordia,' now in the public gallery at Lucca.

TURIN,
Oct. 10, 1826.

MY DEAR FATHER,

We travelled from delightful Florence through the luxuriant Val d'Arno to Pisa, where the Cathedral and its more wonderful Baptistery, the leaning tower, and the Campo Santo riveted our attention. . . . The country from Pisa to Lucca, and, indeed, the whole of that little state is most lovely. Sated as we were with scenery, and desirous almost to avoid any mention of the subject, yet we have yet scarcely ceased to talk in wonder and admiration of the shores of the Mediterranean. The journey from Spezzia to Genoa baffles all idea. . . . For two days we wandered among the most exquisite and the wildest parts of the Apennines, not the Apennines that we had before been used to, but the Apennines of romance and Mrs. Ratcliffe, with streamy blue distances and unfathomable woody dells and ruined castles, and constant views of the blue Mediterranean and its thousand bays. On the third day we descended nearly to its shore, but what a shore! It required no stretch of the imagination to fancy ourselves in Asia and under an Oriental sky, for aloes, huge everlasting aloes, here grow on the shingles, and groves of olive trees, dates and figs, and clusters of Eastern trees abound upon the green mountains, which descend into the sea, and whose only artificial ornaments are towns of colored marble and amphitheatres of palaces. The shore, as I said before, is broken into innumerable bays, which vie with each other for superiority, until they all yield to their Queen—the gorgeous bay of Genoa, on whose mountain banks rises in a crescent Genoa la Superba, a crowd of palaces, villas, and convents. But I am writing of that which should be seen. However, the scenery of the Mediterranean would alone repay me for twice ten thousand the fatigues I have suffered.

Two days' travelling, during one of which we again crossed the great chain of the Apennines and entered Northern Italy, have brought us to Turin. The mighty chain of the High Alps covered with snow now meets our eyes, and tomorrow we shall cross Mont Cenis. . . . I expect to be on the 24th at Dover. Thus end my travels. I trust I have not travelled in vain. Nature and Art have been tolerably well revealed to me. The Alps, the Apennines, and two seas have pretty well done for the first, and though I may see more cities I cannot see more varieties of European nature. Five capitals and twelve great cities, innumerable remains of antiquity and the choicest specimens of modern art have told me what man has done and is doing. I feel now that it is not prejudice, when I declare that England, with all her imperfections, is worth all the world together, and I hope it is not misanthropy when I feel that I love lakes and mountains better than courts and cities, and trees better than men. That is to say, men in general. Yours I must always be most affectionately. In a fortnight I shall have the inexpressible happiness of joining you.

B. DISRAELI.

To Sarah Disraeli.

LYONS,
Oct. 15, 1826.

DEAREST SA,

We arrived at this city last night. . . . Nothing can have been more prosperous than our whole journey. Not a single *contretemps* and my *compagnons de voyage* uniformly agreeable. Everything that I wished has been realized, and more than I wished granted. I have got all the kind of knowledge that I desired, and much more, but that much more, I am convinced, was equally necessary. To discover new wants and find them instantly gratified, or rather to discover unexpected necessities anticipated, is the most pleasing of all things. From Turin we travelled to Susa and crossed Mont Cenis, which, considering the mountain pass merely, is not to be compared to the Simplon. It is vast without being sublime, and dreary without any of the grand effects of desolation. Some points, however, are wonderful; a small lake at the top of the range in the midst of eternal snow, a small blue lake with banks of white marble, attracted my attentive admiration. It is about half a mile from the road, and I walked there while our trout were cooking. Cenis, however, leads to Savoy, which I prefer to Switzerland. The valley of the Arc is even finer than the valley of the Rhone; it is as sublime, and yet not gloomy. The lofty mountains are covered with firs, and tipped with the snows of centuries; brilliant cascades falling from elevations of 200 to 300 feet contrasted with the variety of autumnal tints, and banished monotony without disturbing reflection. . . .

I am glad that I at last get some account of my mother—my best love to her; we meet soon. My father says that he has been very idle, and I fear from his tone that I am to believe him. I have been just the reverse, but I would throw all my papers into the Channel only to hear that he had written fifty pages. This continued inertia makes me sad, but I have hopes that if we get on without fresh vexations for six months more his spirits may be raised. I had a great row about the portrait of Charles 1st, but was quite successful. The consequence is that I have got a new miniature,[1] in which the likeness is exactly hit, and at a cheaper rate.

With best love to all,

Most affectionately yours,

B. D.

On the homeward journey through France Disraeli turned aside with the Austens to see the Layards at school, and Sir Henry Layard, then a boy at school, caught a passing glimpse of his future chief. 'I still retain a vivid recollection of his appearance, his black curly hair, his affected manner, and his somewhat fantastic dress.'[2] Mrs. Austen's letters to Sarah Disraeli testify to his possession of that rare virtue—excellence as a travelling companion. 'Your brother,' she writes, 'is so easily pleased, so accommodating, so amusing, and so actively kind, that I shall always reflect upon the domestic part of our journey with the greatest pleasure.' And, again, more dubiously :—'Your brother has behaved excellently, except when there is a button, or, rather, buttons to be put on his shirt; then he is violently bad, and this happens almost daily. I said once, "They cannot have been good at first"; and now he always threatens to "tell my Mother you have abused my linen."'

The methodical Austen kept careful statistics of the journey. They posted more than 2,000 miles, and Disraeli's share of the expenses, including about £20 for prints and other purchases, was £150.

[1] This miniature is still at Hughenden.
[2] Layard's *Autobiography*, I., p. 18.

CHAPTER VIII.

Illness and Despondency.

1827-1830.

In a letter from Lyons to his sister, Disraeli, as we saw, remarked that he had been the 'reverse of idle' during his Continental journey; a few months after his return a sequel to *Vivian Grey* appeared in three volumes, and we may safely assume that it was at these volumes he had been working. This sequel, or 'second part,' need not long detain us. In Mr. Gladstone's diary for March 20, 1874, we find the entry, 'Finished *Vivian Grey*. The first quarter extremely clever, the rest trash.'[1] Mr. Gladstone was never a sympathetic critic of Disraeli's novels, or of anything else for which Disraeli was responsible, and perhaps at the moment of that entry he was less likely than usual to be in a sympathetic mood. But there is little reason to quarrel with his judgment on the present occasion. What is still worth reading in the five original volumes of *Vivian Grey* is the first. For the second, trash is hardly too strong a word; and of the remaining three volumes almost the best that can be said is that they are void of offence.

After the wreck of his ambitious plans, Vivian Grey, it will be remembered, took refuge in Germany, and his adventures in that country are the subject of the second

[1] Morley's *Life of Gladstone*, II., p. 499.

part. It is a curious illustration of Disraeli's brooding temperament that he should thus have recurred in fancy to the scenes he had visited two years before, leaving the impressions of his Italian journey for future use and record. Perhaps the romantic genius of the Rhine was more in harmony with the mood in which he now found himself. Ill-health and the many misfortunes of the last two years had given to his thoughts a melancholy bias ; and it is not surprising then to find when we meet Vivian Grey again that he has become a Byronic exile who makes a luxury of the sorrow which he believes to be incurable. But energy is of the essence of the true Byronic manner, and there is an air of languor over these volumes that makes them ineffective. The sparkling and audacious hero whom we knew in the original novel has become tame and lifeless, and if there is less extravagance now we feel that the change is owing to loss of vigour by the author rather than to the growth of that conscious self-restraint which comes with maturing power. 'The springiness of my mind is gone,' cries Vivian Grey himself in the agony of remorse that follows the death of Cleveland ; and as we read his subsequent adventures we cannot help feeling that the 'springiness' of his creator's mind is gone no less. Now and then we see flashes of the old epigrammatic spirit :—'Though a great liar he was a dull man'[1] ; 'Like all great travellers, I have seen more than I remember and remember more than I have seen.'[2] Now and then we hear the welcome note of that subtle ironic laughter which Disraeli has always in store for his own most cherished affectations, and which goes so far to redeem them ; as when he mocks at his Byronic enthusiasm :—'The English youth . . . travel now, it appears, to look at mountains and catch cold in spouting trash on lakes by moonlight.'[3] There are isolated episodes that show vigour and invention ; there are scenes that show an advance in descriptive

[1] Bk. VI. ch. 2. [2] Bk. VIII. ch. 5. [3] Bk. V. ch. 8.

power. The picture of life at the little German Court of Reisenberg is cleverly painted, and lacks neither movement nor variety. But the book as a whole is flat and dull, and the story leads to nothing. Our interest has no sooner been awakened in a character or a situation than we are whisked away to something else, and the result is a novel which is fragmentary and inconsecutive, and always unsatisfying. The author in fact was not sufficiently recovered from the strain of the previous year for a fresh creative effort.

The most interesting character in the book is Beckendorff, the Prime Minister of Reisenberg, Disraeli's first attempt at a finished portrait of a statesman. Beckendorff is a man of plebeian origin who has raised himself to power by the force of his own 'master-mind.' He is of a type that recurs more than once in Disraeli's other novels, and is made the medium for the exposition of some of Disraeli's favourite doctrines. 'Fate, Destiny, Chance, particular and special Providence—idle words. Dismiss them all, Sir! A man's Fate is his own temper.' 'Man is not the creature of circumstances. Circumstances are the creatures of men. We are free agents, and man is more powerful than matter.' 'No conjuncture can possibly occur, however fearful, however tremendous it may appear, from which a man, by his own energy, may not extricate himself.'[1] In Beckendorff Vivian Grey sees a man with his own principles of conduct whose ambition has been crowned with success.

Apparently the philosophy on which Beckendorff had regulated his extraordinary career was exactly the same with which he himself, Vivian Grey, had started in life; which he had found so fatal in its consequences; which he believed to be so vain in its principles. How was this? What radical error had he committed? It required little consideration. Thirty, and more than thirty, years had passed over the head of Beckendorff, ere the world felt his power, or indeed was conscious of his existence. A deep

[1] Bk. VI. ch. 7.

student not only of man in detail but of men in groups . . . when that opportunity, which in this world comes to all men, occurred to Beckendorff, he was prepared. With acquirements equal to his genius, Beckendorff depended only upon himself, and succeeded. Vivian Grey, with a mind inferior to no man's, dashed on the stage, in years a boy, though in feelings a man. Brilliant as might have been his genius, his acquirements necessarily were insufficient. He could not depend only upon himself; a consequent necessity arose to have recourse to the assistance of others; to inspire them with feelings which they could not share; and humour and manage the petty weaknesses which he himself could not experience. His colleagues were at the same time to work for the gratification of their own private interests, the most palpable of all abstract things; and to carry into execution a great purpose which their feeble minds, interested only by the first point, cared not to comprehend. The unnatural combination failed; and its originator fell. To believe that he could recur again to the hopes, the feelings, the pursuits of his boyhood, he felt to be the vainest of delusions.[1]

The passage throws an illuminating flash on some of Disraeli's most cherished ideals of character, and on the significance of *Vivian Grey* in relation to those ideals; and incidentally it makes visible the clouds of despondency which were now settling upon Disraeli's mind as they had settled upon his hero's.

It was many a long day before the clouds finally lifted. The three years that followed the publication of the Second Part of *Vivian Grey* are almost a blank in Disraeli's life. As he had now definitely renounced the intention of becoming a solicitor, it was decided that he should at least formally qualify for the other branch of the legal profession; and in April, 1827, he was entered at Lincoln's Inn with a view, in due course, to being called to the Bar. He seems to have kept his terms regularly for nearly a couple of years, but there is nothing to show that beyond eating his dinners and paying his dues he gave any serious labour to preparation for a barrister's career. During all this time, in fact, a

[1] Bk. VII. ch. 1.

mysterious disease held him in its grip and paralysed his energies. In the summer of 1827 we hear of him seriously ill at Fyfield, in Oxfordshire, where the Disraelis and the Austens were spending their holidays together. In the summer of 1828 he is ill again and with his family at Lyme Regis, in Dorset. 'I am at present quite idle,' he says in a letter to Sharon Turner in March, 1828, 'being at this moment slowly recovering from one of those tremendous disorganisations which happen to all men at some period of their lives, and which are perhaps equally necessary for the formation of both body and constitution. Whether I shall ever do anything which may mark me out from the crowd, I know not. I am one of those to whom moderate reputation can give no pleasure, and who in all probability am incapable of achieving a great one.' 'My son's life,' writes Isaac D'Israeli to a friend in January, 1829, 'within the last year and a half, with a very slight exception, has been a blank in his existence. His complaint is one of those perplexing cases which remain uncertain and obscure, till they are finally got rid of. Meanwhile patience and resignation must be his lot—two drugs in human life, bitter of digestion, in an ardent and excitable mind.' Ten years later a doctor who had attended him in this illness described the complaint as 'chronic inflammation of the membranes of the brain,' adding that his patient had made a perfect recovery.

To Benjamin Austen.

June 14, 1827.

MY DEAR AUSTEN,

It has given me great pleasure to find that the accounts from you this morning continue favorable, and that you have arranged for a further enjoyment of your native air—the atmosphere of Ramsgate, that glory of Kent and first of watering places and worthy rival of Ems and Wiesbaden. As, however, you have postponed your return, I cannot refrain from writing to you, if it be only to inform you of my existence and that I continue just 'as ill' as ever. Little else have I to tell you, being in the situation of those youthful jackanapes at school who write home to their parents every week to tell them that they have nothing to say. Your good lady, I am aware, sends you daily bulletins, and I am quite sure that nothing certain or contingent in this odd world can possibly escape the comprehensive circuit of her lively pen. . . .

As I understand you are in want of a book I send you the most amusing in any language—for such I do not hesitate to style the *Memoirs of Benvenuto Cellini*. It is many years since I read it, and I was then enchanted. I should have been entranced with rapture had I then been in Italy. The whole scene lies at Rome, Florence (especially), Milan, Padua, Paris, Fontainebleau, Lyons, &c. You will read it with great delight and sympathise with all his scrapes. The part that will least please you will not be his interesting history of his Perseus—his beautiful Perseus—which you will remember in the more beautiful Palazzo Vecchio at Firenze. . . . I shall be very happy when we are all together again and at Fyfield. . . . Jem is richer than ever and struts about town in a kind of cloth shooting jacket made by the celebrated Hyde of Winchester—almost as celebrated as a tailor as Dr. Chard is as a musician. In this quaint costume, with the additional assistance of a sporting handkerchief, he looks very much like one of those elegant, half blackguard, half gentleman speculators in horseflesh who crowd Winchester market and dine at the 'good ordinary at two o'clock,' for which great grub, if you remember, the bell rang loud and long as we crossed from the Cathedral. . . .

Your sincere friend,

B. D.

In some interval of comparative health during the first year of his illness, Disraeli recurred to the idea of a satire on contemporary society, which he had attempted to carry into execution in his twentieth year; and 'The Adventures of Mr. Aylmer Papillon,' which had been rejected by John Murray, soon grew into *The Voyage of Captain Popanilla*, which was accepted by Colburn and was given to the world as the work of 'The author of *Vivian Grey*' in the late spring of the year 1828. The main object of the piece is to ridicule the then rising sect of the Utilitarians. Popanilla is a native of the Isle of Fantaisie, an earthly paradise in the Indian Ocean, where men lead lives of careless happiness amid the resources provided by a bountiful nature. Finding on the seashore a box of books crammed with useful knowledge, he learns from them that his countrymen are nothing more than 'a horde of useless savages'; and full of his new conception of the blessings of civilisation in the Utilitarian sense, he endeavours to make converts of the King and people of the island. He talks to them 'of men in a savage state, the origin of society, and the elements of the social compact in sentences which would not have disgraced the mellifluous pen of Bentham.' He shows them that 'the interests of the body are alone to be considered and not those of the individual, and that a nation might be extremely happy, extremely powerful, and extremely rich, although every individual member of it might at the same time be miserable, dependent, and in debt.' If they will only adopt his principles and carry out his schemes of development, 'no long time could elapse ere, instead of passing their lives in a state of unprofitable ease and useless enjoyment, they might reasonably expect to be the terror and astonishment of the universe, and to be able to annoy every nation of any consequence.'

Finally Popanilla makes himself so much of a nuisance that the King to get rid of him ironically professes himself a convert and appoints him to the command of an expedition for the extension of the international relations of the island. 'As the axiom of your school seems to be that everything can be made perfect at once, without time, without experience, without practice, and without preparation, I have no doubt, with the aid of a treatise or two, you will make a consummate naval commander, although you have never been at sea in the whole course of your life. Farewell, Captain Popanilla!' Popanilla is launched alone upon the waters, but after giving himself up for lost is carried by a storm to the great city of Hubbabub, which is the capital of the island of Vraibleusia, the most famous island in the world, and a paradise of wealth and freedom, and also of competition. Henceforth the piece is a satire on English social life and the English Constitution. It is not very deep, it abounds in crudities and at times it is a little wearisome; but it is worth reading still as Disraeli's first political essay. In so far as his political faith in the form which it ultimately assumed was the product of temperament, its main features are already visible: on the one hand, the deep-seated popular sympathies and the essentially liberal outlook; on the other, the instinctive aversion of a mind imbued with the historic spirit and full of an imaginative sense of the romance and mystery of life from the hard and self-sufficing dogmatism, the cramped philosophy, and somewhat repellent ideals of the school of thought which was becoming dominant in England. Needless to say, Disraeli was very far from having sounded the depths of Utilitarianism, and made no attempt to do justice to what was best in the teaching of the Benthamites; between them and one of his romantic temper warfare was inevitable, and he struck at them instinctively. Needless also to say, the outlines of his own philosophy are not yet firmly drawn nor his views on questions of party politics consistently elaborated. No one therefore need be surprised to find the future leader of the Protectionists ridiculing the Corn Laws, or the future founder of Imperialism ridiculing the Colonial system; in either case quite heedless of the fact that he was aligning himself with the school which was the immediate object of his ridicule in an attack upon those who were to be his own future allies. John Bright, it is said,[1] greatly admired *Popanilla*, and in these vagaries of the author we may see perhaps in part the reason for his admiration.

Popanilla appeared with a dedication to Plumer Ward, who showed himself no niggard in his appreciation of the compliment. 'Since the days of Swift and Voltaire,' he wrote, 'I have not read anything so witty. Je riais

1 By Mr. George Russell in the *Cornhill Magazine* for January, 1907.

aux éclats and made others do so too. In my opinion it is equal to the *Tale of a Tub* and *Candide*, and superior to *Zadig* and *Babouk*.' The critics, however, took a more moderate view of the merits of the piece, and the public, who perhaps expected stronger meat from the author of *Vivian Grey*, gave it little attention.

In the course of many holiday visits the Disraelis had tasted the pleasures of country life in Bucks, and in the summer of 1829 they gave up their London residence altogether and moved out to Bradenham, an old manor house on the slopes of the Chilterns, a few miles to the west of the town of High Wycombe. 'The precarious health of several members of my family,' writes D'Israeli the elder to Southey, 'has decided me on this movement, and I quit London with all its hourly seductions. My House is described by the "Nourrisse of Antiquitie," venerable Camden, as built by the Lord Windsor in the reign of Henry VIII—for the salubrity of the soil and air.' In this peaceful spot Isaac D'Israeli spent the remainder of his days. Half a century after it first became their home, when his own life was drawing to a close, his son's thoughts recurred to the scene associated with his father's declining years, and in *Endymion* he sketched it with loving fidelity.

At the foot of the Berkshire Downs [Chiltern Hills], and itself on a gentle elevation, there is an old hall with gable ends and lattice windows, standing in grounds which once were stately, and where there are yet glade-like terraces of yew trees, which give an air of dignity to a neglected scene. In the front of the hall huge gates of iron, highly wrought, and bearing an ancient date as well as the shield of a noble house, opened on a village green, round which were clustered the cottages of the parish with only one exception, and that was the vicarage house, a modern building, not without taste, surrounded by a small but brilliant garden. The church was contiguous to the hall, and had been raised by the lord on a portion of his domain. Behind the hall and its enclosure the country was common land but picturesque. It had once been a beech forest, and though the timber had been greatly cleared,

BRADENHAM MANOR.
From a water-colour by MRS. PARTRIDGE.

[To face page 120.

the green land was still occasionally dotted, sometimes with groups and sometimes with single trees, while the juniper which here abounded, and rose to a great height, gave a rich wildness to the scene and sustained its forest character.[1]

For nearly twelve months, with rare and brief visits to London, Disraeli lived quietly at Bradenham. In addition to the trials of bad health the burden of his debts weighed heavily upon him. 'I am desperately ill,' he writes to Austen in November, 'and shall be in town in a day or two, incognito of course. . . . . . Tell Madam I shall call upon her if possible, but I can only call, because I am necessarily betrayed by her and in consequence "the heathen rage most furiously."' The rage of the heathen did not, however, hinder his framing large projects which called for more expenditure. He had somehow conceived the ambition of acquiring an estate and settling down to the life of a country gentleman, and at this very moment was pressing the scheme upon his father. But Isaac D'Israeli was frightened by the prevailing agricultural depression, and declined to invest his money on the advice of a son who confesses that he had 'more than once interfered with his affairs and never with any particular success.' The son, however, had another project. A year or more before he had been attracted by the career of David Alroy, the Jewish hero of the twelfth century, and he had begun the novel on this subject which he completed and published some years later; and his awakening interest in the history of his race had aroused in him a passionate longing to seek rest for his troubled mind and body in the East. At first his father would not hear of it.

To Benjamin Austen.

BRADENHAM,
Dec. 8, 1829.

MY DEAR AUSTEN,

. . . I am sorry to say that my other and still more important plan prospers as badly. I have partly broken it,

[1] *Endymion*, ch. 11.

and it was at once fairly knocked on the head in a calmer manner than I should have expected from my somewhat rapid but too indulgent sire. But I will not quite despair. A sanguine temper supports me still. There is yet *time*, and that, according to the great Frederick, is everything. The fact is I am

'Spellbound within the clustering Cyclades'

and go I must, though I fear I must hack for it. A literary prostitute I have never yet been, though born in an age of literary prostitution, and though I have more than once been subject to temptations. . . . Tempting mother Colburn! However, as Frederick says, I have yet *time*, and I may be saved.

Keep this letter to yourself *without exception*, and indeed all I write to you. Though generally accused of uncommunicativeness, I like a gentle chat with a friend provided it be strictly confidential and he be a tried and trusty one like yourself. Women are delightful creatures, particularly if they be pretty, which they always are; but then they chatter—they can't help it—and I have no ambition in case my dearest project fails to be pointed out as the young gentleman who *was* going to Constantinople. Let it be secret as the cave of the winds, and then perhaps a friendly breeze may yet bear me to Syria!

Farewell, *mon ami*,

B. D.

By the bye, I advise you to take care of my letters, for if I become half as famous as I intend to be you may sell them for ten guineas apiece to the *Keepsake* for 1840, that being the price, as *on dit*, at which that delicate creature D[ouglas] K[innaird] furnishes a Byronic epistle to the Annuals.

To Mrs. Austen.

BRADENHAM HOUSE,
March 7, 1830.

MY DEAR MADAME,

Your repeated kind messages require my personal acknowledgment, and deserve something better. With regard to myself, in a word, I cannot be worse. With regard to London, it is of all places the one, in my present situation, least suited to me. Solitude and silence do not make my existence easy, but they make it endurable.

My plans about leaving England are more unsettled than ever. I anticipate no benefit from it, nor from anything else, but I am desirous of quitting England that I may lead even a more recluse life than I do at present, and emancipate myself from perpetual commiserations. When I was in town last, I consulted secretly many eminent men. I received from them no consolation. Without any exception they approved of Mr. Bolton's treatment, though they were not surprised that it produced no benefit. . . .

I grieve to say my hair grows very badly, and I think more grey, which I can unfeignedly declare occasions me more anguish than even the prospect of death.

Yours ever,

B. D.

In *Popanilla* Disraeli had gone out of his way to ridicule the novel of fashionable life; but this was precisely the novel that Colburn and the public wanted, and the outcome apparently of Disraeli's determination to hack was that he began *The Young Duke*. By the end of March, 1830, he had nearly finished, and he came to town with his manuscript in quest of a publisher. 'It is a series of scenes,' he told his friend Meredith, 'every one of which would make the fortune of a fashionable novel: I am confident of its success, and that it will complete the corruption of the public taste.' If there was anything serious in this, the complacent view of the merits of his work did not long survive. Colburn's reader told him that it was certain to be severely criticised for the egoism and other sins of the writer. Lytton Bulwer, for whom *Pelham* had won celebrity a couple of years before, sounded the same note of warning. Disraeli and he had exchanged volumes in the previous year, and a correspondence had sprung up between them, which somewhere about this time ripened into personal acquaintance. Bulwer was shown the manuscript, and was not sparing of eulogy; but he suggested that the author's judgment was not equal to his genius, that if he had attained more than the excellences of *Vivian Grey* he had not sufficiently avoided its faults, and that the pruning knife might well be applied to the many flippancies and otiose antitheses of the book. The sensitive author was at first so discouraged that he talked of casting aside the work altogether, but money was needed, and a bargain was soon concluded with Colburn, who gave £500 for the book. What proved even more attractive, he consented to pay by post-dated bills, which were no doubt promptly discounted; and in this way and with the aid of a friendly advance from Austen, the tour in the East at last became possible. Meredith, Disraeli's companion in his visit to the Rhine, and now engaged to his sister, was again to accompany him, and at the end of May the travellers were to set forth on their journey.

An entry in Meredith's diary during Disraeli's visit to London with the manuscript of *The Young Duke* gives us a picture that is worth preserving.

Mar. 29.—B. D. to dine with me. He came up Regent Street, when it was crowded, in his blue surtout, a pair of military light blue trousers, black stockings with red stripes, and shoes! 'The people,' he said, 'quite made way for me as I passed. It was like the opening of the Red Sea, which I now perfectly believe from experience. Even well-dressed people stopped to look at me.' I should think so! He was in excellent spirits, full of schemes for the projected journey to Stamboul and Jerusalem; full, as usual, also of capital stories, but he could make a story out of nothing.

A note by Disraeli himself deals with another incident which can probably be referred to this same visit to London.

Just at the commencement of the spring of 1830, if spring it could be called, I made the acquaintance of Lytton Bulwer, and dined with him at his house in Hertford Street. He was just married, or about just married: a year or two. We were both of us then quite youths; about four and twenty. I met three men at dinner of much the same standing; all full of energy and ambition, and all unknown to fame. Bulwer and I had, at least, written something; I *Vivian Grey*, and he two or three years afterwards *Pelham*. The other three were Henry Bulwer, Charles Villiers, and Alexander Cockburn. Writing this, nearly five and thirty years afterwards, it is curious to mark what has been the result of the careers of these five young men. I have been twice leader of the House of Commons, Edward Bulwer has been Secretary of State, Henry Bulwer is at this moment H.M. Ambassador at Constantinople, Charles Villiers is at this moment a Cabinet Minister, and Alexander Cockburn is Lord Chief Justice of England.[1]

Henry Bulwer has also left his recollections of this occasion. Disraeli, he tells us, 'wore green velvet trousers, a canary coloured waistcoat, low shoes, silver buckles, lace at his wrists, and his hair in ringlets. . . . If on leaving the table we had been severally taken aside and asked which was the cleverest of the party we should have been obliged to say "the man in the green velvet trousers."'[2]

When in the course of his preparations for the long journey before him Disraeli came to review his position and affairs, he bethought him of the unlucky partner of his boyish speculations, and wrote the letter that follows.

To T. M. Evans.

UNION HOTEL, COCKSPUR ST.,
May 9, 1830.

MY DEAR EVANS,

We have been too long silent. It has been my fault, but if you could form the slightest idea of the severe visitation under which I have been long, and am still, suffering, I am confident you would not only accept my excuses, but sympathise with their cause. For the last three years—I will not talk of enjoyment—life has not afforded me a moment's ease; and after having lived in perfect solitude for nearly eighteen months, I am about to be shipped off for the last resource of a warmer climate.

To leave England at all, particularly in the state in which I am, is to me most distressing; to leave it without finally arranging my distracted affairs costs me a pang, which is indeed bitter. But I can assure you at this moment, when so many harrowing interests solicit the attention of my weakened mind, there is no subject on which I oftener think,

[1] There is an obvious reminiscence of this party in the dinner given by Mr. Bertie Tremaine and his brother, Mr. Tremaine Bertie, in chapter 37 of *Endymion*.

[2] Article on Lord Beaconsfield in the *Encycl. Brit.*

than our past relations, and no person who more constantly occurs to me than yourself.

I assure you, dear Evans, that it would be very difficult to find one who is really more interested in the welfare of another than I am in yours, and although you may perhaps doubt the sincerity of this declaration, I nevertheless make it. It would be a great consolation for me if before my departure I could hear from yourself that you were prospering in the world, a great satisfaction if you could communicate to me with the candor which I wish to be the characteristic of our letters.

Although I have not been fortunate enough in finally arranging my affairs, I flatter myself I have succeeded in making some temporary dispositions. Nothing of importance has been done with M., but he is inclined to wait till my return if possible, and if he cannot, to be silent. I feel less for him than for others, because I now see too well what was the cause of all our errors, and curse the hour he practised, as he thought so cunningly, upon our inexperienced youth. But this only to yourself, for he is after all an object of pity, and I would to God that I could do something for him more than I am bound to do.

For yourself, who—most unintentionally on my part—have suffered from my madness—it is for you I feel, indeed keenly, you, whose generous and manly soul I have ever honored, and credit me, have ever done justice to. All I can say is, that the first step I take, when the power is mine, shall be in your favor, and that sooner, or later, the power will be mine; and that, some day or other, we may look back to these early adventures, rather as matter of philosophical speculation than individual sorrow, I confidently believe.

For there is something within me, which, in spite of all the dicta of the faculty, and in the face of the prostrate state in which I lie, whispers to me I shall yet weather this fearful storm, and that a more prosperous career may yet open to me.

My father has quitted London, and now resides at Bradenham House, near Wycombe, Bucks—a place where I hope some day to see you, though at present I am only the inmate of an unsocial hotel, and preparing for my embarkation in the course of this current month. Anything addressed to me at the Union will reach one who will always consider himself

Your sincere friend, B. D.

Disraeli at first had thought of making *The Young Duke* an occasion for the resumption of relations with his old friend Murray, and during his visit to London in March he sought an interview with that purpose. 'It has always,' he explained, 'been my wish, if it ever were my fate to write anything calculated to arrest public attention, that you should be the organ of introducing it to public notice. If you feel any inclination to pursue this affair, act as you like, and fix upon any critic you please. I have no objection to Mr. Lockhart, who is certainly an able one, and is, I believe, influenced by no undue partiality towards me.' Murray icily declined the interview, but 'Mr. Disraeli was assured' that if he cared to submit his manuscript 'the proposal would be entertained with the strictest honour and impartiality.' Disraeli took the manuscript to Colburn, but before he left for the East he wrote the following letter :—

To John Murray.

BRADENHAM, BUCKS,
May 27, 1830.

SIR,

I am unwilling to leave England, which I do on Saturday, without noticing your last communication, because I should regret very much if you were to misconceive the motives which actuated me in not complying with the suggestion therein contained. I can assure you I leave in perfect confidence both in your 'honor' and your 'impartiality,' for the first I have never doubted, and the second it is your interest to exercise.

The truth is, my friend and myself differed in the estimate of the MS. alluded to, and while I felt justified, from his opinion, in submitting it to your judgment, I felt it due to my own to explain verbally the contending views of the case, for reasons which must be obvious.

As you forced me to decide, I decided as I thought most prudently. The work is one which, I dare say, would neither disgrace you to publish, nor me to write; but it is not the kind of production which should recommence our connection, or be introduced to the world by the publisher of Byron and *Anastasius*.

I am now about to leave England for an indefinite, perhaps a long period. When I return, if I do return, I trust it will be in my power for the *third time*[1] to endeavour that you should be the means of submitting my works to the public. For this I shall be ever ready to make great sacrifices, and let me therefore hope that when I next offer my volumes to your examination, like the Sibylline Books, their inspiration may at length be recognised.

I am, Sir,
Your obedient servant
B. DISRAELI.[2]

The novel which was thus thought unworthy of presentation by the publisher of Byron is a picture at once flashy and conventional of a society of which Disraeli had little direct knowledge when he wrote. '*The Young Duke*!' exclaimed his father, according to a family tradition, when he first heard of the book. 'What does Ben know of dukes?'[3] The Duke of St. James himself is not wholly uninteresting, for he possesses certain qualities which appear again and again in the heroes of Disraeli's novels, and appear because they are reflected from the author's own personality. 'He was a sublime coxcomb, one of those rare characters whose finished manner and shrewd sense combined prevent their conceit from being contemptible.' But his career of dissipation and prodigality soon grows wearisome, and that in some degree through the unskilfulness of the author. In the well-known gambling scene at Brighton he writes with genuine power; but too often where he endeavours to produce an effect he falls into more extravagance. The figure of May Dacre, however, partially redeems the book, even as she redeemed the hero. She is one of the most charming of Disraeli's women, a forerunner of Sybil, and

[1] The first attempt, no doubt, had been with the manuscript of *Aylmer Papillon*.

[2] Smiles, II., pp. 332-334.

[3] An attempt indeed has been made to show that Disraeli had shared the life of the young bucks whose dissipations he professes to describe; but there is no real evidence to support the theory, and his own testimony is decisive against it. 'Until my return from the East on the eve of the '32 election,' he once said to Lord Rowton, 'I had lived a very secluded life, and mixed not at all with the world.'

like Sybil, it is worthy of note, an adherent of 'the old faith.' The Young Duke finally wins her heart by a speech in favour of Catholic Emancipation, in which of course she was an enthusiastic believer; and so clearly in 1829 was Disraeli himself. This is not the only indication in the novel of a steady movement of his mind towards an interest in political questions. He treats us in one chapter to a disquisition on eloquence, and illustrates it with miniature literary sketches of the leading orators in Parliament which are both interesting and characteristic in themselves and significant as an index to the preoccupations of the artist's mind.

I like a good debate; and, when a stripling, used often to be stifled in the Gallery, or enjoy the easier privileges of a member's son. I like, I say, a good debate, and have no objection to a due mixture of bores, which are a relief. I remember none of the giants of former days; but I have heard Canning. He was a consummate rhetorician; but there seemed to me a dash of commonplace in all that he said, and frequent indications of the absence of an original mind. To the last, he never got clear of 'Good God, Sir!' and all the other hackneyed ejaculations of his youthful debating clubs. The most commanding speaker that I ever listened to is, I think, Sir Francis Burdett. I never heard him in the House,—but at an election. He was full of music, grace, and dignity, even amid all the vulgar tumult; and, unlike all mob orators, raised the taste of the populace to him, instead of lowering his own to theirs. . . .

Mr. Brougham, at present, reigns paramount in the House of Commons. I think the lawyer has spoiled the statesman. He is said to have very great powers of sarcasm. From what I have observed there, I should think very little ones would be quite sufficient. Many a sneer withers in those walls, which would scarcely, I think, blight a currant-bush out of them; and I have seen the House convulsed with raillery which, in other society, would infallibly settle the rallier to be a bore beyond all tolerance. Even an idiot can raise a smile. They are so good-natured, or find it so dull. . . .

I hear that Mr. Babington Macaulay is to be returned. If he speak half as well as he writes, the House will be in fashion again. I fear that he is one of those who, like the individual whom he has most studied, will 'give up to party what was meant for mankind.' At any rate, he must get rid of his rabidity. He writes now on all subjects, as if he certainly intended to be a renegade, and was determined to make the contrast complete.

Mr. Peel is the model of a minister, and improves as a speaker; though, like most of the rest, he is fluent without the least style. He should not get so often in a passion either, or, if he do, should not get out of one so easily. His sweet apologies are cloying. His candour—he will do well to get rid of that. He can make a present of it to Mr. Huskisson. . . .

In the Lords, I admire the Duke. The readiness with which he has adopted the air of a debater, shows the man of genius. There is a gruff, husky sort of a downright Montaignish *naïveté* about him, which is quaint, unusual, and tells. You plainly perceive that he is determined to be a civilian; and he is as offended if you drop a hint that he occasionally wears a uniform, as a servant on a holiday, if you mention the word *livery*.[1]

In the matter of party allegiance Disraeli in the same chapter professes himself a Gallio.

Am I a Whig or a Tory? I forget. As for the Tories, I admire antiquity, particularly a ruin; even the relics of the Temple of Intolerance have a charm. I think I am a Tory. But then the Whigs give such good dinners, and are the most amusing. I think I am a Whig; but then the Tories are so moral, and morality is my forte; I must be a Tory. But the Whigs dress so much better; and an ill-dressed party, like an ill-dressed man, must be wrong. Yes! I am a decided Whig. And yet——I feel like Garrick between Tragedy and Comedy. I think I will be a Whig and Tory alternate nights, and then both will be pleased; or I have no objection, according to the fashion of the day, to take a place under a Tory ministry, provided I may vote against them.

The Young Duke is remarkable for its long and frequent digressions of autobiographic interest. It is dangerous indeed, as it always is in Disraeli's case, to interpret these too literally. Some of the personal touches are obviously deliberate mystifications, the pretence, for instance, above that his father was a member of Parliament or elsewhere that he himself was writing the novel in Rome. In others

[1] Bk. V. ch. 6.

there is probably a good deal of Byronic exaggeration. It was the fashion in those days for a clever youth to pose as the victim of despair, and though Disraeli's illness was real enough, 'there certainly is a dark delight in being miserable,' as he says himself in the book, and we need not suppose that he took such a hopeless view of his future as in some passages he would have us believe.

I have lost the power of conveying what I feel, if indeed that power were ever mine. I write with an aching head and quivering hand ; yet I must write if but to break the solitude.[1]

The drooping pen falls from my powerless hand, and I feel—I keenly feel myself what indeed I am—far the most prostrate of a fallen race ![2]

Where are now my deeds and aspirations, and where the fame I dreamed of when a boy ? I find the world just slipping through my fingers, and cannot grasp the jewel ere it falls. I quit an earth, where none will ever miss me, save those whose blood requires no laurels to make them love my memory. My life has been a blunder and a blank, and all ends by my adding one more slight ghost to the shadowy realm of fatal precocity ![1]

What I am, I know not, nor do I care. I have that within me, which man can neither give nor take away, which can throw light on the darkest passages of life, and draw, from a discordant world, a melody divine. For it I would live, and for it alone. Oh ! my soul, must we then part ! Is this the end of all our conceptions, all our musings, our panting thoughts, our gay fancies, our bright imaginings, our delicious reveries, and exquisite communing ? Is this the end, the great and full result, of all our sweet society ? I care not for myself ; I am a wretch beneath even pity. My thousand errors, my ten thousand follies, my infinite corruption, have well deserved a bitterer fate than this. But thou !—I feel I have betrayed thee. Hadst thou been the inmate of more spiritual clay, bound with a brain less headstrong, and with blood less hot, thou mightest have been glorious.[1]

There is more sincerity, we may believe, in the following confession :—

I am one, though young, yet old enough to know, Ambition is a demon ; and I fly from what I fear. . . . Think of

[1] Bk. III. ch. 18. [2] Bk. IV. ch 3.

unrecognised Cæsar, with his wasting youth, weeping over the Macedonian's young career! Could Pharsalia compensate for those withering pangs? View the obscure Napoleon starving in the streets of Paris! What was St. Helena to the bitterness of such existence? The visions of past glory might illumine even that dark imprisonment; but to be conscious that his supernatural energies might die away without creating their miracles—can the wheel, or the rack rival the torture of such a suspicion? Lo! Byron, bending o'er his shattered lyre, with inspiration in his very rage. And the pert taunt could sting even this child of light! To doubt of the truth of the creed in which you have been nurtured, is not so terrific as to doubt respecting the intellectual vigour on whose strength you have staked your happiness.[1]

Or in this apostrophe to his father:—

Oh, my father! . . . our friendship is a hallowed joy:—it is my pride, and let it be thy solace. O'er the waters that cannot part our souls, I breathe good wishes. Peace brood o'er thy lettered bowers, and Love smile in the cheerful hall, that I shall not forget upon the swift Symplegades, or where warm Syria, with its palmy shore, recalls our holy ancestry![2]

Or, even in spite of the dithyrambs, in the following outburst of patriotism:—

Oh, England! Oh, my country—although full many an Eastern clime and Southern race have given me something of their burning blood, it flows for thee! I rejoice that my flying fathers threw their ancient seed on the stern shores which they have not dishonoured:—I am proud to be thy child. Thy noble laws have fed with freedom a soul that ill can brook constraint. Among thy hallowed hearths, I own most beautiful affections. In thy abounding tongue, my thoughts find music; and with the haughty fortunes of thy realm, my destiny would mingle! . . . Few can love thee better than he who traces here these idle lines. Worthier heads are working for thy glory and thy good; but if ever the hour shall call, my brain and life are thine.[3]

In lighter vein, he laughs, as he was always ready to do, at his own faults and foibles:—

I sometimes think I write a pretty style, though spoiled by that confounded puppyism; but, then, mine is the puppy

[1] Bk. II. ch. 7. [2] Bk. III. ch. 8. [3] Bk. III. ch. 18.

age, and that will wear off. Then, too, there are my vanity, my conceit, my affectation, my arrogance, and my egotism; all very heinous, and painfully contrasting with the imperturbable propriety of my fellow-scribblers,—'All gentlemen in stays, as stiff as stones.' But I may mend, or they fall off, and then the odds will be more equal.[1]

But by far the most remarkable of all these asides is the following truly astonishing bit of prescient impertinence:—

One thing is quite clear,—that a man may speak very well in the House of Commons, and fail very completely in the House of Lords. There are two distinct styles requisite: I intend, in the course of my career, if I have time, to give a specimen of both. In the Lower House, *Don Juan* may perhaps be our model; in the Upper House, *Paradise Lost*.[2]

By reason of Colburn's many delays the book did not make its appearance till the year after it was completed, when Disraeli was in the East. It was never a favourite of its author's. Even before publication he had lost interest in it, so far that he was able to write to his sister: 'I don't care a jot about *The Young Duke*. I never staked any fame on it; it may take its chance.' In the General Preface to the novels, written in 1870, when passing his early novels in review, he ignores it altogether, and to the severely expurgated edition issued with his collected works in 1853 he thought it necessary to prefix the apology: 'Young authors are apt to fall into affectation and conceit, and the writer of this work sinned very much in these respects; but the affectation of youth should be viewed leniently, and every man has a right to be conceited until he is successful.' In one quarter it was assured of an admiring welcome from the first.

From Sarah Disraeli.

April 4, '31.

For *The Young Duke*, it is excellent,—most excellent. There is not a dull half page,—not a dull half line. Your

[1] Bk. III. ch. 18. [2] Bk. V. ch. 6.

story is unparalleled, for though it ends in a marriage which one can tell without peeping it grows more exciting as it winds towards its close. Your heroine is fit to be worshipped—your first sight of her is inimitable. The Young Duke is as you say 'the noblest animal in the world.' The two scenes of rejection and the Alhambra supper, and the gambling scene all wonderful,—the last so utterly unlike all gambling scenes in novels, no thumping of the table or the forehead, but all so desperate and so cool that it makes your hair stand on end. The *last stake* beats Hogarth. You must expect to be rated for bringing your fair innocent readers into such company as pseudo Mrs. Annesley and pseudo Lady Squib. I say nothing of your moral episodes, for they touch my heart too keenly to let me be at all aware of what effect they will have upon others. One reading has repaid me for months of suspense, and that is saying everything if you knew how much my heart is wrapt up in your fame.

The reception of the book by the critics was at least as good as it deserved, and it at once became popular.

From Sarah Disraeli.

May 1, 1831.

Wherever we go, *The Young Duke* is before us, and its praises for ever resounding. But I know you care nothing for family commendation. . . . Jerdan has at last discovered that its author is gifted with every quality that constitutes a man of splendid genius. The highest power of imagination that creates and combines the most brilliant wit, the keenest sense of the ridiculous, a fullness of knowledge that conveys a characteristic trait in a slight phrase, and a long *etcetera* of truths which I suppose he has acquired from his friend Bulwer. To balance such an extraordinary venture of commendation, he is obliged to find a fault or two. . . . The book is reviewed in all weekly and Sunday papers—all with excessive praise.

Subsequently the admiring sister reports, on the authority of 'some Americans who have just come to England,' that '*The Young Duke* is the text-book of the United States, from which they preach and read, and learn that important requisite manners.' The one conspicuous exception to the general friendliness of the critics was supplied by the *Westminster Review*, the organ of the Benthamites. 'To parasites, sycophants, toad-eaters, tuft-hunters, and humble companions,' this paper urbanely remarked, 'it will be a book full of comfort and instruction in their callings.' Disraeli, it must be said, had given much provocation; for not only had ridicule of the Benthamites been the express purpose of *Popanilla*, but in *The Young Duke* itself there is some bitter satire of their 'screw and lever' philosophy. Sarah Disraeli wrote before publication that the book had not been puffed 'in anything to find fault with'; but this was hardly just to Colburn, who was practising his customary arts with his customary activity and address—and that in spite of the fact that the author had tried in the preface to deprive him of one of the most potent weapons in his armoury by expressly disclaiming portraiture.

The great mass of my readers (if I have a mass, as I hope,) will attribute the shades that flit about these volumes to any substances they please. That smaller portion of society, who are most competent to decide upon the subject, will instantly observe, that however I may have availed myself of a trait, or an incident, and often inadvertently, the whole is ideal. To draw caricatures of our contemporaries is not a very difficult task: it requires only a small portion of talent, and a great want of courtesy.

CHAPTER IX.

TOUR IN THE EAST.

1830-1831.

The journey on which Disraeli now embarked with his friend Meredith proved a capital event in his life and had marked effects on his whole subsequent career, both literary and political. It not only enlarged his experience beyond that of most young Englishmen of his day, but, what was even more important to one of his peculiar temperament, it helped to give definite purpose and significance to that Oriental tendency in his nature which, vaguely present before, was henceforth to dominate his imagination and show itself in nearly all his achievements. We can see the influence of the Eastern journey in *Contarini Fleming*, in *Alroy*, in *Tancred*, and in *Lothair*; but we can see it not less clearly in the bold stroke of policy which laid the foundations of English ascendancy in Egypt, in the Act which gave explicit form to the conception of an Indian Empire with the Sovereign of Great Britain at its head, and in the settlement imposed on Europe at the Berlin Congress. The letters [1] written to his family during the journey have been published since his death; and after the lapse of eighty years they retain their freshness and interest in a way that is rare with such compositions. Keen observation, a graphic

[1] The references here will be to the 1887 edition of *Lord Beaconsfield's Letters*, in which the *Home Letters* and *Lord Beaconsfield's Correspondence with his Sister* are combined in one volume.

and vivacious style, the power of concentrating a picture into a phrase, and a strain of joyous raillery running through all are the elements of their charm. 'C'est une si jolie chose que de savoir écrire ce que l'on pense,' says Madame de Sévigné, a favourite of Disraeli's, who well knew herself the vivid delight of easy and perfect expression. Meredith, Disraeli's companion, was much better educated, much more methodical, and much more conscientiously laborious in profiting by the opportunities of the journey; but his diary and letters which, with other material beyond what has been already published, are available for this chapter, help one to realise how easily the scenes and incidents to which the man of imagination can lend an abiding interest may become in the hands of another the subject of a prosy and lifeless chronicle.

The travellers left London by steamer on the 28th of May, and after a week's detention at Falmouth proceeded by the mail packet to Gibraltar.

To Isaac Disraeli.

GIBRALTAR,
July 1, 1830.

MY DEAR FATHER

I write to you from a country where the hedges consist of aloes all in blossom: fourteen, sixteen feet high. Conceive the contrast to our beloved and beechy Bucks. I say nothing of geraniums and myrtles, bowers of oranges and woods of olives, though the occasional palm should not be forgotten for its great novelty and uncommon grace. We arrived here after a very brief and very agreeable passage, passed in very agreeable society. . . . This Rock is a wonderful place, with a population infinitely diversified. Moors with costumes radiant as a rainbow or an Eastern melodrama; Jews with gaberdines and skull-caps; Genoese, Highlanders, and Spaniards, whose dress is as picturesque as that of the sons of Ivor. There are two public libraries—the Garrison Library, with more than 12,000 volumes; and the Merchants', with upwards of half that number. In the Garrison are all your works, even the last edition of the *Literary Character*; in the Merchants' the greater part. Each possesses a copy of another book, supposed to be written by a member of our family, and which is looked upon at Gibraltar as one of the masterpieces of the nineteenth century. You may feel their intellectual pulse from this. At first I apologised and talked of youthful blunders and all that, really being ashamed; but finding them, to my astonishment, sincere, and fearing they were stupid enough to adopt my last opinion, I shifted my position just in time, looked very grand, and passed myself off for a child of the Sun, like the Spaniard in Peru.

We were presented to the Governor, Sir George Don, a general and G.C.B., a very fine old gentleman, of the Windsor Terrace school, courtly, almost regal in his manner, paternal, almost officious in his temper, a sort of mixture of Lord St. Vincent and the Prince de Ligne, English in his general style, but highly polished and experienced in European society. His palace, the Government House, is an old convent, and one of the most delightful residences I know, with a garden under the superintendence of Lady Don, full of rare exotics, with a beautiful terrace over the sea, a berceau of vines, and other delicacies which would quite delight you. . . . He[1] behaved to us with great kindness, asked us to dine, and gave us a route himself for an excursion to the Sierra da Ronda, a savage mountain district, abounding in the most beautiful scenery and bugs!

We returned from this excursion, which took us a week, yesterday, greatly gratified. The country in which we travelled is a land entirely of robbers and smugglers. They commit no personal violence, but lay you on the ground and clean out your pockets. If you have less than sixteen dollars they shoot you; that is the tariff, and is a loss worth risking. I took care to have very little more, and no baggage which I could not stow in the red bag which my mother remembers making for my pistols. . . . You will wonder how we managed to extract pleasure from a life which afforded us hourly peril for our purses and perhaps for our lives, which induced fatigue greater than I ever experienced, for here are no roads, and we were never less than eight hours a day on horseback, picking our way through a course which can only be compared to the steep bed of an exhausted cataract, and with so slight a prospect of attaining for a reward either food or rest.—I will tell you. The country was beautiful, the novelty of the life was great, and above all we had Brunet. What a man! Born in Italy of French

[1] Meredith testifies that Disraeli's lectures on morals and politics had made a great impression on Sir George.

parents, he has visited, as the captain of a privateer, all countries of the Mediterranean: Egypt, Turkey, Syria. Early in life, as valet to Lord Hood, he was in England, and has even been at Guinea. After fourteen years' cruising he was taken by the Algerines, and was in various parts of Barbary for five or six years, and at last he obtains his liberty and settles at Gibraltar, where he becomes *cazador* to the Governor for he is, among his universal accomplishments, a celebrated shot. He can speak all languages but English, of which he makes a sad affair—even Latin, and he hints at a little Greek. He is fifty, but light as a butterfly and gay as a bird; in person not unlike English at Lyme, if you can imagine so insipid a character with a vivacity that never flags, and a tongue that never rests. Brunet did everything, remedied every inconvenience, and found an expedient for every difficulty. Never did I live so well as among these wild mountains of Andalusia, so exquisite is his cookery. Seriously, he is an artist of the first magnitude, and used to amuse himself by giving us some very exquisite dish among these barbarians; for he affects a great contempt of the Spaniards, and an equal admiration for the Moors. Whenever we complained he shrugged his shoulders with a look of ineffable contempt, exclaiming, 'Nous ne sommes pas en Barbarie!' Recalling our associations with that word and country, it was superbly ludicrous. . . .

At Castellar we slept in the very haunt of the banditti, among the good fellows of José Maria, the Captain Rolando of this part, and were not touched. In fact, we were not promising prey, though picturesque enough in our appearance. Imagine M. and myself on two little Andalusian mountain horses with long tails and jennet necks, followed by a larger beast of burthen with our baggage, and the inevitable Brunet cocked upon its neck with a white hat and slippers, lively, shrivelled and noisy as a pea dancing upon tin. Our Spanish guide, tall, and with a dress excessively *brodé* and covered with brilliant buttons, walking by the side and occasionally adding to the burthen of our sumpter steed. The air of the mountains, the rising sun, the rising appetite, the variety of picturesque persons and things we met, and the impending danger, made a delightful life, and had it not been for the great enemy I should have given myself up entirely to the magic of the life; but that spoiled all. It is not worse; sometimes I think it lighter about the head, but the palpitation about the heart greatly increases, otherwise my health is wonderful. Never have I been better; but what use is this when the end of all existence is debarred me? I say no more upon this melancholy subject, by which I am ever and infinitely depressed, and often most so when the world least imagines it; but to complain is useless, and to endure almost impossible; but existence is certainly less irksome in the mild distraction of this various life. . . .

Tell my mother that as it is the fashion among the dandies of this place—that is, the officers, for there are no others—not to wear waistcoats in the morning, her new studs come into fine play, and maintain my reputation of being a great judge of costume, to the admiration and envy of many subalterns. I have also the fame of being the first who ever passed the Straits with two canes, a morning and an evening cane. I change my cane as the gun fires, and hope to carry them both on to Cairo. It is wonderful the effect these magical wands produce. I owe to them even more attention than to being the supposed author of—what is it?—I forget!

These Straits, by-the-bye—that is, the passage for the last ten miles or so to Gib, between the two opposite coasts of Africa and Europe, with the ocean for a river, and the shores all mountains—is by far the sublimest thing I have yet seen. . . . When I beg you to write, I mean my beloved Sa, because I know you think it a bore; but do all as you like. To her and to my dearest mother a thousand kisses. Tell Ralph I have not forgotten my promise of an occasional letter; and my dear pistol-cleaner, that he forgot to oil the locks, which rusted in conveyance. I thank the gods daily I am freed of Louis Clement, who would have been an expense and a bore. Tell [Washington] Irving he has left a golden name in Spain. Few English visit Gibraltar. Tell Lord Mahon, inquiries made after his health. Adieu, my beloved *padre*.

Your most affectionate son,

B. D.[1]

CADIZ,
July 14.

We passed a very pleasant week at Gibraltar, after our return from Ronda. We dined with the Governor at his cottage at Europa, a most charming pavilion, and met a most agreeable party. Lady Don was well enough to dine with us, and did me the honour of informing me that I was the cause of the exertion, which, though of course a fib, was nevertheless flattering. She is, though very old, without exception one of the most agreeable personages that I ever met, excessively

1 *Letters*, pp. 3-10.

acute and *piquante*, with an aptitude of detecting character, and a tact in assuming it, very remarkable. To listen to her you would think you were charming away the hour with a blooming beauty in Mayfair ; and, though excessively infirm, her eye is so brilliant and so full of *moquerie* that you quite forgot her wrinkles. Altogether the scene very much resembled a small German Court. There was his Excellency in uniform covered with orders, exactly like the old Grand Duke of Darmstadt, directing everything ; his wife the clever Prussian Princess that shared his crown ; the aides-de-camp made excellent chamberlains, and the servants in number and formality quite equalled those of a Residenz. The repast was really elegant and *recherché* even for this curious age. Sir George will yet head his table and yet carve, recommend a favourite dish, and deluge you with his summer drink, half champagne and half lemonade.

After dinner Lady Don rode out with the very pretty wife of Colonel Considine, and the men dispersed in various directions. It was the fate of Meredith and myself to be lionised to some cave or other with Sir George. What a scene, and what a procession ! First came two grooms on two Barbs ; then a carriage with four horses ; at the window at which H. E. sits, a walking footman, and then an outrider, all at a funeral pace. We were directed to meet our host at the cave, ten minutes' walk. During this time Sir G. tries one of the Arabians, but at the gentlest walk, and the footman changes his position in consequence to his side ; but it is windy, our valiant but infirm friend is afraid of being blown off, and when he reaches the point of destination, we find him again in the carriage. In spite of his infirmities he will get out to lionise ; but before he disembarks, he changes his foraging cap for a full general's cock with a plume as big as the Otranto one ; and this because the hero will never be seen in public in undress, although we were in a solitary cave looking over the ocean, and inhabited only by monkeys. The cave is shown, and we all get in the carriage, because he is sure we are tired ; the foraging cap is again assumed, and we travel back to the Cottage, Meredith, myself, the Governor, and the cocked hat, each in a seat. In the evening he has his rubber, which he never misses, and is surprised I do not play ' the only game for gentlemen ! You should play ; learn.' However, I preferred the conversation of his agreeable lady, although the charms of Mrs. Considine were puzzling, and I was very much like Hercules between —you know the rest.

I am sorry to say my hair is coming off, just at the moment it had attained the highest perfection, and was universally mistaken for a wig, so that I am obliged to let the women pull it to satisfy their curiosity. Let me know what my mother thinks. There are no wigs here that I could wear. Pomade and all that is quite a delusion. Somebody recommends me cocoa-nut oil, which I could get here; but suppose it turns it grey or blue or green! I made a very pleasant acquaintance at Gibraltar, Sir Charles Gordon, a brother of Lord Aberdeen, and Colonel of the Royal Highlanders. He was absent during my first visit. He is not unlike his brother in appearance, but the frigidity of the Gordons has expanded into urbanity, instead of subsiding into sullenness—in short, a man with a warm heart though a cold manner, and exceedingly amusing, with the reputation of being always silent. As contraries sometimes agree, we became exceedingly friendly. . . .

The Judge Advocate at Gibraltar is that Mr. Baron Field who once wrote a book, and whom all the world took for a noble, but it turned out that Baron was to him what Thomas is to other men. He pounced upon me, said he had seen you at Murray's, first man of the day, and all that, and evidently expected to do an amazing bit of literature; but I found him a bore, and vulgar, a Storks without breeding, consequently I gave him a lecture on canes, which made him stare, and he has avoided me ever since. The truth is, he wished to saddle his mother upon me for a *compagnon de voyage*, whom I discovered in the course of half an hour to be both deaf, dumb, and blind, but yet more endurable than the noisy, obtrusive, jargonic judge, who is a true lawyer, ever illustrating the obvious, explaining the evident, and expatiating on the commonplace. . . .

I have met here Mr. Frank Hall Standish, once a celebrated dandy, and who wrote a life of Voltaire, you remember. We have heard of the King's death, which is the destruction of my dress waistcoats. I truly grieve. News arrived last night of the capture of Algiers, but all this will reach you before my letter. My general health is excellent. I have never had a moment's illness since I left home, not counting an occasional indigestion, but I mean no fever and so on. The great enemy, I think, is weaker, but the palpitation at the heart the reverse. I find wherever I go plenty of friends and nothing but attention.[1]

[1] *Letters*, p. 10.

The Governor's agreeable lady,' made a great impression on Disraeli. 'While I remember it,' he wrote later, 'a copy of *The Young Duke* must be sent to Lady Don. Tell Ralph to attend to it. Write in the title "Lady Don, by desire of the author." . . . You will be surprised at my sending a light novel, and finding a muse in an old lady of seventy; but in truth she is the cleverest and most charming woman I ever met . . . and the only person I know who gives one the least idea of the Madame du Tencins and the other *brillantes*, who flirted with Hénault, chatted with Montesquieu, and corresponded with Horace Walpole.'

The original intention of the two friends had been to hasten on to Malta, but they were so delighted with their first glimpse of Spain that they lingered for a couple of months. 'I travelled through the whole of Andalusia on horseback,' Disraeli wrote to Austen; 'I was never less than ten hours out of the twenty-four on my steed, and more than once saw the sun set and rise without quitting my saddle, which few men can say, and which I never wish to say again. I visited Cadiz, Seville, Cordova, and Granada, among many other cities which must not be named with these romantic towns. I sailed upon the Guadalquivir, I cheered at the bull fights; I lived for a week among brigands and wandered in the fantastic halls of the delicate Alhambra. Why should I forget to say that I ate an *olla podrida*? I will not weary you with tales of men of buckram; they must be reserved for our fireside. I entered Spain a sceptic with regard to their robbers, and listened to all their romances with a smile. I lived to change my opinion. I at length found a country where adventure is the common course of existence.' Leaving Gibraltar he rode in a couple of days to Cadiz, gazing by the way across those 'sublime' Straits, where 'Europe and Africa frown on each other,' at the picturesque beauty of the 'sultry sister.' Cadiz he found brilliant beyond description. '"Fair Florence" is a very dingy affair compared with it. The white houses and the green jalousies sparkle in the sun. Figaro is in every street; Rosina in every balcony.'

To Isaac D'Israeli.

SEVILLE,
July 26.

Cadiz I left with regret, though there is little to interest except its artificial beauty. It is not unlike Venice in its situation, but there the resemblance ceases. Cadiz is without an association—not a church, a picture, or a palace. The family of the Consul is a most agreeable one: you must not associate with this somewhat humble title a character at all in unison. Mr. Brackenbury is great enough for an ambassador, and lives well enough for one; but with some foibles, he is a very hospitable personage, and I owe many agreeable hours to its exercise. You see what a Sevillian *écritoire* is by this despatch. I have already expended on it more time than would have served for writing many letters. I am almost in a state of frenzy from the process of painting my ideas in this horrible scrawl. It is like writing with blacking and with a skewer. Mr. Standish returned to Seville, where he resides at present, and called on me the next day. We dined with him yesterday. He is a most singular character—a spoiled child of fortune, who thinks himself, and who is perhaps now, a sort of philosopher. But all these characters must be discussed over our fireside or on the Terrace.[1]

Fleuriz, the Governor of Cadiz, is a singular brute. When we meet I will tell you how I Pelhamised him. All the English complain that when they are presented to him he bows and says nothing, uttering none of those courtly inanities which are expected on such occasions, and for which crowned heads and all sorts of viceroys are celebrated. Brackenbury had been reading a review of the *Commentaries*[2] in the *Courier* in the morning, and full thereof, announced me to Fleuriz as the son of the greatest author in England. The usual reception, however, only greeted me; but I, being prepared for the savage, was by no means silent, and made him stare for half an hour in a most extraordinary manner.

[1] The Yew Terrace at Bradenham, where Disraeli in these early years was wont to compose his novels or con his speeches as he walked up and down.

[2] His father's *Commentaries on the Life and Reign of Charles I.*

He was sitting over some prints just arrived from England—a view of Algiers, and the fashions for June. The question was whether the place was Algiers, for it had no title. Just fresh from Gibraltar, I ventured to inform his Excellency that it was, and that a group of gentlemen intended to represent A——— and a couple of his friends, but displaying those extraordinary coats and countenances that Mr. Ackermann offers monthly as an improvement upon Nature and Nugee, were personages no less eminent than the Dey and his two principal *conseillers d'état*. The dull Fleuriz took everything *au pied de lettre*, and after due examination insinuated scepticism. Whereupon I offer renewed arguments to prove the dress to be Moorish. Fleuriz calls a mademoiselle to translate the inscription, but the inscription only proves that they are 'fashions for June';—at Algiers, I add, appealing to every one whether they had ever seen such beings in London. Six Miss Brackenburys, equally pretty, protest they have not. Fleuriz, unable to comprehend *badinage*, gives a Mashallah look of pious resignation, and has bowed to the ground every night since that he has met me. . . .

We came here up the Guadalquivir, and to-morrow proceed by a diligence to Cordova. . . . We have found here a most agreeable friend in Mr. Williams, an English merchant married to a Spanish lady, and considered the greatest connoisseur in paintings in Spain. He has nearly thirty of the finest Murillos. I had a letter to him from Brackenbury. It is astonishing with what kindness he behaves to us. His house is open to us at all times, and we pass our evenings most agreeably sitting in his *patio*, turning over the original drawings of Murillo, while his Spanish sister-in-law, Dolores, sings a *bolero*. It is the mode to call all the ladies here by their Christian name directly you are introduced. So much for Spanish etiquette. On the other hand, my tailor is offended if I do not ask him to take a chair, and always address him Signor. It is all banished to the lower classes. When he brought home my jacket, he told me his whole fortune was at my command.[1]

Disraeli was enchanted with Murillo. 'Run, my dear fellow, to Seville,' he wrote to Austen, 'and for the first time in your life know what a great artist is—Murillo, Murillo, Murillo!' 'The most original of artists,' he says in a letter to Bradenham. 'No man has painted

[1] *Letters*, p. 14.

more, or oftener reached the ideal. He never fails. Where can his bad pictures be?'

I parted with my friend Standish at Seville with regret. He is excessively fantastic and odd, but a good fellow. The Spaniards cannot make him out, and the few English that meet him set him down only as exceedingly affected. He is something more. The man of pleasure, who, instead of degenerating into a *roué*, aspires to be a philosopher, is to my mind certainly a respectable, and I think, an interesting character.[1]

At Cordova Disraeli saw and was impressed by the great Cathedral Mosque, and noted therein the beautiful 'shrine and chapel of a Moorish saint, with the blue mosaic and the golden honeycombed roof as vivid and as brilliant as when the saint was worshipped'; and then he set forth on the long ride to Granada.

To Sarah Disraeli.

What a country have I lived in! I am invited by 'a grand lady of Madrid'—I quote our host at Cordova—to join her escort to Granada: twenty foot soldiers, four servants armed, and *tirailleurs* in the shape of a dozen muleteers. We refused, for reasons too long here to detail, and set off alone two hours before, expecting an assault. I should tell you we dined previously with her and her husband, having agreed to meet to discuss matters. It was a truly Gil Blas scene. My lord in an undress uniform, slightly imposing in appearance, greeted us with dignity; the signora, exceedingly young and really very pretty, with infinite vivacity and grace. A French valet leant on his chair, and a duenna, such as Stephanoff would draw, broad and supercilious, with jet eyes, mahogany complexion, and cocked-up nose, stood by my lady bearing a large fan. She was most complaisant, as she evidently had more confidence in two thick-headed Englishmen with their Purdeys and Mantons than in her specimen of the once famous Spanish infantry. She did not know that we are cowards on principle. I could screw up my courage to a duel or a battle, but I think my life worth five pounds in the shape of ransom to José Maria. In spite of her charms and their united eloquence, which,

[1] *Letters*, p. 27.

as they only spoke Spanish, was of course most persuasive, we successfully resisted. The moon rises on our course: for the first two leagues all is anxiety, as it was well known that a strong band was lying in wait for the 'great lady.' After two leagues we began to hope, when suddenly our guide informs us that he hears a trampling of horses in the distance. Ave Maria! A cold perspiration came over me. Decidedly they approached, but rather an uproarious crew. We drew up out of pure fear, and I had my purse ready. The band turned out to be a company of actors travelling to Cordova. There they were, dresses and decorations, scenery and machinery, all on mules and donkeys, for there are no roads in this country. The singers rehearsing an opera; the principal tragedian riding on an ass; and the buffo, most serious, looking as grave as night, with a cigar, and in greater agitation than them all. Then there were women in side-saddles, like sedans, and whole panniers of children, some of the former chanting an *ave*, while their waists (saving your presence, but it is a rich trait) were in more than one instance encircled by the brawny arm of a more robust devotee. All this irresistibly reminded me of Cervantes. We proceed and meet a caravan (*corsario* they call it, but I spell from sound) of armed merchants, who challenged us, with a regular piquet, and I nearly got shot for not answering in time, being somewhat before my guide. Then come two travelling friars who give us their blessing, and then we lose our way. We wander about all night, dawn breaks, and we stumble on some peasants sleeping in the field amid their harvest. We learn that we cannot regain our road, and, utterly wearied, we finally sink to sound sleep with our pack-saddles for our pillows.[1]

At Granada Disraeli was of course delighted with the Alhambra, which he placed 'with the Parthenon, the Pantheon, and York Minster.'

To Isaac D'Israeli.

The Saracenic architecture is the most inventive and fanciful, but at the same time the most fitting and the most delicate that can be conceived. There would be no doubt about its title to be considered among the first inventions of men if it were better known. It is only to be found in any

[1] *Ibid.*, pp. 23-25.

degree of perfection in Spain. When a man sneers at the Saracenic, ask him what he has seen. Perhaps a barbarous though picturesque building, called the Ducal Palace, at Venice! What should we think of a man who decided on the buildings of Agrippa by the architecture of Justinian, or judged the age of Pericles by the restorations of Hadrian? Yet he would not commit so great a blunder. . . .

The great efforts of antique architecture are confined to temples or theatres, which at the best can be only a room. The Alhambra is a palace, and the opportunity for invention is, of course, infinitely increased. It is not a ruin, as I expected, scarcely in a state of dilapidation. Certainly, under the patronage of our late monarch, it might have been restored to all its pristine splendour, though I think a compliant Parliament would have been almost as necessary as Sir Jeffrey Wyatville. Everything about it, though exquisitely proportioned, is slight and small and delicate. Murphy makes the Court of Pillars too large and coarse. Around this court are chambers with carved and purple roofs studded with gold, and walls entirely covered with the most fanciful relief, picked out with that violet tint which must have been copied from their Andalusian skies. In these you may sit in the coolest shade, reclining upon cushions, with your beads or pipe, and view the most dazzling sunlight in the court, which assuredly must scorch the flowers if the faithful lions ever ceased from pouring forth that element which you must travel in Spain or Africa to honour. Pindar was quite right.[1] These chambers are innumerable. There is the Hall of the Ambassadors, always the most sumptuous; the Hall of Justice; the rooms of the sultanas and of the various members of the family, quite perfect, not a single roof has given. What a scene! Ah, that you were here! But conceive it in the times of the Boabdils; conceive it with all its courtly decoration, all the gilding, all the imperial purple, all the violet relief, all the scarlet borders, all the glittering inscriptions and costly mosaics, burnished, bright and fresh; conceive it full of still greater ornaments, the living groups with their rich and vivid and picturesque costume, and, above all, their shining arms; some standing in groups conversing, some smoking in sedate silence, some telling their beads, some squatting round a storier. Then the bustle and the rush, and the arming horsemen all in motion, and all glancing in the most brilliant sun.[2]

[1] Ἄριστον μὲν ὕδωρ—Water is best.

[2] *Letters*, pp. 28, 29.

Benjamin Disraeli 1828.
From a drawing by D. Maclise R.A.
at Hughenden

Meredith records a curious incident of their first visit.

The old lady who showed us over the Alhambra, talkative and intelligent, would have it that Benjamin D. was a Moor, many of whom come to visit this palace, which they say will yet be theirs again. His southern aspect, the style in which he paced the gorgeous apartments, and sat himself in the seat of the Abencerrages, quite deceived her; she repeated the question a dozen times, and would not be convinced of the contrary. His parting speech, 'Es mi casa,' 'This is my palace,' quite confirmed her suspicions.

From Granada Disraeli wrote a letter to his mother 'on an elephantine sheet, all about Spanish ladies and tomato sauce.' No one would dream that it was from the pen of an invalid to whom 'the least exertion of mind' was instantly painful.

To Maria D'Israeli.

GRANADA,
Aug. 1.

MY DEAR MOTHER,

Although you doubtless assist, as the French phrase it, at the reading of my despatches, you will, I am sure, be pleased to receive one direct from your absent son. It has just occurred to me that I have never yet mentioned the Spanish ladies, and I do not think that I can address anything that I have to say upon this agreeable subject to any one more suitable than yourself. You know that I am rather an admirer of the blonde; and, to be perfectly candid, I will confess to you that the only times which I have been so unfortunate as to be captivated, or captured, in this country were both by Englishwomen. But these Espagnolas are nevertheless very interesting personages. What we associate with the idea of female beauty is not common in this country. There are none of those seraphic countenances, which strike you dumb or blind, but faces in abundance which will never pass without commanding a pleasing glance. Their charm consists in their sensibility; each incident, every person, every word touches the far eye of a Spanish lady, and her features are constantly confuting the creed of Mahomet, and proving that she has a soul: but there is nothing quick, harsh, or forced about her. She is extremely unaffected, and not at all French. Her eyes gleam rather than sparkle, she speaks with quick vivacity but in sweet tones, and there is in all her carriage, particularly when she walks, a certain dignified grace which never leaves her, and which is very remarkable. . . .

I sat next to a lady of high distinction at a bull-fight at Seville. She was the daughter-in-law of the Captain-General, and the most beautiful Spaniard I have yet met. Her comb was white, and she wore a mantilla of blonde, I have no doubt extremely valuable, for it was very dirty. The effect, however, was charming. Her hair was glossy black, and her eyes like an antelope's, but all her other features deliciously soft; and she was further adorned, which is rare in Spain, with a rosy cheek, for here our heroines are rather sallow. But they counteract this defect by never appearing until twilight, which calls them from their bowers, fresh, though languid, from the late siesta. To conclude, the only fault of the Spanish beauty is that she too soon indulges in the magnificence of embonpoint. There are, however, many exceptions to this. At seventeen a Spanish beauty is poetical, tall, lithe, and clear, though sallow. But you have seen Mercandotti.[1] As she advances, if she does not lose her shape, she resembles Juno rather than Venus. Majestic she ever is; and if her feet are less twinkling than in her first career, look on her hand and you'll forgive them all.

There is calm voluptuousness about the life here that wonderfully accords with my disposition, so that if I were resident, and had my intellect at command, I do not know any place where I could make it more productive. The imagination is ever at work, and beauty and grace are not scared away by those sounds and sights, those constant cares and changing feelings, which are the proud possession of our free land of eastern winds. You rise at eight, and should breakfast lightly, although a table covered with all fruits renders that rather difficult to one who inherits, with other qualities good and bad, that passion for the most delightful productions of nature, with which my beloved sire can sympathise. I only wish I had him here over a medley of grape and melon, gourd and prickly-pear. In the morning you never quit the house, and these are hours which might be profitably employed under the inspiration of a climate which is itself poetry, for it sheds over everything a golden hue which does not exist in the objects themselves illuminated. At present I indulge only in a calm reverie, for I find the least exertion of mind instantly aggravate all my symptoms; and even this letter

[1] A famous dancer of the day.

is an exertion, which you would hardly credit. My general health was never better. You know how much better I am on a sunny day in England ; well, I have had two months of sunny days infinitely warmer. I have during all this period enjoyed general health of which I have no memory during my life. All the English I have met are ill, and live upon a diet. I eat everything, and my appetite each day increases. . . . The Spanish cuisine is not much to my taste, for garlic and bad oil preponderate ; but it has its points : the soups are good, and *the most agreeable dish* in the world is an olio. I will explain it to you, for my father would delight in it. There are two large dishes, one at each end of the table. The one at the top contains bouilli beef, boiled pork sausage, black-pudding ; all these not mixed together, but in their separate portions. The other dish is a medley of vegetables and fruits, generally French beans, caravanseras, slices of melons, and whole pears. Help each person to a portion of the meats, and then to the medley. Mix them in your plate together, and drown them in tomato sauce. There is no garlic and no grease of any kind. I have eaten this every day, it is truly delightful. . . .

After dinner you take your siesta. I generally sleep for two hours. I think this practice conducive to health. Old people, however, are apt to carry it to excess. By the time I have risen and arranged my toilette it is time to steal out, and call upon any agreeable family whose Tertullia you may choose to honour, which you do, after the first time, uninvited, and with them you take your tea or chocolate. This is often *al fresco*, under the piazza or colonnade of the *patio*. Here you while away the time until it is cool enough for the *alameda* or public walk. At Cadiz, and even at Seville, up the Guadalquivir, you are sure of a delightful breeze from the water. The sea breeze comes like a spirit. The effect is quite magical. As you are lolling in listless languor in the hot and perfumed air, an invisible guest comes dancing into the party and touches them all with an enchanted wand. All start, all smile. It has come ; it is the sea breeze. There is much discussion whether it is as strong, or whether weaker, than the night before. The ladies furl their fans and seize their mantillas, the cavaliers stretch their legs and give signs of life. All rise. I offer my arm to Dolores or Florentina (is not this familiarity strange ?), and in ten minutes you are in the *alameda*. What a change ! All is now life and liveliness. Such bowing, such kissing, such fluttering of fans, such gentle criticism of gentle friends !

But the fan is the most wonderful part of the whole scene. A Spanish lady with her fan might shame the tactics of a troop of horse. Now she unfurls it with the slow pomp and conscious elegance of a peacock. Now she flutters it with all the languor of a listless beauty, now with all the liveliness of a vivacious one. Now, in the midst of a very tornado, she closes it with a whir which makes you start, pop! In the midst of your confusion Dolores taps you on the elbow; you turn round to listen, and Florentina pokes you in your side. Magical instrument! You know that it speaks a particular language, and gallantry requires no other mode to express its most subtle conceits or its most unreasonable demands than this slight, delicate organ. But remember, while you read, that here, as in England, it is not confined alone to your delightful sex. I also have my fan, which makes my cane extremely jealous. If you think I have grown extraordinarily effeminate, learn that in this scorching clime the soldier will not mount guard without one. Night wears on, we sit, we take a *panal*, which is as quick work as snapdragon, and far more elegant; again we stroll. Midnight clears the public walks, but few Spanish families retire till two. A solitary bachelor like myself still wanders, or still lounges on a bench in the *warm* moonlight. The last guitar dies away, the cathedral clock wakes up your reverie, you too seek your couch, and amid a gentle, sweet flow of loveliness, and light, and music, and fresh air, thus dies a day in Spain.

Adieu, my dearest mother. A thousand loves to all.[1]

B. DISRAELI.

To Sarah Disraeli.

GIBRALTAR,
Aug. 9.

MY DEAR SA,

We arrived here[2] yesterday tired to death, but very well. The Mediterranean packet is expected hourly, and I lose not a moment in writing to you, which I do in compliment to your most welcome letter which awaited me here, and which, though short enough, was most sweet. The very long one about all the things I want to know makes my mouth water. . . . In regard to any plans, we are certainly off next packet. No farther can I aver. What use are plans? Did I dream six months ago of Andalusia, where I have spent some of the most agreeable hours of my existence? Such a trip! Such universal novelty, and such unrivalled luck in all things! . . .

[1] *Letters*, p. 17. [2] They returned from Granada by Malaga and the sea.

This is the country for a national novelist. The *al fresco* life of the inhabitants induces a variety of the most picturesque manners; their semi-savageness makes each district retain with barbarous jealousy its own customs and its own costumes. A weak government resolves society into its original elements, and robbery becomes more honourable than war, inasmuch as the robber is paid and the soldier in arrear. Then a wonderful ecclesiastical establishment covers the land with a privileged class, who are perpetually producing some effect on society. I say nothing, while writing these lines—which afterwards may be expanded into a picture—of their costume. You are awakened from your slumbers by the *rosario*—the singing procession by which the peasantry congregate to their labours. It is most effective, full of noble chants and melodious responses, that break upon the still fresh air and your even fresher feelings in a manner truly magical.

Oh, wonderful Spain! Think of this romantic land covered with Moorish ruins and full of Murillo! Ah that I could describe to you the wonders of the painted temples of Seville! ah that I could wander with you amid the fantastic and imaginative halls of delicate Alhambra! Why, why cannot I convey to you more perfectly all that I see and feel? I thought that enthusiasm was dead within me, and nothing could be new. I have hit perhaps upon the only country which could have upset my theory—a country of which I have read little and thought nothing—a country of which indeed nothing has been of late written, and which few visit. I dare to say I am better. This last fortnight I have made regular progress, or rather felt perhaps the progress which I had already made. It is all the sun. Do not think that it is society or change of scene. This, however occasionally agreeable, is too much for me, and even throws me back. It is when I am quite alone and quite still that I feel the difference of my system, that I miss old aches, and am conscious of the increased activity and vitality and expansion of my blood. Write to me whenever you can, always to Malta, from whence I shall be sure to receive my letters sooner or later. If I receive twenty at a time, it does not signify; but write: do not let the chain of my domestic knowledge be broken for an instant. Write to me about Bradenham, about dogs and horses, orchards, gardens, who calls, where you go, who my father sees in London, what is said. This is what I want. Never mind public news, except it be private in its knowledge, or about private friends. I see all newspapers sooner or later. . . . Keep on writing, but don't *bore* yourself. Mind this. A thousand thousand loves to all. Adieu, my beloved. We shall soon meet. There is no place like Bradenham, and each moment I feel better I want to come back. . . .

B. D.[1]

From Gibraltar to Malta the two friends had 'a very rough and disagreeable voyage, the wind—a devil of a levanter, and sometimes sirocco—full in our teeth half the time, and not going, even with the steam, more than four knots an hour.' Their ship called at Algiers, and there, though they did not land, they 'observed with interest that the tricolor flag was flying,' a reminder that this was the summer of 'the three glorious days of July.' At Malta they found an old acquaintance in James Clay, in later years a well-known member of Parliament and the great authority on whist.

To Isaac D'Israeli.

MALTA,
Aug. 27.

He has been here a month, and has already beat the whole garrison at rackets and billiards and other wicked games, given lessons to their prima donna, and seccatura'd the primo tenore. Really he has turned out a most agreeable personage, and has had that advantage of society in which he had been deficient, and led a life which for splendid adventure would beat any young gentleman's yet published in three vols. post 8vo. Lord Burghersh wrote an opera for him, and Lady Normanby a farce. He dished Prince Pignatelli at billiards, and did the Russian Legation at écarté. I had no need of letters of introduction here, and have already 'troops of friends.' The fact is, in our original steam-packet there were some very agreeable fellows, officers, whom I believe I never mentioned to you. They have been long expecting your worship's offspring, and have gained great fame in repeating his third-rate stories at second-hand : so in consequence of these messengers I am received with branches of palm. Here the younkers do nothing but play rackets, billiards, and cards, race and smoke. To govern men, you must either

[1] *Letters*, p. 22.

excel them in their accomplishments, or despise them. Clay does one, I do the other, and we are both equally popular. Affectation tells here even better than wit. Yesterday, at the racket court, sitting in the gallery among strangers, the ball entered, and lightly struck me and fell at my feet. I picked it up, and observing a young rifleman excessively stiff, I humbly requested him to forward its passage into the court, as I really had never thrown a ball in my life. This incident has been the general subject of conversation at all the messes to-day! [1]

Long afterwards, when Disraeli had become famous, Clay appears to have given a somewhat discrepant account of his friend's popularity with those whom that friend believed to be the admiring audience of his affectations. 'It would not have been possible to have found a more agreeable, unaffected companion when they were by themselves; but when they got into society, his coxcombry was intolerable. . . . He made himself so hateful to the officers' mess that, while they welcomed Clay, they ceased to invite "that damned bumptious Jew boy."' [2] There seems, indeed, at this time to have been hardly any limit to Disraeli's 'buffooneries,' as he has the grace himself to call them. He dined at a regimental mess in an Andalusian dress. He 'paid a round of visits,' writes Meredith, 'in his majo jacket, white trousers, and a sash of all the colours in the rainbow; in this wonderful costume he paraded all round Valetta, followed by one-half the population of the place, and, as he said, putting a complete stop to all business. He, of course, included the Governor and Lady Emily in his round, to their no small astonishment.' The Governor, a brother of Lady Caroline Lamb's, was 'reputed a very nonchalant personage, and exceedingly exclusive in his conduct to his subjects.' Disraeli, however, was undismayed.

To Isaac D'Israeli.

SUNDAY,
Aug. 29.

Yesterday I called on Ponsonby, and he was fortunately at home. I flatter myself that he passed through the most

[1] *Ibid.*, pp. 31, 32. [2] Sir William Gregory's *Autobiography*, p. 95.

extraordinary quarter of an hour of his existence. I gave him no quarter, and at last made our nonchalant Governor roll on the sofa, from his risible convulsions. Then I jumped up, remembered that I must be breaking into his morning, and was off; making it a rule always to leave with a good impression. He pressed me not to go. I told him I had so much to do! . . . When I arrived home I found an invitation for Tuesday. . . . Clay confesses my triumph is complete and unrivalled.[1]

To Benjamin Austen.

MALTA,
Sept. 14.

From Gibraltar I arrived here, a place from which I expected little and have found much. Valetta surprises me as one of the most beautiful cities I have ever visited, something between Venice and Cadiz. . . . It has not a single tree, but the city is truly magnificent, full of palaces worthy of Palladio. I have still illness enough to make my life a burthen, and as my great friend the Sun is daily becoming less powerful, I daily grow more dispirited and resume my old style of despair. Had I been cured by this time, I had made up my mind to join you in Italy—as it is, I go I know not where, but do not be surprised if you hear something very strange indeed. . . . The smallpox rages here so desperately that they have put a quarantine of three weeks at Sicily, which has prevented my trip to an island I much desire to visit. . . . Write to me about your movements, in order that, if possible, I may meet you and see the Coliseum by moonlight with Madame, and all that. I was told here by a person of consideration that my father was to be in the new batch of baronets, but I suppose this is a lie. If it be offered I am sure he will refuse, but I have no idea that it will.

To Ralph Disraeli.

MALTA.

MY DEAR RALPH,

Mashallah! Here I am sitting in an easy chair, with a Turkish pipe six feet long, with an amber mouthpiece and a porcelain bowl. What a revolution! But what if I tell you that I not only have become a smoker, but the greatest smoker in Malta. The fact is I find it relieves my head. Barrow,[2] who is here in the 'Blonde,' . . . has

[1] *Letters*, p. 33.

[2] Younger son of Sir John Barrow.

given me a meerschaum, and Anstruther a most splendid Dresden green china, set in silver—an extremely valuable pipe ; but there is nothing like a meerschaum.

I have spent some weeks here. Ponsonby, the Governor, is a most charming fellow, and has been most courteous to me. His wife is very plain and not very popular, being grand, but I rather like her. . . . Do you remember in ancient days in Windsor, the Royal Fusiliers being quartered there, and James swearing that the two young subs, Liddell and Lord Amelius Paulet, were brothers of his schoolfellows, and all that ? How curious life is. That Liddell is now quartered here, and being senior captain on the station in the absence of Fitzclarence, who has gone home to see his papa, he commands the regiment, and has become my most intimate friend. . . . He and another Fusilier, by name Pery, the future Lord Limerick, are my usual companions. They are both men of the world and good company, forming a remarkable contrast to all their brother officers forsooth. A visit to Gibraltar and Malta, our two crack garrisons, has quite opened my eyes to the real life of a *militaire*. By heavens ! I believe these fellows are boys till they are majors, and sometimes do not even stop there. . . .

A week ago I knew not what I should do. All is now settled. On Wednesday morning I quit this place, where on the whole I have spent very agreeable hours, in a yacht which Clay has hired, and in which he intends to turn pirate. The original plan was to have taken it together, but Meredith was averse to this, and we have become his passengers at a fair rate, and he drops us whenever and wherever we like. You should see me in the costume of a Greek pirate. A blood-red shirt, with silver studs as big as shillings, an immense scarf for girdle, full of pistols and daggers, red cap, red slippers, broad blue striped jacket and trousers. . . . There is a Mrs. Pleydell Bouverie here, with a pretty daughter, *cum multis aliis*. I am sorry to say among them a beauty, very dangerous to the peace of your unhappy brother. But no more of that, and in a few weeks I shall be bounding, and perhaps seasick, upon the blue Ægean, and then all will be over. Nothing like an emetic in these cases. I find I have very little to tell you, for although each day brings an infinite deal of nothings, which might authorise a record over a wood fire in the old hall, they are too slight to bear any communication but an oral one. So let us hope that may soon take place. I often think of you all. . . . If you hear of my marriage or death, don't believe it, any more than I shall of our father being in the new batch of baronets, which is here currently reported. Clay is immensely improved, and a very agreeable companion indeed, with such a valet, Giovanni[1] by name. Byron died in his arms, and his mustachios touch the earth. Withal mild as a lamb, though he has two daggers always about his person. Our yacht is of fifty-five tons, an excellent size for these seas, with a crew of seven men. She is a very strong sea boat, and bears the unpoetical title of 'Susan,' which is a bore; but as we can't alter it we have painted it out. And now, my dear boy, adieu. . . .

Your very affectionate brother,

B. D.[2]

The 'something very strange' which he had in contemplation when he wrote to Austen from Malta is explained in his next letter.

To Benjamin Austen.

When I wrote to you last I had some thoughts, indeed had resolved, to join the Turkish Army as volunteer in the Albanian war. I found, however, on my arrival at Corfu, whither for this purpose I had repaired instead of going to Egypt, that the Grand Vizier, whilst all your newspapers were announcing the final loss of Albania to the Porte, had proceeded with such surprising energy that the war which had begun so magnificently had already dwindled into an insurrection. I waited a week at Corfu to see how affairs would turn out; at the end of which came one of the principal rebels flying for refuge, and after him some others. Under these circumstances I determined to turn my intended campaign into a visit of congratulation to headquarters, and Sir Frederick Adam gave me a letter, and with Meredith and Clay, our servants, and a guard of Albanians we at last reached Yanina, the capital of the province.

I can give you no idea in a letter of all the Pashas, and all the Silictars, and all the Agas that I have visited and visited me; all the pipes I smoked, all the coffee I sipped, all the sweetmeats I devoured. . . . For a week I was in a scene equal to anything in the *Arabian Nights*—such processions, such dresses, such corteges of horsemen, such caravans of camels. Then the delight of being made much of by a man who was daily decapitating half the Province. Every morning we paid visits, attended reviews, and crammed ourselves

[1] See Appendix A. [2] *Letters*, p. 34.

with sweetmeats; every evening dancers and singers were sent to our quarters by the Vizier or some Pasha. . . .

I am quite a Turk, wear a turban, smoke a pipe six feet long, and squat on a divan. Mehemet Pasha told me that he did not think I was an Englishman because I walked so slow: in fact I find the habits of this calm and luxurious people entirely agree with my own preconceived opinions of propriety and enjoyment, and I detest the Greeks more than ever. You have no idea of the rich and various costume of the Levant. When I was presented to the Grand Vizier I made up such a costume from my heterogeneous wardrobe that the Turks, who are mad on the subject of dress, were utterly astounded. . . . I had a regular crowd round our quarters and had to come forward to bow like Don Miguel and Donna Maria. Nothing would persuade the Greeks that we were not come about the new King, and I really believe that if I had £25,000 to throw away I might increase my headache by wearing a crown.

Meredith gives details of the costume which produced so great an impression. 'Figure to yourself,' he writes, 'a shirt entirely red, with silver studs as large as sixpences, green pantaloons with a velvet stripe down the sides, and a silk Albanian shawl with a long fringe of divers colours round his waist, red Turkish slippers, and to complete all his Spanish majo jacket covered with embroidery and ribbons.' 'Questo vestito Inglese o di fantasia?' asked a 'little Greek physician who had passed a year at Pisa in his youth.' 'Inglese e fantastico' was the oracular reply.

A long letter written immediately after the return from Yanina gives a highly-coloured account, full of vivid and picturesque detail, of all Disraeli saw and felt during 'this wondrous week' in Albania; it contains among other things an excellent piece of comedy in the description of a festive evening on the journey up from Arta.

To Isaac D'Israeli.

Prevesa,
Oct. 25.

. . . Two hours before sunset, having completed only half our course in spite of all our exertions, we found ourselves at a vast but dilapidated khan as big as a Gothic castle, situated on a high range, and built as a sort of half-way house for travellers by Ali Pasha when his long, gracious, and unmolested reign had permitted him to turn this unrivalled country, which combines all the excellences of Southern Europe and Western Asia, to some of the purposes for which it is fitted. This khan had now been turned into a military post; and here we found a young Bey, to whom Kalio[1] had given us a letter in case of our stopping for an hour. He was a man of very pleasing exterior, but unluckily could not understand Giovanni's Greek, and had no interpreter. What was to be done? We could not go on, as there was not an inhabited place before Yanina; and here were we sitting before sunset on the same divan with our host, who had entered the place to receive us, and would not leave the room while we were there, without the power of communicating an idea. We were in despair, and we were also very hungry, and could not therefore in the course of an hour or two plead fatigue as an excuse for sleep, for we were ravenous and anxious to know what prospect of food existed in this wild and desolate mansion. So we smoked. It is a great resource, but this wore out, and it was so ludicrous smoking, and looking at each other, and dying to talk, and then exchanging pipes by way of compliment, and then pressing our hand to our heart by way of thanks.

The Bey sat in a corner, I unfortunately next, so I had the onus of mute attention; and Clay next to me, so he and M. could at least have an occasional joke, though of course we were too well-bred to exceed an occasional and irresistible observation. Clay wanted to play écarté, and with a grave face, as if we were at our devotions; but just as we were about commencing, it occurred to us that we had some brandy, and that we would offer our host a glass, as it might be a hint for what should follow to so vehement a schnaps. Mashallah! Had the effect only taken place 1830 years ago, instead of in the present age of scepticism, it would have been instantly voted a first-rate miracle. Our mild friend smacked his lips and instantly asked for another cup; we drank it in coffee cups. By the time that Meredith had returned, who had left the house on pretence of shooting, Clay, our host, and myself had despatched a bottle of brandy in quicker time and fairer proportions than I ever did a bottle of Burgundy, and were extremely gay. Then he would drink again with Meredith and ordered some figs, talking I must tell you all the time, indulging in the most

[1] The Governor of Arta.

graceful pantomime, examining our pistols, offering us his own golden ones for our inspection, and finally making out Giovanni's Greek enough to misunderstand most ludicrously every observation we communicated. But all was taken in good part, and I never met such a jolly fellow in the course of my life. In the meantime we were ravenous, for the dry, round, unsugary fig is a great whetter. At last we insisted upon Giovanni's communicating our wants and asking for bread. The Bey gravely bowed and said, 'Leave it to me; take no thought,' and nothing more occurred. We prepared ourselves for hungry dreams, when to our great delight a most capital supper was brought in, accompanied, to our great horror, by—wine. We ate, we drank, we ate with our fingers, we drank in a manner I never recollect. The wine was not bad, but if it had been poison we must drink; it was such a compliment for a Moslemin; we quaffed it in rivers. The Bey called for the brandy; he drank it all. The room turned round; the wild attendants who sat at our feet seemed dancing in strange and fantastic whirls; the Bey shook hands with me; he shouted English—I Greek. 'Very good' he had caught up from us. 'Kalo, kalo' was my rejoinder. He roared; I smacked him on the back. I remember no more. In the middle of the night I woke. I found myself sleeping on the divan, rolled up in its sacred carpet; the Bey had wisely reeled to the fire. The thirst I felt was like that of Dives. All were sleeping except two, who kept up during the night the great wood fire. I rose lightly, stepping over my sleeping companions, and the shining arms that here and there informed me that the dark mass wrapped up in a capote was a human being. I found Abraham's bosom in a flagon of water. I think I must have drunk a gallon at the draught. I looked at the wood fire and thought of the blazing blocks in the hall at Bradenham, asked myself whether I was indeed in the mountain fastness of an Albanian chief, and, shrugging my shoulders, went to bed and woke without a headache. We left our jolly host with regret. I gave him my pipe as a memorial of having got tipsy together. . . .

In the same letter there is a vivid description of the scene in the Hall of Audience at Yanina.

An hour having been fixed for the audience, we repaired to the celebrated fortress-palace of Ali, which, though greatly battered in successive sieges, is still inhabitable, and yet affords a very fair idea of its old magnificence. Having passed the gates of the fortress, we found ourselves in a number of small streets, like those in the liberties of the Tower, or any other old castle, all full of life, stirring and excited; then we came to a grand place, in which on an ascent stands the Palace. We hurried through courts and corridors, all full of guards, and pages, and attendant chiefs, and in fact every species of Turkish population, for in these countries one head does everything, and we with our subdivision of labour and intelligent and responsible deputies have no idea of the labour of a Turkish Premier. At length we came to a vast, irregular apartment, serving as the immediate ante-chamber to the Hall of Audience. This was the finest thing I have ever yet seen. In the whole course of my life I never met anything so picturesque, and cannot expect to do so again. I do not attempt to describe it; but figure to yourself the largest chamber that you ever were perhaps in, full of the choicest groups of an Oriental population, each individual waiting by appointment for an audience, and probably about to wait for ever. In this room we remained, attended by the Austrian Consul who presented us, about ten minutes—too short a time. I never thought that I could have lived to have wished to kick my heels in a minister's ante-chamber. Suddenly we are summoned to the awful presence of the pillar of the Turkish Empire, the man who has the reputation of being the mainspring of the new system of regeneration, the renowned Reschid, an approved warrior, a consummate politician, unrivalled as a dissembler in a country where dissimulation is the principal portion of their moral culture.

The Hall was vast, built by Ali Pasha purposely to receive the largest Gobelins carpet that was ever made, which belonged to the chief chamber in Versailles, and was sold to him in the Revolution. It is entirely covered with gilding and arabesques. Here, squatted upon a corner of the large divan, I bowed with all the nonchalance of St. James's Street to a little ferocious-looking, shrivelled, care-worn man, plainly dressed, with a brow covered with wrinkles, and a countenance clouded with anxiety and thought. I entered the shed-like divan of the kind and comparatively insignificant Kalio Bey with a feeling of awe; I seated myself on the divan of the Grand Vizier (' who,' the Austrian Consul observed, ' has destroyed in the course of the last three months,' *not* in war, ' upwards of four thousand of my acquaintance ') with the self-possession of a morning call. At a distance from us, in a group on his left hand, were his secretary and his immediate suite; the end of the saloon was lined by lacqueys in waiting, with an odd name which I now forget, and which you will find in the glossary of *Anastasius*. Some compliments now passed between us, and pipes and coffee were then brought by four of these lacqueys; then his Highness waved his hand, and in an instant the chamber was cleared. Our conversation I need not repeat. We congratulated him on the pacification of Albania. He rejoined, that the peace of the world was his only object, and the happiness of mankind his only wish; this went on for the usual time. He asked us no questions about ourselves or our country, as the other Turks did, but seemed quite overwhelmed with business, moody and anxious. While we were with him, three separate Tartars arrived with despatches. What a life! and what a slight chance for the gentlemen in the ante-chamber![1]

This letter to his father, like the previous letter to Austen, breathes in nearly every line a spirit of intense delight in all the splendour and circumstance of the East. The buzz and bustle of the swarming population, 'arrayed in every possible and fanciful costume'; the brilliant colours of the military chieftains; the scribe with the writing material in his girdle; the call of the muezzin from the minaret; the salute of the passing dervish; the 'wild unearthly drum' that heralds the approach of a caravan and the stately camel that follows at the head of 'an almost interminable procession of his Arabian brethren'; for all such sights and sounds he has eager eyes and ears, and he records them with an exultation that betrays an access of Orientalism. But before the letter closes Europe triumphs over Asia and with perhaps unconscious art he ends with the following palinode:—

I write you this from that Ambracian Gulf where the soft Triumvir gained more glory by defeat than attends the victory of harsher warriors. The site is not unworthy of the beauty of Cleopatra. From the summit of the land this gulf appears like a vast lake walled in on all sides by mountains more or less distant. The dying glory of a Grecian eve bathes with warm light a thousand promontories and gentle bays, and infinite modulations of purple outline. Before me is Olympus,

[1] *Letters*, pp. 40-47.

whose austere peak glitters yet in the sun; a bend of the land alone hides from me the islands[1] of Ulysses and of Sappho. When I gaze upon this scene I remember the barbaric splendour and turbulent existence which I have just quitted with disgust I recur to the feelings in the indulgence of which I can alone find happiness, and from which an inexorable destiny seems resolved to shut me out.[2]

'I wander in pursuit of health,' he wrote in another letter, 'like the immortal exile in pursuit of that lost shore, which is now almost glittering in my sight. Five years of my life have been already wasted, and sometimes I think my pilgrimage may be as long as that of Ulysses.' Their 'yacht,' he told Austen, was 'the only mode of travel for this sea, where every headland and bay is the site of something memorable, and which is studded with islands that demand a visit.'

To Isaac D'Israeli.

We sailed from Prevesa through the remaining Ionian islands, among which was Zante, pre-eminent in beauty; indeed, they say none of the Cyclades is to be compared to it, with its olive trees touching the waves and its shores undulating in every possible variety. For about a fortnight we were for ever sailing on a summer sea, always within two or three miles of the coast, and touching at every island or harbour that invited. A cloudless sky, a summer atmosphere, and sunsets like the neck of a dove, completed all the enjoyment which I anticipated from roving in a Grecian sea. We were, however, obliged to keep a sharp look-out for pirates, who are all about again. We exercised the crew every day with muskets, and their increasing prowess and our pistol exercise kept up our courage.[3]

They spent a week at Navarino, 'the scene of Codrington's bloody blunder, a superb, perhaps unrivalled harbour, with the celebrated Sphacteria

[1] Ithaca and Leucadia. Disraeli no doubt had in mind his Byron (*Childe Harold*, II., 39). It was from

'Leucadia's far projecting rock of woe'

that Sappho, according to the very doubtful story, flung herself into the sea. Lesbos, her island home, was of course far away, off the coast of Asia Minor.

[2] *Letters*, p. 47. [3] *Ibid.*, p. 48.

on one side and old Pylus on the other. Here we found the French in their glory. They have already covered the scene of Spartan suffering with cafés and billiard rooms and make daily picnics to the grotto of Nestor.' From Napoli, where they also lingered, the travellers made excursions to Corinth, Argos, and Mycenae; and finally, on November 24, they cast anchor in the Piræus.

To Isaac D'Israeli.

ATHENS,
Nov. 30.

On the afternoon of our arrival in Piræus, which is about five miles from the city, I climbed a small hill, forming the side of the harbour. From it I looked upon an immense plain covered with olive woods and skirted by mountains. Some isolated hills rise at a distance from the bounding ridge. On one of these I gazed upon a magnificent temple, bathed in the sunset; at the foot of the hill was a walled city of considerable dimensions, in front of which a Doric temple apparently quite perfect. The violet sunset—and to-day the tint was peculiarly vivid—threw over this scene a colouring becoming its beauty, and if possible increasing its delicate character. The city was Athens; but independent of all reminiscences, I never witnessed anything so truly beautiful, and I have seen a great deal.

We were fortunate. The Acropolis, which has been shut for nine years, was open to us, the first Englishmen. Athens is still in the power of the Turks, but the Grecian Commission to receive it arrived a short time before us. When we entered the city, we found every house roofless; but really, before the war, modern Athens must have been no common town. The ancient remains have been respected; the Parthenon, and the other temples which are in the Acropolis, have necessarily suffered during the siege, but the injury is only in the detail; the general effect is not marred. We saw hundreds of shells and balls lying about the ruins. The temple of Theseus looks at a short distance as if it were just finished by Pericles.[1]

'Of all that I have yet visited,' he wrote to Mrs. Austen, 'nothing has more completely realized all that I imagined and all that I could have wished than Athens.'

[1] *Ibid.*, p. 49. In *Contarini Fleming* he corrected Pericles into Cimon.

In spite, however, of this momentary enthusiasm, there was not much real sympathy between Disraeli's genius and the pure Hellenic spirit, and education had done little to foster any that nature had implanted in him. 'Pleasant Argos and rich Mycenae, the tomb of Agamemnon and the palace of Clytemnestra,' inspired in Contarini Fleming thoughts that were not unworthy of the scene :—

> The fortunes of the House of Atreus form the noblest of all legends. I believe in that destiny before which the ancients bowed. Modern philosophy, with its superficial discoveries, has infused into the breast of man a spirit of scepticism ; but I think that, ere long, science will again become imaginative, and that as we become more profound, we may become also more credulous. Destiny is our will, and our will is our nature. . . . All is mystery, but he is a slave who will not struggle to penetrate the dark veil. [1]

In the legend of the House of Atreus and the tragic idea of destiny that underlies it we are in touch with the Oriental background of Hellenic civilisation, and here Disraeli is at home. Within sight of the Parthenon his thoughts are still turned towards the East. 'In art the Greeks were the children of the Egyptians,' observes Contarini, and there was more originality in the observation in those days than there would be in ours. But Athens stands for literature as well as art, and presently the memory of early sufferings from grammar and lexicon supervenes. 'The Greeks, who were masters of composition, were ignorant of all languages but their own.' Now that every nation has in its own tongue a record of all knowledge, let education be confined to the national literature. To the few who have leisure or inclination to study foreign literatures he would say, 'Why not study the Oriental ? Surely in the pages of the Persians and the Arabs we might discover new sources of emotion, new modes of expression, new trains of ideas, new principles of invention, and new bursts of

[1] *Contarini Fleming*, Pt. V. ch. 18.

fancy.' These are Contarini's 'meditations amid the ruins of Athens'; these and one of those defiant outbursts of racial scorn for the Northern barbarians among whom he lived, which became more frequent with Disraeli at a later date :—

> With horror I remember that, through some mysterious necessity, civilisation seems to have deserted the most favoured regions and the choicest intellects. The Persian, whose very being is poetry, the Arab, whose subtle mind could penetrate into the very secret shrine of Nature, the Greek, whose acute perceptions seemed granted only for the creation of the beautiful—these are now unlettered slaves in barbarous lands. The arts are yielded to the flat-nosed Franks. And they toil, and study, and invent theories to account for their own incompetence. Now it is the climate, now the religion, now the government; everything but the truth, everything but the mortifying suspicion that their organization may be different, and that they may be as distinct a race from their models as they undoubtedly are from the Kalmuck and the Negro.[1]

The travellers made, of course, an expedition to Marathon, where, however, discomfort seems to have effaced in Disraeli's mind the memory of its heroic past. 'I can give you no idea of the severe hardship and privation of present Grecian travel. Happy are we to get a shed for nightly shelter, and never have been fortunate enough to find one not swarming with vermin. My sufferings in this way are great.' They 'lived for a week on the wild boar of Pentelicus and the honey of Hymettus, both very good,' though the former, apparently, was 'not as good as Bradenham pork': and then early in December they continued their voyage round Sunium, of which they had 'a most splendid view,' and through 'the clustering Cyclades' to Constantinople.

> We have reached the Dardanelles, a capital passage—what a road to a great city!—narrower and much longer than the Straits of Gibraltar, but not with such sublime shores. Asia and Europe look more kindly on each other than Europe and her more sultry sister.

[1] *Ibid.*, Pt. V. ch. 19.

The breeze has again sprung up; we have one hundred and thirty miles to Constantinople.

It is near sunset, and Constantinople is in full sight; it baffles all description, though so often described. An immense mass of buildings, cupolas, cypress groves, and minarets. I feel an excitement which I thought was dead.[1]

On a closer view the far-famed city did not disappoint him.

To Isaac D'Israeli.

CONSTANTINOPLE,
Jan. 11, 1831.

I leave Constantinople to your imagination. Cypress groves and mosquish domes, masses of habitations grouped on gentle acclivities rising out of the waters, millions of minarets, a sea like a river covered with innumerable long thin boats as swift as gondolas, and far more gay, being carved and gilt—all these, and then when filled with a swarming population in rich and brilliant and varied costume, will afford you a more lively, and certainly not a more incorrect, idea than half a dozen pages worthy of Horace Smith.

There are two things here which cannot be conceived without inspection—the Bosphorus and the Bazaar. Conceive the ocean not broader than the Thames at Gravesend, with shores with all the variety and beauty of the Rhine, covered with palaces, mosques, villages, groves of cypress, and woods of Spanish chestnuts; the view of the Euxine at the end is the most sublime [and mystical][2] thing I can remember. The Bazaar would delight you more than the Bosphorus. Fancy the Burlington Arcade, or some of the Parisian passages and panoramas; fancy perhaps a square mile of ground covered with these arcades intersecting each other in all directions and full of every product of the empire, from diamonds to dates. The magnificence, novelty, and variety of the goods on sale, the whole nation of shopkeepers all in different dress, the crowds of buyers from all parts of the world, are just to be hinted at.

Here every people have a characteristic costume. Turks, Greeks, Jews, and Armenians are the staple population; the latter seem to predominate. The Armenians wear round and very unbecoming black caps and robes; the Jews a black hat wreathed with a white handkerchief; the Greeks

[1] *Letters*, p. 50.
[2] The words in brackets are from a letter to Mrs. Austen.

black turbans; the Turks indulge in all combinations of costume. The meanest merchant in the Bazaar looks like a Sultan in an Eastern fairy tale. This is merely to be ascribed to the marvellous brilliancy of their dyes, which is one of the most remarkable circumstances in their social life, and which never has been explained to me. A common pair of slippers that you push on in the street is tinged of a vermilion or a lake so extraordinary that I can compare their colour to nothing but the warmest beam of a summer sunset.

We have seen the Sultan [1] several times. He affects all the affable activity of a European prince, mixes with his subjects, interferes in all their pursuits, and taxes them most unmercifully. He dresses like a European, and all the young men have adopted the fashion. You see young Turks in uniforms which would not disgrace one of our crack cavalry regiments, and lounging with all the bitterness of Royal illegitimates. It is on the rising generation that the Sultan depends, and, if one may form an opinion, not in vain. After all his defeats, he has now 60,000 regular infantry excellently appointed and well disciplined. They are certainly not to be compared to French or English line, but they would as certainly beat the Spanish and the Dutch, and many think, with fair play, the Russian. Fair play their monarch certainly had not during the last campaign; the secret history would not now interest, but it was by other means than military prowess that the Muscovites advanced so successfully. The Sultan had to struggle against an unprecedented conspiracy the whole time, and the morning that Adrianople was treacherously delivered up, the streets of Stamboul were filled with dead bodies of detected traitors.[2]

He lingered there for more than a month, lounging daily in the shop of 'Mustapha the Imperial perfumer,' attending 'masquerade balls and diplomatic dinners,' and leading a life of rapturous, but far from inattentive, indolence. The Ambassador, a brother of Lord Aberdeen's, received him 'with a kindness which he should always remember with gratitude'; though in a game of forfeits one day his Excellency showed so little respect for the Oriental gravity which his guest was anxious to cultivate as to make him 'tumble over head and heels. Can you conceive anything more dreadful?' 'My health

[1] Mahmud II., destroyer of the Janissaries. [2] *Letters*, pp. 53-55.

improved, but my desire of wandering increased. I began to think that I should now never be able to settle in life. The desire of fame did not revive. I felt no intellectual energy; I required nothing more than to be amused.' This was Contarini's mood during his stay in the 'Capital of the East,' and Disraeli's seems to have been not very different. 'All,' as he wrote to Mrs. Austen, 'was like life in a pantomime or Eastern tale of enchantment.'

To Edward Lytton Bulwer.

CONSTANTINOPLE,
Dec. 27, 1830.

I confess to you that my Turkish prejudices are very much confirmed by my residence in Turkey. The life of this people greatly accords with my taste, which is naturally somewhat indolent and melancholy. And I do not think it would disgust you. To repose on voluptuous ottomans and smoke superb pipes, daily to indulge in the luxuries of a bath which requires half a dozen attendants for its perfection; to court the air in a carved caïque, by shores which are a perpetual scene; and to find no exertion greater than a canter on a barb; this is, I think, a far more sensible life than all the bustle of clubs, all the boring of drawing-rooms, and all the coarse vulgarity of our political controversies. And all this, I assure you, is, without any coloring or exaggeration, the life which may be here commanded. A life accompanied by a thousand sources of calm enjoyment, and a thousand modes of mellowed pleasure, which it would weary you to relate, and which I leave to your own lively imagination. . . . I mend slowly, but mend. The seasons have greatly favoured me. Continual heat. And even here, where the winter is proverbially cold, there is a summer sky.[1]

At the beginning of the year Meredith had parted from 'his amusing but idle' companions and gone overland to Smyrna, and a fortnight later Disraeli and Clay sailed in the 'Susan' for the same place. There they found their companion intent on an expedition to 'the unseen relics of some unheard-of cock-and-a-bull city,' and as

[1] *Life of Bulwer*, II., p. 323.

Disraeli was bent on a pilgrimage to the Holy Sepulchre, he and Clay continued their voyage to the south.

To Sarah Disraeli.

We found ourselves again in an archipelago—the Sporades—and tried to make Rhodes; but a contrary wind, although we were off it for two days, prevented us. After some days we landed at Cyprus, where we passed a day on land famous in all ages, but more delightful to me as the residence of Fortunatus than as the rosy realm of Venus or the romantic kingdom of the Crusaders. Here we got a pilot to take us to Jaffa.

One morning, with a clear blue sky and an intense sun, we came in sight of the whole coast of Syria, very high and mountainous, and the loftiest ranges covered with snow. We passed Beyrout, Sur, the ancient Tyre, St. Jean d'Acre, and at length cast anchor in the roads of Jaffa. Here we made a curious acquaintance in Damiani, the descendant of an old Venetian family, but himself a perfect Oriental. We had read something about his grandfather in Volney, and as he had no conception of books, he was so appalled by our learning that, had we not been Englishmen, he would have taken us for sorcerers. We found him living among the most delightful gardens of oranges, citrons, and pomegranates, the trees as high and the fruit as thick as in our English apple orchards; himself a most elegant personage in flowing robes of crimson silk, &c., &c. I am obliged to hint rather than describe, and must reserve all detail till our meeting. He wished us to remain with him for a month, and gave us an admirable Oriental dinner, which would have delighted my father—rice, spices, pistachio nuts, perfumed rôtis, and dazzling confectionery.

From Jaffa, a party of six, well mounted and well armed, we departed for Jerusalem. Jaffa is a pretty town, surrounded by gardens, and situated in a fruitful plain. After riding over this, we crossed a range of light hills and came into the plain of Ramle, vast and fertile. Ramle, the ancient Arimathea, is the model of our idea of a beautiful Syrian village, all the houses isolated, and each surrounded by palm trees, the meadows and the exterior of the village covered with olive trees or divided by rich plantations of Indian fig. Here we sought hospitality in the Latin convent, an immense establishment, well kept up, but with only one monk.[1]

[1] *Letters*, p. 58.

The next day they continued their journey towards the east.

In the distance rose a chain of severe and savage mountains. I was soon wandering, and for hours, in the wild, stony ravines of these shaggy rocks. At length, after several passes, I gained the ascent of a high mountain. Upon an opposite height, descending as a steep ravine, and forming, with the elevation on which I rested, a dark and narrow gorge, I beheld a city entirely surrounded by what I should have considered in Europe an old feudal wall, with towers and gates. The city was built upon an ascent, and, from the height on which I stood, I could discern the terrace and the cupola of almost every house, and the wall upon the other side rising from the plain; the ravine extending only on the side to which I was opposite. The city was in a bowl of mountains. In the front was a magnificent mosque, with beautiful gardens, and many light and lofty gates of triumph; a variety of domes and towers rose in all directions from the buildings of bright stone.

Nothing could be conceived more wild, and terrible, and desolate than the surrounding scenery, more dark, and stormy, and severe; but the ground was thrown about in such picturesque undulations, that the mind, full of the sublime, required not the beautiful; and rich and waving woods and sparkling cultivation would have been misplaced. Except Athens, I had never witnessed any scene more essentially impressive. I will not place this spectacle below the city of Minerva. Athens and the Holy City in their glory must have been the finest representations of the beautiful and the sublime; the Holy City for the elevation on which I stood was the Mount of Olives and the city on which I gazed was JERUSALEM.[1]

The week they spent at Jerusalem was to him 'the most delightful of all our travels.' He visited the Holy Sepulchre of course, and the so-called Tombs of the Kings, and was so fascinated by the Mosque of Omar, standing on the supposed site of the temple of his forefathers, that he 'endeavoured to enter it at the hazard of his life.'

I was detected, and surrounded by a crowd of turbaned fanatics, and escaped with difficulty; but I saw enough to

[1] *Contarini Fleming*, Pt. VI. ch. 4.

feel that minute inspection would not belie the general character I formed of it from the Mount of Olives. I caught a glorious glimpse of splendid courts, and light airy gates of Saracenic triumph, flights of noble steps, long arcades, and interior gardens, where silver fountains spouted their tall streams amid the taller cypresses. [1]

Returning to Jaffa, the two companions continued their voyage thence, and arrived at Alexandria on March 12, 1831. In 'the ancient land of Priestcraft and of Pyramids,' which next to Syria had from the beginning 'formed the most prominent object of his travels,' Disraeli remained for more than four months.

To Sarah Disraeli.

From Alexandria, I crossed the desert to Rosetta. It was a twelve hours' job, and the whole way we were surrounded by a mirage of the most complete kind. I was perpetually deceived, and always thought I was going to ride into the sea. At Rosetta I first saw the mighty Nile, with its banks richly covered with palm groves. A grove of palms is the most elegant thing in nature. From Rosetta five days in a capital boat which the Consul had provided for us, with cabins and every convenience . . . . took us to Cairo through the famous Delta. This greatly reminded me of the rich plains in the Pays Bas, quite flat, with a soil in every part like the finest garden mould, covered with production, but more productive than cultivated. The banks of the river studded with villages of mud, but all clustered in palm groves; beautiful moonlight on the Nile, indescribably charming, and the palms by this light perfectly magical. Grand Cairo, a large town of dingy houses of unbaked brick, looking terribly dilapidated, but swarming with population in rich and various costume. Visited the Pyramids, and ascended the great one, from the top of which, some weeks afterwards, a man, by name Maze, whom I had slightly known in Spain, tumbled, and dashed himself to a mummy. Very awful, the first accident of the kind.

A voyage of three weeks in the same boat to Thebes: banks of the river very different. The Delta ceases at Cairo, and Egypt now only consists of a valley, formed by a river running through a desert. The land is, however, equally rich, the

[1] *Alroy*, note 35.

soil being formed by the Nile; but on each side at the distance of three or four miles, and sometimes much nearer, deserts. The Libyan desert on the African side is exactly our common idea of a desert, an interminable waste of burning sand; but the Arabian and Syrian deserts very different, in fact, what we call downs. Landing on the African side, one might, where the desert stretches to the very banks, find a ship of Hadgees emptied on the shore, in the most picturesque groups, some squatting down with their pipes, some boiling coffee, some performing their devotions. It was excessively close, but had been a fine clear day. I walked nearly a mile from the shore; in an instant very dark, with a heat perfectly stifling; saw a column of sand in the distance. It struck me directly what it was. I rushed to the boat with full speed, but barely quick enough. I cannot describe the scene of horror and confusion. It was a simoom. The wind was the most awful sound I ever heard. Five columns of sand, taller than the Monument, emptied themselves on our party. Every sail was rent to pieces, men buried in the earth. Three boats sailing along overturned; the crews swam to shore. The wind, the screaming, the shouting, the driving of the sand, were enough to make you mad. We shut all the windows of the cabin, and jumped into bed, but the sand came in like fire. . . .

As for Dendera and Thebes, and the remains in every part of Upper Egypt, it is useless to attempt to write. Italy and Greece were toys to them, and Martin's inventions commonplace. Conceive a feverish and tumultuous dream, full of triumphal gates, processions of paintings, interminable walls of heroic sculpture, granite colossi of gods and kings, prodigious obelisks, avenues of sphinxes, and halls of a thousand columns, thirty feet in girth, and of a proportionate height. My eyes and mind yet ache with a grandeur so little in unison with our own littleness. Then the landscape was quite characteristic: mountains of burning sand, vegetation unnaturally vivid, groves of cocoa trees, groups of crocodiles, and an ebony population in a state of nudity, armed with spears of reeds.

Having followed the course of the Nile for seven hundred miles, to the very confines of Nubia, we returned. As an antiquary I might have been tempted to advance, to have witnessed further specimens, but I was satisfied, and I wish not to lose time unnecessarily. We were a week at Thebes, with the advantage of the society of Mr. Wilkinson,[1] an

[1] Afterwards well known as Sir Gardner Wilkinson.

Englishman of vast learning, who has devoted ten years to the study of hieroglyphics and Egyptian antiquity, and who can read you the side of an obelisk or the front of a pylon as we would the last number of the *Quarterly*.[1]

By the end of May he is back in Cairo, which, in spite of its dinginess, he finds 'a luxurious and pleasant place.' Clay, however, is ill and likely to leave him, and this is a serious trouble. 'You know that though I like to be at my ease I want energy in those little affairs of which life greatly consists ; here I found Clay always ready.' As Clay expressed it to Meredith, Disraeli was one of those people who 'ought never to travel without a nurse.'

To Sarah Disraeli.

CAIRO,
May 28.

I am sorry also to say that his faithful servant Giovanni, better known by the name of Tita (he was Byron's chasseur of renown), who is a Belzoni in appearance and constitution, is also very ill, which is a great affliction. Thus you see the strong men have all fallen, while I, who am an habitual invalid, am firm on my legs ; but the reason is this, that I, being somewhat indolent and feeble, live *à la Turque*, while Clay and Giovanni are always in action, have done nothing but shoot and swim from morning to night. As I am on the chapter of domestic troubles, you will hear with regret that my favourite servant, a Greek of Cyprus, gave me warning yesterday, his father being very ill at Alexandria. He leaves me directly, which is a great bore at this moment, especially as I am about to be alone, and would annoy me at all times, because he wore a Mameluke dress of crimson and gold, with a white turban thirty yards long, and a sabre glittering like a rainbow. I must now content myself with an Arab attendant in a blue shirt and slipperless. How are the mighty fallen !

I cannot sufficiently commend your letters ; they are in every respect charming, very lively and witty, and full exactly of the stuff I want. If you were only a more perfect mistress of the art of punctuation, you might rival 'Lady Mary' herself. Thank my mother for her remembrance of me. I cannot write to say I am quite well, because the enemy still

[1] *Letters*, pp. 65-67.

holds out, but I am sanguine, very, and at any rate quite well enough to wish to be at home. . . . . I am quite delighted with my father's progress. How I long to be with him, dearest of men, flashing our quills together and opening their minds, 'standing together in our chivalry,' which we will do, now that I have got the use of my brain for the first time in my life. Tell Ralph to write as often and as much as he likes, and that I have become a most accomplished smoker, carrying that luxurious art to a pitch of refinement of which he has no idea. My pipe is cooled in wet silken bag, my coffee is boiled with spices, and I finish my last chibouque with a sherbet of pomegranate. Oh the delicious fruits that we have here, and in Syria! Orange gardens miles in extent, citrons, limes, pomegranates; but the most delicious thing in the world is a banana, which is richer than a pineapple.

I don't care a jot about *The Young Duke*. I never staked any fame on it. It may take its chance. I meant the hero to be a model for our youth; but after two years' confinement in these revolutionary times, I fear he will prove old-fashioned. Goethe [1] and *Vivian Grey* of course gratifying. I hear the Patriarch is dead: perhaps a confusion with his son. I saw it in *Galignani*, an excellent publication which keeps me *au jour*. . . . The death of Max [2] has cut me to the heart.[3]

When Disraeli wrote this letter his thoughts, as can be seen, were all directed homeward, and in fact he was 'only waiting for a ship to convey him to Malta'; but 'the more he saw of Oriental life the more he liked it,' and he lingered on that he might return with Meredith, who was now in Upper Egypt. His first glimpse of the redoubtable Mehemet Ali was curious.

Wandering in the gardens of his palace at Shubra, I suddenly came upon him one afternoon, surrounded by his Court, a very brilliant circle, in most gorgeous dresses, particularly the black eunuchs in scarlet and gold, and who ride white horses. I was about to retire, but one of his

1 A friend of the Austens and Disraelis had just returned from Weimar and reported that 'the old man himself, and Madame Goethe, his son's wife, were among the warmest admirers of *Vivian Grey*; they had it on their own particular bookshelves, and they spoke enthusiastically of it as being after Scott the first of their English favourites. They could find but one fault, that the author had misconceived the German character in his youthful Princess.' Goethe, according to his daughter-in-law, 'considered that there was more true originality in the work than in any he had seen for years.'

2 A favourite puppy at Bradenham.

3 *Letters*, pp. 62-64.

principal attendants took me by the arm and led me to the circle. The Pasha is exceedingly fond of the English. His Highness was playing chess with his fool, and I witnessed a very curious scene. I stayed about a quarter of an hour, and had I waited till his game was finished, I am informed that he would have spoken to me; but as I had no interpreter with me, and am pretty sure that he was in the same state, I thought it best to make my bow.[1]

He seems, however, before he left to have had more than one audience of the Pasha, to have succeeded in engaging his attention 'by the readiness or patience of his replies,' and to have had the honour of being consulted as to a scheme his Highness was considering for the introduction of Parliamentary institutions into his dominions. The traveller pointed out the immediate difficulties that occurred to him, and the Pasha listened in silence; but at the next levée he welcomed his visitor with a favouring smile and beckoned to him to advance:—

'God is great!' said Mehemet Ali to the traveller; 'you are a wise man—Allah! Kerim, but you spit pearls. Nevertheless I will have a Parliament, and I will have as many Parliaments as the King of England himself. See here!' So saying, his Highness produced two lists of names. . . . 'See here!' said he, 'here are my Parliaments; but I have made up my mind, to prevent inconvenience, to elect them myself.'[2]

Meredith arrived in Cairo at the end of June, and the two friends were about to start on their homeward journey when a calamity befell which was a terrible shock to Disraeli at the time and threw a cloud over the whole of his sister's remaining life. Meredith was stricken with smallpox, and, after a short illness, died on the 19th of July.

To Isaac D'Israeli.

CAIRO,
July 20, 1831.

MY DEAREST FATHER,

If you were not a great philosopher as well as a good man, I do not think that I could summon courage to communicate

[1] *Ibid.*, p. 67. [2] *Vindication of the English Constitution*, p. 103.

to you the terrible intelligence which is now to be imparted by this trembling pen; but I have such confidence in your wisdom as well as in your virtue, that it is your assistance to which I look in the saddest office that has ever yet devolved upon me, because I know that the joint influence of your experience and your benevolent soul will at the same time assist the sufferers in forming a juster estimate of the loss than can perhaps occur in the first pangs of affliction, and offer the only solace which is dear to a refined soul, the sympathy of one as refined.

You have already guessed the fatal truth—our William is lost to us. I feel that I must repeat it. It is too terrible to believe. . . . I would willingly have given my life for his. . . . . Oh! my father, why do we live? The anguish of my soul is great. Our innocent lamb, our angel is stricken. Save her, save her. I will come home directly. . . . I wish to live only for my sister. I think of her all day and all night. It is some satisfaction that I was with our friend to the last. Oh! my father, I trust a great deal to you and my dear mother. I do not know what to write, what to think. I have not said anything that I wanted, yet I have said too much. God bless you, my dear father. Embrace them all. I wish that I could mingle my tears with yours.

To Sarah Disraeli.

MY OWN SA,

Ere you open this page, our beloved father will have imparted to you with all the tenderness of parental love the terrible intelligence which I have scarcely found energy enough to communicate to him. It is indeed true. Yes! our friend of many years, our hope and joy and consolation, is lost to us for ever. He has yielded to his Creator without a bodily or mental pang that pure, and honorable, and upright soul which we all so honored and so esteemed. He has suddenly closed a life unsullied by a crime, scarcely by a weakness. Oh! my sister, in this hour of overwhelming affliction my thoughts are only for you. Alas! my beloved, if you are lost to me where, where am I to fly for refuge? I have no wife, I have no betrothed; nor since I have been better acquainted with my own mind and temper have I sought them. Live then, my heart's treasure, for one who has ever loved you with a surpassing love, and who would cheerfully have yielded his own existence to have saved you the bitterness of this letter. Yes, my beloved, be my genius, my solace, my companion, my joy. We will never part, and if I cannot be to you all our lost friend [was ?], at least we will feel that life can never be a blank while gilded by the perfect love of a sister and a brother.

Disraeli had thought of returning through Italy, that he might see Naples and Rome, but he now abandoned the project, and took what was then the direct route by Gibraltar; though owing to a long detention in quarantine at Malta it was late in October before he reached England. At Bradenham he found a sorrowing household, and the beloved sister on whom the blow had directly fallen almost crushed by its force. 'I cannot trust myself to write of her,' he says in a letter to Meredith's sister on his arrival, 'but her sweet and virtuous soul struggles under this overwhelming affliction.' Sarah Disraeli was a woman, as her letters show her and as she is described by her friends, of intensely loving and sympathetic nature, of real nobility of character, and of no small intellectual capacity. Henceforth her life was dedicated to others; above all to her father and her family, for whom the desolation that had come upon her seemed to have quickened her affection. For her eldest brother especially this affection now became a passion. From the first she had a romantic faith in his coming greatness, which never wavered even in the darkest hour, and her chief solace in her loneliness was to watch the progress of his fame. It is not given to a man in the stress and turmoil of an active life to pay back in kind the self-forgetting devotion of a lonely woman's heart; but Disraeli's affection for his sister remained of rare depth and tenderness. 'I believe,' wrote an intimate friend,[1] 'he never entirely got over his deep sense of suffering at the crushing disappointment of her early hopes, and, amid the many stirring incidents of his eventful life, the death-bed scene at Cairo was not seldom recalled. He rarely spoke either of his sister or of

[1] The late Sir Philip Rose.

Meredith, but that was his habit where his feelings were deeply concerned. Once I remember his describing Meredith to me as a man of great intellectual powers who would certainly have distinguished himself if he had lived; and on the first occasion of his becoming Prime Minister I remember saying to him, "If only your sister had been alive now to witness your triumph what happiness it would have given her"; and he replied, "Ah, poor Sa, poor Sa! we've lost our audience, we've lost our audience," and at once turned the subject as too painful to dwell upon.'

CHAPTER X.

CONTARINI FLEMING AND ALROY.

1832-1833.

Disraeli's pen had not been idle during the last few months of his residence in the East or during the voyage home. *Contarini Fleming* was not published till May, 1832, and *Alroy* not till March, 1833 ; but when he reached Bradenham in November both works, if not complete, must have been far on the road towards completion. In the Preface to the 1845 edition of *Contarini* he speaks of the book as having been composed 'in a beautiful and distant land' ; in an unpublished letter of later date he couples *Alroy* with *Contarini* as having been written while he was abroad ; and three months after his return, when *Contarini* is already in the hands of the publisher, he tells Austen that he has another work finished in his portfolio, and this can only have been *Alroy.* Whatever the external facts, there is internally, at all events, a close association between the two novels. They are spiritually the product of the same period in Disraeli's life, and that the period of the journey in the East, and they are artistically the most sincere and disinterested of his early works, direct emanations from his own personality and inner experience. 'My works,' he writes in the diary to which reference has already been made, 'are the embodification of my feelings. In *Vivian Grey* I have portrayed my active and real ambition: in *Alroy* my ideal ambition: *The Psychological Romance* is a development of my poetic character. This trilogy is the secret history of my feelings—I shall write no more about myself.'

These two novels are therefore, in common with *Vivian Grey*, of first-rate biographic significance, and *Contarini* especially is in some respects the most self-revealing of all Disraeli's works.

> I am desirous of writing a book which shall be all truth: a work of which the passion, the thought, the action, and even the style, should spring from my own experience of feeling, from the meditations of my own intellect, from my own observation of incident, from my own study of the genius of expression.

So the self-discovering hero tells us in the first chapter of the novel, and the author of course intended that we should apply the words to himself. Contarini's father is a Saxon nobleman in the service of a Northern court; his mother was the daughter of a great Venetian house who had died in giving birth to him: he has thus, like Disraeli himself, though surrounded by the snows and forests of the North, the nervous temperament and glowing imagination of the South. We have seen something already of his sensitive and brooding childhood and the perpetual oscillation of his aims between the fields of art and of action: on the one hand 'his imaginary deeds of conquest, his heroic aspirations, his long dazzling dreams of fanciful adventure'; on the other, 'the first indication of his predisposition (as a poet), the growing consciousness of his powers, his reveries, his loneliness, his doubts, his moody misery, his ignorance of his art, his failures, his despair.' 'To feel the strong necessity of fame, and to be conscious that without intellectual excellence life must be insupportable, to feel all this with no simultaneous faith in your own power, these are moments of despondency for which no immortality can compensate.' While in some such mood as this Contarini falls in with one

Winter, an artist, a man of philosophic mind and wide experience, who, in his serene wisdom and penetrating gaze into the hidden springs of character and the deeper realities of life, is of the same family as Horace Grey and Beckendorff in the earliest of the novels, or as Sidonia in the great trilogy of Disraeli's full maturity. Winter recognises the poetic gift of the child, teaches him that before he can hope to be a great artist he must study his art, and leaves him with some talismanic rules which he had 'copied off an obelisk amid the ruins of Thebes':—

Be patient: cherish hope. Read more: ponder less. Nature is more powerful than education: time will develope everything.

In accordance with this oracular advice the boy determines to be patient and that a book shall be ever in his hand; but the first he reads, a History of Venice, reawakens the love of action that slumbers in him and gives another turn to his aspirations. His 'consular blood demands a sword,' he resolves to be a Doge, and, as a first step, to run away from school and set out for Venice; and so end his schooldays.

After many other youthful adventures and many shiftings of ambition Contarini at length becomes private secretary to his father, and developing into a callous and unscrupulous worldling so much distinguishes himself in his new career that in a few years he is made an Under-Secretary of State. In a conference with the ambassadors of the great powers he, by a sudden stroke of audacity, wins a diplomatic success which seems to open a path to the attainment of his highest ambitions. The passage in which he describes his feelings at this moment of triumph is worth quoting at length as a specimen of Disraeli's style at its best.

The conference broke up, my father retired with the King, and desired me to wait for him in the hall. I was alone. I was excited. I felt the triumph of success. I felt that I had done a great action. I felt all my energies. I walked up and down the hall in a frenzy of ambition, and I thirsted for action. There seemed to be no achievement of which I was not capable, and of which I was not ambitious. In imagination I shook thrones and founded empires. I felt myself a being born to breathe in an atmosphere of revolution.

My father came not. Time wore away, and the day died. It was one of those stern, sublime sunsets, which is almost the only appearance in the north in which nature enchanted me. I stood at the window, gazing on the burnished masses that for a moment were suspended in their fleeting and capricious beauty on the far horizon. I turned aside and looked at the rich trees suffused with the crimson light, and ever and anon irradiated by the dying shoots of a golden ray. The deer were stealing home to their bowers, and I watched them till their glancing forms gradually lost their lustre in the declining twilight. The glory had now departed, and all grew dim. A solitary star alone was shining in the grey sky, a bright and solitary star.

And as I gazed upon the sunset, and the star, and the dim beauties of the coming eve, my mind grew calm, and all the bravery of my late reverie passed away. And I felt indeed a disgust for all the worldliness on which I had been late pondering. And there arose in my mind a desire to create things beautiful as that golden sun and that glittering star.

I heard my name. The hall was now darkened. In the distance stood my father. I joined him. He placed his arm affectionately in mine, and said to me, 'My son, you will be Prime Minister of . . . ; perhaps something greater.'[1]

A short time before, a fresh encounter with a lady who had been the object of a boyish passion had reawakened the better feelings of the young egoist and made him recoil in disgust from the thought of his present life. The latent poetry of his being revived; he took up his pen and, in the sudden rush of inspiration, produced in seven days a novel which was published anonymously under the title of *Manstein*. The narrative now runs closely parallel to Disraeli's own experience in the case of *Vivian Grey*. *Manstein* is a rapid sketch of the development of the poetic character, the hero 'a youth whose mind is ever combating with his situation.' It never strikes Contarini that he is delineating his own

[1] Pt. II. ch. 13.

character, and this may have been true of Disraeli when he wrote *Vivian Grey*. In the following passage we may assume that we have an exact account of the feelings with which Disraeli regarded his earliest novel five years after its publication :—

For the work itself, it was altogether a most crude performance, teeming with innumerable faults. It was entirely deficient in art. The principal character, although forcibly conceived, for it was founded on truth, was not sufficiently developed. Of course, the others were much less so. The incidents were unnatural, the serious characters exaggerations, the comic ones caricatures ; the wit was too often flippant, the philosophy too often forced ; yet the vigour was remarkable, the licence of an uncurbed imagination not without charms, and, on the whole, there breathed a freshness which is rarely found, and which, perhaps, with all my art and knowledge, I may never again afford : and, indeed, when I recall the heat with which this little work was written, I am convinced that, with all its errors, the spark of true creation animated its fiery page.[1]

Manstein proves a decisive influence in Contarini's life. In depicting the scenes of society amid which his hero was forced to move, the bitterness of the author's heart finds vent in slashing satire and malignant personality. The anonymity which shelters him is not long preserved, and there is at once a tremendous outcry. Everybody takes a delight in detecting the originals of his portraits.

Various keys were handed about, all different ; and not content with recognizing the very few decided sketches from life which there really were, and which were sufficiently obvious and not very malignant, they mischievously insisted that not a human shadow glided over my pages which might not be traced to its substance.

In the storm that now bursts Contarini's chances of a political career are wrecked ; and even if it were otherwise his desire for worldly success is gone. Analysing his own character, he recognises that he has been 'selfish

[1] Pt. II. ch. 12.

and affected,' 'entirely ignorant of the principles of genuine morality' and with 'a total want of nature in everything connected with him.' He determines to re-educate himself. Considering himself a poet, he resolves to pursue a course which shall develop and perfect his poetic power; and, as the first step must be to gain an acquaintance with men and nature in all their varieties and conditions, he bids farewell to Scandinavia and sets out upon his travels.

In all this there is much that is of the first importance as a picture of Disraeli's childhood and youth: though whether it equally well depicts the formation of the poetic character is quite another matter. Some of the ingredients that go to the making of the true poet are to be found in Contarini as they are to be found in Disraeli himself. The high imagination, the brooding temperament, the wild ecstasy—even in some degree the creative faculty and the self-devotion of the artist are there; and yet there is an indefinable something which we look for in vain. There are elements, moreover, in Contarini's character—a fierce and ravening ambition, a consuming thirst for power and greatness—which assuredly were present in the young Disraeli also, and have very little to do with the true poetic temperament. In those perpetual oscillations of Contarini's will between the active and literary careers it is the author's artistic purpose to have us believe that poetry is the real vocation, and that the bias for action is factitious. But the impression really left on us is exactly the opposite. We see Contarini in action; we are only told that he is a poet; and we feel that Baron Fleming has truly divined the sentiments both of his son and of the author when he thus gives expression to his own:—

What were all those great poets of whom we now talk so much, what were they in their lifetime? The most miserable of their species. . . . A man of great energies aspires that they should be felt in his lifetime, that his existence should be rendered more intensely vital by the constant consciousness of his multiplied and multiplying power. Is posthumous fame a substitute for all this? . . . Would you rather have been Homer or Julius Cæsar, Shakespeare or Napoleon? No one doubts. . . . We are active beings, and our sympathy above all other sympathies is with great action. . . . Mix in society [is his final advice], and I will answer that you lose your poetic feeling; for in you as in the great majority, it is not a creative faculty originating in a peculiar organization, but simply the consequence of a nervous susceptibility that is common to all.[1]

From the moment when Contarini sets out upon his travels the value of the novel as a biographic document rapidly diminishes. The fact is, just as in *Vivian Grey*, after the first volume, the creative impulse is now spent; the author has given us a picture of his inward experience as far as it has been carried, and he has to resort to book making to bring his story to an end. It is better book making than what we get in the second volume of *Vivian Grey*, but little more can be said in its praise. Contarini first of all finds his way to Venice and there meets and marries his predestined bride, the last of his mother's house. Apart from the descriptions, this part of the tale is merely conventional romance, with even less relation than has generally been supposed to Disraeli's own experience. After a year of intense happiness in Crete the bride dies in childbirth, and in a highly melodramatic scene the hero, maddened by his anguish, flings himself from a peak of Mount Ida. For anything that he ever seems to accomplish he might just as well succeed in his purpose of self-destruction; but he is picked up alive and, after a time, begins a course of wandering which is made an excuse for the introduction of the travel scenes in Disraeli's letters from the East. Falling in again with the philosophic Winter, Contarini receives some excellent advice.

I tell you what, my friend, the period has arrived in your life when you must renounce meditation. Action is now

[1] Pt. II. ch. 9.

your part. Meditation is culture. It is well to think until a man has discovered his genius, and developed his faculties, but then let him put his intelligence in motion. Act, act, act; act without ceasing, and you will no longer talk of the vanity of life.

Disraeli himself profited by this advice, but Contarini neglects it. He becomes a mere dilettante, and at the end, having inherited his father's wealth, is found devoting himself to the planning of an earthly paradise at Naples, which is to rival Hadrian's Villa. 'Here let me pass my life in the study and the creation of the beautiful: such is my desire; but,' as the author with prescient scepticism makes him add, 'whether it will be my career is, I feel, doubtful.'

My interest in the happiness of my race is too keen to permit me for a moment to be blind to the storms that lour on the horizon of society. Perchance, also, the political regeneration of the country to which I am devoted may not be distant, and in that great work I am resolved to participate. Bitter jest, that the most civilized portion of the globe should be considered incapable of self-government!

This enthusiasm for the Italian cause proved short-lived in the author, whatever may have been the case with the hero; but in all that is really essential the true completion of *Contarini*, as of *Vivian Grey* before it, and of *Coningsby* and *Tancred* later, is Disraeli's own career.

On nearly every page of *Contarini* the reader who knows Disraeli will find him lifting the veil that hides his own personality. Sometimes in those smaller touches that reveal his tastes and habits: his unaffected joy in woods and trees—'I began to long to be a woodman, to pass a quiet, and contemplative, and virtuous life, amid the deep silence and beautiful scenery of forests'; his love of women's society—'For a long time, I could not detect the reason why I was so charmed with Egyptian life. At last I recollected that I had recurred, after a long estrangement, to the cheerful influence of women'; the incidents of composition—'After writing a book my mind always makes a great spring.' 'I can write only in the morning. It is then I execute with facility all that I have planned the preceding eve.' 'It is my habit to contrive in my head the complete work before I have recourse to the pen which is to execute it. I do not think that meditation can be too long, or execution too rapid.' Or in the Polonius-like advice of Baron Fleming to his son,

Read French authors. Read Rochefoucauld. The French writers are the finest in the world, for they clear our heads of all ridiculous ideas. . . . Do not talk too much at present; do not *try* to talk. But whenever you speak, speak with self-possession. . . . Never argue. In society nothing must be discussed; give only results. . . . Talk to women, talk to women as much as you can. This is the best school. This is the way to gain fluency, because you need not care what you say, and had better not be sensible. They, too, will rally you on many points, and as they are women you will not be offended. Nothing is of so much importance and of so much use to a young man entering life as to be well criticised by women. . . . Read no history, nothing but biography, for that is life without theory.

Or, again, in half-conscious utterances of his deeper self: 'There is that within me which may yet mould the mind and fortunes of my race'; 'the breath of man has never influenced me much, for I depend more upon myself than upon others'; 'I contrasted the smiling indifference of his public appearance with the agonies of ambition which it was my doom alone to witness.' Here, too, are many characteristic formulæ from the Disraelian philosophy of life—'There is little mystery, there is much ignorance'; and with no less conviction, 'Everything is mysterious'; 'at the present day we too much underrate the influence of individual character'; 'patience is a necessary ingredient of genius'; 'The magic of his character was his patience. This made him quicker, and readier, and more successful than all other men.' The stormy passions, violent impulses, and conflicting aspirations which made Contarini's life so fluctuating and tumultuous were present in Disraeli himself ; but in him held in subjection by an all-mastering will, so that if we had to select any single quality as the keynote to his character the choice might best fall on patience—patience and that unbroken continuity of mind and purpose and endeavour which patience renders possible.

In accordance with the promise which he had given to John Murray before departing for the East, Disraeli sent his manuscript to Albemarle Street as soon as he had it ready. On the suggestion of Lockhart, whose own judgment was perplexed between the 'affectations and absurdities' on the one hand and 'the life and brilliancy' of the descriptions on the other, Murray submitted the work to Milman,[1] withholding the name of the author, and obtained a report so favourable that he at once accepted it for publication. 'Very wild, very extravagant, very German, very powerful, very poetical,' wrote Milman. 'It will, I think, be much read, . . . much admired, and much abused. It is much more in the Macaulay than in the Croker[2] line, and the former is evidently in the ascendant. . . . The latter part . . . . is a rapid volume of travels, a *Childe Harold* in prose.'[3] Disraeli had called his novel 'A Psychological Romance,' and to this title he reverted in subsequent editions ; but at the suggestion of Milman and under pressure from Murray he now consented to change it into 'Contarini Fleming : A Pyschological Autobiography.' The work appeared in four volumes and with nothing on the title-page to indicate the authorship,

[1] The well-known historian of Latin Christianity, later Dean of St. Paul's.

[2] Macaulay had just been 'dusting that varlet's jacket' in a number of the 'Blue and Yellow.'

[3] Smiles, II., p. 338.

but the anonymity was only thinly veiled, many of the reviewers mentioning Disraeli by name.

To Sarah Disraeli.

May 26, 1832.

I received your letter yesterday, and the note you enclosed was from Beckford, to whom I had sent a copy of *Contarini*. His answer is short, but very courteous. It commences with four exclamations. 'How wildly original! How full of intense thought! How awakening! How delightful!' This really consoles one for Mr. Patmore's criticism in the *Court Journal*.

May 28.

Amid abundance of praise and blame of *Contarini*, one thing which we all expected is very evident, that not one of the writers has the slightest idea of the nature or purposes of the work. As far as I can learn it has met with decided success. Among others Tom Campbell, who, as he says, never reads any books but his own, is delighted with it; 'I shall review it myself,' he exclaims, 'and it will be a psychological review.' Have you read the review in the *Monthly*, where I am accused of atheism, because I retire into solitude to write novels?

July 5.

Contarini seems universally liked, but moves slowly. The staunchest admirer I have in London, and the most discerning appreciator of *Contarini*, is old Madame d'Arblay. I have a long letter, which I will show you—capital! [1]

In the course of the following year Disraeli wrote in the diary from which we have already quoted:—

Beckford was so enraptured when he read *The Psychological* that he sent Clarke, his confidential agent and publisher, with whom alone he corresponds, to call upon me on some pretence or other, and give him a description of the person, converse, &c., of the author of what he was pleased to style 'that transcendent work.' Clarke called accordingly and wrote back to Beckford that Disraeli was the most conceited person he had ever met in the whole course of his life. B. answered and rated C. roundly for his opinion,

[1] *Letters*, pp. 76, 77.

telling him that what 'appeared conceit in D. was only the irrepressible consciousness of superior power.' Some time after this, when Clarke knew me better, he very candidly told me the whole story and gave me a copy of B.'s letter.

I shall always consider *The Psychological* as the perfection of English prose and a chef d'œuvre. It has not paid its expenses. *Vivian Grey*, with faults which even youth can scarcely excuse, in short, the most unequal, imperfect, irregular thing that indiscretion ever published, has sold thousands, and eight years after its publication a new edition is announced to-day—so much for public taste.

In fact, in spite of the comparative unfriendliness of the critics and the praise it received from some of those whose praise was best worth having, *Contarini* was a failure.

I published *Contarini Fleming* anonymously and in the midst of a revolution. It was almost still-born, and having written it with deep thought and feeling, I was naturally discouraged from further effort. Yet the youthful writer who may, like me, be inclined to despair, may learn also from my example not to be precipitate in his resolves. Gradually *Contarini Fleming* found sympathising readers; Goethe [1] and Beckford were impelled to communicate their unsolicited opinions of this work to its anonymous author, and I have seen a criticism on it by Heine, of which any writer might be justly proud.[2]

The criticism by Heine is worthy of citation as the judgment of the only Hebrew contemporary with Disraeli who might dispute with him the primacy in genius :—

Modern English letters have given us no offspring equal to *Contarini Fleming*. Cast in our Teutonic mould, it is nevertheless one of the most original works ever written : profound, poignant, pathetic ; its subject the most interesting, if not the noblest, imaginable—the development of a poet ; truly

[1] Disraeli must have been thinking of the incident already related (p. 176) in connexion with *Vivian Grey* ; Goethe died in March, 1832, a month or more before *Contarini* was published.

[2] General Preface to the Novels, 1870.

psychological; passion and mockery; Gothic richness, the fantasy of the Saracens, and yet over all a classic, even a death-like, repose.[1]

One of the most discerning critics[2] of Disraeli's novels has noted the excellence of his style in early life as compared with what we find after the habits of Parliamentary oratory had grown upon him; and though we may not be able to adopt his own too complacent judgment that *Contarini* is 'the perfection of English prose,' his style perhaps is here at its best. It has a rhythm and swing that carry us along, and is full of sparkle and vitality; and though it is deficient in some of the finer graces of consummate prose, in the unerring instinct of the scholar for the most appropriate word, in tenderness, in delicacy, in all that prose may legitimately borrow from poetry, there is no lack of any rhetorical excellence. At times the fervour of the rhetoric carries us to real heights of imaginative eloquence, and it is not often that the eloquence degenerates into bombast or that the glitter of the style becomes merely meretricious; while we find comparatively little of the affected prettiness or careless verbiage that are too frequent in the later novels. On the other hand, there is a curious absence in *Contarini* of the special qualities which give to the novels their peculiar flavour. Disraeli is here so full of his high poetic theme that we seldom see the familiar ironic smile playing over his features or catch that note of mocking laughter which is heard so often in his other works.

Alroy, the second direct product of the Eastern journey, though, as already noted, not published till March, 1833, was begun two years earlier during Disraeli's visit to Jerusalem: indeed, in later life Disraeli ascribed to it an even earlier origin.

[1] I am indebted for this passage to Dr. F. C. Brewster's work *Disraeli in Outline*, but have not succeeded in tracing the original reference.

[2] Sir Leslie Stephen: *Hours in a Library*, II., p. 139.

I had commenced *Alroy* the year after my first publication, and had thrown the manuscript aside. Being at Jerusalem in the year 1831, and visiting the traditionary Tombs of the Kings, my thoughts recurred to the marvellous career which had attracted my boyhood, and I shortly after finished a work which I began the year after I wrote *Vivian Grey*.[1]

The novel appeared as '*The Wondrous Tale of Alroy*, by The Author of *Vivian Grey* and *Contarini Fleming*,' and with a dedication to Sarah Disraeli; and like *Vivian Grey* and *The Young Duke* it was published by Colburn. Murray, 'out of heart with the frightful aspect of coming events,' and 'his incessant ill luck in the publication of works of fiction,' and not encouraged by the comparative failure of *Contarini Fleming*, had returned the manuscript unread when the author submitted it.

The period of the novel is the twelfth century, when the Caliphate was in a state of rapid decay and the empire of Western Asia was divided among the Seljuks: its purpose, in Disraeli's own words, 'the celebration of a gorgeous incident in the annals of that sacred and romantic people from whom I derive my blood and name.'[2] The real David Alroy appears to have been little better than a vulgar impostor, but Disraeli has idealised him into a figure worthy to be compared with Judas Maccabaeus. A scion of the House of David and one of those Hebrew rulers who under the title of 'Princes of the Captivity' exercised a certain authority over their own people by the tolerant permission of the Mahomedan conquerors, Alroy conceives the idea of winning back the independence of Israel and restoring her departed glory. The slaying of a Seljuk chief, who has offered violence to his sister, compels him to fly from his home, and encouraged by a visit to Jabaster, a priest who had been the mentor of his youth, and who had diligently

[1] General Preface to the Novels.

[2] Preface to *The Revolutionary Epick*, 1834.

fostered his high ideals and ambitions, he sets out on a pilgrimage to Jerusalem to win the token of his election. There, after manifold sufferings and adventures, he arrives; and there in the Tombs of the Kings, amid incidents of supernatural awe, he receives the sceptre of King Solomon from the hands of his great ancestor himself. With full assurance of his mission, and supported by Jabaster, he now raises the standard of revolt and sweeps through Western Asia on a tide of victory and conquest. But with constant success his belief in himself grows overweening, and he begins to dream of other things than Jabaster's lofty but narrow aim of re-establishing the theocracy.

> The world is mine; and shall I yield the prize, the universal and heroic prize, to realise the dull tradition of some dreaming priest and consecrate a legend? . . . Is the Lord of Hosts so slight a God, that we must place a barrier to His sovereignty, and fix the boundaries of Omnipotence between the Jordan and the Lebanon? . . . Universal empire must not be founded on sectarian prejudices and exclusive rights.[1]

Convincing himself by such reasoning as this, he makes Bagdad the centre of his kingdom, and is there ensnared by a Delilah in the form of the daughter of the Caliph. Jabaster and the more fanatical spirits presently rise in revolt, and the friend of Alroy's youth falls a victim to the vindictive hatred of the Sultana. From that moment Alroy's good fortune is at an end; his enemies begin to close upon him; and a crushing defeat in battle at the hands of the Sultan of Karasmé causes his mushroom empire to disappear. Taken captive Alroy redeems his fame, and wins the crown of martyrdom by refusing life and liberty as the reward of apostasy from his faith. His epitaph is written in the words with which his beloved

[1] Pt. VIII. ch. 1.

sister Miriam—a character modelled on Disraeli's own sister—endeavours to console him in his failure and remorse :—

> You have shown what we can do and shall do. Your memory alone is inspiration. A great career, although baulked of its end, is still a landmark of human energy. Failure, when sublime, is not without its purpose. Great deeds are great legacies, and work with wondrous usury. By what Man has done, we learn what Man can do ; and gauge the power and prospects of our race.[1]

Did the young Disraeli himself ever dream that the legacy of Alroy had descended to him, or feel the inspiration of his memory as a motive not merely to literary effort, but to an active career ? It is probable enough. As he stood in the Tombs of the Kings at Jerusalem, or gazed on Mount Zion, the thought may have passed through his mind that the true aim of the political ambition which was beginning to shape itself within him should be to win back the Holy Land for the chosen people and restore the sceptre to Judah. To any young Hebrew of genius such thoughts would naturally—nay, inevitably—occur ; and in no other way can Disraeli's own declaration that *Alroy* represented his ' ideal ambition ' be construed. Men of great achievement have often, in addition to the imaginative aims which are the inspiration of their practical careers, their merely visionary fancies which they never realise, which they never seriously try to realise, and which are perhaps neither capable nor deserving of realisation, but which cling to them through life and, though they may not seriously deflect their energies, give a certain bias to their character and colour to their outlook. With all his dreaminess Disraeli's genius was far too practical to permit him to devote his life to the pursuit of a mere phantom ; but it is probable that these early visions never wholly forsook him. They

[1] Pt. X. ch. 19.

had a soil of genuine racial sentiment from which perennially to spring, and though it would be easy to exaggerate their significance, yet to know them is to get a glimpse into the inmost recesses of Disraeli's mind. Therein lies the value of *Alroy* for us now. Before the novel was published Disraeli boasted to a lady of evangelical turn, who inquired after his spiritual welfare, that it would show he read his Bible. He read his Bible, indeed, though less to edification as his pious friend would have interpreted the word than as a record of exclusive interest to the race to which he belonged. In this esoteric sense *Alroy* is saturated with the language and spirit of the Old Testament; and more than any of Disraeli's works, more even than *Tancred*, it reveals the Hebraic aspect of his many-sided nature.

Apart from this biographic interest not much can be said in commendation of the novel. We are impressed, in the dialogue especially, by the quickness and success with which Disraeli has caught the spirit of the East, but his story as a story never really grips us. The East may give us pictures or the embryonic tales which are little more than pictures; but where events lead to nothing and life is a troubled sea with no definite current setting through it, an historical novel is impossible. The remoteness and unreality of the surroundings destroy the interest for Western readers, and the effect of unreality is increased by the author's too faithful adherence to his Eastern models in the things in which they are least deserving of imitation. In his descriptions he falls into a mechanical magnificence and in his action into a mechanical hyperbole which are certainly in harmony with the spirit of the East, but no less certainly wearisome and absurd; and he needlessly introduces a crude supernatural machinery which we like none the better for being told in the preface that it is 'cabalistical and correct.' Disraeli had to pay for the faults of his education, and the mysticism which was such a marked feature of his character, and which on its higher and imaginative side was a source of power and insight, too often degenerated into a taste for mere hocus-pocus.

But the most obvious defect of the novel is the style in which it is written. In *Contarini* we had a strain of fervid rhetoric rarely without distinction. In *Alroy* we get in its place a sort of prose poetry which the author only adopted, as he tells us in the preface to the original edition, 'after long meditation and a severe examination of its qualities.' His tale is 'essentially dramatic,' and therefore he introduces 'occasional bursts of lyric melody for that illustrative music without which all dramatic representations are imperfect.' His subject is essentially poetical and therefore

> I never hesitate although I discard verse to have recourse to rhythm whenever I consider its introduction desirable, and occasionally even to rhyme. There is no doubt that the style in which I have attempted to write this book is a delicate and difficult instrument for an artist to handle. He must not abuse his freedom. He must alike beware the turgid and the bombastic, the meagre and the mean. He must be easy in his robes of state, and a degree of elegance and dignity must accompany him even in the camp and the market house. The language must rise gradually with the rising passions of the speakers and subside in harmonious unison with their sinking emotions.

Whether it would ever be possible to use such an instrument with effect it is not necessary to inquire ; suffice it to say that Disraeli has not succeeded. When he tries to be most impressive he is often simply grotesque, and at times we ask in amazement if his sense of the ridiculous has wholly deserted him. Take for instance such a piece of intolerable bombast as the following :—

> Pallid and mad he swift upsprang, and he tore up a tree by its lusty roots, and down the declivity, dashing with rapid leaps, panting and wild, he struck the ravisher on the temple with the mighty pine.

That fantastical genius Beckford was enchanted with it all, and wished 'the truly wondrous tale had been extended to twenty volumes'; this in spite of some distress at the discovery that 'Disraeli and company were smoking away like vulgar factories.' Disraeli wrote [1] to his sister immediately after publication :—

Of *Alroy* I hear golden opinions, and I doubt not of its success. . . . . I hear no complaints of its style, except from the critics. The common readers seem to like the poetry and the excitement. Mrs. Jameson told Otley that 'reading it was like riding an Arab.' Slade, the traveller, said 'it was the most thoroughly Oriental book he had ever read.'

In spite, however, of these encouraging pronouncements, the author's hopes were hardly realised: the subject was too remote and, his own opinion notwithstanding, the style presented too easy a mark for ridicule [2]; so that the book, if not a failure, had at best only a moderate success.

With *Alroy* was published a short story entitled *The Rise of Iskander*, which Disraeli appears to have written while he was on a visit to Bath with Bulwer. Iskander is the Scanderbeg of Gibbon, the Albanian prince who won his independence in the days of Mahommed the Conqueror; and the piece was designed to provide a contrast to *Alroy* by setting forth 'the history of a Christian hero placed in a somewhat similar position but achieving a very different end.' It is a pretty tale, as the author claimed, and it shows to what good

[1] March 26, 1833; *Letters*, p. 81.

[2] There was an amusing parody by Maginn, Disraeli's old acquaintance of *Representative* days :—'O reader dear! do pray look here, and you will spy the curly hair and forehead fair, and nose so high and gleaming eye of Benjamin Dis-ra-e-li, the wondrous boy who wrote *Alroy*, in rhyme and prose, only to show, how long ago victorious Judah's lion-banner rose,' &c. There is a good deal of this prose poetry in *The Young Duke*, and Disraeli never wholly lost the habit. Even in his last novel we find him in the middle of a passage of ordinary prose suddenly breaking into verse: 'And now and then was heard a silver laugh, and now and then was breathed a gentle sigh.' (*Endymion*, ch. 2.)

account he could turn his brief visit to Albania; but apart from this it has nothing that is peculiar to Disraeli nor any special significance in the story of his inner development.

CHAPTER XI.

Entry into Politics.

1832-1833.

'Poetry is the safety valve of my passions, but I wish to act what I write.' Disraeli was not the man to degenerate into a dilettante recluse like Contarini or to waste his life in fanciful dreams of Hebrew conquest after the manner of Alroy. The journey to the East had restored him to health and vigour. He arrived in England 'in famous condition—better indeed than I ever was in my life and full of hope and courage in spite of the overwhelming catastrophe'; so he wrote to Austen. One of his first acts was to withdraw his name from the books of Lincoln's Inn; he would not even pay the tribute to convention of cloaking his vague ambitions under the dress of an acknowledged profession. His debts were a heavy burden, but he had one tangible asset in his literary reputation. 'Mr. Disraeli, Sir, is come to town—young Mr. Disraeli,' said Colburn to Bulwer. 'Won't he give us a nice light article about his travels?' In his pen Disraeli had a permanent source of income; but during his absence he had developed new ambitions that were more likely to increase expenditure than income. In the East, as health and courage returned, his thoughts had begun to dwell on the attractions of an active political career. Even before he left England Parliament seems to have been in his mind. 'I should have liked you,' writes Austen in July, 1830, 'to have had a picking out of this general election; it would be a famous opening and lots to say.' During his sojourn in the East, Disraeli had been a diligent reader of *Galignani*, and he used in later life to say that it was in studying a file of that 'excellent publication' during his long detention in quarantine at Malta that he first began to understand politics.[1] Through *Galignani* he was able to follow the fortunes of the Reform movement, and he followed them with the keenest interest. 'What a confusion you are all in,' he wrote to Austen from Constantinople, when he read of that 'bold act of cowardice'[2] on the part of the Wellington Ministry, the postponement of the King's visit to the City in November, 1830. 'I have just got through a batch of *Galignanis*. What a capital Pantomime it would make: "The Lord Mayor's Day or Harlequin Brougham"'; and the fancy pleased him so much that by a habit that was already forming he repeated it in almost the same words in letters to his father and Bulwer, adding to Bulwer, 'Oh for the days of Aristophanes, or Foote, or even Scaramouch! Damn the Licenser!' 'The wonderful news which meets me here in a pile of *Galignanis* has quite unsettled my mind,' he writes from Cairo on reading of the introduction of the first Reform Bill. 'I am of course very anxious to hear of the progress of the Bill. I have heard up to the majority of one.'

Disraeli arrived in England on the day that Parliament was prorogued after the rejection of the second Reform

[1] *Life of Jowett*, II., p. 109.

[2] The phrase was Lord Wellesley's. Disraeli has an interesting note on this occurrence, written in 1836:—

'Sir Robert Peel told me that Hume was the real cause of the King's not going into the City. They had received many warnings and much information, when suddenly Joseph sought a confidential interview at the Home Office and told Peel he was in possession of information of an extraordinary character and that an insurrection was certain. Afterwards Joseph had the impudence to make a speech in the House of Commons abusing the Ministers for not letting the King go, and declaring that it was his solemn belief that the outcry was all an alarming invention of their own. "I might have risen and crushed him, the impudent dog," said Peel. Why did he not? The interview was certainly confidential, but the speech absolved the Minister, in my opinion.'

Bill by the Lords. A fortnight later, during the riotous weeks that followed the prorogation, he writes to Austen somewhat in the spirit of an old Tory: 'The times are damnable. I take the gloomiest view of affairs, but we must not lose our property without a struggle.' 'In the event of a new election,' he adds, 'I offer myself for Wycombe.' No new election, however, came at present, and he spent the greater part of the winter at Bradenham 'working like a tiger,' no doubt at *Contarini*. By the middle of February he is in London, 'most comfortably located in Duke Street,' and enjoying his first real taste of the pleasures of London society. Through his friend Bulwer, already at the height of his fame, Disraeli at once found his way into the charmed circle of Mayfair, and in his letters to his sister he has left us a graphic and vivacious record of his adventures in this paradise.

To Sarah Disraeli

Feb. 18, 1832.

We had a very brilliant *réunion* at Bulwer's last night. Among the notables were Lords Strangford[1] and Mulgrave,[2] with the latter of whom I had a great deal of conversation; Count D'Orsay, the famous Parisian dandy; there was a large sprinkling of blues—Lady Morgan, Mrs. Norton, L.E.L., &c. Bulwer came up to me, said 'There is one blue who insists upon an introduction.' 'Oh, my dear fellow, I cannot really; the power of repartee has deserted me.' 'I have pledged myself, you must come'; so he led me up to a very sumptuous personage, looking like a full-blown rose, Mrs. Gore. Albany Fonblanque,[3] my critic, was in the room, but I did not see him. . . . The Mr. Hawkins who made a wonderful speech, and who, although he squinted horribly, was the next day voted a Cupidon, and has since lost his beauty by a failure, and many others, whom in this hurry I cannot recall—Charles Villiers,

1 6th Viscount (1780-1855): A diplomatist of some distinction who had been for many years Minister at Lisbon and afterwards for some years Ambassador at Constantinople.

2 Afterwards 1st Marquis of Normanby.

3 Editor of the *Examiner*.

Henry Ellis, &c. I avoided L.E.L., who looked the very personification of Brompton—pink satin dress and white satin shoes, red cheeks, snub nose, and her hair *à la* Sappho.

Feb. 22.

I am writing a very John Bull book, which will quite delight you and my mother. I am still a Reformer, but shall destroy the foreign policy of the Grey faction. They seem firmly fixed at home, although a storm is without doubt brewing abroad. I think peers will be created, and Charley Gore has promised to let me have timely notice if Baring[1] be one. He called upon me, and said that Lord John often asked how I was getting on at Wycombe. He fished as to whether I should support them. I answered, 'They had one claim upon my support; they needed it,' and no more.

April 28.

The *soirée* last night at Bulwer's was really brilliant, much more so than the first. There were a great many dames there of distinction, and no blues. I should, perhaps, except Sappho, who was quite changed; she had thrown off Greco-Bromptonian costume and was perfectly *à la Française*, and really looked pretty. At the end of the evening I addressed a few words to her, of the value of which she seemed sensible. I was introduced, 'by particular desire,' to Mrs. Wyndham Lewis, a pretty little woman, a flirt, and a rattle; indeed, gifted with a volubility I should think unequalled, and of which I can convey no idea. She told me that she liked 'silent, melancholy men.' I answered 'that I had no doubt of it.' . . .

I had a long conversation with Lord Mulgrave, and a man talked to me very much who turned out to be Lord William Lennox. In the course of the evening I stumbled over Tom Moore, to whom I introduced myself. It is evident that he has read or heard of *The Young Duke*, as his courtesy was marked. 'How is your head?' he enquired. 'I have heard of you, as everybody has. Did we not meet at Murray's once?' He has taken his name off the Athenæum, 'really Brooks is sufficient; so I shall not see your father any more. . . .' I remained in Hertford Street after the breaking up, smoking. Colonel Webster, who married Boddington's daughter, said to me, 'Take care, my good fellow; I lost the most beautiful woman

[1] Sir Thomas Baring, father of the first Lord Northbrook, and at this time M.P. for Wycombe.

in the world by smoking. It has prevented more *liaisons* than the dread of a duel or Doctors' Commons.' Then I replied, 'You have proved that it is a very moral habit.' W., you know, although no Adonis, is a terrible *roué*.

May 15.

I very much fear that the Whigs are again in, and on their own terms. Such, indeed, is the report, but that is only a shot founded on last night's debate; but it is, I apprehend, a conjecture that will turn out to be a prophecy. I dined at [Lord] Eliot's[1] on Saturday, and met Colonel and Captain A'Court, brothers of Lord Heytesbury, and Lord Strangford. We had some delightful conversation and remained till a late hour. Strangford is an aristocratic Tom Moore; his flow is incessant and brilliant. The A'Courts very unaffected, hearty fellows.

Yesterday I dined at Eliot's—a male party consisting of eight. I sat between Peel and Herries,[2] but cannot tell you the names of the other guests, although they were all members of one or other House; but I detected among them Captain York, whom I had met in the Levant. Peel was most gracious. He is a very great man, indeed, and they all seem afraid of him. By-the-bye, I observed that he attacked his turbot most entirely with his knife, so Walker's story is true. I can easily conceive that he could be very disagreeable, but yesterday he was in a most condescending mood and unbent with becoming haughtiness. I reminded him by my dignified familiarity both that he was ex-Minister and I a present Radical. Herries—old, grey-headed, financial Herries—turned out quite a literary man—so false are one's impressions. The dinner was sumptuous, and we broke up late.[3]

The 'John Bull book,' of which he wrote in February and which was to 'destroy the foreign policy of the Grey faction,' was published by Murray in April under the title of 'England and France; or a Cure for the Ministerial Gallomania.' It appeared anonymously and with an ironical dedication to the Prime Minister as 'the most eminent Gallomaniac of the day.' 'With regard to the authorship of this work,' Disraeli wrote to Murray, 'I should never be ashamed of being considered the

1 Afterwards 3rd Earl of St. Germans.
2 Chancellor of the Exchequer in Goderich's Ministry.
3 *Letters*, pp. 70-75.

author. I should be proud to be; but I am not. It is written by Legion, but I am one of them, and I bear the responsibility.'[1] His chief coadjutors appear to have been Baron d'Haussez, a legitimist exile, who had been Minister of Marine in the last Ministry of Charles X., and Baron de Haber, 'a mysterious German gentleman of Jewish extraction,' as Dr. Smiles describes him. 'Beware, my dear, of secret agents,' wrote Isaac D'Israeli to his son, who had told him that he was about to startle Europe; 'beware of forgeries and delusions.' His son had all his life a certain weakness for mystery and intrigue, and disregarded the warning; but Murray, who, as publisher, bore the real responsibility, was less disposed to be venturesome, and insisted, to Disraeli's great annoyance, on the proofs being read by Croker. 'I have no desire,' writes the irritated author, 'to thrust my acquaintance on your critic. More than once I have had an opportunity to form that acquaintance, and more than once I have declined it.' It will be remembered that at the time of *The Representative* affair Disraeli had found reason for resenting Croker's interference, and the prejudice which had slumbered in his mind since then had just been reawakened by an incident of the present year. A few weeks before the letter to Murray Disraeli had failed in an attempt to secure election[2] to the Athenæum, a club of which his father was one of the original members and Croker practically the founder; and rightly or wrongly the Bradenham family laid the failure to the charge of Croker. We shall hear again of the antipathy which these things combined to foster.

The pamphlet, or book—for it runs to 300 pages—is a violent diatribe against the foreign policy of Palmerston and against the friendly understanding with France upon which this policy was for the moment based. The alliance between the two countries is, we are assured, 'un-

[1] Smiles's *Life of Murray*, II., p. 344.

[2] Under the rule allowing the committee to elect annually a limited number of persons 'who have attained to distinguished eminence.' Disraeli did not become a member till 1866.

natural,' and their friendship 'fictitious.' Their 'permanent interests are incompatible from natural passions and prejudices, if from no other reasons.' 'The resolution to be supreme, and the consequent hatred of England, are rooted in the breast of every Frenchman.' Louis Philippe and his Government are attacked with a bitterness for which d'Haussez no doubt was responsible; and with a great parade of secret information the writer professes to set forth the true history of 'that mean and monstrous incident which hitherto we have been pleased to style a Glorious Revolution.'

I have endeavoured to show that the English Minister, in sacrificing all the ancient principles of our policy to ally himself with our hereditary foe, has not even succeeded in the object for which he has thus imprudently and previously paid the dearest price; and that we have, in fact, deserted Portugal and outraged Holland, not for the friendship of the French nation, but for a mere transient connexion with two individuals—the French King and the French Minister; one of whom that nation despises and the other of whom that nation detests.[1]

Disraeli afterwards became a personal friend and admirer of Louis Philippe's, and a consistent supporter of the policy of friendship with France through all her many changes of Government. No one would dream of turning to this hastily-written pamphlet, in which he made his pen the instrument for setting forth the views of others, in order to obtain light on his real and permanent convictions in the region of foreign affairs. Both at the time of publication and afterwards he was unusually silent as to his connexion with the book. 'I am anxious,' he wrote to Mrs. Austen, 'that my name should not be mentioned in reference to the work you have been lately reading. . . . You are so familiar with my writings that you will not give me credit for every idiotism you meet in its columns.' What is of real interest now is the choice of subject for his first venture in the domain

[1] *Gallomania*, p. 255.

of practical politics. Though it was not until near the end of his career that he was able to assert himself effectively in the field of foreign affairs, he had early divined the truth that it is in this field far more than in the noisy and exaggerated strife of parties over questions of internal politics that history is really made. 'There is no subject,' he writes in the *Gallomania*, 'on which, as a society, we are so misinformed as our foreign policy. . . To my mind it is of primary, of paramount, importance: upon our foreign policy the safety as well as the glory of this country as a great Empire depends.' After the experience of a lifetime his judgment remained the same. 'Real politics,' says Lady Montfort to Endymion, 'are the possession and distribution of power. I want to see you give your mind to foreign affairs.'

One passage of the *Gallomania*, which is clearly not the outcome of any extraneous inspiration, has a curious and picturesque interest.

> An Englishman recently resident in Egypt discovered by an accident that a secret agent in the employ of France was in the habit of being honoured with private interviews by the Pasha. It was immediately after the events of July. As the Englishman was well cognisant of the constant intrigues of the French in Egypt—a country of which we may some day hear, although it is not at present much thought of at the Foreign Office—he resolved to ascertain the nature of their conferences. By what means he succeeded, it matters not at present. . . . Let it suffice that he did ascertain that, in the event of any collision with England, a French army was to be received in Egypt and that India was to be threatened. . . . The feelings of the Moslemin population of India were to be excited, and even the Hindus were to be reminded that the most ancient temples of their creed rose on the palmy banks of Nile. . . . We possess no diplomatic agent in Egypt. A Consul-General, indeed, resides there, but his residence is the seaport of Alexandria. . . . But it so happened that about this time an eminent person[1] distinguished by his talents and by the confidence of our Sovereign, was travelling in Egypt, and the Englishman

[1] Some erased words in the original MS. show that the 'eminent person' was Sir John Malcolm.

seized this opportunity of impressing upon that eminent person his conviction of the French intrigues. The eminent person was not deficient in that frankness which we flatter ourselves to be characteristic of our nation. . . . He took an opportunity in an early interview to communicate to the Pasha his apprehensions. 'God is great!' exclaimed his Highness, as he drew his pipe from his mouth. 'It is an infamous falsehood.' . . . 'It is an infamous falsehood,' repeated the eminent person to his informant on the first opportunity. 'His Highness declares that we are the greatest nation in the world and dear to him as his own children. Depend upon it, he is devoted to us. Has he not presented me during my visit with his finest palace? Does not his European band, by his special command, play every day under my window during my dinner? Does he not always proffer me the pipe of honour? And has he not condescended to accept from my hands the finest shawl that Cashmere ever produced?' The reasoning was unanswerable, and the solitary Englishman, who was rather a poet than a politician, proceeded on his pilgrimage.[1]

The pamphlet received the honour of a leading article in *The Times*,[2] in which recognition was freely given to the cleverness and curious information of the authors; though it was also broadly hinted that the real motive which animated them was hostility to the Reform Bill. The third Reform Bill had now been launched, and as it proceeded on the perilous voyage which eventually was to carry it into port, Disraeli's sympathy with the cause whose fortunes it carried seemed rapidly to cool. 'I am still a Reformer,' he wrote, as we have seen, in the last week of February; but a fortnight later he pronounced the Bill to be in a most crazy state, and added that he 'would not be overwhelmed if it failed altogether.' Yet he erased some passages in the *Gallomania* that were adverse to Reform, and, when Croker wanted to restore them, he entered an emphatic protest.

To John Murray.

March 30, 1832.

It is quite impossible that anything adverse to the general measure of Reform can issue from my pen or from anything

[1] *Gallomania*, p. 40. [2] April 20, 1832.

to which I contribute. Within these three months I have declined being returned for a Tory borough, and almost within these four days, to mention slight affairs, I have refused to inscribe myself a member of 'The Conservative Club.' I cannot believe that you will place your critic's feelings for a few erased passages against my permanent interest.[1]

That curious phrase, 'the general measure of Reform,' is not without significance. It seems to suggest that Disraeli's attitude on the question was already not far different from that which he was soon openly to adopt—sympathy with the movement for broadening the electorate and bringing the House of Commons into touch with popular aspirations combined with deep distrust of the motives by which the Whigs were animated and of the principles on which they were founding their reconstruction of the constituency. His political creed, however, was still somewhat vague, and in the matter of party allegiance his position was still wholly unsettled. 'I am neither Whig nor Tory,' he explains in the *Gallomania*. 'My politics are described by one word, and that word is England.' His political stock-in-trade consisted, in fact, of a sincere and ardent patriotism, genuine popular sympathies, a strong and apparently instinctive antipathy to Whiggery, and an hereditary disposition to Toryism derived from his father with an imaginative interest in its romantic aspects that was native to himself. These apparently conflicting principles and elements had not yet been fused into the popular or democratic Toryism for which his name stands in history, and by the eccentricity of his views and his rather light-hearted detachment from party he was to get himself and his friends into no small amount of trouble. 'I, too, have read the *Gallomania*,' writes his sister, 'and I long to see you that you may read me many riddles. The principal one is, how you will reconcile

[1] Smiles, II., p. 344.

your constituents to your politics.' His 'constituents,' indeed, were sorely perplexed by the behaviour of their candidate.

From Sarah Disraeli.

You can imagine the astonishment and consternation of old and young Wycombe. Huffam [Disraeli's chief supporter] is in a great fright that you are going to betray him by proving yourself a Tory after he has for so many months sworn to all Wycombites that you were not one. What will happen ? I should be sorry to give up the plan of regenerating Wycombe and turning them all unconsciously into Tories.

'You are probably acquiring an European name,' writes his father in the same connexion, 'but invention and imagination are not the qualities for a representative of our modern patriots.'

High Wycombe, or Chepping Wycombe, as it was alternatively called, a few miles from Bradenham on the London side, was a typical close borough of the time before the Reform Act, returning to Parliament two members whose election rested exclusively with the Corporation and burgesses. The sitting members were the Hon. Robert Smith, the son and heir of the local magnate, Lord Carrington, and Sir Thomas Baring, both supporters of the Grey Ministry. When Disraeli began to cast eyes on the borough there was the possibility of an election with the old constituency owing to a dissolution in the course of the struggle over the Reform Bill, and there was also the certainty of an election with the new constituency, and at no distant date, if the Reform Bill passed. The Royal assent was given to the Bill on June 7, and a few days before Disraeli posted down from London to begin his canvass. 'I start on the high Radical interest,' he wrote to Austen, 'and take down strong recommendatory epistles from O'Connell, Hume, Burdett, and *hoc genus*. Toryism is worn out, and I cannot condescend to be a Whig.' Edward Bulwer, himself a member of Parliament and a

Reformer of the Radical type, had procured the letters from O'Connell and Hume, and to him O'Connell's was addressed. It regretted that the writer had 'no acquaintance at Wycombe to whom he could recommend Mr. Disraeli.'

I am as convinced as you are of the great advantage the cause of genuine Reform would obtain from his return. His readiness to carry the Reform Bill into practical effect towards the production of cheap government and free institutions is enhanced by the talent and information which he brings to the good cause. I should certainly express full reliance on his political and personal integrity, and it would give me the greatest pleasure to assist in any way in procuring his return, but that, as I have told you, I have no claim on Wycombe, and can only express my surprise that it should be thought I had any.

Hume was more explicit; but his knowledge of Disraeli and of the situation at Wycombe seems to have been extremely meagre, and he presently discovered that he had lent the use of his name against 'his best friend' Baring, and another staunch Reformer, whereas, by some confusion between Wycombe and Wendover, he had believed that Disraeli was opposing a couple of anti-Reformers. A letter of explanation which he wrote to Smith and Baring, and in which he expressed a hope that their seats would not be disturbed, was of course published by their agents, and gave something of a check to Disraeli at the opening of his campaign. But Disraeli was not easily discouraged, and he persevered with his candidature.

To Benjamin Austen.

RED LION, WYCOMBE.

I write you a hurried note after a hard day's canvass. Whigs, Tories, and Radicals, Quakers, Evangelicals, Abolition of Slavery, Reform, Conservatism, Cornlaws—here is hard work for one who is to please all parties. I make an excellent canvasser, and am told I shall carry it if the borough be opened.

His canvass had at first for its objective the new constituency of ten-pound householders; but before it had proceeded many days the situation was suddenly changed. A chance vacancy occurred for one of the seats in Hampshire, and in order to contest it Sir Thomas Baring resigned his seat at Wycombe, thus precipitating a single election under the unreformed system. Bulwer tried hard to secure his friend from opposition, but they seem to have had no love for Disraeli at the Whig headquarters in London, and Bulwer's efforts were in vain.

To Mrs. Austen.

[*June* 10, 1832.]

We are hard at it. Sir Thomas you know has resigned. His son was talked of; I have frightened him off and old Pascoe Grenfell and Buxton. Yesterday the Treasury sent down Colonel Grey with a hired mob and a band. Never was such a failure. After parading the town with his paid voices, he made a stammering speech of ten minutes from his phaeton. All Wycombe was assembled. Feeling it was the crisis, I jumped up on the portico of the Red Lion and gave it them for an hour and a quarter. I can give you no idea of the effect. I made them all mad. A great many absolutely *cried.* I never made as many friends in my life or converted as many enemies. All the women are on my side and wear my colors, pink and white. Do the same. The Colonel returned to town in the evening absolutely astounded out of his presence of mind, *on dit* never to appear again. If he come I am prepared for him.

B. D.

There is some reason for suspecting that the terror inspired in 'old Pascoe Grenfell' and others by Disraeli's prowess was purely imaginary, and that they had never had any thought of standing; and certainly the official candidate, however astounded he may have been, soon reappeared. Colonel Grey was the second son of the Prime Minister, and was afterwards to be well known to Disraeli and the world as Private Secretary to Queen Victoria. In the brief and stammering speech which he delivered from his phaeton he admitted that he had never addressed a public meeting before. The same may have been true of Disraeli, but in his case there was none of the diffidence or hesitation of the beginner. Tales are still told in Wycombe of that famous first speech from the portico of the Red Lion. The youthful orator was now at the height of his dandyism, and his 'curls and ruffles' played no small part in the election. Standing on the top of the porch beside the figure of the lion, with his pale face set off by masses of jet-black hair and his person plenteously adorned with lace and cambric, he must have seemed to the spectators better fitted for his *rôle* of fashionable novelist than for that of strenuous politician. Great, then, was their surprise when this 'popinjay,' as a hostile newspaper called him, began to pour forth a torrent of eloquence with tremendous energy of action and in a voice that carried far along the High Street. He had an instinct for the dramatic effects which hold the attention of a mob. 'When the poll is declared, I shall be there,' he exclaimed, according to a Wycombe tradition, pointing to the head of the lion, 'and my opponent will be there,' pointing to the tail. By the admission even of the opposite party the speech was a complete success and his popularity with the crowd was thenceforth assured.

In the days of unreformed constituencies, however, elections were not to be won by popularity alone. The official Whigs and Reformers of course opposed him, and their county organ[1] gave him a first taste of that malignant and rancorous abuse of which he was to have such full measure throughout his political career and which a certain cynical truculence on his own part no doubt did much to provoke. The Tory organ,[2] on the other hand, welcomed him as an independent in preference to the official Whig, and gave him a qualified blessing. He had placed his interests in the hands of one Nash, the local representative of the great county magnate, the Duke of Buckingham, whose son, Lord Chandos, was the leader of the Buckinghamshire Tories; and though Disraeli

[1] The *Bucks Gazette*. [2] The *Bucks Herald*.

THE HIGH STREET, HIGH WYCOMBE—LOOKING WEST.
From an engraving of a picture by E. J. Niemann.

[To face page 214.

declared on the hustings that he had never had any communication with Lord Chandos, his choice of an agent gave no little point to the charge with which the Whigs persistently assailed him that whatever his Radical protestations he was all the time a Tory at heart. What is really of interest now is the undoubted fact that in this his first election he succeeded in effecting an alliance between Radicals and Tories, between the popular elements in the constituency and the supporters of privilege and tradition. When the day of nomination came he explained his position in a long speech on the hustings. He wore, he declared, the badge of no party; if the Tories had supported him the people had supported him first; as regards the Reform Act, it was only a means to a great end; he expected to derive from it financial, ecclesiastic, and legal reform: he would seek the amelioration of the condition of the poor; the happiness of the many must now be preferred to the happiness of the few: and as regards himself he had never received one shilling of the public money and he belonged to a family who never had; he was sprung, moreover, from the people and had none of the blood of the Plantagenets in his veins. But in spite of this popular programme and these many popular qualifications he speedily found it useless to persevere, the poll at its close on June 26 being—

Grey, 20.
Disraeli, 12.

The defeated candidate consoled himself with another lengthy speech, in which he fiercely assailed the Corporation and poured the vials of his wrath on all his enemies. He ended, according to his opponents, with the words, 'The Whigs have cast me off and they shall repent it'; but in a letter to *The Times*[1] Disraeli repudiated this version.

Whatever may be the disposition of the Whigs to me they never could have cast me off since I never had the

[1] Nov. 12, 1832.

slightest connexion with them. I believe that the phrase I did use, and I am sanctioned in my recollection by every person to whom I have applied, was the following :—'The Whigs have opposed me, not I them, and they shall repent it.' I am in no wise ashamed of this observation and I adhere to it.

The defiant note in the hour of defeat was highly characteristic; but the speech very nearly involved him in a duel. As he flung his gibes and sarcasms right and left he pointed to Lord Nugent[1] and retorting to the charge that he himself was a Tory in disguise declared that the nearest thing to a Tory in disguise was a Whig in office. Lord Nugent construed these words as a personal affront and sent a challenge; but when the seconds met they agreed that the affair was absurd and arranged for such an interchange of explanations as averted a meeting.[2]

To Sarah Disraeli.

[LONDON,]
July 5, 1832.

Giovanni[3] called on me (announced by the servant as *Don Giovanni*). He has left Clay and brought me a lock of Byron's hair from Venice, which he cut himself off the corpse at Missolonghi. I have been very idle, the natural consequence of former exertion, but shall soon buckle to among our beeches.

Aug. 4.

Town is fast emptying. I have been lately at the House of Commons, and one night had a long conversation with my late antagonist and present representative. We are more than friendly.

Aug. 8.

On Friday I shall pitch my tent in the green retreats of Bradenham, and Bulwer accompanies me. He wants absolute retirement, really, to write, and all that. He is to do what he likes, and wander about the woods like a madman. I am anxious that he and my father should become better

[1] Younger brother of the 1st Duke of Buckingham and author of those *Memorials of Hampden* which gave occasion for one of Macaulay's Essays.

[2] Lord Ebrington acted as Lord Nugent's second and Captain Angerstein of the Grenadier Guards as Disraeli's. A notice containing the explanations agreed upon and signed by them is to be seen in the *Bucks Gazette* for July 7, 1832.

[3] See above, p. 158.

acquainted. Our sire never had a warmer votary. . . . I saw Tita to-day, who suggests that he shall return with me to Bradenham, and try our place.[1]

The general election could not long be delayed, and the campaign at Wycombe proceeded almost without intermission. The unreformed Parliament was not actually dissolved till December 3, but on October 1 Disraeli issued a fresh address which is interesting as the first full and authentic exposition of his political opinions that has survived the chances of time. He comes forward again 'wearing the badge of no party and the livery of no faction.' He is 'prepared to support that ballot which will preserve us from that unprincipled system of terrorism with which it would seem we are threatened even in this town.' He is 'desirous of recurring to those old English triennial Parliaments of which the Whigs originally deprived us ; and by repealing the taxes upon knowledge' he 'would throw the education of the people into the hands of the philosophic student, instead of the ignorant adventurer.' He is already occupied with that great question of the condition of the people in which he took an abiding interest.

While I shall feel it my duty to enforce on all opportunities the most rigid economy, and the most severe retrenchment, to destroy every useless place and every undeserving office, and to effect the greatest reduction of taxation consistent with the maintenance of the public faith and the real efficiency of the Government, I shall withhold my support from every Ministry which will not originate some great measure to ameliorate the condition of the lower orders—to rouse the dormant energies of the country, to liberate our shackled industry, and reinstate our expiring credit.

With regard to the Corn Laws,

I will support any change the basis of which is to relieve the customer without injuring the farmer ; and for the Church I am desirous of seeing effected some commutation which, while it prevents the tithe from acting as a tax on industry and enterprise, will again render the clergy what I am always

[1] *Letters*, p. 77.

desirous of seeing them, fairly remunerated, because they are valuable and efficient labourers, and influential, because they are beloved.

And then in a fine rhetorical conclusion he appeals for support in his struggle

Against that rapacious, tyrannical, and incapable faction, who, having knavishly obtained power by false pretences, sillily suppose that they will be permitted to retain it by half measures, and who, in the course of their brief but disastrous career, have contrived to shake every great interest of the Empire to its centre. Ireland in rebellion, the colonies in convulsion, our foreign relations in a state of such inextricable confusion, that we are told that war alone can sever the Gordian knot of complicated blunders ; the farmer in doubt, the shipowner in despair, our merchants without trade, and our manufacturers without markets, the revenue declining, and the army increased, the wealthy hoarding their useless capital, and pauperism prostrate in our once-contented cottages. Englishmen, behold the unparalleled Empire raised by the heroic energies of your fathers ; rouse yourselves in this hour of doubt and danger ; rid yourselves of all that political jargon and factious slang of Whig and Tory—two names with one meaning, used only to delude you—and unite in forming a great national party which can alone save the country from impending destruction.

At a dinner given to him by his supporters in the course of the campaign he elaborated his programme, leaning on this occasion somewhat more towards the Tory side of the argument, probably because there were a good many Tories among his hosts and audience as certainly there was a Tory in the chair. He is still, indeed, defiantly independent. 'I care not for party. I stand here without party. I plead the cause of the people, and I care not whose policy I arraign': but he rejoices that 'the Tories have joined the popular party' in that town, and it is now that, for the first time, we are taken back to the principles of primitive Toryism and introduced to 'Sir William Wyndham and my Lord Bolingbroke,' of whom we shall hear a good deal in future. A Whig organ had denounced Disraeli as 'a destructive Radical.' A few short months ago, he retorted, they had described him as 'a disappointed Tory candidate.' 'I need scarcely say to you that I have undergone no change. I am as I ever was in motive, principle, and determination.' In advocating triennial Parliaments he was only supporting 'the true principles, the just spirit of our admirable constitution.' They had been advocated by the Tory Party in 'the most laudable period of its career,'—by Sir William Wyndham 'in a speech which for sound argument, keen research, close reasoning, and bitter invective, is, I think, unequalled,' and by Lord Bolingbroke, 'one of the ablest men who ever lived': and he was not ashamed to be 'as great and as destructive a Radical as Sir William Wyndham and my Lord Bolingbroke.' The ballot again was decidedly a Conservative measure, and he supported it as much against the passions of the many as the prejudices of the few. He was, in fact, 'a Conservative to preserve all that is good in our constitution, a Radical to remove all that is bad.' As the people had been invested with power, he wished to see them fitted for its exercise; therefore, he wished to see the taxes on knowledge repealed and the Press really free. In the matter of foreign affairs 'he shewed how the policy of the present Administration must lead to an ultimate loss of the sovereignty of the seas, the destruction of our commerce, and finally of our country. Peace is now the policy of England. We have gained everything: now it is our duty to preserve.' He was a sincere friend of the slave population, but he was not 'one of those precious politicians who wish to deliver the Colonies of England to the United States of America.' Finally, Free Trade was a theory which 'as a theory he much admired,' but a word of warning was necessary as to its practical application.

I cannot resist the conviction that if we have recourse to any sudden alteration of the present system, we may say farewell to the county of Bucks, farewell to the beautiful Chilterns. . . . You will ask is bread, then, always to be dear? By no means, but it is surely better to have dear bread than to have no bread at all. Reduce the burdens that so heavily press upon the farmer, and then reduce his protection in the same ratio. That is the way to have cheap bread. I do not doubt that when the question of tithes is eventually settled, when the poor laws are brought back to the system of 1795, and when we employ our surplus revenue in relieving the agricultural interest instead of sending forth fantastic expeditions to attack our ancient allies—I do not doubt that then we may have the blessing of cheap bread without destroying the interest which is the basis of all sound social happiness.[1]

'If I gain my election I think I have doubled the Cape of my destiny,' Disraeli wrote to Evans, his old comrade of the solicitor's office. He was not to gain his election. The Whigs put forth all their efforts to defeat him, and on the hustings he angrily declared that 'the secret of their enmity was that he was not nobly born.' When the poll closed on Dec. 12 the figures were—

Smith, 179.
Grey, 140.
Disraeli, 119.

To Benjamin Austen.

Sunday.

Had my agent attended to our registration, which for various reasons he did not, I should have succeeded at Wycombe, as upwards of 18 ratted from Grey, but the rates of many of my old supporters were not paid up. The election, or rather contest, did not cost me £80, the expense of hustings, &c., and Grey not short of £800. Had I let money fly I should have come in. I make no doubt of success another time.

Beaten at Wycombe, he on the same day issued an address to the electors of the county.

[1] This speech is preserved in the *Wycombe Sentinel* (Nov. 30), a weekly publication, of which eight numbers were issued gratis by the Disraeli party during the campaign. There is also a report in the *Bucks Herald* of Dec. 1.

I come forward as the supporter of that great interest which is the only solid basis of the social fabric, and, convinced that the sound prosperity of this country depends upon the protected industry of the farmer, I would resist that spirit of rash and experimental legislation which is fast hurrying this once glorious Empire to the agony of civil convulsion.

Lord Chandos [1] was the only Tory in the field, opposed to two Reformers; but when Disraeli arrived at Aylesbury on the day after the issue of his address he found that he had been anticipated, and he at once withdrew his own pretensions, and appeared on the hustings as a supporter of the second Tory candidate. The incident marked a distinct advance towards formal alliance with the Tory Party. As the hostile Journal put it, having been beaten at Wycombe as a Tory Radical he endeavoured to come forward for the County as a Radical Tory.

To The Rev. Alfred Beaven.

HUGHENDEN MANOR,
Jan. 17, 1874.

On the loss of my election in 1832 I started for the County, and issued my address on the same day that Mr. Scott Murray, unknown to me, agreed to become a candidate. I acted throughout the Wycombe election and on this occasion entirely with the approval and under the advice of Lord Chandos, then one of the principal leaders of the Tory party. We felt it would not do for me to stand in the way of Mr. Scott Murray, a gentleman of large estate. He was an amiable man, totally unfit to be a County candidate in those stormy days, and lost his election, which seemed difficult, as there was no doubt, from the enthusiasm of the farmers in my favour, I should have been returned by five or six hundred majority.

Though it is now a mere point of historical curiosity, I must observe, that I advocated the ballot in 1832 because it was part of the Tory scheme of a century before; and for the same reason, as it was suggested by Sir W. Wyndham, and particularly Sir John Hinde Cotton, almost as distinguished a leader of the Country party, in the days of the

[1] Afterwards 2nd Duke of Buckingham.

first Georges. It seemed to me, that the Borough constituency of Lord Grey was essentially, and purposely, a dissenting and low Whig constituency, consisting of the principal employers of labour—and that the ballot was the only instrument to extricate us from these difficulties. . . .

Political history is not sufficiently known now, but when I started in life, it is not an exaggeration to say, that the mind of the country, even in the Houses of Parliament, was a complete blank upon it. The Tory party had lost all their traditions, and this led to their fall : to the mess they made about the Roman Catholics, and Parliamentary Reform. I have, for forty years, been labouring to replace the Tory party in their natural and historical position in this country. I am in the sunset of life, but I do not despair of seeing my purpose effected.

To General The Hon. Charles Grey.[1]

10, DOWNING-STREET, WHITEHALL,
Nov. 30, 1868.

MY DEAR GENERAL,

I reciprocate all your feelings, and shall cherish your friendship, which I highly esteem. Your conduct to me, during my tenure of Office, has been admirable, and in quitting my post, it is a consolation to me to know that Her Majesty has near her a gentleman in whose abilities, experience, judgment, honor, and devotion she may place implicit reliance.

Let me know when Her Majesty would wish to receive me to-morrow ; and believe me,

Yours sincerely,

B. DISRAELI.

Meanwhile during those autumn months at Bradenham, in the intervals of electioneering, *Alroy* had been completed ; and early in the new year Disraeli was at Bath writing *The Tale of Iskander*.

To Sarah Disraeli.

BATH,
Jan. 19, 1833.

Bulwer and I arrived here on Monday, and have found the change very beneficial and refreshing. Such is the power

[1] His antagonist at Wycombe.

of novelty, that the four or five days seem an age. . . . We are great lions here, as you may imagine, but have not been anywhere, though we have received several invitations, preferring the relaxation of our own society, and smoking Latakia, which as a source of amusement, I suppose, will last a week. I like Bath very much. Bulwer and I went in late to one public ball, and got quite mobbed.

LONDON,
Jan. 29.

I dined with Bulwer *en famille* on Sunday, 'to meet some truffles'—very agreeable company. His mother-in-law, Mrs. Wheeler, was there; not so pleasant, something between Jeremy Bentham and Meg Merrilies, very clever, but awfully revolutionary. She poured forth all her systems upon my novitiate ear, and while she advocated the rights of woman, Bulwer abused system-mongers and the sex, and Rosina played with her dog.

Feb. 7.

Went to the House of Commons to hear Bulwer adjourn the House; was there yesterday during the whole debate—one of the finest we have had for years. Bulwer spoke, but he is physically disqualified for an orator; and, in spite of all his exertions, never can succeed. He was heard with great attention, and is evidently backed by a party. Heard Macaulay's best speech, Sheil and Charles Grant. Macaulay admirable; but, between ourselves, I could floor them all. This *entre nous*; I was never more confident of anything than that I could carry everything before me in that House. The time will come. . . . Grey spoke highly of my oratorical powers to Bulwer, said he never heard 'finer command of words.' *Ixion* is thought the best thing I ever wrote.[1]

Ixion in Heaven was one of several short pieces which he contributed about this time to the *New Monthly*, a magazine owned by Colburn, of which Bulwer was the editor. A companion piece *The Infernal Marriage* was published in the following year. Light, satirical dialogues conceived in the manner of Lucian they are reminiscences, as has been noted before, of Disraeli's schoolboy admiration for that author, though they surpass even Lucian in the audacity of their persiflage. There was an element

[1] *Letters*, pp. 79, 80.

of sheer irreverence in Disraeli strangely mingled, as in Heine, with the more obvious characteristics of the Semitic temperament—a spirit of revolutionary mockery ever struggling in both with the mysticism of the Hebrew, so that they both of them appear to be the most impossible compounds of Spinoza and Voltaire; and nowhere has Disraeli given more perfect expression to this side of his complex nature than in these dialogues, because nowhere else is its expression so genial and inoffensive. His father thought them the most original of all his writings; and more than one critic since, charmed by their wit and vivacity and sparkle, their entire freedom from malice, and the spirit of innocent mischief which breathes through them, has repeated the contemporary judgment, and pronounced them to be the best things that their author ever wrote.

To Sarah Disraeli.

April 8.

I have agreed to stand for Marylebone, but I shall not go to the poll unless I am certain, or very confident; there is even a chance of my not being opposed. In the *Town* yesterday, I am told, 'some one asked Disraeli, in offering himself for Marylebone, on what he intended *to stand*. "On my head," was the reply.'

I have heard nothing more from ————, who appears to have pocketed more than I should like to do. It was impossible to pass over attacks from such a quarter in silence. The only way to secure future ease is to take up a proper position early in life, and show that you will not be insulted with impunity.[1]

The allusion in this passage is to a correspondence with Dashwood, the Whig member for Bucks, who in a speech at Wycombe had elaborately depicted a type of political profligacy in language that had been interpreted as applying to the late candidate for the borough. More perhaps in a spirit of calculation than out of real sensitiveness or irritability Disraeli was in these years

[1] *Letters*, p. 82.

something of a fire-eater, ready to fly out at every fancied insult; in marked contrast to his contemptuous disregard in later days of the shower of venomous abuse that unceasingly descended on him. He succeeded on this occasion in intimidating his critic, but at the expense of alarming his family.

The candidature for Marylebone began and ended with the issue of an address. Appealing to an urban constituency, Disraeli stands forth again as a militant democrat, the comparative Toryism of his views on Church and land fading into the background. 'Supported by neither of the aristocratic parties,' he appears before the electors 'as an independent member of society who has no interest, either direct or indirect, in corruption or misgovernment, and as one of a family untainted by the receipt of public money.' He asks for their votes 'as a man who has already fought the battle of the people and as one who believes that the only foundation on which a beneficent and vigorous government can now be raised is an unlimited confidence in the genius of the British nation.' And then he repeats the principal items of his Wycombe programme: triennial Parliaments, election by ballot, the repeal of the taxes on knowledge, reduction of the public burdens, and the elevation of the moral and improvement of the physical condition of the people.

The vacancy did not occur, and Disraeli had recourse to his pen in order to explain and, at the same time, draw attention to his somewhat anomalous political position. A short pamphlet presently appeared entitled '"What is He?" By the Author of *Vivian Grey*'; the title finding its explanation in the legend beneath it—'"I hear that * * * * is again in the field; I hardly know whether we ought to wish him success. 'What is he?'"—*Extract from a letter of an Eminent Personage.*' The 'Eminent Personage' was supposed to be Lord Grey, the Prime Minister, but he is just as likely to have been a figment of Disraeli's imagination. The pamphlet is an argument in favour of a National Party and an explanation of the principles on which it should be founded.

> The Tories have announced [it begins] that they could not carry on the government of this country with the present state machinery; every day the nation is more sensible that the Whigs cannot. . . . The first object of a statesman is a strong Government, without which there can be no security. . . . By what means are we to obtain a strong Government? We must discover some principles on which it can be founded. We must either revert to the *aristocratic* principle, or we must advance to the *democratic*. . . . The moment the Lords passed the Reform Bill, from menace instead of conviction, the aristocratic principle of government in this country, in my opinion, expired for ever. From that moment, it became the duty of every person of property, talents, and education, unconnected with the unhappy party at present in power, to use his utmost exertions to advance the democratic principle, in order that the country should not fall into that situation, in which, if I mistake not, it will speedily find itself—absolutely without any Government whatever.
>
> A Tory and a Radical, I understand; a Whig—a democratic aristocrat, I cannot comprehend. If the Tories indeed despair of restoring the aristocratic principle, and are sincere in their avowal that the State cannot be governed with the present machinery, it is their duty to coalesce with the Radicals, and permit both political nicknames to merge in the common, the intelligible, and the dignified title of a National Party. He is a mean-spirited wretch who is restrained from doing his duty by the fear of being held up as insincere and inconsistent by those who are incapable of forming an opinion on public affairs. . . . A great mind, that thinks and feels, is never inconsistent and never insincere. . . . The insincere and the inconsistent are the stupid and the vile. Insincerity is the vice of a fool and inconsistency the blunder of a knave.

What then in practice are 'the easiest and most obvious methods by which the democratic principle may be made predominant'? The answer, it must be confessed, is somewhat disappointing. They are, we are told, 'the instant repeal of the Septennial Act, the institution of

Election by Ballot, and the immediate dissolution of Parliament.' We feel at once that the current of thought has lost itself in the shallows of formula, and we hasten on with some impatience to the much-quoted passage which brings the tract to an eloquent conclusion.

It is wise to be sanguine in public as well as in private life; yet the sagacious statesman must view the present portents with anxiety, if not with terror. It would sometimes appear that the loss of our great Colonial Empire must be the necessary consequence of our prolonged domestic dissensions. Hope, however, lingers to the last. In the sedate but vigorous character of the British nation, we may place great confidence. Let us not forget also an influence too much underrated in this age of bustling mediocrity—the influence of individual character. Great spirits may yet arise to guide the groaning helm through the world of troubled waters; spirits whose proud destiny it may still be at the same time to maintain the glory of the Empire and to secure the happiness of the People!

'Who will be the proud spirit?' was Isaac D'Israeli's pointed query when he read the pamphlet; but his son vouchsafed no answer. The whole performance is a characteristically Disraelian blend of eloquence and bathos, of sincerity and pose, of insight and fantasy.

April 30, 1833.

There is an attack in the *Morning Herald* on *What is He?* where the author is advised to adhere to the region of romance. Such attacks are not very disagreeable, for you have no idea of the success of the pamphlet, which is as much a favourite with the Tories as the Rads. The recent *exposé* of the Whigs proves me a prophet.[1]

In spite of this complacent view the world was as far as ever from an answer to the question which supplied a title to the pamphlet. A year had now elapsed since Disraeli's first appearance on the stage of practical politics, and he had done little more than win for himself the reputation of a political adventurer with unintelligible opinions. As he became more famous, controversy began

[1] *Letters*, p. 82.

to rage around the details of these first campaigns and it has never wholly died away; pamphleteering biographers striving with one another—some eager to prove that he was a consistent Tory from the beginning, others no less eager to convict him as an unscrupulous time-server, careless of everything but his own advancement. The outlines of the truth will now begin to be apparent. Disraeli in 1832 was impatiently eager to get into Parliament; but his opinions were the opinions of a man in complete isolation from the ordinary schools of political thought and he was almost cynically indifferent to the conventions of party allegiance. Experience soon taught him that this indifference could not be maintained; he learnt in due course to pay the necessary tribute to convention, and as time went on he acquired some of the freedom which is the privilege of greatness. But in these early days his extreme detachment in the matter of opinion and allegiance was ascribed by the multitude of humdrum politicians to absence of political convictions. That he was without political convictions, however, was the exact opposite of the truth. He was a man over-burdened with political convictions, not yet fully elaborated or harmonised into a system, but dear to him as the product of original and independent thought. If he had been content to wear the livery of either party he could with half the energy and ability he showed have speedily forced his way into Parliament. But it was not in his nature to accept a political creed or programme ready made or to stifle the instinct of criticism which was so strong within him. He was a political free-thinker at the beginning of his career as he remained a political free-thinker to the end.

Born in a library and trained from early childhood by learned men who did not share the passions and the prejudices of our political and social life, I had imbibed on some subjects conclusions different from those which generally prevail, and especially with reference to the history of our own country. How an oligarchy had been substituted for a kingdom, and a narrow-minded and bigoted fanaticism flourished in the name of religious liberty, were problems long to me insoluble, but which early interested me. But what most attracted my musing, even as a boy, was the elements of our political parties, and the strange mystification by which that which was national in its constitution had become odious, and that which was exclusive was presented as popular.[1]

We are not bound to suppose that the Disraeli of 1832 would have set forth his difficulties in the precise manner in which the Disraeli of 1870 set them forth in retrospect: the language of the foregoing extract is the language of his finished political creed, of the *Vindication* or of *Coningsby*; but even in 1832 all the elements of his finished political creed can already be detected. His faith in democracy on the one hand, his reverence for tradition and our traditional institutions on the other; his dislike of the selfish Whig oligarchy; his desire to secure a modification of the Corn Laws, but without the sacrifice of agriculture; his interest in the condition of the people, and that, too, at a time when the subject had not become fashionable; these are all to be found in the speeches and writings of Disraeli's first year in politics precisely as they run through his subsequent political life. If we study his first campaigns in the light of what followed, putting aside party prepossessions and ignoring party labels, what they demonstrate is not any tendency to mental fickleness in the man, but an amazing continuity, not to say rigidity, of thought in the principles which underlie his whole political career. We need never look in Disraeli for the self-conscious consistency of the moral precisian; but there is no lack of the far deeper consistency which has its roots in a highly original mind, in a strong intellectual grasp of certain cardinal ideas, in a temperament of marked idiosyncrasy, and in a character of exceptional persistence.

[1] General Preface to the Novels, 1870.

CHAPTER XII.

Life in London.

1833-1834.

In *Endymion* we are shown the contrast between the social world of London as Disraeli first knew it in his youth and the same world as he saw it half a century later.

The great world then, compared with the huge society of the present period, was limited in its proportions, and composed of elements more refined though far less various. . . . There were then, perhaps, more great houses open than at the present day, but there were very few little ones. The necessity of providing regular occasions for the assembling of the miscellaneous world of fashion led to the institution of Almack's, which died out in the advent of the new system of society, and in the fierce competition of its inexhaustible private entertainments. The season then was brilliant and sustained, but it was not flurried. People did not go to various parties on the same night. They remained where they were assembled, and, not being in a hurry, were more agreeable than they are at the present day. Conversation was more cultivated; manners, though unconstrained, were more stately; and the world, being limited, knew itself much better.[1]

On his return from the East Disraeli had, as we have seen, at once found admission to a society which if not the highest stood in close relationship to the highest —a curious blend of literature, fashion, politics, and

[1] *Endymion*, ch. 5.

bohemianism; and here and in even more Olympian circles he made rapid headway from the first. He had all the qualities that enable a man to shine in such an atmosphere: he was by instinct a social artist, as his earliest novels prove; in those days dandyism was in fashion, and he was a dandy by nature, practice, and conviction; he was 'at that time a very handsome young man, with a countenance in which beauty of feature and intellectual expression were strikingly combined'[1]; and he could when he liked be so brilliant in conversation as to extort admiring testimony even from unsympathetic listeners.

To Sarah Disraeli.

Feb. 21, 1833.

Yesterday I dined with the Nortons; it was her eldest brother's birthday, who, she says, is 'the only respectable one of the family, and that is because he has a liver complaint.' There were there her brother Charles and old Charles Sheridan, the uncle, and others. The only lady beside Mrs. Norton, her sister Mrs. Blackwood,[2] also very handsome and very Sheridanic. She told me she was nothing. 'You see Georgy's the beauty, and Carry's the wit, and I ought to be the good one, but then I am not.' I must say I liked her exceedingly; besides, she knows all my works by heart, and spouts whole pages of 'V.G.' and 'C.F.' and the 'Y.D.' In the evening came the beauty, Lady St. Maur, and anything so splendid I never gazed upon. Even the handsomest family in the world, which I think the Sheridans are, all looked dull. Clusters of the darkest hair, the most brilliant complexion, a contour of face perfectly ideal. In the evening Mrs. Norton sang and acted, and did everything that was delightful. Ossulston came in—a very fine singer, unaffected and good-looking. Old Mrs. Sheridan—who, by the bye, is young and pretty, and authoress of *Carwell*—is my greatest admirer; in fact, the whole family have a very proper idea of my merits! and I like them all.[3]

Many years later Lady Dufferin gave a description of the appearance presented at this dinner party by her

[1] Sir Henry Layard in the *Quarterly Review* for Jan., 1889.
[2] Afterwards Lady Dufferin. [3] *Letters*, p. 80.

sister's fantastic guest. He wore, she said, 'a black velvet coat lined with satin, purple trousers with a gold band running down the outside seam, a scarlet waistcoat, long lace ruffles, falling down to the tips of his fingers, white gloves with several brilliant rings outside them, and long black ringlets rippling down upon his shoulders.'[1] Lady Dufferin protested that there was not the slightest exaggeration in this picture; but we may at least suspect or hope that time had not deprived it of any of its colour. It may have been to the same occasion that she referred in a well-known anecdote.

He was once dining with my insufferable brother-in-law, Mr. Norton, when the host begged him to drink a particular kind of wine, saying he had never tasted anything so good before. Disraeli agreed that the wine was very good. 'Well,' said Norton, 'I have got wine twenty times as good in my cellar.' 'No doubt, no doubt,' said Disraeli, looking round the table; 'but, my dear fellow, this is quite good enough for such *canaille* as you have got to-day.'

To Sarah Disraeli.

April 25, 1833.

I have done nothing but go to the play lately, one night with Mrs. Norton to see Sheridan Knowles's new play, which was successful. Public amusements are tedious, but in a private box with a fair companion less so.

May 22.

There was a review in Hyde Park, and the Wyndham Lewis's gave a *déjeuner*, to which I went. By the bye, would you like Lady Z—— for a sister-in-law, very clever, £25,000 and domestic? As for 'love,' all my friends who married for love and beauty either beat their wives or live apart from them. This is literally the case. I may commit many follies in life, but I never intend to marry for 'love,' which I am sure is a guarantee of infelicity.[2]

The meeting with this lady was at the Opera, and an entry in her diary gives us a glimpse of Disraeli in the company of a clever and romantic girl.

[1] Motley's *Correspondence*, I., p. 264. [2] *Letters*, p. 82.

The younger Disraeli was in the box. He and I soon got acquainted. He is wild, enthusiastic, and very poetical. He told me he thought Southey the greatest man of the age; he was really a great man, he said. . . . The brilliancy of my companion infected me, and we ran on about poetry and Venice and Baghdad and Damascus. He tells me that repose is the great thing and that nothing repays exertion. Yet noise and light are his fondest dreams, and nothing could compensate him for an obscure youth—not even glorious old age. It was beautiful to hear him talk of Southey.

The girl was herself a great admirer of Southey's, but her companion's enthusiasm, we may suspect, began and ended in that opera box. 'Lady Z.' presently found a less poetical husband, and nearly fifty years later Disraeli had the satisfaction of recommending her son for a peerage. Marriage at this time was a good deal in his thoughts, and in the letters from Bradenham there are frequent allusions to a matrimonial scheme to which, though probably having its origin less in his own feelings than in the wishes of his family, he seems seriously for a time to have given his attention. The lady was a sister of his lost friend Meredith, but whether through her own reluctance or her suitor's lack of zeal the project came to nothing.

To Sarah Disraeli.

June 29.

My table is literally covered with invitations, and some from people I do not know. I dined yesterday with the St. Maurs, to meet Mrs. Sheridan. An agreeable party: the other guests, Lady Westmorland, very clever; Mrs. Blackwood, Lord Clements, and Brinsley. Lord St. Maur, great talent, which develops itself in a domestic circle, though otherwise shy-mannered. In the evening a good *soirée* at Lady Charleville's. I met Lady Aldboro', but the lion of the evening was Lucien Bonaparte, the Prince of Canino. I went to the Caledonian Ball after all, in a dress from my Oriental collection. Particulars when we meet. Yesterday, at Mrs. Wyndham's, I met Joseph Bonaparte and his beautiful daughter.

July 20.

I am putting my house in order and preparing for a six months' sojourn and solitude amid the groves of Bradenham. . . . London is emptying fast, but gay. Lady Cork[1] had two routs. 'All my best people, no blues.' At a concert at Mrs. Mitford's I was introduced to Malibran, who is to be the heroine of my opera. She is a very interesting person.

Aug. 4.

My letters are shorter than Napoleon's, but I love you more than he did Josephine. I shall be down to-morrow.[2]

'I wish,' wrote his father on some occasion, 'that your organization allowed you to write calmer letters, and that you could sober yourself down to a diary before you went to bed.' To a diary in the ordinary sense Disraeli never did succeed in sobering himself down, but in these quiet autumn months at Bradenham he began a document which has unfortunately not escaped the ravages of time and is known to those who have engaged in the exploration of his papers as the 'Mutilated Diary.'

Sept. 1, 1833.

I have passed the whole of this year in uninterrupted lounging and pleasure—with the exception of offering myself for Marylebone and writing a pamphlet, but the expected vacancy, thank God, did not occur: and one incident has indeed made this year the happiest of my life. How long will these feelings last? They have stood a great test, and now absence, perhaps the most fatal of all. My life has not been a happy one. Nature has given me an awful ambition and fiery passions. My life has been a struggle, with moments of rapture—a storm with dashes of moonlight—Love, Poetry

* * * * * * * * * * * *
* * * * * achieve the difficult undertaking. With fair health I have no doubt of success, but the result will probably be fatal to my life.

[1] Mary Countess of Cork (1746-1840), widow of the 7th Earl, who died in 1798. Before her marriage she was the Miss Monckton whom we meet in Boswell; whose 'vivacity enchanted the sage'; and whom Johnson crushed in argument with the retort, 'Dearest, you're a dunce,' adding, when she reproached him afterwards, 'Madam, if I had thought so, I certainly should not have said it.' She was a lion-hunter all her life and, beside the members of Johnson's circle, had known the Prince Regent, Castlereagh, Canning, Byron, Scott, and a hundred other celebrities. We shall find her appearing in *Henrietta Temple* as Lady Bellair.

[2] *Letters*, pp. 83, 84.

My disposition is now indolent. I wish to be idle and enjoy myself, muse over the stormy past and smile at the placid present. My career will probably be more energetic than ever, and the world will wonder at my ambition. Alas! I struggle from Pride. Yes! It is Pride that now prompts me, not Ambition. They shall not say I have failed. It is not Love that makes me say this. I remember expressing this feeling to Bulwer as we were returning from Bath together, a man who was at that moment an M.P., and an active one, editing a political journal and writing at the same time a novel and a profound and admirable philosophical work. He turned round and pressed my arm and said in a tone the sincerity of which could not be doubted: 'It is true, my dear fellow, it is true. We are sacrificing our youth, the time of pleasure, the bright season of enjoyment—but we are bound to go on, we are *bound*. How our enemies would triumph were we to retire from the stage! And yet,' he continued in a solemn voice, 'I have more than once been tempted to throw it all up, and quit even my country, for ever.'

All men of high imagination are indolent.

I have not gained much in conversation with men. Bulwer is one of the few with whom my intellect comes into collision with benefit. He is full of thought, and views at once original and just. The material of his conversation and many a hint from our colloquies he has poured into his *England and the English*, a fine series of philosophic dissertations. Lockhart is good for *tête-à-têtes*, if he like you, which he did me once. His mind is full of literature, but no great power of thought. He is an overrated man. But the man from whom I have gained most in conversation is Botta,[1] the son of the Italian historian, whom I knew in Egypt, travelling as a physician in the Syrian dress—the most philosophic mind that I ever came in contact with. Hour after hour has glided away, while, *chibouque* in mouth, we have disserted together upon our divan, in a country where there are no journals and no books. My mind made a jump in these high discourses. Botta was wont to say that they formed also an era in his intellectual life. If I add to these my father, the list comprises the few men from whose conversation I have gained wisdom. I make it a rule now never to throw myself open to men. I do not grudge them the knowledge

[1] Paul Emile Botta, 1805-1870. He was afterwards French Consul at Mosul, and shares with Layard the honour of founding Assyrian archæology.

I could impart, but I am always exhausted by composition when I enter society, and little inclined to talk, and as I never get anything in return, I do not think the exertion necessary. In the conversation of society the most brilliant men I know are perhaps Spencer (now in Paris) and Tom Moore. As a lively companion, of ceaseless entertainment and fun, no one perhaps equals Charles Mathews, the son of the comedian, but far excelling his father, who is, I understand, jealous of him. James Smith, though gouty, will nevertheless not easily find a rival as a *diseur des bons mots.* I met him at General Phipps's this year, and he divided mankind into those who walked to get an appetite for their dinner and those who walked to get a dinner for their appetite. *Jeemes* Smith, as the good old General (who, by the bye, gives as pleasant little dinners as anybody in town) ever calls him. 'General,' says Lady Cork, 'when am I to dine with you?' 'Name your day and your party, Lady Cork.' 'Well then, the 20th, and you may ask whom you like—only not Jeemes Smith or Jekyll, I am tired of them.'

But I am not Lady Cork, and was very much amused with Jeemes. Jekyll has his faculties, but is deaf, like Lady Aldboro'. I cannot bear deaf people. I feel for them so much, and I never can repeat what I say, not even to Princes.

The world calls me *conceited.* The world is in error. I trace all the blunders of my life to sacrificing my own opinion to that of others. When I was considered very conceited indeed I was nervous and had self-confidence only by fits. I intend in future to act entirely from my own impulse. I have an unerring instinct—I can read characters at a glance; few men can deceive me. My mind is a continental mind. It is a revolutionary mind. I am only truly great in action. If ever I am placed in a truly eminent position I shall prove this. I could rule the House of Commons, although there would be a great prejudice against me at first. It is the most jealous assembly in the world. The fixed character of our English society, the consequence of our aristocratic institutions, renders a career difficult. Poetry is the safety-valve of my passions, but I wish to act what I write. My works are the embodification of my feelings. In *Vivian Grey* I have portrayed my active and real ambition. In *Alroy* my ideal ambition. The *Psychological Romance* is a development of my poetic character. This trilogy is the secret history of my feelings. I shall write no more about myself.

The Utilitarians in politics are like the Unitarians in religion; both omit imagination in their systems, and imagination governs mankind.

Oct. 21.

Seven weeks! and not a line in my book.

These strange rhapsodies show that Disraeli's mind was in a state of unusual exaltation and excitement, and prepare us for that which followed. In the course of the autumn months at Bradenham he embarked on a literary venture which is one of the most curious enterprises of an enterprising life. The habit of verse-making, apart from any genuine poetic impulse, was more in fashion among the educated in those days than now; Isaac D'Israeli was much addicted to it, and his son hardly less, in spite of his discovery proclaimed in *Contarini*, and repeated in *Alroy*, that the age of versification was past. Full of a vague consciousness of power, which had hardly yet been directed into definite channels, he was now seized, as he wrote to Austen, by 'an unconquerable desire of producing something great and lasting,' and he seems to have indulged for a moment in the dream that he might become a supreme poet. He had achieved already no small reputation as a writer of prose fiction; in imagination, at all events, he had scaled the steepest heights of political ambition; and turning his thoughts to poetry he characteristically aimed at the highest. Let him tell the tale himself.

It was in the plains of Troy that I first conceived the idea of this work. Wandering over that illustrious scene, surrounded by the tombs of heroes and by the confluence of poetic streams, my musing thoughts clustered round the memory of that immortal song, to which all creeds and countries alike respond, which has vanquished Chance, and defies Time. Deeming myself, perchance too rashly, in that excited hour a Poet, I cursed the destiny that had placed me in an age that boasted of being anti-poetical. And while my Fancy thus struggled with my Reason, it flashed across my mind, like the lightning which was then playing over Ida, that in those great poems which rise, the pyramids of poetic art, amid the falling and the fading splendour of less creations, the Poet hath ever embodied the spirit of his Time. Thus the most heroick incident of an heroick age produced in the *Iliad* an Heroick Epick; thus the consolidation of the most superb of Empires produced in the *Aeneid* a Political Epick; the revival of learning and the birth of vernacular genius presented us in the *Divine Comedy* with a National Epick; and the Reformation and its consequences called from the rapt lyre of Milton a Religious Epick.

And the spirit of my time, shall it alone be uncelebrated?

Standing upon Asia, and gazing upon Europe, with the broad Hellespont alone between us, and the shadow of night descending on the mountains, these mighty continents appeared to me, as it were, the rival principles of government that, at present, contend for the mastery of the world. 'What!' I exclaimed, 'is the revolution of France a less important event than the siege of Troy? Is Napoleon a less interesting character than Achilles? For me remains the Revolutionary Epick.'[1]

To the development of this great conception he now accordingly applied himself. 'I live here like a hermit, he writes to Mrs. Austen from Bradenham, 'and have scarcely seen my family. I rise at seven, and my day passes in study and composition.' A little later he is at Southend, staying 'at an old grange with gable ends and antique windows,' 'living solely on snipes and riding a good deal,' but still 'passing his days in constant composition.' By the beginning of December he is far enough advanced to set forth his argument.

To Mrs. Austen.

Dec. 1, 1833.

Since the revolt of America a new principle has been at work in the world to which I trace all that occurs. This is the Revolutionary principle, and this is what I wish to embody in the *Revolutionary Epick*. I imagine the Genius of Feudalism and the Genius of Federalism appearing before the Almighty Throne and pleading their respective and antagonistic causes. The pleading of the Feudal Genius, in which I say all that can be urged in favour of the aristocratic system of society, forms

[1] Preface to the *Revolutionary Epick*.

the first book : the pleading of the Federal, the second : the decree of the Omnipotent is mystical. It declares that a man is born of supernatural energies and that whichever side he embraces will succeed, or to that effect. The man is Napoleon just about to conquer Italy. The spirits descend to earth to join him. He adopts the Federal or Democratic side. The Feudal stirs up the Kings against him. Hence my machinery! The next two books contain the conquest of Italy, very little vulgar fighting but highly idealised. This is all—about 4,000 lines—that I shall now venture to print; the whole of it is matured in my mind, though probably it could not be completed under 30,000 lines. What do you think of it? The conception seems to me sublime. All depends on the execution. I have finished the three first books. The two first cost me much the most trouble; the rest is play work.

Mrs. Austen was still his literary Egeria. 'You appear,' he tells her, 'to be the only person in the world except myself who have any energy. What would I give to have you always at my right hand?' When he wants a description of Josephine he appeals to her. 'Are you sure that a Creole is dark? No matter, I will make her brunette. . . . I was introduced to the King of Spain and the Prince of Canino (Lucien) last year, but do not like to write to them.' Or again,

I have got a grand simile about a S. Wester, I think they call it: and am perfectly ignorant of the geography of the wind and have no atlas here. I mean that wind that blows, I think, about the Cape and knocks the Honourable Company's ships about. Daniel has a famous picture about it, consisting of one ship and one wave. Is it a S. Wester that I mean, and whence does it blow, and all about it? Get it up for the 16th.

On the 16th of January he was to dine with the Austens, and he promised to put a canto of his work in his bag and if they were alone 'to perform the part of the Importunate Author and bore them with a grand recitation.' They were not alone, but the grand recitation was given all the same. 'There was something irresistibly comic,' writes an eye-witness[1] of the scene that followed, 'in the young man dressed in the fantastic, coxcombical costume

[1] Sir Henry Layard in the *Quarterly Review* for January, 1889.

that he then affected—velvet coat of an original cut thrown wide open, and ruffles to its sleeves, shirt collars turned down in Byronic fashion, an elaborately embroidered waistcoat whence issued voluminous folds of frill, and shoes adorned with red rosettes—his black hair pomatumed and elaborately curled, and his person redolent with perfume—announcing himself as the Homer or Dante of the age.' Thus arrayed, and standing with his back to the fire, our poet unfolded in grandiloquent language his great conception; and he then declaimed in pretentious tones the whole of his first canto. But unfortunately for the effect produced he had no sooner left the room than Samuel Warren,[1] who was present, recited in perfect mimicry of style and voice and manner a number of heroic verses improvised for the occasion; and the company, which had no doubt been hovering between admiration and amusement, hardly knowing whether to regard the poem as a work of genius or of coxcombry, settled the question at once by going into fits of laughter.

The *Epick* was published in the spring of 1834, the first book separately in March, the second and third together in June. 'My poem turns out a terrible labor,' he wrote to Austen on the eve of publication, but presently added with some complacency:—

I have executed the work to my satisfaction and, what is of more importance, to the satisfaction of my father, a critic difficult to please. I await the great result with composure, though I am not sanguine of pleasing the million. I feel that I have now done enough for my reputation and that I am at length justified in merely looking to my purse.

The preface showed more becoming diffidence:—

I have ventured to submit to the public but a small portion of my creation, and even that with unaffected distrust and sincere humility. Whatever may be their decision I shall

[1] Author of *Ten Thousand a Year*.

bow to it without a murmur ; for I am not one who find consolation for the neglect of my contemporaries in the imaginary plaudits of a more sympathetic posterity. The public will then decide whether this work is to be continued and completed ; and if it pass in the negative, I shall, without a pang, hurl my lyre to Limbo.

The reading public gave the would-be successor of Homer, Virgil, Dante, and Milton no encouragement, and with or without a pang he accordingly 'hurled his lyre to Limbo'; though not, it would seem, at once. Thirty years later, when the poem had long been buried, the stress of political controversy brought it to the light again. In debate in the House of Commons in 1864 Disraeli had occasion to denounce certain well-known opinions of Mazzini's ; whereupon Mr. Bright retorted that if what he had somewhere read was true Disraeli himself in one of his earlier works had propounded doctrines not dissimilar in tendency. The statement was at once denied and the denial accepted : but some lines of swelling rhetoric were subsequently quoted in the newspapers from the *Revolutionary Epick* and eagerly repeated to prove that in his youth the Conservative leader had advocated regicide. Disraeli might very well have followed his usual practice and laughed at the charge, the more so as the lines in question,[1] occurring in the rival pleadings before the throne of Demogorgon, could no more be held with justice to incriminate the author than Milton could be held responsible for every sentiment

[1] They have a double dramatic shelter in their place in the poem, being quoted by Lyridon as the utterance of the maiden Opinion. In the orignal edition the passage runs :—

Pharaoh's doom
Shall cool those chariot wheels now wet with blood,
And blessed be the hand that dares to wave
The regicidal steel that shall redeem
A nation's sorrow with a tyrant's blood.

In the edition of 1864 this became

Dark Pharaoh's doom
Shall cool your chariot wheels, and hallowed be
The regicidal steel that shall redeem
A nation's woe.

—Bk. II. sect. 22.

of the fallen spirits in the debate in *Paradise Lost*: but he chose instead to make the incident the occasion for a new edition of the poem with substantial variations from the original, and in a dedicatory address to Lord Stanley prefixed to this edition he thus explained the variations :—

> The *Revolutionary Epick* is printed from the only copy in my possession, and which, with slight exceptions, was corrected in 1837, when, after three years' reflection, I had resolved not only to correct but to complete the work. The corrections are purely literary. The somewhat sudden accession of her Most Gracious Majesty occasioned in that year a dissolution of Parliament, and being then returned to the House of Commons, in which I have since sat without an interval, these dreams for ever vanished.

No one who has read *Contarini* will think it strange that the dreams should have visited him. Disraeli was indeed something of a poet, though his proper medium was neither the prose poetry of *Alroy* nor the heroic verse of the *Revolutionary Epick*. 'I am only truly great in action'; when he wrote that, his insight into character did not fail him. He carried into the field of action, indeed, a good deal of the spirit of the poet and the artist, but action was his true province all the same. For supreme greatness in the field of creative literature he had neither the self-restraint nor the self-devotion that are needed; and though he could make verses, he had none of the peculiar and divine gift which gives to verses the quality of lasting poetry. No one need be surprised then at the failure of the *Epick*. The conception, if not, according to his own word, sublime, has a certain largeness which a happier execution might have raised to the pitch of grandeur, and which even as it is gives an air of spaciousness to the poem. But the execution, on which, as he saw, all would depend, falls far short of the conception. Disraeli's verse is fluent, but where we look for poetry we find only the dull and cloudy rhetoric into which a man invariably falls who writes poetry not because he must, but because he thinks it a fine thing to do. There is a brave pretence of poetic rapture, but rarely any gleam of genuine inspiration; a succession of brilliant fancies clothed in eloquent language, image piled upon image with gorgeous though bewildering prodigality; but nowhere the passionate thought that goes direct to the heart, or the inevitable phrase that lingers by its beauty in the memory. Where we find merit in the verse it is usually a merit that reflects the writer's studies in poetry rather than his own native gift. Take, for instance, the following description of Athens from the second book:—

A city like the dream of youthful bard,
Reposing in the shade of summer trees,
And pressing to his eyes his magic hand,
To call up visions of a fairer world:
Blue ocean, bowery plain, and azure sky,
And marble walls, and free-born citadel,
Glittering with snowy columns in the sun;
Statues of ivory, tablets like the blaze
Of the far-flashing twilight of the land;
And choral theatres, where the Poet's voice
Blends with the whisper of the delicate air,
The messenger of nature to his soul;
And gardens of delight, in whose green glades
And fragrant groves, or by the mossy verge
Of sparkling fountain or serener stream,
Conversing Sages teach to genial youth
Ennobling precepts; to be wise and free,
Refined and virtuous, is their theme sublime;
Or for the high and passionate hour prepare,
When from the Bema's all-subduing throne
A voice may sway the fortunes of a world!
Divine Equality, thou art a God
Omnipotent indeed! Thy sacred fire
Burns now in later temples, not to fall
Like thine old shrines; yet who can e'er forget,
Whose soul indeed thy noble faith inflames,
Thy broken altar on Athena's hill!

We feel at once that our poet has studied his Milton and is engaged in a vain endeavour to mimic him. Original as was his genius, Disraeli was always a liberal borrower, both from others and himself; and here, whether he is at his best or at his worst, he is invariably imitative. He had early been a devoted student of Shelley, and if the diction and versification of the poem are feebly reminiscent of Milton, the matter and machinery, and often even the sentiment, are still more reminiscent of Shelley, though unfortunately of Shelley in his least inspired moments. The word Demogorgon, which meets us in the opening lines, recalls Shelley at once, and in the first two books we have not only Demogorgon and the rival genii Magros and Lyridon, but a bewildering mixture of subordinate agents, Faith and Fealty, Religion and Loyalty, the Monster Change, the beautiful maiden Opinion, daughter of Physical and Moral Strength, and so forth—all vague impersonations in the Shelleyan manner, but not, alas! the manner of *Prometheus* or *Adonais*.

'Standing upon Asia and gazing upon Europe, . . . these mighty continents appeared to me as it were the Rival Principles of Government that at present contend for the mastery of the world.' What is still of profound interest in the poem to the student of Disraeli is the development of this contention between Asia and Europe which forms its essential subject. In his choice of the poetical form for the clothing of his thoughts there was no doubt a large element of pose, with the result that he produced poetry which is rhetorical, imitative, and, in a sense, insincere. But in his choice of the subject itself there was no insincerity. The conflict between Asia and Europe and all that they symbolise ran through Disraeli's life, as it runs through the poem, and never wholly found an issue in the triumph of either principle or in their harmonious reconcilement. 'My mind is a revolutionary mind': that was true, and perhaps especially true when it was written and when the *Revolutionary Epick* was conceived. Disraeli had been fascinated by the great drama in which the modern spirit was unfolding itself, and hence we get in the *Epick* the triumph of the 'Federal' side and the apotheosis of Napoleon. The third book closes with Napoleon's entry into Milan; but if the poem had been continued one wonders how the action could ever have been brought to a climax or to any natural conclusion. It is safe indeed to assume that even if Disraeli had received the encouragement which he looked for, he could never have completed the *Epick*; as in the case of *Vivian Grey* or *Contarini Fleming*, the impulse of creation must before long have spent itself and the current of his story have lost itself in shallows. He was able to remain at ease with his revolutionary theme through the space of a book or more, but he could not long have pursued it without acute spiritual discomfort. Revolutionary as he really was on one side of his complex nature, there was another side which is exposed in the first book of the *Epick* and which was to be the front presented to the world in his subsequent career. Reverence for the past, a Semitic feeling for religion, an instinct for the positive, for order, for tradition, for everything that Carlyle embodies in the phrase 'the everlasting yea'—all these things were strong within him, and it was in their development and expression and not in the *rôle* of revolutionary leader that his mission really lay. Yet to the end the revolutionary side was there; and it is just because Disraeli never lost his sympathy with the modern spirit, never felt any of that timorous shrinking from new political ideals which afflicts Conservatives of a narrower type, that his conservatism is so sane, so robust, and so fruitful; without forgetting the things which are behind he is always found reaching forth unto the things which are before.

To Sarah Disraeli.

THE GRANGE, SOUTHEND,
Thursday. [*Feb.* 13, 1834.]

MY DEAR CHILD,

Although I have only half a sheet in my desk, you shall not be a loser thereby. I continue here quite alone, my only companion little Eva, who with her golden locks and rosy cheeks is a most beautiful child, and prattles without ceasing. The Sykes have not returned, and their return is indefinite, for the Baronet is very unwell, and confined to his room.

Solitude at this moment suits me very well. The book surpasses all my hopes, but so little of the original sketch remains that you will scarcely recognise it. Assure my father that it is not now at all like Pye, which he seemed to fear. I think of dedicating it to the Duke in a long political prose ; if so, I shall request his permission ; but upon this dedication I have not determined.

Montagu Gore has accepted the Chiltern Hundreds, and asked me to stand for Devizes, which I have refused. Any place but Parliament at present. The time will, however, come, and is coming speedily. Gore, according to his address, resigns for two reasons ; his health, and also because he has recanted and turned Tory ! His health and head seem equally weak. He is an ass, who has terminated an asinine career with a very characteristic bray.

I hunted the other day with Sir Henry Smythe's hounds, and although not in scarlet was the best mounted man in the field, riding Lady Sykes's Arabian mare, which I nearly killed, a run of 30 miles, and I stopped at nothing. I gained great *kudos*. The only Londoner I met was Henry Manners Sutton, who had come over to cover from Mistley Hall. He asked me to return with him, but as Lady Manners was not there, I saw no fun, and refused.

Write directly. Love to all,

Your affectionate D.

I told you, I believe, that Mrs. Norton had given me her portrait.

From the Duke of Wellington.

STRATHFIELDSAYE,
March 7, 1834.

SIR,

I am really much flattered by your desire to dedicate to me by permission your Epic Poem.

Unfortunately I found myself under the necessity twenty years ago of determining that I would never give a formal permission that any work should be dedicated to me. I will not trouble you with the reasons for this determination. They were founded upon a sense of the necessity for this course, or for the adoption of another—viz., that I should peruse every work which it was wished that I should give permission that it should be dedicated to me, before I should grant the required permission. This last alternative was impracticable; and I have found myself under the painful necessity in many instances, as in this, of declining to give such formal permission.

If, however, you should think proper to dedicate your poem to me without such formal permission, you are at full liberty to take that course[1]; assuring you at the same time that I feel greatly flattered by the expression of your desire that I should permit it,

I have the honour to be, Sir

Your most obedient humble servant,

WELLINGTON.

The *Epick* off his mind, Disraeli plunged with renewed zest into the dissipations of society.

May, 1834.

On Monday I dined with Lady Blessington—the Prince of Moskova, Charles Lafitte, Lords Castlereagh, Elphinstone, and Allen, Mr. Talbot, myself; and Lord Wilton was the absent guest, having to dine with the King, but he came in the evening. He is very handsome. Hope's ball on Monday was the finest thing this year—supped off gold and danced in the sculpture gallery. To-day is the Drawing-room; but nobody thinks of anything but politics. I dine with O'Connell on Saturday.[2]

Disraeli, as has been seen, had met Count D'Orsay, 'the famous Parisian dandy,' at a reception at Bulwer's a couple of years before, but this is the first time we hear of an acquaintance with Lady Blessington. Still in the fulness of her mature beauty, she had now been a widow for several years, and her house in Seamore Place, though shunned by the great ladies of society, had become a meeting ground for most of the social, literary, and political celebrities of the day. D'Orsay, the husband of her stepdaughter, had succeeded after an interval to the empire of Brummell and was now at the height of his fame as leader of the dandies, arbiter of fashion, and gambler and

1 The poem appeared without a dedication.

2 *Letters*, p. 85.

spendthrift. With both him and Lady Blessington Disraeli soon formed an intimate and enduring friendship.

June 4, 1834.

I was at Lady Dudley Stuart's on Sunday—a pleasant circle—and made the acquaintance of Lord Hertford.[1] I dine with Lady Cork to-day, to meet the Mulgraves, Tavistocks, and Lincolns.

June 16.

I made Beckford's acquaintance at the Opera on Thursday. Conversation of three hours [he adds in the Mutilated Diary]; very bitter and *malin*, but full of warm feelings for the worthy.

I dined yesterday with Lady Blessington, and Durham among the guests, and he talked to me nearly the whole evening; afterwards to Lady Salisbury's.[2]

A gossiping American journalist was one of the guests at this last dinner and wrote an account of it in his paper a few years later when Durham had crossed the Atlantic for his memorable work in Canada.

The guests dropped in, announced but unseen, in the dim twilight, and when Lord Durham came, I could only see that he was of middle stature, and of a naturally cold address. Bulwer spoke to him, but he was introduced to no one—a departure from the custom of that *maison sans gêne*, which was either a tribute to his Lordship's reserve or a ruse on the part of Lady Blessington to secure to Disraeli the advantage of having his acquaintance sought: successful, if so, for Lord Durham after dinner requested a formal introduction to him. But for D'Orsay, who sparkles, as he does everything else, out of rule, and in splendid defiance of others' dullness, the soup and first half hour of dinner would have passed off with the usual English fashion of earnest silence. . . . Bulwer and Disraeli were silent altogether. I should have foreboded a dull dinner if in the open brow, and clear sunny eye, and unembarrassed repose of the beautiful and expressive mouth of Lady Blessington I had not read the promise of a change.

It came presently. With a tact of which the subtle ease and grace can in no way be conveyed into description,

[1] The 'Lord Monmouth' of *Coningsby* and the 'Lord Steyne' of *Vanity Fair*.

[2] *Letters*, p. 86.

she gathered up the cobweb threads of conversation going on at different parts of the table, and, by the most apparent accident, flung them into Disraeli's fingers. It was an appeal to his opinion on a subject he well understood, and he burst at once, without preface, into that fiery vein of eloquence which, hearing many times after, and always with new delight, has stamped Disraeli in my mind as the most wonderful talker I have ever had the fortune to meet. He is anything but a declaimer. You would never think him on stilts. If he catches himself in a rhetorical sentence, he mocks at it in the next breath. He is satirical, contemptuous, pathetic, humorous, everything in a moment. Add to this that Disraeli's is the most intellectual face in England—pale, regular, and overshadowed with the most luxuriant masses of raven-black hair, and you will scarce wonder that meeting him for the first time Lord Durham was impressed. . . . Disraeli and he formed at the moment a finely-contrasted picture. Understanding his game perfectly, the author deferred constantly and adroitly to the opinion of his noble listener, shaped his argument by his suggestions, allowed him to say nothing without using it as the nucleus of some new turn to his eloquence, and all this with an apparent effort against it, as if he had desired to address himself exclusively to Lady Blessington, but was compelled by a superior intellectual magnetism to turn aside to pay homage to her guest. . . . Without meaning any disrespect to Disraeli, whom I admire as much as any man in England, I remarked to my neighbour, a celebrated artist, that it would make a glorious drawing of Satan tempting an archangel to rebel.

Well, Disraeli is in Parliament, and Lord Durham on the last round but one of the ladder of subject greatness. The Viceroy will be Premier, no doubt, but it is questionable if the author of *Vivian Grey* does more than carry out the moral of his own tale. Talking at a brilliant table, with an indulgent and superb woman on the watch for wit and eloquence, and rising in the face of a cold, commonsense House of Commons on the look out for froth and humbug, are two different matters. In a great crisis, with the nation in a tempest, Disraeli would flash across the darkness very finely, but he will never do for the calm right hand of a Premier.[1]

[1] N. P. Willis—known among his countrymen, for reasons which any reader of the above excerpt will understand, as 'Namby Pamby' Willis—in the *New York Mirror* for Aug. 11, 1838.

This testimony as to Disraeli's powers of conversation is confirmed in a less exuberant manner by another witness. 'I frequently met Mr. Disraeli at Lady Blessington's,' writes her biographer.

Though in general society he was habitually silent and reserved, he was closely observant. It required generally a subject of more than common interest to produce the fitting degree of enthusiasm to animate him and to stimulate him into the exercise of his marvellous powers of conversation. When duly excited, however, his command of language was truly wonderful, his power of sarcasm unsurpassed; the readiness of his wit, the quickness of his perception, the grasp of mind that enabled him to seize on all the parts of any subject under discussion, those only would venture to call in question who had never been in his company at the period I refer to.[1]

To Sarah Disraeli.

June 19, 1834.

I was at the Duchess of St. Albans on Monday, but rather too late for the fun. It was a most brilliant *fête*. The breakfast a real banquet; but I missed the Morris dancers, &c. In the evening at Lady Essex, where the coterie consisted of the new Postmaster-General and his lady, the Chesterfields, George Ansons, and Albert Conynghams, and Castlereagh. Tuesday after the Opera I supped with Castlereagh, who gave a very *recherché* party. Ossulston,[2] myself, Massey Stanley, and a Forester, not Cecil. Wednesday a good dinner at Lady Sykes: to-night, after paying my respects to their Majesties at the Opera, I am going to the Duchess of Hamilton's.

I have had great success in society this year in every respect. . . . I make my way easily in the highest set, where there is no envy, malice, &c., and where they like to admire and be amused. Yesterday Lord Durham called upon me, being the first day he has been in town since we met. I was not at home; but this Lady Blessington told me. I am also right in politics as well as society, being now backed by a very powerful party, and I think the winning one.

A good story! On Monday, I think, Lady Sykes was at Lady Cork's, and Lord Carrington paid her a visit.

[1] Madden's *Countess of Blessington*, III., p. 81.

[2] Castlereagh was afterwards 4th Marquis of Londonderry and Ossulston 6th Earl of Tankerville.

Lady C.: Do you know young Disraeli ?

Lord C.: Hem! Why ? Eh ?

Lady C.: Why, he is your neighbour, isn't he, eh ?

Lord C.: His father is.

Lady C.: I know that. His father is one of my dearest friends. I dote on the Disraelis.

Lord C.: The young man is a very extraordinary sort of person. The father I like; he is very quiet and respectable.

Lady C.: Why do you think the young man extraordinary ? I should not think that *you* could taste him.

Lord C.: He is a great agitator. Not that he troubles us much *now*. He is never amongst us now. I believe he has gone abroad again.

Lady C., *literatim*: You old fool! Why, he sent me this book this morning. You need not look at it; you can't understand it. It is the finest book ever written. Gone abroad, indeed! Why, he is the best *ton* in London! There is not a party that goes down without him. The Duchess of Hamilton says there is nothing like. Lady Lonsdale would give her head and shoulders for him. He would not dine at your house if you were to ask him. He does not care for people because they are lords; he must have fashion, or beauty, or wit, or something: and you are a very good sort of person, but you are nothing more.

The old Lord took it very good-humoredly, and laughed. Lady Cork has read every line of the new book. I don't doubt the sincerity of her admiration, for she has laid out 17s. in crimson velvet, and her maid is binding it. . . .

D.

Monday morning. [*July* 7.]

My dearest,

I have quite recovered, but I am taking quinine and shall yet for a few days. I was very unwell unto Friday evening. I had promised to join a water party in Sir Frank's yacht, which has returned without its master, to witness the Royal embarkation on Saturday morning, and the exertion, which I dreaded, cured me. It was almost the only party of pleasure that ever turned out pleasant. Lady Sykes and Sir M. and Lady Georgiana Cholmely, the Burdett daughters, Castlereagh, Ossulston, and myself. The day was beautiful. The ladies went off the night before. Ossulston drove me down in his cab. We arrived just in time, half past 9, in spite of a long debate on tithes, which had kept him and Cas. up till

2. Cas. rode down and arrived covered with dust and sulky, but just in time also ; and regained his good humor after breakfast. After the show we breakfasted, and sailed up to Greenwich. After lionising the hospital and sentimentalising in the Park, we had a magnificent banquet on deck, and had nothing from shore except whitebait piping hot. Ossulston was our minstrel, and a most musical one ; and we all arrived in town in time for the ballet. I never knew a more agreeable day, and never drank so much champagne in my life. I woke, quite well, and, after a very dull dinner party at the Wyndham Lewis's, went to Lady Salisbury's. So you see I am on my legs again. I am sorry for dear Jem, but he has many fellow-sufferers. The influenza, however, is not so severe as last year.

My love to all.

Your own D.

Ossulston asked me to allow him to put me up for Crockford's. I told him that I was sure I should be blackballed ; but he was sanguine of the reverse, and is to consult his friends.

Disraeli was not elected to Crockford's, the famous gaming house in St. James's Street, till 1840, shortly before the retirement of the founder and the consequent dissolution of the club. Another social institution of the day was Almack's, a periodical subscription ball held at Willis's Rooms and presided over by an oligarchy of fashionable ladies, who wielded their powers with a jealous and vigilant exclusiveness.

To Sarah Disraeli.

July 11, 1834.

I made my *début* at Almack's with a subscription from Lady Tankerville,[1] but it was not a very brilliant *réunion*. Yesterday I met Lord Lyndhurst, whom I like very much. The next time he goes the Norfolk circuit he is to sleep at Bradenham. He says the Duke of Wellington never reads any book but the *Commentaries*,[2] and assured me it was a positive fact !

[1] Daughter of Antoine Duc de Gramont and sister of the Duc de Gramont who married Count Alfred D'Orsay's sister.

[2] Isaac D'Israeli's *Commentaries on the Life and Reign of Charles the First*.

July 23.

I still adhere to my plan of being down with you in a week or ten days, and tell Tita to get my pipes in order, as I look forward to a batch of smoking with great zest.

I go every day to fêtes and water parties. Lady Tavistock's at Richmond on Saturday. Monday, another party to Blackwall with D'Orsay. To-morrow to Lord Hertford's. I find the end of the season more fatiguing than the beginning, owing to the morning festivities.

The water party at the 'Cedars' most delightful. We embarked at five o'clock, the heavens very favourable, sang all the way down, wandered in beautiful gardens worthy of Paul Veronese full not only of flowers, but fountains and parroquets : the dinner first-rate and much better than cold, miserable picnics, in which all bring the same things. People are still in town, but Goodwood will, I think, clear us.[1]

'You give me the same advice as my father ever has done,' he wrote on some occasion to Lady Blessington, 'about dotting down the evanescent feelings of youth; but, like other excellent advice, I fear it will prove unprofitable. I have a horror of journalising, and indeed of writing of all description. With me execution is ever a labour and conception a delight. Although a great traveller, I never kept a diary in my life.' His book of jottings and reflections, if we are not to call it a diary, had been forgotten since October, but in the seclusion of Bradenham he returned to it once more.

BRADENHAM,
Aug. 4, 1834.

And now nearly a year has elapsed. And what an eventful one ! Let me sketch it. The end of 1833 and spring of 1834 passed in Essex, writing the three first books of the *Revolutionary Epick* : returned to Bradenham before Easter, then to town and remained there until this moment. A season of unparalleled success and gaiety. What a vast number of extraordinary characters have passed before me or with whom I have become acquainted. Interviews with O'Connell, Beckford, and Lord Durham, three men all making a great noise. Will they be remembered when this book turns up, if ever it do ? Perhaps O'Connell. The first [he

[1] *Letters*, pp. 87, 88.

added in a letter to his sister] is the man of the greatest genius; the second of the greatest taste; and the last of the greatest ambition.

Conversation of three hours with O'Connell, next whom I sat at dinner. Very communicative. Said that from being the son of a gentleman farmer he had raised himself to be *une des puissances du monde* (his very words). Said that the Clare Election was the most nervous moment of his life. I think he said he did not sleep a wink for three days. Had he failed he would have been ridiculous for life. Did not determine on the step until he had tried every country gentleman favorable to the Catholics. Two days after the election a legal flaw was detected in the registration of his voters by which, had it been discovered in time, his majority, and much more, would have been cut off.

How sorry I am that I did not keep some record of the last four months. I revived my acquaintance with the Sheridans, with whom I was so intimate last year, Mrs. Norton, Helen Blackwood, Lady Seymour—three matchless sisters, and the mother and Lady Graham.

Mrs. Norton's house was the scene of the famous encounter with Lord Melbourne, of which the story has been so often told.

It was in 1834 that I met Lord Melbourne at Storey's Gate and was introduced to him. Lord Melbourne asked how he could advance me in life, and half proposed that I should be his private secretary, enquiring what my object in life might be. 'To be Prime Minister.' It was then that Lord Melbourne, with a gravity not common with him, set to work to prove to me how vain and impossible to realise, in those days, was this ambition. It was a long speech, and I think I could repeat every word of it still.

So Disraeli himself told the story to Lord Rowton, and Melbourne's biographer supplies what is missing. Lord Grey, it will be borne in mind, had not yet resigned, and Melbourne was still Home Secretary. Disraeli was presented to him after dinner, and the two had a long conversation.

The Minister was attracted more and more as he listened to the uncommonplace language and spirit of the youthful politician, and thought to himself he would be well worth serving. Abruptly, but with a certain tone of kindness which took away any air of assumption, he said, 'Well now, tell me, what do you want to be?' The quiet gravity of the reply fairly took him aback—'I want to be Prime Minister.' Melbourne gave a long sigh, and then said very seriously: 'No chance of that in our time. It is all arranged and settled. Nobody but Lord Grey could perhaps have carried the Reform Bill; but he is an old man, and when he gives up, he will certainly be succeeded by one who has every requisite for the position, in the prime of life and fame, of old blood, high rank, great fortune, and greater ability. Once in power, there is nothing to prevent him holding office as long as Sir Robert Walpole. Nobody can compete with Stanley. I heard him the other night in the Commons, when the party were all divided and breaking away from their ranks, recall them by the mere force of superior will and eloquence: he rose like a young eagle above them all, and kept hovering over their heads till they were reduced to abject submission. There is nothing like him. If you are going into politics and mean to stick to it, I daresay you will do very well, for you have ability and enterprise; and if you are careful how you steer, no doubt you will get into some port at last. But you must put all these foolish notions out of your head; they won't do at all. Stanley will be the next Prime Minister, you will see.'[1]

There is a sequel to the story which is not so well known. Melbourne lived till near the close of 1848; and when, after the death of Lord George Bentinck and shortly before his own, he heard of Disraeli's approaching elevation to the leadership of the Tory party in the House of Commons, he exclaimed in some excitement, 'By God! the fellow will do it yet.'

I have become this year [the diary resumes] very popular with the dandies. D'Orsay took a fancy to me, and they take their tone from him. Lady Blessington is their muse, and she declared violently in my favor. I am as popular with first-rate men as I am hated by the second-rate: D'Orsay, Massey Stanley, Talbot, Marquis of Worcester. Revived my acquaintance with Angerstein,[2] who thought I meant to cut him—an error! I am very blind.

[1] Torrens's *Life of Melbourne*, p. 275.
[2] His second, it will be remembered, in the affair with Lord Nugent.

What a happy or rather amusing society H[enrietta][1] and myself commanded this year. What delicious little suppers after the Opera! Castlereagh ever gay, a constant attendant, and Ossulston, the pet of all the women, with his beautiful voice. What a singular character is Ossulston. He requires studying. Then we made it a point always to have some very pretty women. Charles Mathews ever there. Inimitable mime! His animal spirits are extraordinary. Landseer (Edwin), Grantley Berkeley, Seymour de Constant. This last hero reminds me of that extraordinary woman Lady Dudley Stuart[2] and she again of her family—most of whom I know, Lucien Prince of Canino, Joseph Count of Survilliers. Lady Dudley's little son, like the Emperor. And Lord Dudley must not be forgotten with his handsome melancholy face, and then Lady Tankerville and her lovers. How much I could write of this singular coterie! But this is a mem. which will recall them perhaps to my memory.

Old Lady Salisbury and old Lady Cork. Met the Duke of Wellington at Lady Cork's in his blue ribbon the eve of the day Lord Grey resigned. 'He always wears his blue ribbon when mischief is going on,' whispered Ossulston to me.

Rogers hates me. I can hardly believe, as he gives out, that V.G. is the cause. Considering his age I endeavoured to conciliate him, but it is impossible. I think I will give him cause to hate me. When Shee was elected P.R.A. Rogers (his friend) said it was the greatest compliment ever paid to *Literature*.

Lord Wilton and his Italian. The story I thought too good but I believe *true*.

{ Come sto Signor Rubini }
{ Come sta Signora Grisi }

Dined with him at Lady B.'s.

Lady Blessington and Lady Manners Sutton [her sister]. The Speaker appeared to me a *bête* when I was introduced to him by his wife.

Long conversation with Lord Lyndhurst. He said that if he were to choose a career *now* it would to be at once editor and proprietor of a firstrate newspaper.

To Lady Blessington.

BRADENHAM HOUSE,
Aug. 5. [1834.]

I was so sorry to leave London without being a moment alone with you; but although I came to the Opera last night on

[1] See below, p. 339. [2] Daughter of Lucien Bonaparte.

purpose, Fate was against us. I did not reach this place until Sunday, very ill indeed from the pangs of parting. Indeed, I feel as desolate as a ghost, and I do not think that I ever shall be able to settle to anything again. It is a great shame, when people are happy together, that they should be ever separated; but it seems the great object of all human legislation that people never should be happy together.

My father I find better than I expected, and much cheered by my presence. I delivered him all your kind messages. He is now very busy on his History of English Literature, in which he is far advanced. I am mistaken if you will not delight in these volumes. They are full of new views of the history of our language, and indeed of our country, for the history of a State is necessarily mixed up with the history of its literature.

For myself, I am doing nothing. The western breeze favors an *al fresco* existence, and I am seated with a pipe under a spreading sycamore, solemn as a pasha.

I wish you would induce Hookham to entrust me with *Agathon*,[1] that mad Byronic novel.

What do you think of the modern French novelists, and is it worth my while to read them, and if so, what do you recommend me? What of Balzac, is he better than Sue and Geo: Sand Dudevant and are these inferior to Hugo? I ask you these questions because you will give me short answers, like all people who are masters of their subject.

I suppose it is vain to hope to see my dear D'Orsay here; I wish indeed he would come. Here is a cook by no means contemptible. He can bring his horses if he like, but I can mount him. Adieu, dear Lady Blessington, some day I will try to write you a more amusing letter; at present I am in truth ill and sad.[2]

BRADENHAM HOUSE,
Friday, Aug. 15. [1834.]

MY DEAR LADY BLESSINGTON,

I have been very unwell, or I should sooner have acknowledged the receipt of your kind letter. I can assure you that your friendship is a great consolation to me. The change of life was too sad and sudden. Indeed I am quite at a loss how to manage affairs in future as I find separation more irksome than even my bitterest imagination predicted. God however is great, and the future must regulate itself, for I can't. I

[1] A translation from the German of Wieland.

[2] From Mr. Alfred Morrison's collection of autograph letters.

have done nothing but scribble one day a third part of *The Infernal Marriage* with which fantasy Colburn pretends now to be much pleased. I suppose your letter is at the bottom of his rapture.

I am delighted with *Agathon*. It left me musing which is a test of a great work. I invariably close one in a reverie. Wieland indeed always delights me. I sympathise with him much. There is a wild Oriental fancy blended with his Western philosophy which is a charming union. I like a moral to peep out of the wildest invention, to assure us that, while we have been amused, we have also all the time been growing a little wiser. The translation of the *Agathon* is very clumsy. I wish I could read it in the original but I have no talent for languages and invariably lose my command over English in an exact proportion as I gain any hold over another tongue. . . . My kind regards to his Highness, King Alfred: a wise man though not a Saxon.

Your faithful

D.

From Lady Blessington.

Aug. 20, 1834.

I am very sorry indeed to hear that you have been ill and sad; we are all but poor machines, easily put out of order, when the mind, or the heart, or both—for they always like true friends sympathise—are deranged or chagrined. What poor philosophers even the wisest of us are proved to be, when influenced by some master passion, and authors who, like yourself, can make others think, are among those who can the least govern their own thoughts, when once under the rule of love. Genius is, and must ever be, accompanied by passions proportionately strong, and I therefore reserve all my sympathies for its calamities, which is exactly the reverse of the practice of the world.

From Count D'Orsay.

[*Undated.*]

C'est une injustice que fait le cher Disraeli que de supposer qu'il ne peut approcher son ami que comme un Pacha à trois queues, chargé de présents orientaux. Ces chevaux arabes, ces sabres damas, ne sont que des présents matériels, mais lorsqu'il s'agit de dons spirituels, de ceux qu'une belle Nature seule peut engendre, c'est alors qu'il regrette de ne pas voir celui qui possède toute la vivacité et le feu du coursier arabien dans le caractère et le tranchant dans l'esprit du damas. Ces richesses sont les seules dont l'homme ait le droit de se glorifier et le cher Disraeli a donc extrêmement tort, d'être injuste envers cette belle Nature, qui a été si généreuse à son égard.

Son ami affectionné,

D'ORSAY.

To Lady Blessington.

BRADENHAM,

Friday. [*Oct.* 17, 1834.]

MY DEAR LADY BLESSINGTON,

. . . I sympathise with your sufferings; my experience unhappily assures me how ably you describe them. This golden autumn ought to have cured us all. I myself, in spite of the sunshine, have been a great invalid. Indeed, I know not how it is, but I am never well save in action, and then I feel immortal. I am ashamed of being 'nervous.' Dyspepsia always makes me wish for a civil war. In the meantime I amuse myself by county politics. . . .

My father sends his kindest regards. As for myself, I am dying for action, and rust like a Damascus sabre in the sheathe of a poltroon.

Adieu! dear friend, we shall meet on your return.

B. DISRAELI.[1]

To Benjamin Austen.

BRADENHAM,

Oct. 24, 1834.

I have been prevented in bringing out a novel [*Henrietta Temple*] in November by a strange illness which kept me to my sofa exactly two months. It was something of the kind of attack you experienced at Fyfield—great pain in the legs and extraordinary languor. It came upon me suddenly. I struggled against it for some time, but mounting my horse one day, I had a slight determination of blood to my head, and was obliged to throw myself on the floor of the hall. This frightened me, remembering old sufferings, and I laid up. Quiet, diet and plenteous doses of ammonia (heavenly maid!) not only restored me, but I have felt better and more hearty this last fortnight than I long remember.

[1] From Mr. Alfred Morrison's collection.

CHAPTER XIII.

JOINS THE CONSERVATIVES.

1834-35.

The last letters prepare us for another period of mainly political activity. Nearly two years had now elapsed since the second Wycombe election, and during that interval, while the politician slumbered in Disraeli, public events had been moving swiftly on. 'There is nothing more remarkable,' he writes in *Endymion*,[1] 'than the sudden break-up of the Whig party after their successful revolution of 1832. It is one of the most striking instances on record of all the elements of political power being useless without a commanding individual will.' Durham, whose place was at the extreme left of the party, had abandoned the Grey Ministry in March, 1833; Stanley and Graham at the extreme right had followed in May, 1834; and Lord Grey himself retired a couple of months later. Melbourne succeeded as Prime Minister; but in November his position was weakened by the succession of Lord Althorp to the peerage, and his consequent withdrawal from the House of Commons, of which he had been leader, and King William IV. seized the opportunity of dismissing his Ministers to make way for Peel and Wellington. During the crisis that followed the retirement of Stanley and

[1] Ch. 14

Graham, Disraeli had anticipated the course of events with curious prescience.

To Sarah Disraeli.

June 4, 1834.

There is a lull in the storm; it is supposed the session will now be hurried over quietly, and then something must be determined on. The Whigs cannot exist as a party without taking in Lord Durham, and the King will not consent to it. Durham is not in a hurry, and becomes each day more violent in his demands. Triennial Parliaments to be a Cabinet measure, and an extension of the constituency, the ballot to stand on its merits—in short, a revolution; for this must lead to a fatal collision with the House of Lords. The Tories will not take office unless the Whigs give it up in despair. My own opinion is, that in the recess the King will make an effort to try and form a Conservative Government with Peel and Stanley; but the Tories think that Durham will have his way. I fear a dissolution must be the end of it.[1]

Incidentally this letter reveals a growing estrangement on the part of the writer from the Radicalism of his first political campaigns: triennial Parliaments and the ballot, the nostrums which had figured so prominently in his earlier political programmes, had now come to spell 'a revolution.' Disraeli's acquaintance with Durham may have checked for a moment the progress of his conversion; but Durham's influence was soon overshadowed by the influence of another and more congenial spirit. At the end of the season, as has been seen, he had met Lord Lyndhurst, and their acquaintance soon ripened into a friendship which became a capital fact in Disraeli's life. Lyndhurst was already over sixty, but he had still nearly thirty years of life before him, and he was still in the full vigour of those splendid faculties which might have given him an even higher place among his contemporaries and in the eyes of posterity than that to which he attained, if he had only possessed in larger measure the power of inspiring confidence, which is so essential to the success of a states-

[1] *Letters*, p. 86.

man in England. But he suffered from a certain lack of seriousness, and the crowning gifts of lofty purpose and severe integrity were denied him.

To Sarah Disraeli.

Nov. 4, 1834.

I dined on Saturday with Lyndhurst *en famille*. A more amiable and agreeable family I never met. The eldest daughter, 'Sa,' is just like her mother, and, although only thirteen, rules everything and everybody—a most astounding little woman. Yesterday I went to see the new actor, Denvil. He is deplorable, has not the slightest feeling, nor one physical or mental qualification for the stage. I saw Chandos to-day, and had a long conversation with him on politics. He has no head, but I flatter myself I opened his mind a little. . . . D'Orsay has taken my portrait.[1]

Lord Chandos, as has been seen, was one of the members for Bucks; but, as the author or reputed author of the famous clause in the Reform Bill which enfranchised the agricultural occupiers, and as the recognised spokesman for the farmers in the House of Commons, he was a person of more than local importance. With his genius for intrigue Disraeli was not long in devising a plot in which his county member and his new friend Lyndhurst might be usefully combined. Let him tell the tale himself.[2]

I became acquainted with Lord L. at the latter end of the summer of 1834. We took to each other instantly. I sat next to him at dinner at Henrietta's. He went abroad in the autumn with a family party which he asked me to accompany, but I refused. On his return we again met with much intimacy. It was the latter end of October that he first began to speak to me in confidence on political affairs. It was his opinion at that moment that the end of Whiggism was at hand. The secession of the Stanley party, the subsequent intrigues of the Whigs with O'Connell and the consequent retirement of Lord Grey on their

[1] *Letters*, p. 88.

[2] What follows is from a memorandum inscribed over date 'Hughenden, 1863'—the year of Lyndhurst's death—'I cut this out of an old paper book. It was written at Bradenham in 1836, and is very authentic.' Its accuracy in certain points of detail is confirmed by contemporary letters from Lyndhurst and Chandos themselves.

BENJAMIN DISRAELI, 1834.
From a portrait by COUNT D'ORSAY.

[To face page 262.

discovery had reduced the mighty reform Parliament in spite of their apparently overwhelming majority to a very low ebb in public opinion; but the nation at large was impressed with an idea that from their reconstruction of the constituency they were our masters for life. I had then no political relations, though I had had overtures from Durham, who offered to return me to Parliament. I had conversation with him, but he appeared to me to have no definite plan. Lord L. thought the time had arrived when the movement might be stopped. He was looking about for a party to put in motion which might not seem factious. After some consultation he resolved that the Ministers should be thrown in a minority on some agricultural amendment at the meeting of Parliament, and I agreed to see Lord Chandos, with whom I had a county acquaintance, on the subject.

I went into the country therefore to attend some meeting of our agricultural committee. We agreed to petition Parliament on the Malt Tax, and I was requested to prepare the county petition to the House of Commons, which I did. After business was over I took Lord C. aside and it was settled that I should go over with him to Wotton and talk over affairs. The result of our conference was this—being, I think, the 11th November—that he undertook to organise a country party and throw the Government in a minority on Parliament meeting by an agricultural amendment on the address. He required for himself the First Lord of the Admiralty, but told me then that he was assured, from some communication he had received, that the Duke would recommend Peel as Premier. He made no terms for any other country leader except Knatchbull, who, he stipulated, should have a seat in the Cabinet.

In the evening of the 12th I arrived in town on my return and immediately had an interview with L. who told me the Duke of W. had arrived that day and that Lord Spencer was dead, which, by-the-bye, I had heard at Wotton as I was departing, Chandos hurrying my departure, as he said he thought this was the last blow to the Cabinet. Lord L. immediately wrote to the D. requesting an interview, and afterwards appointed me to meet him at his private room in the Exchequer[1] the morning of the 14th, at 2 o'clock, to hear the result. The Duke fixed the evening of the 13th for the interview, and I wrote to Lord C. accordingly.

Lord L. had accordingly his interview with the D. on the evening of the 13th, and opened his plan; but the D,

[1] Lyndhurst was Chief Baron.

threw cold water upon it. The interview finished thus :—'At this moment I will make no movements—to-morrow morning I depart for Strathfieldsaye. If the King is well advised he will now send for me—but I will not even be in London.' In spite of what occurred Lord L. does not believe that the D. was at the time in any communication with the Court. The D. accordingly departed for Strathfieldsaye the following morning, and I wrote to Lord C. notifying his Grace's refusal to concur in our plan, of which I had been apprised by Lord L. on the morning of the 14th. On the same day (the 14th) the Ministry were dismissed at Brighton, and a messenger arrived for the Duke at Apsley House. The letter was, I believe, brought up by Lord Melbourne himself. It was immediately forwarded to Strathfieldsaye.

15th Nov.—Dismissal of the Ministry publicly announced. The Duke at Brighton—whence he wrote to Lyndhurst, informing him that he had recommended H.M. to send for Peel, and requesting him to meet his Grace the following morning at Apsley House. This L. communicated to me in the evening. After that interview I met L. The Duke was in good spirits. He said 'It will be a month perhaps before he comes. All that we have got *to do now is to get the Government of the country into our hands*. I shall sit at the Treasury and take all the Secretary's seals; you must take the Great Seal—you and I must be the government of the country. Things are quiet, the people will not murmur.' Thus the government of the country was efficiently carried on, L. retaining his C[hief] B[aron]y and sitting also in the Chancery. Nobody murmured. The general opinion was that the Tories would succeed. Bonham calculated we might just get a Tory majority, but the chief hope was in the goodness of our measures and the impossibility of the Conservative Whigs *à la* Grey, &c., coalescing with Papists and Republicans. Lord L. was, however, in the habit of saying to me 'You will see that there will be a coalition of all parties against us.' 'You will see that these fellows will coalesce.'

Great was the suspense until Peel arrived. At last one evening we were informed that he had indeed come. The messenger, Mr. Hudson, a King's page, reached him at Rome, about to depart for Naples. P. immediately had an audience of the King and undertook the Government, and then interviews with the D. and L. He immediately offered the F. Secretary to the Duke and the Great Seal to L., who accepted it, though at a sacrifice. He then wrote to Lord

Stanley offering him four places in the Cabinet, at his choice, with the above exceptions. Never was such an offer before —never will it be made again. The refusal of Lord Stanley was expected, but it was not expected that the reason would have been his unwillingness to act with the D. on account of foreign policy. This was frivolous. Sir J[ames] G[raham] was inclined to join, but, of course, went with Lord S.

From this moment P. only consulted Goulburn, which astonished all and disgusted many. Sir H[enry] H[ardinge] was dissatisfied at being offered Ireland, which, however, he accepted. G[oulburn] was Secretary for Home; a very unpopular appointment. Lord Ashburton accepted the Board of Trade on the condition of being Lord Ashburton—a good name, but Mr. B[aring] has had no success in the Upper House. The man who gained most was Scarlett—a Chief [Barony of the Exchequer] and a peerage [as Lord Abinger] after having been apparently shelved. Chandos, entangled in our agricultural intrigues and pledged to the repeal of the Malt Tax, was obliged to decline office, as Peel would not consent to his panacea. Knatchbull was less nice and deserted the Country party.

The Cabinet was necessarily a weak one, and contained many feeble and some odious names. And yet never did a Cabinet mature such admirable and comprehensive measures! But all was owing to P. and L. The law appointments were excellent and popular. To the astonishment of Lord L. Sugden accepted the Irish Chancellorship. Before he offered it to him L. was prepared for an indignant refusal. Pollock was Attorney, a weak man but the leader of his circuit: the Solicitor, Follett, who had great success in the House as well as at the Bar, though the youngest Solicitor, I believe, ever appointed. So excellent were the projected measures of the Cabinet that with 300 Tories or Conservatives—for the Stanley section of 25 votes was counted among them—Lord L. became sanguine and thought that they had weathered the storm. The vote on the Speakership, however, opened all eyes, and after that no one could hesitate about the ultimate fate of the Cabinet. Had Lord S. joined, the movement would have been arrested: this junction would have been a golden bridge for rats, of which there were numbers who only wanted a leader.

This memorandum has anticipated—anticipated both in the order of the events which it narrates and still more in the point of view from which they are surveyed. When it was written, nearly two years later than the time our narrative has reached, Disraeli had definitely taken his place in the Tory ranks; at present all was confusion and unsettlement both for him and others.

It was a lively season, that winter of 1834! What hopes, what fears, and what bets! From the day on which Mr. Hudson was to arrive at Rome to the election of the Speaker, not a contingency that was not the subject of a wager! People sprang up like mushrooms; town suddenly became full. Everybody who had been in office, and everybody who wished to be in office; everybody who had ever had anything, and everybody who ever expected to have anything, were alike visible. All of course by mere accident; one might meet the same men regularly every day for a month, who were only 'passing through town.' . . .

But, after all, who were to form the government, and what was the government to be? Was it to be a Tory government, or an Enlightened-Spirit-of-the-Age Liberal-Moderate-Reform government; was it to be a government of high philosophy or of low practice; of principle or of expediency; of great measures or of little men? A government of statesmen or of clerks? Of Humbug or of Humdrum? Great questions these, but unfortunately there was nobody to answer them. They tried the Duke; but nothing could be pumped out of him. All that he knew, which he told in his curt, husky manner, was, that he had to carry on the King's government. As for his solitary colleague, he listened and smiled, and then in his musical voice asked them questions in return, which is the best possible mode of avoiding awkward inquiries. It was very unfair this, for no one knew what tone to take; whether they should go down to their public dinners and denounce the Reform Act or praise it; whether the Church was to be remodelled or only admonished; whether Ireland was to be conquered or conciliated.[1]

Disraeli, unlike the majority, was in no doubt at all as to his opinions; but he was still in great doubt as to his party affiliations, and, decided only in his hostility to the Whigs, was still straddling between the extremes

[1] *Coningsby*, Bk. II. ch. 4.

of Toryism on the one side and Radicalism on the other. The formation of the Peel Government had made a general election a certainty, and he was of course anxious to obtain a seat. 'I saw your son yesterday,' writes Bulwer to Isaac D'Israeli one day in the middle of November, 'restless and ambitious as usual: such dispositions always carve out their way.' The son was indeed determined to carve out his way, and restlessness and ambition marked all his conduct at this time of crisis. His first appeal appears to have been addressed to a high Radical quarter.

To Lord Durham.

BRADENHAM HOUSE, HIGH WYCOMBE,
Monday, Nov. 17, 1834.

MY DEAR LORD DURHAM,

My electioneering prospects look gloomy. The squires throughout my own county look grim at a Radical, and the Liberal interest is split and pre-engaged in our few towns, that I fear I shall fail. At present I am looking after Aylesbury, where young Hobhouse was beat last time, and will be beat this, if he try, but where, with my local influence, your party would succeed. If you have influence with Hobhouse, counsel him to resign in my favour, and not of another person, as 'tis rumoured he will. At the same time if Nugent return, he will beat us all. So my dear Lord, my affairs are black; therefore, remember me and serve me if you can. My principles you are acquainted with; as for my other qualifications, I am considered a great popular orator.

What do you think of the Tories! at a moment when decision and energy would be pearls and diamonds to them, they have formed a provisional Government! 'The voice of one crying in the wilderness, prepare ye the way of the—Lords.' Such is Wellington's solitary cry; a Baptist worthy of such a Messiah as—Peel.

In great haste,
Dear Lord Durham,
Your faithful,
BENJ. DISRAELI.[1]

Durham's reply was sympathetic. He had not, indeed, sufficient acquaintance with Hobhouse to justify

[1] Reid's *Life of Durham*, I., p. 408.

his interference at Aylesbury; but, he added, 'these are times which require the presence in Parliament of every true and honest politician. I trust and hope, therefore, that you will find your way there yet. If an occasion offers when I can forward your views I shall not fail to do so.' Disraeli, however, was in quest of something more substantial, and he soon turned to his friends at the opposite pole of politics.

To Sarah Disraeli.

Nov. 28, 1834.

The Duke and the Chancellor are besetting old Carrington in my favour, that they say he must yield. I am not sanguine, but was recommended to issue the address.[1] D'Orsay is working Bob Smith very hard. The Duke wrote a strong letter to the chairman of election committees, saying that if Wycombe were not insured something else must be done for Disraeli, as 'a man of his acquirements and reputation must not be thrown away.' L. showed me the letter, but it is impossible to say how things will go. *Entre nous*, Parliament will not be dissolved as speedily as is imagined, which is all in my favour, both as regards Wycombe or any other place. It is impossible for anyone to be warmer than the Duke or Lyndhurst, and I ought to say the same of Chandos.[2]

In spite of all these blandishments Lord Carrington and his son remained courteously obdurate, and Lyndhurst, foiled in this quarter, employed his good offices elsewhere, as the following entries in Greville's *Diary* show:—

Dec. 6, 1834.—The Chancellor called on me yesterday about getting young Disraeli into Parliament (through the means of George Bentinck) for Lynn. I had told him George wanted a good man to assist in turning out William Lennox, and he suggested the above-named gentleman, whom he called a friend of Chandos. His political principles must, however, be in abeyance, for he said that Durham was doing all he could to get him by the offer of a seat, and so forth; if therefore he is undecided and wavering between Chandos and Durham, he must be a mighty impartial personage. I

[1] To the electors of High Wycombe.

[2] *Letters*, p. 88.

don't think such a man will do, though just such as Lyndhurst would be connected with.

Dec. 7.—Disraeli he [George Bentinck] won't hear of.

Eventually Disraeli decided to enter on a third contest at Wycombe, the other candidates being his old opponents Smith and Grey. To Wycombe accordingly he repaired, and delivered[1] a long speech on the situation which he at once reissued as a pamphlet under the title of 'The Crisis Examined.' This speech has an important place in the story of Disraeli's political development. He begins with the usual assurance of the fixity of his principles. Since he last addressed them 'great revolutions have occurred—revolutions of government and revolutions of opinion: I can, however, assure you that I remain unchanged.' But as he cannot condescend, to obtain even the honour of a seat in Parliament 'by Jesuitical intrigue or casuistical cajolery,' as he 'cannot condescend at the same time to be supported by the Tories because they deem me a Tory, and by the Liberals because they hold me a Liberal,' he proceeds to unfold his programme as adapted to the new circumstances which have arisen. In the foreground stands relief for the agricultural interest, which is suffering from severe depression. 'We may hope that the Exchequer may grant them at least the partial relief of the malt tax, although I recommend them to petition for the whole. I would not at the same time make a request and intimate a compromise.' The popular cry of the country is Church Reform; but he dislikes that 'cant phrase,' and hopes to hear less of Church reform and more of Church improvement. Pluralities must be abolished, the great evil of non-residence must be terminated, and to achieve these all-important objects there must be an increase in 'the value of the lesser livings and the incomes in general of the inferior clergy.' Church reform leads him on to Ireland.

I deem it absolutely necessary, even for the existence of the Protestant Establishment itself, that the question of the

1 On Dec. 16.

Irish Church should be forthwith grappled with; that it should be the object of a measure in its nature as final, in its operation as conclusive, as human wit can devise. It is now impossible to avoid, and too late to postpone it; it must be met immediately—the question is, how may it be met efficiently? Twelve months, therefore, must not pass over without the very name of tithes in that country being abolished for ever; nor do I deem it less urgent that the Protestant Establishment in that country should be at once proportioned to the population which it serves. But, gentlemen, I for one will never consent that the surplus revenues of that branch of our Establishment shall ever be appropriated to any other object save the interests of the Church of England, because experience has taught me that an establishment is never despoiled except to benefit an aristocracy. . . . I know the love that great lords, and especially Whig lords, have for abbey lands and great tithes: I remember Woburn, and I profit by the reminiscence.

Then there are the claims of the Dissenters.

In my opinion these are claims which must not be eluded by any Government that wishes to stand. I would grant every claim of this great body that the spirit of the most comprehensive toleration required, consistent with the established constitution of the country. Therefore, I think that the registration and the marriage claims should be conceded. As for the question of the church-rate, it is impossible that we can endure that every time one is levied, a town should present the scene of a contested election. The rights of the Establishment must be respected, but, for the sake of the Establishment itself, that flagrant scandal must be removed. These are concessions which, I think, are due to a numerous and powerful portion of our fellow-subjects; due, I repeat, to their numbers, their intelligence, and their property, and consistent, in my opinion, with the maintenance of an Established Church, a blessing with which I am not prepared to part, and which I am resolved to uphold, because I consider it a guarantee of civilisation, and a barrier against bigotry.

In the matter of the Municipal Corporations he is also in favour of reform; but what is to be his attitude to the Government that had just been constituted? If they will adopt and carry measures similar to those he has enumerated, he indicates that he will be ready to support them ; though, as Peel had not yet explained his policy, he is careful not to commit himself. 'I am for measures, gentlemen, and not men, and for this simple reason, that for four years we have had men and not measures, and I am wearied of them.' It was said, however, that they ought not to accept any measures from the hands of those who had opposed the Reform Bill. But he shows at length how little claim the Whigs themselves can lay to consistency even in the matter of reform, and how little right they have to call other men renegades and apostates : and then, in a famous and daring passage, he expounds his doctrine of consistency.

The truth is, gentlemen, a statesman is the creature of his age, the child of circumstances, the creation of his times. A statesman is essentially a practical character ; and when he is called upon to take office, he is not to inquire what his opinions might or might not have been upon this or that subject ; he is only to ascertain the needful and the beneficial, and the most feasible measures are to be carried on. The fact is, the conduct and the opinions of public men at different periods of their career must not be too curiously contrasted in a free and aspiring country. The people have their passions, and it is even the duty of public men occasionally to adopt sentiments with which they do not sympathise, because the people must have leaders. Then the opinions and prejudices of the Crown must necessarily influence a rising statesman. I say nothing of the weight which great establishments and corporations, and the necessity of their support and patronage, must also possess with an ambitious politician. All this, however, produces ultimate benefit ; all these influences tend to form that eminently practical character for which our countrymen are celebrated. I laugh, therefore, at the objection against a man, that at a former period of his career he advocated a policy different to his present one. All I seek to ascertain is whether his present policy be just, necessary, expedient ; whether at the present moment he is prepared to serve the country according to its present necessities.

If on Peel and his Ministry he suspends judgment, to the Whigs he gives no quarter. He has always believed that they intended to make themselves masters for life, and they would certainly have gained their object if they had succeeded in overpowering the House of Lords as they have succeeded in packing the House of Commons. What then would have become of the liberties of England ?

I will allow for the freedom of the Press ; I will allow for the spirit of the age ; I will allow for the march of intellect ; but I cannot force from my mind the conviction that a House of Commons, concentrating in itself the whole power of the State, might—I should rather say would—notwithstanding the great antagonistic forces to which I have alluded, establish in this country a despotism of the most formidable and dangerous character.

He reminds his hearers of the consequences of such an arrangement in the reign of Charles I.

Looking at such consequences I think we may feel that we have some interest in maintaining the prerogative of the Crown and the privileges of the Peers. I, for one, shall ever view with jealous eye the proceedings of any House of Commons, however freely chosen.

Already he sees symptoms of jobbery and servility in the Reformed Parliament, and what of the Reform Ministry ? 'The Reform Ministry indeed ! Why scarcely an original member of that celebrated Cabinet remained' at the time of their dismissal. And then we have the famous Ducrow simile, a characteristic specimen of Disraeli's early political eloquence, full of the broad humour which appeals effectively to the mob and yet with the indefinable quality which suggests the born man of letters.

The Reform Ministry ! I dare say, now, some of you have heard of Mr. Ducrow, that celebrated gentleman who rides upon six horses. What a prodigious achievement ! It seems impossible ; but you have confidence in Ducrow. You fly to witness it ; unfortunately, one of the horses is ill, and a donkey is substituted in its place. But Ducrow is still admirable ; there he is, bounding along in a spangled jacket and cork slippers ! The whole town is mad to see Ducrow riding at the same time on six horses. But now two more of the steeds are seized with the staggers, and lo! three jackasses in their stead! Still Ducrow persists, and still announces to the public that he will ride round the circus every night on his six steeds. At last all the horses are knocked up, and now there are half-a-dozen donkeys. What a change! Behold the hero in the amphitheatre, the spangled jacket thrown on one side, the cork slippers on the other. Puffing, panting, and perspiring, he pokes one sullen brute, thwacks another, cuffs a third, and curses a fourth, while one brays to the audience, and another rolls in the sawdust. Behold the late Prime Minister and the Reform Ministry—the spirited and snow-white steeds have gradually changed into an equal number of sullen and obstinate donkeys; while Mr. Merryman, who, like the Lord Chancellor, was once the very life of the ring, now lies his despairing length in the middle of the stage, with his jokes exhausted and his bottle empty!

One can imagine how this kind of thing was relished by his audience. 'I stand astonishingly well at Wycombe,' he wrote to Austen, 'and may beat the Colonel yet. Had I the money, I might canter over the county, for my popularity is irresistible.' On the day following the speech at Wycombe he spoke again at Aylesbury at an agricultural dinner where he was introduced to the audience as a firm friend of the agricultural interest, and where he declared that his confidence in the present Administration was greatly abated by the exclusion of Lord Chandos from office. The Duke of Buckingham was in the chair, so this declaration was not only good politics for the audience, but a courtly compliment which, however touched with irony, was in the style Disraeli loved. His presence at such a gathering marked a distinct advance towards identification with the Tories; and in sending the reprint of the Wycombe speech to Durham, whom he had described in it as the only man of any decision of character in the Reform Ministry, he shows a consciousness of the widening of the interval between them.

As for the opinions contained in these pages [he writes] they are those I have ever professed, and I should grieve if your

Lordship's juncture with the Whigs and [my ?] continued resistance to a party which has ever opposed me, even with a degree of personal malignity, should ever place me in opposition to a nobleman whose talents I respect, and who, I am confident, has only the same object in view with myself—to maintain this great Empire on a broad democratic basis, which I am convinced is the only foundation on which it can now rest.[1]

Radicals and Whigs, as usual, were drawing closer to each other in opposition, and Disraeli, resolute in his detestation of the Whigs, was moving in the opposite direction ; but in Wycombe at all events he still clung to his Radical friends, and this third election was fought on the old basis of an alliance between Radicals and Tories. On the day of nomination, 'it is not enough to say of Mr. Disraeli,' writes a hostile witness, 'that he delivered himself with his usual ability ; the difficulties he had to encounter were most ably met and judiciously avoided ; to steer between the shoals of Toryism on the one hand and the quicksands of Radicalism on the other (for he was supported by the two parties) required his utmost skill, and well did he acquit himself.'[2] All his adroitness, however, did not avail to carry the election. When the poll closed on January 7 the figures were—

Smith, 289.
Grey, 147.
Disraeli, 128.

'It would be injustice to Mr. Disraeli,' the same writer adds, 'not to say that he conducted himself throughout the whole proceedings in the handsomest manner : there was a total absence of those personalities which disgraced the last election ; and in his concluding speech the unfortunate candidate admitted that he had had fair play, and no cause to complain.' A fortnight later, at a Conservative dinner at Wycombe with Chandos in the chair, the unfailing note of hopefulness and faith was sounded.

[1] Reid's *Life of Durham*, I., p. 371.
[2] From a letter in the *Bucks Gazette* for Jan. 16, 1835.

I am not at all disheartened. I do not in any way feel like a beaten man. Perhaps it is because I am used to it. I will say of myself like the famous Italian general, who being asked in his old age why he was always victorious, replied, it was because he had always been beaten in his youth.

To the Duke of Wellington.

[*Jan.* 7, 1835.]

I have fought our battle and I have lost it by a majority of 14.[1] . . . . Had Lord Carrington exerted himself even in the slightest degree in my favour I must have been returned; but he certainly maintained a *neutrality*—a neutrality so strict that it amounted to a blockade. . . . Grey made a violent anti-Ministerial speech, and I annihilated him in my reply; but what use is annihilating men out of the House of Commons. . . . I am now a cipher; but if the devotion of my energies to your cause, *in* and *out*, can ever avail you, your Grace may count upon me, who seeks no greater satisfaction than that of serving a really great man.[2]

From the Duke of Wellington.

Jan. 10, 1835.

The Duke of Wellington presents his compliments to Mr. Disraeli, and has received his letter of Wednesday night, for which he is much obliged. He very much regrets the result of the election at Wycombe.

The failure of this third attempt at Wycombe seems finally to have convinced Disraeli that he could not hope for a political career unless he definitely identified himself with one or other of the two great parties; and there could no longer be any doubt as to which he would choose. The formation of the Peel Government entirely changed the problem for him, and thousands of others who were still unsettled in their political allegiance. When he published his Wycombe speech of December 16 as a pamphlet, he told Austen that he was acting by 'the Minister's desire'; and if Peel read the speech at all he

[1] This does not agree with the figures given above, but those were the days of open voting, and Disraeli may have written before the final figures were available.

[2] Maxwell's *Life of Wellington*, II., p. 305.

could hardly have failed to read it with approval. On the very day after its delivery Peel himself submitted to his Cabinet the draft of the address to his constituents which has become famous in history as the Tamworth manifesto, and there is a very remarkable coincidence, for it can hardly have been more, between the policy of moderate reform therein unfolded and the practical measures upon which Disraeli had insisted in his speech. The Tamworth manifesto was too opportunist in its spirit, too much of a programme and too little of a creed, long to satisfy Disraeli ; but at all events it showed that Toryism had ceased to spell reaction or—a thing even more repugnant to one of his temperament—stagnation, and was in process of adapting itself to the spirit of the age. The greatest obstacle in the way of his entering the Tory camp had now been removed, and not many weeks after the Wycombe election he was nominated [1] at his own request as a candidate for the Carlton Club, which had been founded a few years before by the Duke of Wellington and his friends, and had at once become the recognised social citadel of Toryism. The decisive step had now been taken. He had been exactly three years in politics, and his apparent course in those years had been that of a political comet, highly eccentric and irregular. Henceforward his place in the political firmament is fixed, or his orbit at all events conforms to the accepted laws of political motion.

It is no accident that there is a certain ambiguity about the party affiliations of nearly all our greater statesmen : Chatham, Pitt, Burke, Canning, Peel, Palmerston, Disraeli, and Gladstone—none of these has an absolutely consistent party record ; and, indeed, a man with such a record would be more likely to win distinction as a good partisan than as a great statesman. If we are to measure consistency by ideas, Disraeli is the most consistent of them all, and yet more than any of the others he was to suffer throughout his career from the reputa-

[1] Lord Strangford proposer and Lord Chandos seconder.

tion of political time-server and adventurer acquired in these early and errant years. In one sense this reputation was wholly unjust; in another it had not been unprovoked nor, indeed, wholly undeserved. In his guiding principles and ideas he had changed far less than most of his judges and critics, but the world, which looks only to externals, saw that he had been in communication, if not in co-operation, with men at the opposite poles of politics, and drew its conclusions accordingly. He had been too eager in his desire for tangible and immediate success, too reckless in his disregard for the conventions of political life; and he had thus aroused in many a distrust which he was never wholly to allay, and which to the very end of his days was to be a cause of weakness to himself and a formidable weapon at the disposal of his enemies.

To Sarah Disraeli.

Jan. 20, 1835.

Last Saturday a dinner by the Chancellor to Lord Abinger and the Barons of the Exchequer. There were also George Dawson, myself, Praed, young Gladstone, Sir M. Shee, Sir J. Beresford, and Pemberton: rather dull, but we had a swan very white and tender, and stuffed with truffles, the best company there.[1]

In 'young Gladstone's' recollections of this dinner apparently neither the swan nor Disraeli found a place; but he noted for his future guidance some counsel given them by Lyndhurst: 'Never defend yourself before a popular assembly, except with and by retorting the attack; the hearers, in the pleasure which the assault gives them, will forget the previous charge'[2]—a piece of wisdom which, if Disraeli failed to note it at the time, he was afterwards, as Lord Morley reminds us, to make his

[1] *Letters*, p. 90.

[2] Morley's *Life of Gladstone*, I., p. 122.

own, compressing it into one of his most effective phrases, '*Never complain and never explain.*'

To Sarah Disraeli.

Feb. 20, 1835.

About last night's debate [on the election of the Speaker], Peel did not speak well; Stanley with great point and power. . . . O'Connell is so powerful that he says he will be in the Cabinet. How can the Whigs submit to this? It is the Irish Catholic Party that has done all the mischief.

Feb. 26.

Here there is only one topic, the division on the Address. Peel made a powerful speech; Stanley constrained and qualifying. His way is evidently not clear; I cannot understand the game he is playing. On the Speakership he had no party. Now fifty men meet at his house every morning. Lyndhurst squabashed Brougham on Tuesday.

April 1.

I do not doubt myself that the Government will be in a minority on the present question, but this is not the cause of the *malaise* of the Tories. The fact is, their chief is worried by his wife, and she is nervous lest he should fight and all that. There is no more reason now that the Tories should go out than two months ago, and I cannot help believing that they will not. On Sunday I dined at the Chancellor's, and ever since I have had a severe cold and been nowhere.

April 4.

I have not seen the Chancellor since Thursday. Peel is much firmer and the King quite so, but his Majesty cannot sleep. The decisive battle is to be fought on the Irish Tithe Bill, and we expect to win. Everybody has got the influenza; the Lord Chancellor has had an attack; and, as you rightly expected, myself, though mine was much modified to former years.[1]

The decisive battle, however, was lost, and Peel resigned. We are now admitted to some knowledge of a curious episode in unwritten political history.

In April, 1835, when Sir R. P[eel] resigned and great difficulties and time experienced in forming a Government

[1] *Letters*, pp. 90-92.

by the Whigs, my old friend Mrs. Norton opened a communication with me in order to form a coalition between the constitutional Whigs and Sir R. P. Melbourne was her prompter, and he and she wished the affair to be arranged by Lord L[yndhurst]. Lord M. would, I think, have thrown over the Appropriation Clause. He expressed, according to her, an absolute horror of O'Connell—with whom, he said, nothing should induce him to form a connexion. He had authorised none of the intrigues.

I had several conferences with her, prompted by L., and paid her visits sometimes of two hours (though our acquaintance otherwise had quite ceased). Admitting the possibility of arranging the Appropriation Clause, which of course rested with M., I enquired whether M. would serve under P. She assured me he had positively agreed to do so, and that he would throw over Brougham as Chancellor for L.

I think the idea of throwing over B. occurred in this manner, as I know the resolution was taken lately. Although our negotiation failed, very friendly feelings subsisted at that time between M. and L., and when all was over M. consulted L. through Mrs. Norton as to putting the Seals in commission. The difficulty was to communicate to B. that he was thrown over. At last M. resolved to do it himself, which he did. What an interview![1]

To Isaac D'Israeli.

Good Friday Morn [*April 17th*], 1835.

My dearest Father,

The Whigs cannot form a Government. It is impossible to describe to you the extraordinary state of affairs. On Wednesday Mrs. N. sent for me, and I was closeted with her from 3 until 5. Lords Grey, Melbourne, and all the old constitutional aristocratic Whigs are desirous of forming a coalition with Peel, Lyndhurst, &c. They will have nothing to do with the Radicals, and a considerable section of the Opposition, headed by Lord Seymour, no doubt acting under the auspices and instigation of Mrs. N., back them. They (Melbourne, &c.) will have nothing to do with O'Connell and the English and Scotch Rads., and will not make Brougham Chancellor or anything. Melbourne disapproved of the attack on Manners Sutton and Londonderry and the whole course of John Russell's career on the Irish Church.

[1] From the Memorandum of 1836, already quoted.

From Mrs. N. I went to the Lord Chancellor's, with whom I remained in close conference until half-past 7, so I could not write to you. Yesterday I was obliged to be at the House of Commons until half-past 5, then to see Lord Seymour, and afterwards with the Chancellor again until 8 o'clock, so it was impossible to write again. There seem great, I fear insuperable, difficulties in the way of an immediate coalition, though eventually it must take place.

I cannot say now whether Peel will immediately resume office or Melbourne form an Administration of his friends by way of blind, and which may last a few months. But at present the Whigs have absolutely not advanced a jot. I need not say that we are all in the highest spirits, and that the excitement is unparalleled. I think myself Peel will be again sent for by the King. If there be any more this morning and I have an opportunity to write by post, I will. That we shall win in the long run, and triumphantly, I have no doubt. You now know all the secrets of affairs which not ten people do in the realm, and you must burn this letter when read. Mulgrave and the more useful and desperate Whiglings are for pushing on to Durham. . . . I intended to have come down to Bradenham to-day or to-morrow, but can say nothing of my movements now, as all is on my shoulders.

Love to all,

B. D.[1]

To Sarah Disraeli.

April 13, 1835.

As *coalition*, or, as the Whigs call it, *amalgamation*, is at the present moment impossible. Lord Melbourne has, I understand, formed his Cabinet, and some of the writs will be moved for this evening. It is purely Whig, and consists entirely of the old hacks—Palmerston, Auckland, Duncannon, &c. Granville Somerset sent for me to the Woods and Forests this morning to say if there was a fair opening the Tories would start me, &c. I was astonished at his courtesy and strong expressions of desire to see me in.[2]

The fair opening soon presented itself. Mr. Henry Labouchere, the member for Taunton, vacated his seat on his appointment as Master of the Mint in the new

[1] From an original in the possession of Mr. Walter V. Daniell.
[2] *Letters*, p. 92.

Melbourne Government, and at the last moment Disraeli was sent down by the Tories to oppose his re-election.

To Sarah Disraeli.

Wednesday night [*April* 23].

There is no place like *Taunton*, not that I can win this time, for Labouchere, who was twenty-four hours in advance of me, has picked up many blues (my colour); but come in at the general election I must, for I have promises of two-thirds of the electors. I live in a rage of enthusiasm; even my opponents promise to vote for me *next time*. The fatigue is awful. Two long speeches to-day, and nine hours' canvass on foot in a blaze of repartee. I am quite exhausted, and can scarcely see to write.

CASTLE, TAUNTON,
April 27.

The county gentlemen for ten miles round flock to me every day, but I am obliged to decline all their invitations. As for Taunton itself, the enthusiasm of Wycombe is a miniature to it; and I believe in point of energy, eloquence, and effect I have far exceeded all my former efforts. Had I arrived twenty hours sooner the result might have been in my favour. . . . It is astonishing how well they are informed in London of all that passes here, and how greatly they appreciate my exertions. They have opened a subscription for me at the Carlton, headed by Chandos, who has written twice to me in the warmest manner. To-morrow is nomination day.[1]

An eye-witness of the election scenes has recorded his impressions of the candidate's appearance.

Never in my life had I been so struck by a face as I was by that of Disraeli. It was lividly pale, and from beneath two finely-arched eyebrows blazed out a pair of intensely black eyes. I never have seen such orbs in mortal sockets, either before or since. His physiognomy was strictly Jewish. Over a broad, high forehead were ringlets of coal-black, glossy hair, which, combed away from his right temple, fell in luxuriant clusters or bunches over his left cheek and ear, which it entirely concealed from view. There was a sort of half-smile, half-sneer, playing about his beautifully-formed mouth, the upper lip of which was curved as we see it in the portraits of Byron.

[1] *Ibid.*, p. 93.

. . . . He was very showily attired in a dark bottle-green frock-coat, a waistcoat of the most extravagant pattern, the front of which was almost covered with glittering chains, and in fancy-pattern pantaloons. He wore a plain black stock, but no collar was visible. Altogether he was the most intellectual-looking exquisite I had ever seen.[1]

Now that he had definitely emerged as a Tory, Disraeli heard, of course, a good deal about the ambiguity of his previous performance.[2] 'It is absolutely essential,' wrote D'Orsay on the eve of the election, 'for you to explain to them that though a Tory you are a reforming one; because it is generally understood that you committed yourself in some degree with the other party.' In his speech on nomination day Disraeli essayed the task thus proposed to him.

Gentlemen, if there be anything on which I pique myself it is my consistency. I shall be ready to prove that consistency either in the House of Commons or on the hustings at Taunton. Every man may be attacked once; but no one ever attacked me twice. Gentlemen, here is my consistency. I have always opposed with my utmost energy the party of which my honorable opponent is a distinguished member. That party I have opposed for reasons I am prepared to give and to uphold. I look upon the Whigs as an anti-national party. When I first entered political life I found the high places of the realm filled by the party of which my opponent is a member. I found they had an immense majority in the House of Commons, acquired by a system of nomination not less equivocal than that of the boroughmongers they affected to destroy. Believing that the policy of the party was such as must destroy the honour of the kingdom abroad and the happiness of the people at home, I considered it my duty to oppose the Whigs, to ensure their discomfiture, and, if possible, their destruction.

[1] *Pen and Ink Sketches of Poets, Preachers, and Politicians.* London, 1846.

[2] There was much pother then and subsequently about a certain Westminster Club of which Disraeli had been nominally a member, and which after his resignation assumed a political character and became the Westminster Reform Club; but it is now fortunately unnecessary to enter on the details of a tiresome controversy from which Disraeli emerges quite unscathed. 'Life is too short,' as he said himself in connexion with this affair, 'to refute every misrepresentation of every malicious fool.'

Let me recall to your recollection the extraordinary characteristic of the political world when I entered it. Gentlemen, the great safeguard of our liberties, the balance of parties, was destroyed. There was then no constitutional Opposition to keep the Government in check The great Tory party, now so strongly constituted, was a shattered, a feeble, and a disheartened fragment, self-confirming their own inability to carry on the King's Government, and announcing an impending revolution. Had I been a political adventurer I had nothing to do but to join the Whigs; but, conscientiously believing that their policy was in every respect pernicious, I felt it my duty to oppose them. But how were they to be opposed? Where were the elements of a party to keep the Government in check and to bring back the old constitutional balance? I thought they existed in the Liberal Tories, and in those independent Reformers who had been returned to Parliament independent of the Whigs. I laboured for the union, and I am proud of it. Gentlemen, remember the Whig policy. They had a packed Parliament. They had altered the duration of Parliaments once before. They had the whole power of the State in their hands. I believed, and I still believe, that we were nearer to a Long Parliament than we imagined. I wished to break the strength of the Whigs by frequent elections, and by frequent appeals to a mis-governed people; therefore I advocated a recurrence to those triennial Parliaments which it was once the proudest boast of the Tories to advocate. I wished to give the country gentlemen a chance of representing the neighbouring towns, where they are esteemed, instead of the nominees of a sectarian oligarchy; therefore I proposed the adoption of the ballot, in the only constituencies willing to assume it. . . .

Had the Whigs remained in power—and it seemed to me, and the wisest men in England shared my conviction, that they were our masters for life—had, I repeat, they remained in power I considered the dismemberment of the Empire inevitable; and, therefore, I tried to root them out. But, Gentlemen, great, ay, almost illimitable as was my confidence in Whig incapacity, I confess they far surpassed even my most sanguine expectations. The mighty Whig party which had consented to a revolution to gain power fell to pieces; the vessel of the State righted itself; and now there is no necessity to cut away its masts. Gentlemen, the object for which I laboured is attained; the balance of parties is restored; and I do no longer advocate the measures in question, simply because they are no longer necessary. Is this an answer? Is this inconsistency?[1]

To Sarah Disraeli

April 28.

I have just left the hustings, and have gained the show of hands, which no blue candidate ever did before. This, though an idle ceremony in most places, is of great account here, for the potwallopers of Taunton are as eloquent as those of Athens, and we gain votes by such a demonstration.[2]

In spite, however, of this demonstration, when the poll was closed on the second day the figures were—

Labouchere	452
Disraeli	282
	170

Disraeli did not perhaps overrate the popularity he had acquired during the election. 'His undaunted spirit, his eloquence, his wit, his courtesy and kindness,' says a writer in the local paper in words that appear to be charged with something more than conventional eulogy, 'have acquired him the respect and admiration of all parties and the entire confidence of his own.' After the election the Conservatives of the district made him the central figure in an elaborate festival culminating in a banquet, and great appears to have been the enthusiasm. The writer already quoted was present at the banquet, and has given us a minute description of the manner of Disraeli's oratory.

He commenced in a lisping, lackadaisical tone of voice. . . . He minced his phrases in apparently the most affected manner, and, whilst he was speaking, placed his hands in all imaginable positions; not because he felt awkward, and did not know, like a booby in a drawing-room, where to put them, but apparently for the purpose of exhibiting to the best advantage the glittering rings which decked his white and taper fingers. Now he would place his thumbs in the armholes of his waistcoat, and spread out his fingers on its

[1] *Dorset County Chronicle*, April 30, 1835. [2] *Letters*, p. 93.

flashing surface; then one set of digits would be released and he would lean affectedly on the table, supporting himself with his right hand; anon he would push aside the curls from his forehead. . . . But as he proceeded all traces of this dandyism and affectation were lost. With a rapidity of utterance perfectly astonishing he referred to past events and indulged in anticipations of the future. The Whigs were, of course, the objects of his unsparing satire, and his eloquent denunciations of them were applauded to the echo. In all he said he proved himself to be the finished orator—every period was rounded with the utmost elegance, and in his most daring flights, when one trembled lest he should fall from the giddy height to which he had attained, he so gracefully descended that every hearer was wrapt in admiring surprise. . . . His voice, at first so finical, gradually became full, musical, and sonorous, and with every varying sentiment was beautifully modulated. His arms no longer appeared to be exhibited for show, but he exemplified the eloquence of the hand. The dandy was transformed into the man of mind, the Mantalini-looking personage into a practised orator and finished elocutionist.

Disraeli's speech[1] on this occasion is full of interest. It is the first in which we find the main lines of his creed of democratic Toryism firmly drawn.

He had told them once before that the Conservative party was the really democratic party in the country who surrounded the people with the power of the Throne to shield them from the undue power of the aristocracy. . . . The point to which they were arrived in the history of the country was this: whether the establishments of the realm should be supported or destroyed. The question was between an hereditary monarchy on one side and an elective executive on the other. . . . He was in favour of an hereditary monarchy because a King whose power and authority were so judiciously limited as those of the King of England was in effect the great leader of the people against an usurping aristocracy.

He was, he told them also, a steadfast supporter of the Established Church against

that misty, ambiguous, and impalpable thing, that spectre of unsubstantiality, rising confusedly from the realm of dark-

[1] There is a report in the *Dorset County Chronicle* for June 4, 1835.

ness, that nameless thing called by some 'the voluntary system.' Now when he who was a tower of toleration avowed that he was opposed to this system, he declared that he was so opposed because he regarded it as an essentially aristocratic system devoted to the few and not to the many. It was a system that amounted to this, that no man should be saved who could not pay for salvation. Let them ask whether this was the way by which to instruct a nation. The same system that cared not for the unrepresented many in politics cared little for the unrepresented many in religion.

Incidentally he gives unstinted praise to the policy and achievements of the late Administration.

Nowhere in history could there be found an instance of a council of statesmen who in so short a period had matured a series of measures so vast in their character, so beneficent in their nature, so conducive to the prosperity and the glory of the country, as those which had been brought forward by the late Ministers. He confessed that, great as was his confidence in that great man who stood at the helm, and in his colleagues, sanguine as were his hopes, he was utterly astonished at what they did.

The Taunton election involved Disraeli in a quarrel which became too celebrated. The Peel Ministry had been overthrown by a combination between the Whigs and O'Connell, and it was only by virtue of the same combination that Melbourne could hope to maintain himself in office. Inevitably of course the new alliance between politicians who had been so recently at war became the great mark for invective with Tory orators and writers, and Disraeli could be trusted not to be behindhand. Alluding to the subject in his speech on the hustings, he was reported in the summarised version which appeared in the London papers to have described O'Connell as an incendiary and a traitor. Disraeli then and ever afterwards maintained that the summary misrepresented him, and that he had only quoted from the Whigs the language in which they had but recently denounced their present ally; and his explanation is in full accord with the speech as reported in all the local papers.[1] The unlucky version, however, came before the eyes of O'Connell and much incensed him; and he seized the opportunity of a meeting in Dublin a few days later to take a savage revenge on his supposed assailant.

I must confess, that some of the attacks made on me, particularly one, by a Mr. Disraeli, at Taunton, surprised me. Anything so richly deserving the appellation of superlative blackguardism, or at all equal to that in impudence and assurance, I never before met with. The annals of ruffianism do not furnish anything like it. He is an author, I believe, of a couple of novels, and that was all I knew about him until 1831, or 1832, when he[2] wrote to me, being about to stand for High Wycombe, requesting a letter of recommendation from me to the electors. He took the letter with him to the place, got it printed and placarded all over the place. The next I heard of him was his being a candidate for Marylebone; in this he was also unsuccessful. He got tired of being a Radical any longer after these two defeats, and was determined to try his chance as a Tory. He stands the other day at Taunton, and by way of recommending himself to the electors he calls me an incendiary and a traitor. Now, my answer to this piece of gratuitous impertinence is, that he is an egregious liar. He is a liar both in action and words. What! shall such a vile creature be tolerated in England? Shall the man be received by any constituency who after coming forward on two separate occasions as the advocate of certain opinions, now boldly and unblushingly recants those principles by which his political life had been apparently regulated? He is a living lie: and the British Empire is degraded by tolerating a miscreant of his abominable description. The language is harsh, I must confess; but it is no more than deserved, and if I should apologise for using it, it is because I can find no harsher epithets in the English language by which to convey the utter abhorrence which I entertain for such a reptile. He is just fit now, after being twice discarded by the people,

[1] The best report is that in the *Dorset County Chronicle* for April 30, 1835, reprinted in Kebbel's *Selected Speeches of Lord Beaconsfield*. Here the word 'incendiary' does not occur at all, and the only mention of 'traitor' is in a passage in which the Whigs are described as 'that weak aristocratic party in the state who could only obtain power by leaguing themselves with one whom they had denounced as a traitor.'

[2] This was inaccurate. The application, as has been seen, was made through Bulwer.

to become a Conservative. He possesses all the necessary requisites of perfidy, selfishness, depravity, want of principle, &c., which would qualify him for the change. His name shews that he is of Jewish origin. I do not use it as a term of reproach; there are many most respectable Jews. But there are, as in every other people, some of the lowest and most disgusting grade of moral turpitude; and of those I look upon Mr. Disraeli as the worst. He has just the qualities of the impenitent thief on the Cross, and I verily believe, if Mr. Disraeli's family herald were to be examined and his genealogy traced, the same personage would be discovered to be the heir at law of the exalted individual to whom I allude. I forgive Mr. Disraeli now, and as the lineal descendant of the blasphemous robber, who ended his career beside the Founder of the Christian Faith, I leave the gentleman to the enjoyment of his infamous distinction and family honours.[1]

Vituperation so picturesque was of course irresistible, and 'this terrible philippic,' as the reporter well described it, found its way into nearly every newspaper. Having once killed an antagonist in a duel, O'Connell had taken a vow that he would never fight another; but this self-denying ordinance had not been accompanied by the practice of any similar self-denial in the matter of his language; and the papers had just been full of a quarrel between him and Lord Alvanley, a Tory peer, to whom he had alluded as 'a bloated buffoon.' A duel had resulted, in which Morgan O'Connell, the Liberator's son, had acted in the interest of his father's honour; and as soon, therefore, as Disraeli saw his 'crucifixion' in *The Times* of May 5 he wrote the following letter:—

To Mr. Morgan O'Connell, M.P.

31A, PARK ST., GROSVENOR SQUARE,
Tuesday, May 5

SIR,

As you have established yourself as the champion of your father, I have the honour to request your notice to a very

[1] This, from the *Courier* of May 6, 1835, was the version of O'Connell's speech adopted by Disraeli himself in an explanatory address to the electors of Taunton.

scurrilous attack which your father has made upon my conduct and character.

Had Mr. O'Connell, according to the practice observed among gentlemen, appealed to me respecting the accuracy of the reported expressions before he indulged in offensive comments upon them, he would, if he can be influenced by a sense of justice, have felt that such comments were unnecessary. He has not thought fit to do so, and he leaves me no alternative but to request that you, his son, will resume your vicarious duties of yielding satisfaction for the insults which your father has too long lavished with impunity upon his political opponents.

I have the honour to be, Sir,
Your obedient servant,
B. Disraeli.

Morgan O'Connell very reasonably replied that he was not answerable for what his father might say, and that he had only challenged Lord Alvanley because he conceived the latter had purposely insulted his father. Thereupon Disraeli sent the following letter to the newspapers.

To Mr. Daniel O'Connell, M.P. for Dublin.

London,
May

Mr. O'Connell,

Although you have long placed yourself out of the pale of civilisation, still I am one who will not be insulted, even by a Yahoo, without chastising it. When I read this morning in the same journals your virulent attack upon myself, and that your son was at the same moment paying the penalty of similar virulence to another individual on whom you had dropped your filth, I thought that the consciousness that your opponents had at length discovered a source of satisfaction might have animated your insolence to unwonted energy, and I called upon your son to re-assume his vicarious office of yielding satisfaction for his shrinking sire. But it seems that gentleman declines the further exercise of the pleasing duty of enduring the consequences of your libertine harangues. I have no other means, therefore, of noticing your effusion but this public mode. Listen, then, to me.

If it had been possible for you to act like a gentleman, you would have hesitated before you made your foul and insolent comments upon a hasty and garbled report of a speech which scarcely contains a sentence or an expression as they emanated from my mouth ; but the truth is, you were glad to seize the first opportunity of pouring forth your venom against a man whom it serves the interest of your party to represent as a political apostate.

In 1831,[1] when Mr. O'Connell expressed to the electors of Wycombe his anxiety to assist me in my election, I came forward as the opponent of the party in power, and which I described in my address as 'a rapacious, tyrannical, and incapable faction'—the English Whigs, who in the ensuing year denounced you as a traitor from the Throne, and every one of whom, only a few months back, you have anathematised with all the peculiar graces of a tongue practised in scurrility. You are the patron of these men now, Mr. O'Connell: you, forsooth, are 'devoted' to them. I am still their uncompromising opponent. Which of us is the most consistent ?

You say that I was once a Radical, and now that I am a Tory. My conscience acquits me of ever having deserted a political friend, or ever having changed a political opinion. I worked for a great and avowed end in 1831, and that was the restoration of the balance of parties in the state, a result which I believed to be necessary to the honour of the realm and the happiness of the people. I never advocated a measure which I did not believe tended to this result, and if there be any measures which I then urged, and now am not disposed to press, it is because that great result is obtained.

In 1831 I should have been very happy to have laboured for this object with Mr. O'Connell, with whom I had no personal acquaintance, but who was a member of the Legislature, remarkable for his political influence, his versatile talents, and his intense hatred and undisguised contempt of the Whigs.

Since 1831 we have met only once ; but I have a lively recollection of my interview with so distinguished a personage. Our conversation was of great length ; I had a very ample opportunity of studying your character. I thought you a very amusing, a very interesting, but a somewhat overrated man. I am sure on that occasion I did not disguise from

[1] A slip, of course, for 1832.

you my political views: I spoke with a frankness which I believe is characteristic of my disposition. I told you I was not a sentimental, but a practical politician; that what I chiefly desired to see was the formation of a strong but constitutional Government, that would maintain the Empire, and that I thought if the Whigs remained in office they would shipwreck the State. I observed then, as was my habit, that the Whigs must be got rid of at any price. It seemed to me that you were much of the same opinion as myself; but our conversation was very general. We formed no political alliance, and for a simple reason—I concealed neither from yourself, nor from your friends, that the repeal of the Union was an impassable gulf between us, and that I could not comprehend, after the announcement of such an intention, how any English party could co-operate with you. Probably you then thought that the English Movement might confederate with you on a system of mutual assistance, and that you might exchange and circulate your accommodation measures of destruction; but even Mr. O'Connell, with his lively faith in Whig feebleness and Whig dishonesty, could scarcely have imagined that in the course of twelve months his fellow-conspirators were to be my Lord Melbourne and the Marquis of Lansdowne.

I admire your scurrilous allusions to my origin. It is quite clear that the 'hereditary bondsman' has already forgotten the clank of his fetter. I know the tactics of your Church; it clamours for toleration, and it labours for supremacy. I see that you are quite prepared to persecute.

With regard to your taunts as to my want of success in my election contests, permit me to remind you that I had nothing to appeal to but the good sense of the people. No threatening skeletons canvassed for me; a death's-head and cross-bones were not blazoned on my banners. My pecuniary resources, too, were limited; I am not one of those public beggars that we see swarming with their obtrusive boxes in the chapels of your creed, nor am I in possession of a princely revenue wrung from a starving race of fanatical slaves. Nevertheless, I have a deep conviction that the hour is at hand when I shall be more successful, and take my place in that proud assembly of which Mr. O'Connell avows his wish no longer to be a member. I expect to be a representative of the people before the repeal of the Union. We shall meet at Philippi; and rest assured that, confident in a good cause, and in some energies which have been not altogether unproved, I will seize the first opportunity of inflicting upon you a castigation which will make you at the same time remember and repent the insults that you have lavished upon

BENJAMIN DISRAELI.

The newspapers of those days were anything but squeamish, and most of them published this letter; and as soon as it appeared, Disraeli wrote again to Morgan O'Connell:—

I deduce from your communication that you do not consider yourself responsible for any insults offered by your father, but only bound to resent the insults that he may receive. Now, Sir, it is my hope that I *have* insulted him; assuredly it was my intention to do so. I wished to express the utter scorn in which I hold his character, and the disgust with which his conduct inspires me. If I failed in conveying this expression of my feelings to him, let me more successfully express them now to you. I shall take every opportunity of holding your father's name up to public contempt. And I fervently pray that you, or some one of his blood, may attempt to avenge the unextinguishable hatred with which I shall pursue his existence.

To Sarah Disraeli.

May 6, 1835.

There is but one opinion among *all* parties—viz., that I have *squabashed* them. I went to D'Orsay immediately. He sent for Henry Baillie for my second, as he thought a foreigner should not interfere in a political duel, but he took the management of everything. I never quitted his house till ten o'clock, when I dressed and went to the Opera, and every one says I have done it in first-rate style.

May 9.

This morning as I was lying in bed, thankful that I had kicked all the O'Connells and that I was at length to have a quiet morning, Mr. Collard, the police officer of Marylebone, rushed into my chamber, and took me into custody. . . . We all went in a hackney coach to the office, where I found that the articles were presented by a Mr. Bennett, residing in some street in Westminster, and an acquaintance of the O'Connells. We were soon dismissed, but I am now bound to keep the peace in £500 sureties. As far as the present affair was concerned, it was a most unnecessary precaution, as if all the O'Connells were to challenge me I could not think of meeting them *now*. I consider and every one else that they are lynched. It is very easy for you to criticise, but I do not regret the letter: the expressions were well weighed, and without it the affair was but clever pamphleteering. Critics you must always meet. W. told me the last letter was the finest thing in the English language, but that the letter to Dan was *too long*; others think that perfect. One does not like the Yahoo as coarse, others think it worthy of Swift, and so on. . . . The general effect is the thing, and that is, that all men agree I have shown pluck.[1]

His father and sister had been much alarmed by the ferocity and vindictiveness of the second letter to Morgan O'Connell, and perhaps Disraeli himself may in calmer moments have suspected that his violence had been excessive.

I have no ambition [he wrote[2] to the electors of Taunton] to be considered either ferocious or vindictive. . . . I am, I believe, of a mild and tolerant disposition, not too easily nettled, and quite ready to subscribe to a considerable latitude in the gladiatorial encounter between political opponents. . . . If in those hot and hurried letters I indulged in expressions which my calmer reason may disapprove, I am sure no candid and generous spirit, whatever may be his party, would scan with severity the words of one who had been subjected, without the prospect of redress, to such unparalleled outrage; I am sure no candid and generous spirit but must sympathise with one, who young, alone, supported only by his own energies, and the inspiration of a good cause, dared to encounter, in no inglorious struggle, the most powerful individual in the world who does not wear a crown.

The general effect, however, was the thing, and judged by this test the result was not unsatisfactory. 'Row with O'Connell in which I greatly distinguish myself' is the complacent entry in the Mutilated Diary a year later. The incident had at least made him notorious, and notoriety to Disraeli was at this time as the breath of his nostrils. Some observers may have thought the taste

[1] *Letters*, p. 94.

[2] Address of May 12.

of his letters questionable. D'Orsay declared that they were perfection and added that everybody agreed with him; and one of Disraeli's supporters at Wycombe was so impressed by their eloquence that 'neither he nor his old father could sleep all the night' after their perusal. 'Scarcely a day has elapsed,' Disraeli wrote[1] a month later, 'on which I have not received letters from some part of the United Kingdom congratulating me on my conduct.'

The charge of ingratitude, skilfully exploited by his adversaries, is what did him most injury, both then and afterwards; and it is worth while repeating his own defence:—

Whatever may be Mr. O'Connell's errors, he has an instinctive horror of blockheads. The man who talks or writes of my *ingratitude* to Mr. O'Connell only perverts our language and makes himself ridiculous. Mr. O'Connell, not at my written request, as he has been falsely represented to have stated, but at the verbal request of a third person, wrote a commonplace letter to the electors of Wycombe in my favour *when opposed to Colonel Grey, the son of the Whig Prime Minister*. The letter did me no good, but the reverse, but it was one of those slight courtesies of life, whatever might be its motives, of which a gentleman would always be prepared to show his sense by courtesies as slight. When therefore, long after, I for the first and only time met Mr. O'Connell, *who, in the meantime, had become a Repealer*, I thanked him for his courtesy, and however we differed in politics, I seized with pleasure that opportunity of being civil to him; and very recently when I met his most intimate friend, Mr. Ronayne.[2] . . . I wished to show by the tone of my conversation that, however I was opposed to him or his friend in public life, I was far from desirous of conducting myself towards them in a hostile spirit when we met in serener situations than the hustings or the House of Commons. . . . In the tone of courtesy I then used I should have ever spoken of Mr. O'Connell, had not he,

[1] Letter to the electors of Taunton, June 13, 1835.

[2] In a letter to the *Morning Chronicle* dated May 3, 1835, this gentleman declared that Disraeli 'had within the last month spoken to him in terms of the most extravagant admiration of O'Connell,' to whom also he had asked him 'to communicate his kind remembrances.'

from the intentional misrepresentations of some busy fools in London, thought proper to make his notorious attack upon me in Dublin.[1]

The following note, written in the early sixties, though it anticipates, may be given here as an epilogue.

Croker, Peel, and O'Connell sent me, I may say, messages of peace before they died—literally O'Connell. He was so delighted with my smashing of Peel, and so glad, perhaps, that he had escaped what I once threatened and he now found I could do, that he sent me a message that it had always been heavy on his heart that there should have been a misunderstanding between us, and that he had long known that he had been misinformed and misled in the matter. I sent him a very courteous reply : but avoided any personal communication. He always made me a very reverential bow afterwards.

To Dawson Turner.[2]

May 29, 1835.

All this vulgar electioneering bustle is not worth a few calm hours in your magnificent library among those collections of which you have good cause to be proud ; but we are the creatures of circumstances, and as far as Destiny and tobacco are concerned I am a decided Orientalist.[3]

[1] Letter to the electors of Taunton, June 13, 1835.
[2] Botanist and Antiquary. His library and collection of manuscripts were famous.
[3] From a letter in Mr. Alfred Morrison's collection.

CHAPTER XIV.

POLITICAL WRITINGS.

1835-36.

During the next couple of years Disraeli's political activity was mainly with the pen. He had a mind of the complexion that will not allow a man to feel at ease in a fresh position till he has framed a theory to account for it; and now that he had become a Tory it was necessary for him to justify his faith both to himself and to the world. The times and the Tory party alike called for guidance: in his own words, it was 'a perplexed, ill-informed, jaded and shallow generation.' The reaction which followed the high idealism and strenuous efforts of the French Revolutionary era had produced the Benthamite philosophy and the Ricardian political economy, and when Disraeli entered public life these systems had just emerged from their period of struggle as the peculiar possession of an unpopular sect, and attained to that position of dominating influence over the mind of England, and especially over the mind of the English middle class, which they were to retain for nearly fifty years. It was only in the eighth decade of the century, after Disraeli himself had overthrown the ascendancy of the middle class, and when for the greater part of the decade he was Prime Minister of England, that the authority of these systems began seriously to be shaken. His active career coincides closely with the period of their dominion, and in his life, his writings, and his achievements he stands for all that is their spiritual antithesis, at war with them throughout the whole range of their influence. Not that he was the only or even the first antagonist in the field. The Reform Act of 1832 had marked the triumph of the commercially-minded middle class with their unimaginative ideals. In the summer of 1833 Newman, with 'fierce thoughts against the Liberals,'[1] hastened home from the Mediterranean, writing 'Lead, kindly Light' in the orange boat that carried him from Palermo to Marseilles, to begin the Oxford movement; and in the winter of the same year the book which Carlyle had 'hawked' round the publishers of London appeared in *Fraser's Magazine* under the title of *Sartor Resartus*. Newman, Carlyle, and Disraeli were far different figures; but, little as they may have known it, they were in a sense spiritual brethren, engaged in a desperate fight against a common enemy, working in their several ways with a common purpose. Beneath a thousand superficial differences they had all three the same romantic temperament; all three had in them something of the artist; and all three were deeply imbued with that historical sentiment which is the fatal enemy of Benthamism, as of every kind of system-mongering. Disraeli's sphere of operations being primarily political, in his case the prophet and the teacher had to wear the livery and submit to the routine of the practical politician and statesman; but, though it may have happened not infrequently that in appearance at all events he postponed the higher to the lower, he was nevertheless in the conflict in which all were engaged not the least potent and effective of the three.

[1] *Apologia*, p. 33, 'It was the success of the Liberal cause which fretted me inwardly. I became fierce against its instruments and its manifestations.'

Politically the Utilitarian doctrines were throughout the period of their prevalence an appanage of the Liberal party, and in the political sphere accordingly the problem of resistance was to recreate the Tory party so as to make it a bulwark against all that was devastating in the philosophy of the hour. This was the problem that presented itself to Peel after the Reform Bill, and his assumption of office in 1834 is therefore a critical event in the history of English parties.

> In 1834 England, though frightened at the reality of Reform, still adhered to its phrases; it was inclined, as practical England, to maintain existing institutions; but, as theoretical England, it was suspicious that they were indefensible. No one had arisen, either in Parliament, the Universities, or the Press, to lead the public mind to the investigation of principles; and not to mistake, in their reformations, the corruption of practice for fundamental ideas. It was this perplexed, ill-informed, jaded, shallow generation, repeating cries which they did not comprehend, and wearied with the endless ebullitions of their own barren conceit, that Sir Robert Peel was summoned to govern. It was from such materials, ample in quantity, but in all spiritual qualities most deficient; with great numbers, largely acred, Consoled up to their chins, but without knowledge, genius, thought, truth, or faith, that Sir Robert Peel was to form a 'great Conservative party on a comprehensive basis.'[1]

Disraeli, as we have seen, in his last speech at Taunton praised in the highest terms the policy and measures of the Peel administration; but his maturer view, the view of *Coningsby*, was that the whole attempt was premature, precipitated by 'the tactics of those short-sighted intriguers who persisted in looking upon a revolution as a mere party struggle, and would not permit the mind of the nation to work through the inevitable phases that awaited it.' The result was that Peel, though he did his work of reconstructing the Tory party like a 'dexterous politician,' failed to realise 'those prescient views of a great statesman in which he

[1] *Coningsby*, Bk. II. ch. 4.

had doubtless indulged, and in which, though still clogged by the leadership of 1834, he may yet find fame for himself and salvation for his country.' These last words are probably nothing more than conventional homage to a leader whom the writer still acknowledged, and one seems to detect in them that note of grave irony which is so often heard from Disraeli. When they were written in 1844 Disraeli was well aware that Peel was not the man for a great constructive work such as the formation of a Conservative party on a comprehensive basis. He had already come to see that the Tamworth manifesto was an attempt to construct a party without principles; its basis 'Latitudinarianism'; its inevitable consequence 'Political Infidelity.'

> There was indeed a considerable shouting about what they called Conservative principles; but the awkward question naturally arose, what will you conserve? The prerogatives of the Crown, provided they are not exercised; the independence of the House of Lords, provided it is not asserted; the Ecclesiastical estate, provided it is regulated by a commission of laymen. Everything, in short, that is established, as long as it is a phrase and not a fact[1].

Peel, in fact, was a political opportunist, disinterested and therefore with a certain nobility in his opportunism, but still essentially an opportunist, a man who lived without ideas. Disraeli, if any one will have it so, may in the stress of practical politics have sunk at times to an opportunism that was less disinterested than Peel's, and therefore more ignoble; but he was never without ideas or the courage to follow their guidance. He had what Peel signally lacked, the creative mind, and for him therefore was reserved the task at which Peel so disastrously failed.

Between men so different in temperament and in mental constitution antagonism from the first was perhaps almost inevitable. A division of tendency soon declared itself in the reconstituted Tory party, and

[1] *Coningsby*, Bk. II. ch. 5.

Disraeli not many months after his enrolment found himself in the opposite camp to his newly accepted leader. It was a case in which Peel's policy seemed to him to be 'the conservation of the independence of the House of Lords provided it is not asserted.' The principal measures of the Melbourne Government in the Session of 1835 were the Irish Tithes Bill and the Municipal Corporations Bill. Both parties were agreed as to the policy of the conversion of the Irish tithes into a rent-charge; but through the clumsy strategy of the Whig leaders the Peel Ministry had been overthrown, not on a vote of want of confidence nor on any question that was worth fighting for, but on a motion asserting the barren principle of the appropriation of the surplus revenues of the Irish Church to secular purposes. Eventually, in 1838, the difficulty was settled exactly on the lines of Peel's original proposals, but for the present the Whig Ministers clung to this principle of appropriation with what even the Whig historian is constrained to call 'factious folly.'[1] In the present Session they carried through the House of Commons a Tithe Bill in which, in spite of the protests of Peel, appropriation found a place, and when the House of Lords, under the guidance of Lyndhurst, expunged the offensive clauses, Ministers abandoned the Bill. On the question of the English municipal corporations the two Houses again came into sharp collision. In his speech at Taunton in June Disraeli had spoken contemptuously of the Bill as 'a measure of such utter insignificance that he hoped the Conservatives would not condescend to oppose it'; but he soon found himself strenuously supporting Lyndhurst in a campaign for converting the Government proposals into 'a conservative arrangement.' Under Lyndhurst's direction the Bill was drastically amended in the House of Lords; but Peel, who had approved of its main principles during its passage through the House of Commons, was known to have little sympathy with the

[1] Walpole's *History*, III., p. 312.

action of his late Chancellor, and when the measure came back to the Commons he separated himself from the Lords on some important points, though duly laying stress on their privileges and independence. Ultimately a compromise was arranged which, while making large concessions to the wishes of the Upper House, secured the adoption of the Government plan in most of its important features; but the compromise did not prevent a good deal of angry declamation against the Lords during the Parliamentary recess or an attempt on the part of the Radicals to revive the old Reform cry of 'the Bill, the whole Bill, and nothing but the Bill.' The country, however, refused to respond, and in spite of the Radicals, and to some extent in spite of Peel, the session had for result that the Lords, whose prestige had been almost destroyed by the passage of the Reform Act, had now successfully vindicated the independence of their chamber and reasserted its rights as an organic part of the working constitution.

It appears to be the case that during this crisis the King, who was still eagerly seeking for a way in which to rid himself of his hated Whig Ministers, applied to Lyndhurst to assist him if Peel should refuse; and the terms on which Lyndhurst was to become Prime Minister were discussed and informally arranged. Throughout these events Disraeli was in the closest touch with Lyndhurst, and his account [1] of the transaction is to be found in a fragment among his papers written in the following year.

It was in this session [1835] that Lord L[yndhurst] first formed his great plan of stopping the movement. Tried upon the English Municipal Reform Bill as a basis. His triumphant and able career in the House of Lords. Jealousy of Peel. Lyndhurst determines to accept the Premiership

[1] See also the remarkable memoir of Lyndhurst that appeared in *The Times* of Oct. 13, 1863, the day after his death. The disclosures of this memoir were commonly attributed to Disraeli, who was known to have been in Lyndhurst's confidence during the events in question; but though in full agreement with his own account, they surprised Disraeli himself, and were most probably derived from Barnes, who was Editor of *The Times* in 1835, and in close communication with Lyndhurst.

if offered, having received hints from Windsor. His plan to make Brougham Chancellor—to demand from his party 10 seats in the Commons, which were to be given to 10 young men whom he should select. I was one, Bickham Escott another, Thesiger a third. The Commons to be led by Sir James Graham, whom he had sounded, and Sir William Follett, in whom he had great confidence. Peel came up from Drayton and threw him over, and a party in the Lords, led by Wharncliffe, frightened at not being supported in the Commons, receded from their engagement at a meeting at Apsley House at the end of August or beginning of September.

The D[uke] of W[ellington] would have been firm in spite of Peel and accepted office if Wharncliffe and his friends had not seceded. The secession was only private. L.'s final speech at the close of the business, and Brougham's complimentary oration to him, surprised everybody, but the truth is there was an understanding between B. and L. After the debates they generally went home together, and once B. said : 'You and I, Lyndhurst, can rule this country if we like.' Before L.'s final speech B. took him aside and shook hands with him with great feeling and said : 'Let us embrace. We are both Ex-Chancellors and have both been thrown over by our party.'

The consequence of Peel's conduct was the inevitable demonstration apparently in favour of the Whigs by the corporation elections in November. This alone saved the Cabinet. They had become so unpopular in the country, and the H[ouse] of L[ords] had so rallied, even in spite of Peel, and had done so much that in the autumn all the elections went against the Whigs. Ten days or so before the municipal elections was the death of Lord Milton and the Northamptonshire election. The blow was so great that I heard from a good authority that the Ministers did not intend to meet Parliament.

To Sarah Disraeli.

July 20, 1835.

Nothing has been talked of but the great fancy ball which came off last night, and exceeded in splendor anything ever known in London. My dress was very good, with some additions, such as a silken shirt with long sleeves, lent me by Henry Baillie. D'Orsay, Henry Bulwer, myself, Massey Stanley, Talbot, Herbert, and Regina went in a party with the Chesterfields, Ansons, and Worcesters. We flattered ourselves we were by far the most distinguished there. Lady Chesterfield was a Sultana, and Mrs. Anson a Greek, with her own hair lower than the calf of her leg. She was the most brilliant in the room. Lady Burghersh, Lady Fitzroy Somerset, and Lady Sykes wore powder—the two first Louis XIV., the last a complete copy of a Sir Joshua. Lady Londonderry,[1] as Cleopatra, was in a dress literally embroidered with emeralds and diamonds from top to toe. Castlereagh introduced me to her by her desire, and I was with her a great deal. Mrs. Norton and Mrs. Blackwood beautiful Greeks; but the finest thing was that at half-past 2 Lyndhurst gave a supper in George Street to eighty of the supremest *ton* and beauty, and you can conceive nothing more brilliant than his house illuminated with a banquet to a company so fancifully dressed. The Duke of Wellington, who was at the ball, was too tired to come. This great secession rather knocked up the ball, however, and everybody looked blue who was not going to Lyndhurst's. He looked like a French marshal. Wilton was Philip IV., and the Duke lent him his Golden Fleece set in diamonds for the evening.

July 24.

I have since dined at Rosebank with the Londonderrys. 'Tis the prettiest baby-house in the world—a pavilion rather than a villa, all green paint, white chintz, and looking-glass. The grounds, however, are considerable, and very rich, bordering the Thames. The dinner was admirable, but no plate; porcelain, fresh as the room, with a bouquet by every guest, and five immense pyramids of roses down the table. . . . Lyndhurst was quite delighted with his visit, and certainly Bradenham never looked to greater advantage. Yesterday he and I went to Richmond.

Aug. 5.

I can hardly trust myself to write about politics; the debate[2] was dashing in the extreme. Lyndhurst's speech by far the crack one—most bold and triumphant, and received with tumultuous cheering. I can give you no idea of the excited and at the same time depressed state of Melbourne. He seemed quite wild and scared. Brougham

[1] Daughter and heiress of Sir Henry Vane-Tempest and second wife of the 3rd Marquis of Londonderry.

[2] Of August 3 in the Lords, on the motion that the House should go into Committee on the Municipal Corporations Bill. An amendment was moved from the Tory benches that the House, which had already heard counsel in behalf of the corporations, should now receive evidence, and this amendment, supported by Lyndhurst, was carried against the Government.

spoke very well, but his conduct is perplexing. He rather assists us than the reverse. The course taken was kept secret, and perfectly confounded the Whigs. It is an awful crisis whatever may be the result. I cannot think of the hot weather or anything else.

Aug. 12, 1835.

Lyndhurst has been very ill, and unable to go to the Lords, where he ought not to be absent a moment, as all depends upon him. However, Saturday and Sunday's nursing brought him round. The Duke has formally resigned to him the leadership of the House of Lords, and there is every probability of his being Prime Minister; his own disinclination alone stands in the way. To-morrow the war begins in the Lords. The speeches of counsel made a great impression; the evidence was capital, the Lords united, and Lyndhurst has with his own hand drawn up their counter project. . . . But for him all would have been lost, and now everybody praises the stand the Lords have made, and the Whigs have entirely failed in getting up a crisis.

Aug. 14.

There was a sharp engagement in the House of Lords last night. Melbourne is evidently so annoyed that I cannot help fancying he will come down to-night and withdraw the Bill. . . . Brougham was terribly tipsy. He shook his fist at Lord Wicklow, and quoted Ciceronian braggadoccios. . . . After all this is over, Lyndhurst will like to come down with me for a quiet week at Bradenham.[1]

Aug. 20.

I have sent you the *Morning Post* every day, which is the only paper now read, and in whose columns some great unknown has suddenly risen, whose exploits form almost the sole staple of political conversation, and all conversation is now political. The back numbers for the last week cannot be obtained for love or money, and the sale has increased nearly one-third. All attempts at discovering the writer have been baffled, and the mystery adds to the keen interest which the articles excite.[2]

The mystery, if any mystery there be, is solved by another entry in the Mutilated Diary: 'Write the M.P. during the English Municipal Bill for L.—three leading

[1] 'Lord Lyndhurst's visits this year to Bradenham and our increasing friendship' is the corresponding entry in the Mutilated Diary.

[2] *Letters*, pp. 95-98.

articles a day for nearly a month.' The articles, which have been preserved in a book of cuttings, are in the strain of reckless vituperation which was then the fashion even in responsible journals, with only here and there a flash of wit or a happy phrase to redeem the personalities. That 'meagre-minded rebel Roebuck'[1] has something perhaps of the true Disraelian touch; but what would be thought to-day of a newspaper that described a great officer of State as 'this shrewd, coarse, manœuvring Pict,' 'this base-born Scotchman,' 'this booing, fawning, jobbing progeny of haggis and cocka-leekie,' the pleasant labels affixed in the articles to the Attorney-General, Campbell.[2] For argument there is a great deal of the doctrine that the House of Commons is no more representative of the people than is the House of Lords; but the constitutional theories which Disraeli was now evolving we shall find more systematically set forth in a work which was shortly to appear and which must presently engage our attention.

To Lady Blessington.

BRADENHAM,
Oct. 4 [1835].

I see by the papers that you have quitted the shores of the 'far-resounding sea' and resumed your place in the most charming of modern houses. I therefore venture to recall my existence to your memory, and request the favour of hearing some intelligence of yourself, which must always interest me. Have you been well, happy, and prosperous? And has that pen, plucked assuredly from the pinion of a bird of paradise, been idle or creative? My lot has been as usual here, though enlivened by the presence of Lady Sykes, who has contrived to pay us two visits, and the presence of Lord Lyndhurst, who also gave us a fortnight of his delightful society. I am tolerably busy, and hope to give a good account of myself and doings when we meet, which I trust will be soon. How goes that 'great lubber' the Public, and how fares that mighty hoax, the World? Who of our

[1] The 'meagre-minded rebel' before his death was made a Privy Councillor by Disraeli.

[2] Afterwards Lord Campbell.

friends has distinguished or extinguished himself or herself? In short, as the hart for the waterside, I pant for a little news, but chiefly of your fair and agreeable self. . . . How is the most delightful of men and best of friends, the Admirable Crichton? . . . How and where is Bulwer? How are the Whigs and how do they feel? All here who know you send kind greetings, and all who have not that delight, kind wishes. Peace be within your walls and plenteousness within your palace. Vale.

Yours affectionately,

DIS.[1]

In December of this year there was published as a volume of 200 pages a tract entitled a 'Vindication of the English Constitution in a Letter to a Noble and Learned Lord, by Disraeli the Younger,' the noble and learned Lord being, of course, Lyndhurst. This tract is the most important of Disraeli's early political writings, and the fullest exposition of his political creed that preceded *Coningsby*; while even *Coningsby*, as we shall see, added little that is essential to the statement. There is little in the *Vindication* itself, perhaps, that may not be found in germ in the speeches, letters, and articles of the few preceding years, but all is now brought together, and this is one of the cases where the whole is something more than the mere aggregate of the parts. The *Vindication* gave Disraeli what his fugitive efforts could never have given him, a recognised position as a political writer and thinker, and it not only helped to fix and clarify his own ideas, but, appearing at a moment when party boundaries were shifting and principles in a state of flux, it from the first exerted no inconsiderable influence over the development of political thought.

From Isaac D'Israeli.

Dec. 23, 1835.

Your vulgar birthday was, it seems, last Monday, but your nobler political birth has occurred this week, and truly,

[1] Mr. Alfred Morrison's collection. In the reprint the year is wrongly given as 1837.

like the fable of old, you have issued into existence armed in the full panoply of the highest wisdom. You have now a positive *name* and a *being* in the great political world, which you had not ten days ago. It is for you to preserve the wide reputation which I am positive is now secured. I never doubted your powers—they were not latent to me. With more management on your side they would have been acknowledged long ere now—universally. You never wanted for genius, but it was apt in its fullness to run over. You have now acquired, what many a great genius never could, *a perfect style*, and that's a pickle which will preserve even matter less valuable than what you, I doubt not, will always afford the world. You have rejected the curt and flashy diction which betrayed perpetual effort. All now flows in one continuous stream of thought and expression—at once masculine and graceful. . . . All that now remains for you to do is to register 'a vow in Heaven' that you will never write anything inferior to what you have now written, and never to write but on a subject which may call forth all your energies. Should you ever succeed in getting into Parliament I well know that your moral intrepidity and your rapid combinations of ideas will throw out many 'a Vindication' in the brilliancy and irresistible force of your effusions. No man thinks more deeply, while he delights even common eyes by the beauties of his surface. . . . Take care of your health—that is the only weak part which I fear about you.

Disraeli begins the *Vindication* with an attack on his old enemies the Utilitarians. He had not only the instinctive antipathy of the born romantic to their unimaginative creed, but by training as well as by temperament he had all the intolerance of Burke for their practice of indulging in 'barren assertions of abstract rights,' of dabbling in '*a priori* systems of politics,' and of framing 'new constitutions on the abstract principles of theoretic science.' There are, indeed, frequent passages in the *Vindication* which sound like echoes of Burke, and show that Disraeli was deeply penetrated with the spirit and sentiment of Burke's later writings. 'Nations have characters as well as individuals, and national character is precisely the quality which the new sect of statesmen in their schemes and speculations either deny or overlook.' 'This respect for precedent, this clinging to prescription, this reverence for antiquity, which are so often ridiculed by conceited and superficial minds . . . appear to me to have their origin in a profound knowledge of human nature.' Disraeli had read widely, if not deeply, in history; and, like Burke, indeed like Bolingbroke, in a still earlier generation, and, above all, like Bolingbroke's friend Montesquieu, he carried into his investigation of political problems the spirit of that pregnant historical method which, already triumphant in Germany, was in a subsequent generation to overthrow the pretensions of the dominant school of thinkers in England and present their so-called philosophy in its true historical perspective as a mere insular anachronism in the œcumenical history of thought.

The argument of the *Vindication* is largely based on a favourite doctrine of Disraeli's, the representation in Parliament of separate estates of the realm and the dependence of the balance of the constitution on the maintenance of their several rights. The assailants against whom he was vindicating the constitution were the Radicals, who, as has been seen, had attempted during the recess to stir up agitation against the House of Lords, and O'Connell, who, in a pilgrimage of passion through the north, had especially distinguished himself in this endeavour. With a considerable display of learning the author traces the origin and development of our institutions, and arrives at the conclusion that 'the House of Commons is no more the house of the people than is the House of Lords.' To the Radical conception of the people he opposes his conception of the nation as a living and organized whole; but not even in the narrower or in any reasonable sense of the term can the House of Commons be regarded as the house of the people or its members as the representatives of the people. 'The Commons form still only an estate of the realm, a privileged and limited order of the nation, in numbers a fraction of the mass,' the constituency even since its enlargement by the Reform Act comprising no more than three or four hundred thousand persons. The House of Lords, on the other hand, though not elective, is truly representative, 'the most eminent existing example of representation without election.'

The House of Lords represents the Church in the Lord Bishops, the law in the Lord Chancellor, and often the Lord Chief Justice, the counties in the Lord Lieutenants, the boroughs in their noble recorders. This estate, from the character of the property of its members, is also essentially the representative chamber of the land; and, as the hereditary leaders of the nation, especially of the cultivators of the land, the genuine and permanent population of England, its peasantry.[1]

'In a hasty and factious effort to get rid of representation without election, it will be as well if eventually we do not discover that we have only obtained election without representation.' But if the Lords are representative, what of their responsibility? They are in fact in no greater degree irresponsible than the Commons.

Is a privileged order of three hundred thousand individuals, represented by their deputies, likely to be more responsible than a privileged order of three hundred individuals appearing by themselves? On the contrary, every one sees and feels in an instant that, as far as the nation is concerned, the more limited order, who appear for themselves, and are more in the eye of the world, are in fact in a moral point of view much more responsible to the general body of the people than the more numerous and more obscure class, who shuffle off that moral responsibility on their representatives.[2]

'If I were called upon,' he declares in words which sound like an echo of an often-quoted dictum of Alexander Hamilton's, 'to construct a constitution *a priori* for this country, of which a senate, or superior chamber,

[1] P. 129. [2] P. 145.

was to be a constituent part, I am at a loss to conceive where I could obtain more suitable materials for its construction than in the body of our hereditary peerage.' The tree, his argument runs, shall be known by its fruit. The hereditary peerage has formed an active and powerful branch of our legislature for five centuries, and no statesman can doubt that its peculiar character has mainly contributed to the stability of our institutions. Throughout that period it has given us a senate not inferior in capacity to the elective chamber, and now, as he contends, the hereditary assembly manifestly excels the elective, not only 'in the higher accomplishments of statesmen, in elevation of thought and feeling, in learning and in eloquence,' but also in 'those very qualities, for the possession of which at first sight we should be most disposed to give a House of Commons credit, that mastery of detail and management of complicated commonplaces which we style in this country "business-like habits."'

You cannot, he is careful to observe, obtain a substitute for the House of Lords by merely collecting all the clever men of the country and giving them the august title of a senate. A nation will not allow three hundred men, however ingenious, to make laws for them, just because the sovereign power of the state chooses to appoint that such a number of its subjects shall possess this privilege. 'The King of England may make peers, but he cannot make a House of Lords.'

> The order of men, of whom such an assembly is formed, is the creation of ages. In the first place, they must really be an estate of the realm, a class of individuals who from their property and personal influence alone form an important section of the whole nation. . . . Their names, office, and character, and the ennobling achievements of their order, must be blended with our history and bound up with our hereditary sentiment. They must be felt and recognised as the not unworthy descendants or successors of a class that has always taken the lead in civilisation and formed the advance guard in the march of national progress.[1]

[1] Pp. 159, 161.

Be it observed, moreover, that at the root of the permanence and popularity of our hereditary peerage is its essentially democratic character. The basis of our social fabric is the principle of civil equality. It is this principle which has 'prevented the nobility of England from degenerating into a favoured and odious sect.' It is this principle which has placed the Peers at the head of the people and filled the House of Commons with members connected with the Peers by the most intimate ties of birth and blood.

The English nation, to obtain the convenience of monarchy, have established a popular throne, and to enjoy the security of aristocracy, have invested certain orders of their fellow subjects with legislative functions: but these estates, however highly privileged, are invested with no quality of exclusion; and the Peers and the Commons of England are the trustees of the nation, not its masters. The country where the legislative and even the executive office may be constitutionally obtained by every subject of the land, is a democracy, and a democracy of the noblest character. . . . Neither ancient ages, nor the more recent experience of our newer time, can supply us with a parallel instance of a free government, founded on the broadest basis of popular rights, yet combining with democratic liberty, aristocratic security, and monarchical convenience.[1]

Incidentally Disraeli sets forth his theory of the origin and genius of our English parties—a curious blend of insight and paradox, of which perhaps the paradox will seem less startling when our history has been truly interpreted and freed from the bias it has received from the great Whig historians. The Whigs, according to Disraeli, have always been an anti-national party, always striving to upset the balance of the constitution, always making war on the national institutions in the interest of their own aggrandisement. The party had its origin in the latter part of the 17th century in a combination between the Peers and the

[1] P. 207.

Puritans, the former animated by hostility to the monarchy, the latter by hatred of the establishment. A republican sentiment united the two; but the republican model of the House of Russell was Venice; of their plebeian allies, Geneva. 'Their cry was civil and religious Freedom . . . that is, a doge and no bishops: advocating the liberty of the subject, the Peers would have established an oligarchy; upholding toleration, the Puritans aimed at supremacy.' The Tory party, on the other hand, is the national party, the really democratic party in England. 'It supports the institutions of the country, because they have been established for the common good, and because they secure the equality of civil rights, without which, whatever may be its name, no government can be free.' When the Peers and the Puritans raised their cry of civil and religious liberty as a pretext for the destruction of the Monarchy and the Church—

> The mass of the nation still smarting under the sequestrations and imprisonments of parliamentary committees, and loathing the recollection of the fanaticism and the hypocrisy of the Roundhead apostles of the tub, clung to the national institutions. The clergy, jealous of the Nonconformists, and fearful of another deprivation, exaggerated the power and character of the Crown, in which they recognized their only safeguard. Hence divine right and passive obedience resounded from our Protestant pulpits, echoed with enthusiasm by a free and spirited people who acknowledged in these phrases only a determination to maintain the mild authority of their King and of their Church.[1]

Such was the origin of the Tory party in this country. The position long remained preposterous and paradoxical. 'An oligarchy sought to establish itself by the plan of public freedom; a nation struggled to maintain its rights on the principles of arbitrary power.'

There are periods when the titles and watchwords of political parties become obsolete; and when by adhering

[1] P. 177.

to an ancient and accustomed cry, a party often appears to profess opinions less popular than it really practises, and yields a proportionate advantage to its more dexterous competitor. In times of great political change, and rapid political transition, it will generally be observed that political parties find it convenient to re-baptize themselves. Thus, in the present day, Whigs have become Reformers, and Tories Conservatives. In the early part of the last century, the Tory party required a similar reorganization to that which it has lately undergone; and as it is in the nature of human affairs that the individual that is required shall not long be wanting, so in the season of which I am treating, arose a man remarkable in an illustrious age, who, with the splendour of an organizing genius, settled the confused and discordant materials of English faction, and reduced them into a clear and systematic order. This was Lord Bolingbroke.

Gifted with that fiery imagination, the teeming fertility of whose inventive resources is as necessary to a great statesman or a great general, as to a great poet, the ablest writer and the most accomplished orator of his age, that rare union that in a country of free parliaments and a free press, insures to its possessor the privilege of exercising a constant influence over the mind of his country, that rare union that has rendered Burke so memorable; blending with that intuitive knowledge of his race which creative minds alone enjoy, all the wisdom which can be derived from literature, and a comprehensive experience of human affairs; — no one was better qualified to be the minister of a free and powerful nation than Henry St. John; and destiny at first appeared to combine with nature in the elevation of his fortunes. Opposed to the Whigs from principle, for an oligarchy is hostile to genius, and recoiling from the Tory tenets, which his unprejudiced and vigorous mind taught him at the same time to dread and to contemn, Lord Bolingbroke, at the outset of his career, incurred the commonplace imputation of insincerity and inconsistency, because in an age of unsettled parties with professions contradictory of their conduct, he maintained that vigilant and meditative independence which is the privilege of an original and determined spirit. It is probable that in the earlier years of his career he meditated over the formation of a new party, that dream of youthful ambition in a perplexed and discordant age, but destined in English politics to be never more substantial than a vision. More experienced in political life, he became aware that he had only to choose between the Whigs and the Tories, and his sagacious intellect, not satisfied with the superficial character of these celebrated divisions, penetrated their interior and essential qualities, and discovered, in spite of all the affectation of popular sympathy on one side and of admiration of arbitrary power on the other, that this choice was in fact a choice between oligarchy and democracy. From the moment that Lord Bolingbroke, in becoming a Tory, embraced the national cause, he devoted himself absolutely to his party: all the energies of his Protean mind were lavished in their service; and although the ignoble prudence of the Whig Minister restrained him from advocating the cause of the nation in the Senate, it was his inspiring pen that made Walpole tremble in the recesses of the Treasury, and in a series of writings, unequalled in our literature for their spirited patriotism, their just and profound views, and the golden eloquence in which they are expressed, eradicated from Toryism all those absurd and odious doctrines which Toryism had adventitiously adopted, clearly developed its essential and permanent character, discarded *jure divino*, demolished passive obedience, threw to the winds the doctrine of non-resistance, placed the abolition of James and the accession of George on their right basis, and in the complete re-organisation of the public mind laid the foundation for the future accession of the Tory party to power, and to that popular and triumphant career which must ever await the policy of an administration inspired by the spirit of our free and ancient institutions.[1]

Disraeli had steeped himself in the politics of the age of Anne and the early Georges, had studied Bolingbroke both in his career and in his writings, and drawn freely from the fund of political ideas which he found in him. The English Alcibiades has received something less than justice from the Whig writers who have given us our history, but whether he wholly deserved Disraeli's glowing eulogy is not now the question. It is not as an historical judgment on the character and achievements of Henry St. John that the passage really interests us, but as a statement of the ideal and an anticipation of the

[1] Pp. 185-188.

career of Benjamin Disraeli. The writer proceeds at once to show the need for another Bolingbroke in the circumstances of the hour. The Tories have just carried England through a perilous age of war and revolution, and are burdened in consequence with an accretion of those accidental qualities which are inseparable from all political parties that have long been in power.

> If the Whigs at this moment be pursuing the same desperate and determined policy that they prosecuted so vigorously a century back, it will be well for their rivals to adopt the same cautious yet energetic system of conduct which, developed at the same period by the genius of a Bolingbroke, led in due season to the administration of a Pitt. In the conduct of the Tory party at this moment, it appears to me that there are three points to the furtherance of which we should principally apply ourselves : 1st. That the real character and nature of Toryism should be generally and clearly comprehended : 2ndly. That Toryism should be divested of all those qualities which are adventitious and not essential, and which, having been produced by that course of circumstances which are constantly changing, become in time obsolete, inconvenient, and by the dexterous misrepresentation of our opponents even odious : 3rdly. That the efficient organisation of the party should be secured and maintained.[1]

There surely is a statement of the task Disraeli proposed to himself. 'I do not think,' he adds, 'there ever was a period in our history when the English nation was so intensely Tory in feeling as at the present moment ; but the Reform Act has placed the power of the country in the hands of a small body of persons hostile to the nation, and therefore there is no due proportion between the social and the political power of the national party.' To this partial and sectarian character of the constituency of 1832 he is never tired of recurring. 'I am not one of those,' he tells us elsewhere in a passage that ought to be remembered, 'who believe that the safety of the constitution is consulted by encouraging an exclusive principle in the formation of the constituency

[1] P. 192.

of our third estate. It is not the supposed democratic character which it has assumed under the new arrangement—I wish I could call it settlement—that fills me with any apprehensions. On the contrary, I wish it were even more catholic, though certainly not more Papist.[1] It is its sectarian quality in which I discover just cause of alarm.'[2] In genuine Toryism there is no shrinking from democracy.

It is curious to observe that so difficult is it to destroy the original character and eradicate the first principles of human affairs, that those very members of the Tory party who were loudest in upbraiding the Whig Reform Act as a democratic measure were simultaneously, and have ever since been, urging and prosecuting measures infinitely more democratic than that cunning oligarchical device. . . . No sooner was the passing of the Whig Reform Act inevitable, than the Tories introduced a clause into it which added many thousand members to the estate of the Commons. No sooner was the Whig Reform Act passed, and circumstances had proved that, with all their machinations, the oligarchy was not yet secure, than the Whigs, under the pretence of reforming the corporations, attempted to compensate themselves for the democratic increase of the third estate, through the Chandos clause, by the political destruction of all the freemen of England ; but the Tories again stepped in to the rescue of the nation from the oligarchy, and now preserved the rights of eighty thousand members of the third estate. And not content with adding many thousands to its numbers, and preserving eighty thousand, the Tories, ever since the passing of the oligarchical Reform Act of the Whigs, have organised societies throughout the country for the great democratic purpose of increasing to the utmost possible extent the numbers of the third estate of the realm. The clause of Lord Chandos, your Lordship's triumphant defence of the freemen of England, and the last registration, are

[1] Disraeli's language in this tract is coloured in many places by the Protestant feeling which the Whig attack on the revenues of the Irish Church had aroused into activity ; and his reconstruction of history had not yet been carried to the stage which we shall find it reaches in *Sybil*. James II. is still 'the Popish tyrant' ; Lord Somers is held up to us as the model of a wise statesman ; and the Revolution of 1688 is regarded as salutary and inevitable.

[2] P. 100.

three great democratic movements, and quite in keeping with the original and genuine character of Toryism.[1]

To Sarah Disraeli.

Jan., 1836.

The letter that was sent on to me was from Sir Robert Peel. I sent him a copy, late and grudgingly, with a cold dry note, convinced that he would never notice or even confess to having heard of it, being, as you well know, by reputation the most jealous, frigid, and haughty of men. This is what he says:—'I beg to return you my best thanks for that copy of your recent work respecting the House of Lords for which I am indebted to your kind attention and consideration. It is not the only one in my possession, for, attracted as well by your name as by some extracts from the work in the public papers, which struck me as very forcibly written, I had taken the first opportunity of procuring a copy, and was gratified and surprised to find that a familiar and apparently exhausted topic could be treated with so much of original force of argument and novelty of illustration.

'I thank you, both for the work itself and the satisfaction which the reading of it has afforded me.

'I have the honour to be,
'Your faithful and obedient servant,
'ROBERT PEEL.'

Lyndhurst thinks this is *much*, considering the writer.[2]

'A masterly union of learning, skill, and eloquence,' was Lyndhurst's own judgment.

To Sarah Disraeli.

Jan. 9.

The sale of the *Vindication* continues, and, though not quite so brisk, is in daily demand. I received to-day a letter from Eliot, which, from its length and the extreme warmth of its feeling, would quite surprise you. His copy did not reach him till the 6th. He says, among other things, 'In reading your sketch of Bolingbroke I could not help thinking that if opportunities are not withheld you may become what he might have been.' He wants to know, by the bye, why I

[1] Pp. 201-3. [2] *Letters*, p. 108.

call the Orleans branch the House of Valois. I am sure I don't know. Pray find out for me, and write your answer, if you catch one, as soon as possible.

On Tuesday I dined at Lyndhurst's, and met Lords Roden, Lowther, and Rosslyn, Sir E. Sugden,[1] Sir H. Hardinge, Courtenay, Alderson, &c., and Lockhart, whom L. asked, that he might review the *Vindication*. Chance! he never spoke a word. He is known in society by the name of 'The Viper,' but if he tries to sting me, he will find my heel of iron.[2]

The beginning of the year had found him engaged in an angry quarrel which afforded him abundant opportunity for displaying his 'heel of iron.' 'The letters to *The Times* have made a great sensation,' he writes[3] to his sister. 'I am the first individual who has silenced the Press with its own weapons.' The *Globe*, then a Whig organ, in an abusive notice of the *Vindication*, had revived the old business of Hume, O'Connell, and the first Wycombe election; and a lengthy controversy ensued conducted on Disraeli's side in the columns of *The Times*. His letters add nothing of moment to our knowledge, but one passage is, perhaps, worth preserving, both as a specimen of the manner in which the 'heel of iron' was applied and as an illustration of the controversial methods of the day.

The editor of the *Globe* has been pleased to say that he is disinclined to continue this controversy because it gratifies my 'passion for notoriety.' The editor of the *Globe* must have a more contracted mind and paltrier spirit than even I imagined if he can suppose for a moment that an ignoble controversy with an obscure animal like himself can gratify the passion for notoriety of one whose works at least have been translated into the languages of polished Europe, and circulate by thousands in the New World. It is not then my passion for notoriety that has induced me to tweak the editor of the *Globe* by the nose, and to inflict sundry kicks upon the baser part of his base body; to make him eat dirt, and his own words, fouler than any filth; but because I wished to show to the world what a miserable poltroon, what

[1] Afterwards Lord St. Leonards and Lord Chancellor.
[2] *Letters*, p. 100. [3] On Jan. 4.

a craven dullard, what a literary scarecrow, what a mere thing, stuffed with straw and rubbish, is the *soi-disant* director of public opinion and official organ of Whig politics.[1]

' 'Tis a great thing to have such an organ for response as *The Times*,' wrote Disraeli to his sister. Under the guidance of John Walter, second of the name, *The Times* had already taken a place far ahead of all its rivals ; and, though it had supported the Reform movement and been friendly to the Grey Ministry, it was now in open opposition to Melbourne and bitterly hostile to the alliance between the Whigs and O'Connell. In the previous summer, it will be remembered, Disraeli had used the *Morning Post* as his journalistic medium, but he now transferred his flag to *The Times* and formed a close alliance with Barnes, the Editor. The alliance soon bore fruit. In *The Times* of January 19 there appeared a scathing philippic against the Government and its members in the form of a letter addressed to Lord Melbourne, and written in the style of Junius over the signature of 'Runnymede.' This letter was the first of a series of nineteen[2] in all which appeared in the course of the four months that followed. Three are addressed to Melbourne, two to Peel and Stanley, and most of the others to the leading members of the Government.

To Sarah Disraeli.

[*Jan.*, 1836.]

The *Letters of Runnymede* are the only things talked of in London, especially the latter ones. The author is unknown, and will probably so remain. One or two papers have foolishly ascribed them to me. There is certainly some imitation of my style, and the writer is familiar with my works.

Feb. 5.

The *Letters of Runnymede* are still making a great sensation. They are considered as rising regularly in power, and the two

[1] *The Times*, Jan. 9, 1836.

[2] A few more letters appeared over the same signature in the following year.

last, the characters of Lord J[ohn] R[ussell] and O'C[onnell] are generally esteemed the most powerful. *Fraser*, which is making some noise, is the highest eulogy I ever received, saying: 'Swift observes, the appearance of a great genius in the world may always be known by the virulence of the dunces, and that this has been singularly illustrated in my case,' &c. Peel told Lyndhurst the last letter was the most powerful of all; so it is generally esteemed.[1]

That the letters were immensely effective at the time of their appearance there is no room for doubt, but their style is hardly such as to win appreciation now or to act as a salt to preserve them for posterity. Urbanity was certainly not in those days a characteristic of Disraeli's controversial methods any more than it was a characteristic of the journalism of the time; and whatever wit or wisdom the letters may contain, their tone is too personal, their invective too unmeasured, and even their praise, when they praise, too little under restraint for the taste of the present day. The abuse of O'Connell, for instance, in the letter which Peel thought so powerful exceeds all bounds in its savagery:—'He is a systematic liar and a beggarly cheat, a swindler, and a poltroon. . . . . His public and his private life are equally profligate; he has committed every crime that does not require courage.'[2] In the case of O'Connell there was of course personal animus to add venom to the shaft, but others who were guiltless of provocation are made to suffer hardly less. 'You have a most surprising disdain for the law of libel,' wrote Barnes on some occasion, and the law of libel was evidently less of a terror to newspapers in those days than now. Disraeli never till the end of his life acknowledged the authorship of the letters, and probably he was deterred by a feeling of remorse for the rough handling he had given to men with whom he was afterwards on terms of friendship. Lord John Russell, for instance, is 'a feeble Catiline'; 'an individual, who, on the principle that good vinegar is the corruption of bad wine,

1 *Letters*, pp. 100 and 102.

2 Letter VIII. To the People.

has been metamorphosed from an incapable author into an eminent politician.' In all his conduct 'it is not difficult to detect the workings of a mean and long-mortified spirit suddenly invested with power,—the struggles of a strong ambition attempting, by a wanton exercise of authority, to revenge the disgrace of a feeble intellect.' Palmerston is the 'Lord Fanny of diplomacy,' endowed with a dexterity 'which seems a happy compound of the smartness of an attorney's clerk and the intrigue of a Greek of the lower Empire.' 'The leader of the Whig Opposition was wont to say that your Lordship reminded him of a favourite footman on easy terms with his mistress': that was of course said in Palmerston's Tory days, but those days had been ended by his expulsion from the Duke of Wellington's Cabinet 'for playing a third-rate part in a third-rate intrigue.' 'Our language commands no expression of scorn which has not been exhausted in the celebration of your character; there is no conceivable idea of degradation which has not been at some period or another, associated with your career.' Spring Rice, the Chancellor of the Exchequer, has the reputation of 'a man of business'; 'and, indeed, shrewd without being sagacious, bustling without method, loquacious without eloquence, ever prompt though always superficial, and ever active though always blundering, you are exactly the sort of fussy busybody who would impose upon and render himself indispensable to indolent and ill-informed men of strong ambition and weak minds.' Melbourne himself in a happy phrase is accused of 'sauntering over the destinies of a nation, and lounging away the glory of an Empire.'

I think the Cabinet might take to cricket—they are a choice eleven. With their peculiarly patriotic temperaments, and highly national feelings, they might venture, I think, to play against 'All England.' Lord Palmerston and Lord Glenelg, with their talent for keeping in, would assuredly secure a good score. Lord John, indeed, with all his flourishing, will probably end in knocking down his own wicket; and as for

Sir Cam,[1] the chances certainly are that he will be 'caught out,' experiencing the same fate in play as in politics. If you could only engage Lord Durham to fling sticks at the seals of the Foreign Office, and the agile Mr. Ellice to climb a greasy pole for the Colonial portfolio, I think you will have provided a very entertaining programme of Easter sports.[2]

The letter to Peel is throughout a piece of highly-pitched glorification that reads strangely in the light of subsequent events. 'In your chivalry alone is our hope. Clad in the panoply of your splendid talents and your spotless character we feel assured that you will' conquer.

What a contrast does your administration as Prime Minister afford to that of one of your recent predecessors! No selfish views, no family aggrandisement, no family jobs, no nepotism. . . . Contrast the serene retirement of Drayton, and the repentant solitude of Howick; contrast the statesman, cheered after his factious defeat by the sympathy of a nation, with the coroneted Necker, the worn-out Machiavel, wringing his helpless hands over his hearth in remorseful despair, and looking up with a sigh at his scowling ancestors. . . .

You have an addition to the scutcheon of your fame in the emblazoned memory of your brief but masterly premiership. They cannot taunt you now with your vague promises of amelioration: you can appeal to the deeds of your Cabinet, and the plans which the applause of a nation sanctioned, and the execution of which the intrigues of a faction alone postponed. Never, too, since the peace of Paris, has the great national party of this realm been so united as at the present moment. It is no exaggeration to say, that among its leaders not the slightest difference of opinion exists upon any portion of their intended policy. Pitt himself, in the plenitude of his power, never enjoyed more cordial confidence than that which is now extended to you by every alleged section of the Conservative ranks.

A similar strain of panegyric runs through the letter to Stanley.

When the acerbities of faction have passed away, posterity will do justice to your disinterestedness and devotion. . . . Less than three years ago the Whigs, and loudest among

1 Sir John Cam Hobhouse, afterwards Lord Broughton.

2 Letter XV.

them my Lord Melbourne, announced you as the future Prime Minister of England. Young, of high lineage, of illustrious station, and of immaculate character, and unquestionably their ablest orator,—among your own party you had no rival. . . . You, my Lord, preferred your honour to your interest, the prosperity of your native land to the gratification of your ambition. You sacrificed without a pang the proudest station in your country, to prove to your countrymen that public principle was not yet a jest. You did well. The pulse of our national character was beating low. We required some great example to re-brace the energies of our honour. From the moment that you denounced the disgusting thraldom and the base expedients of your chicaning colleagues, a better feeling pervaded England, and animated Englishmen. . . .

The time is ripe for union and fair for concord. When, some days back, in my letter to Sir Robert Peel—a letter, let me observe in passing, written by one whose name, in spite of the audacious licence of frantic conjecture, has never yet been even intimated, can never be discovered, and will never be revealed—I announced the fact that the great Conservative party was at length completely united, it was a declaration equivalent to England being saved. . . . In a Peel, a Stanley, a Wellington, and a Lyndhurst, the people of England recognise their fitting leaders. Let the priestly party oppose to these the acrid feebleness of a Russell, and the puerile commonplace of a Howick, Melbourne's experienced energy, and Lansdowne's lucid perception!

From Lord Lyndhurst.

[*Feb.*, 1836.]

My dear Dissy,

Lord John is a great, very great success. B[arnes] writes me word that it is the best of the series. I agree entirely with him in this.

It strikes me that one advantage of a strict incognito is this: that people are never jealous of the success of an unknown person: they praise therefore readily, freely, fully. This they will not do when an author is known: other feelings, other considerations raise themselves up in the mind and operate as a minus quantity in the sum of praise. I fear in this case nobody can doubt the author! It should have been discovered later.

Ever,

L.

The letters were republished in the course of the summer with a long dedication to Peel, and bound up with them there was a short tract entitled 'The Spirit of Whiggism,' which could have left little doubt in the mind of any one who had read the *Vindication* as to the identity of 'Runnymede.' From beginning to end we have the argument, the history, and even the language of the *Vindication* repeated, though here and there is a phrase more finished, a point more precisely made, or a position more happily elaborated.

It is a great delusion to believe that revolutions are ever effected by a nation. It is a faction, and generally a small one, that overthrows a dynasty or remodels a constitution. . . . During the last five years the Whigs have been at war with the English constitution. First of all they captured the King; then they vanquished the House of Commons; now they have laid siege to the House of Lords. . . . The House of Lords at this moment represents everything in the realm except the Whig oligarchs, their tools—the Dissenters, and their masters—the Irish priests. In the meantime, the Whigs bawl aloud that there is a 'collision!' It is true there is a collision; but it is not a collision between the *Lords* and the *People*, but between the *Ministers* and the *Constitution*.

It may be as well to remind the English nation that a revolutionary party is not necessarily a liberal one, and that a republic is not indispensably a democracy. . . . The rights and liberties of a nation can only be preserved by institutions. It is not the spread of knowledge or the march of intellect that will be found sufficient sureties for the public welfare in the crisis of a country's freedom. . . . I would address myself to the English Radicals. . . . I mean those thoughtful and enthusiastic men who study their unstamped press, and ponder over a millennium of operative amelioration. Not merely that which is just, but that which is also practicable, should be the aim of a sagacious politician. Let the Radicals well consider whether, in attempting to achieve their avowed object, they are not, in fact, only assisting the secret views of a party whose scheme is infinitely more adverse to their own than the existing system, whose genius I believe they entirely misapprehend. The monarchy of the Tories is more democratic than the republic of the Whigs. It appeals with a keener sympathy to the passions of the millions; it studies their interests with a more comprehensive solicitude.

There is no probability of ever establishing in England a more democratic form of government than the present English constitution. . . . The disposition of property in England throws the government of the country into the hands of its natural aristocracy. I do not believe that any scheme of the suffrage, or any method of election, could divert that power into other quarters. It is the necessary consequence of our present social state. I believe, the wider the popular suffrage, the more powerful would be the natural aristocracy. This seems to me an inevitable consequence; but I admit this proposition on the clear understanding that such an extension should be established upon a fair, and not a factious, basis.

Our revolutions are brought about by the passions of creative minds taking advantage, for their own aggrandisement, of peculiar circumstances in our national progress. They are never called for by the great body of the nation. Churches are plundered, long rebellions maintained, dynasties changed, Parliaments abolished; but when the storm is passed, the features of the social landscape remain unimpaired; there are no traces of the hurricane, the earthquake, or the volcano; it has been but a tumult of the atmosphere, that has neither toppled down our old spires and palaces, nor swallowed up our cities and seats of learning, nor blasted our ancient woods, nor swept away our ports and harbours. The English nation ever recurs to its ancient institutions—the institutions that have alike secured freedom and order; and after all their ebullitions, we find them, when the sky is clear, again at work, and toiling on at their eternal task of accumulation.

There is ever an union in a perverted sense between those who are beneath power and those who wish to be above it; and oligarchies and despotisms are usually established by the agency of a deluded multitude. . . . This union of oligarchical wealth and mob poverty is the very essence of the 'Spirit of Whiggism.'

Meanwhile Disraeli had found a haven of rest in the Carlton.

To Lady Blessington.

Wednesday [*Feb.*, 1836].

MY DEAREST LADY,

Early in March there are to be fifty members elected into the Carlton by the members at large. A strong party of my friends, Lord L., Lord Chandos, Stuart de Rothesay, etc., are very active in my behalf, and I think among the leaders of our party my claims would be recognised; but doubtless there is a sufficient alloy of dunces even among the Conservatives, and I have no doubt there will be a stout opposition to me. Although I will not canvass myself, I wish my friends to do so *most earnestly*. I know from personal experience that one word from you would have more effect upon me than letters from all the lords in Xdom. I wish therefore to enlist you on my side, and will take the liberty of sending you a list to-morrow.

Votre DIS.[1]

To Sarah Disraeli.

[*March*, 1836.]

I carried the Carlton; the opposition was not inconsiderable in the committee, but my friends were firm—400 candidates, and all in their own opinion with equal claims.

THE CARLTON,
April 18.

The Opera is very good this year, and Carlotta Grisi the great dancer. There is a report in *Times* of the Lewes banquet. About my pledging myself to come forward is a mendacious flourish, but does not matter. The Carlton is a great lounge, and I have found a kind friend in Francis Baring—Lord Ashburton's eldest son.[2]

Disraeli knew how to employ to advantage his new connexion with *The Times*. He had gone to Lewes with a friend who was candidate for the borough and addressed a meeting in his interest; and *The Times* gave a column

[1] From Mr. Alfred Morrison's Collection. [2] *Letters*, pp. 103, 104.

of the speech, introducing the speaker as 'Mr. Disraeli, already well known for his literary talents and his opposition to the O'Connell influence in the Government.' The report is worth reading even now for the skill with which the history and constitutional theory of the *Vindication* are woven into a speech that was yet supremely effective as a piece of platform oratory, as is proved by the fact that when the orator sat down 'the most deafening applause prevailed for the space of several minutes.'

To Sarah Disraeli.

June 13.

The crisis goes on. The general impression is that the Ministers are going to play 1832 over again, and resign with the idea we cannot form a Government. Nothing can give you an idea of the excitement prevailing in the political circles, but I am not inclined to change my opinion, viz., that there will be no dissolution. Lyndhurst, who has been dining with the Duke, confirms what I have heard ; the battle cannot be fought better than at present. . . . Lyndhurst's speech was really a masterpiece ; since Canning there has been nothing like it. O'Connell came into the House, but, he will have it, *after* L. had done speaking about him. However, he *was* there, and it was a grand hit, for everybody believed him to be there. The Commons were cowed last night ; Lyndhurst's dash has daunted them ; John Russell was really feeble, and O'Connell furiously tame. In the meantime, I am brought forward with great trumpeting in leading articles of the *Chronicle*. Both Lyndhurst and Sir R. Peel are said to have adopted Mr. Disraeli's view of the Constitution, &c., &c.[1]

The session was in the main an Irish session, and though it opened well for the Government they emerged from it with little credit. Disraeli's account of it, from the same fragment as his account of the session of 1835,[2] and written in the same *staccato* style, is as follows :—

The Tories met Parliament in the most sanguine spirits. It was supposed that the Ministers would not have a majority.

[1] *Ibid.*, p. 104. [2] See above, p. 301.

The Tories had gained in isolated elections since their resignation enough votes to destroy the majority that drove Sir R. P. from office. The Raphael Carlow business was also considered very injurious to O'Connell. To our surprise the Ministers as strong as ever. Our party became dispirited. Peel timid and always acting on the defensive. The Irish Corporations and Church Bill again approaching. The last propitiously postponed by the Ministers for reasons afterwards discovered.

L. has a conference with the Duke of Cumberland. Forms another and still more comprehensive plan for arresting the movement. Conferences with the Duke of Wellington: announces his determination to withdraw if not supported by Sir R. P. Conferences between the D. of W., Sir R. P., and Lord L. Sir R. P. agrees to accept Lord L.'s plan and pledges himself to act upon it. The total extinction[1] of the Irish corporations resolved upon. Strength of the Ministers in the Commons—majority of more than 80. Lords assembled at Apsley House. Each peer individually pledges himself to support Lord L.'s plans at all events. Commencement of the real session of the Lords as late as June. Extraordinary speeches and exertions of Lord L. Attempt at creating a collision. Total failure from the firmness of the Lords. Great courage and eminent services of the D. of Cumberland. Great exertions of the Press and of *The Times* in favour of Lyndhurst. The country sides with the Lords. The threatened collision laughed at. The Ministerial tactics long planned by O'Connell now developed. The Lords Bill on Irish Corporations to be accepted and the appropriation clause to be given [up ?]. Consequent jealousy and discontent of the English Radicals. The Ministers obliged to give up the O'Connell tactics. They reject the Irish Corporations Bill as amended by the Lords and pass the appropriation clause. The Lords follow up the Lyndhurst plan. He becomes virtual leader of the Upper House. All the Whig Radical measures thrown out with the entire approbation of the country: all the elections in favour of the Tories. Rage of the Irish party. The country rallies round Lyndhurst. He delivers his speech called 'The Summary of the Session'—reprinted, and circulates through the country in innumerable editions. The English Radicals announce their provisional

[1] The Government Bill proposed to substitute for the old corrupt corporations a system of elected councils; but the Lords declined to accept the constructive portion of the scheme and converted the Bill into a measure for the abolition of municipal corporations in Ireland.

defection from the Whigs. The Foreign policy of the Whigs. The session closes with the complete triumph of the Tories at home and abroad.

About a month ago (I write this rapid sketch 17 Sept. 1836) at the Carlton Club Lord de L'Isle, son-in-law of the King, informed me that His Majesty wished L. to be Premier, but was afraid he was inextricably bound to Sir R. P. Dined alone with Lord Strangford on the 13th, who was fresh from Walmer, where he had a confidential conversation with the D. of W'n. His Grace said he anticipated a daily break-up of the Government but himself wished it postponed. That he himself would take a seat in the Cabinet but no office: wished L. to throw over his profession. Thought P. must be Premier, but thought L. with the leadership of the House of Lords, an earldom, and the Home Department would be almost the same as Premier. Similar ideas are common—but a large party in the country would hail L.'s accession to the Premiership with satisfaction. His firmness and courage have won all hearts, and the result has proved his sagacity.

On the day that Lyndhurst died nearly thirty years later Disraeli took his pen and placed on paper his impressions of the dead man's mind and character: and the document, which is at once an appreciation guided by the knowledge and warmed by the sympathy of a long and intimate friendship, and a judgment that is almost Rhadamanthine in its penetration and detachment, has happily come down to us.

Oct. 13, 1863

Lord Lyndhurst died this morning.

He had a mind equally distinguished for its vigour and flexibility. He rarely originated, but his apprehension was very quick and he mastered the suggestions of others and made them clearer and more strong. He had a great grasp; thoroughly mastered a subject; deep and acute; and sometimes when you thought him slow, was only exhaustive. In his statements accurate, complete and singularly lucid: the clearest mind on affairs with equal power of conceiving and communicating his perspicuous views.

His soul wanted ardor, for he was deficient in imagination, though by no means void of sensibility. He adapted himself to circumstances in a moment, though he could not create.

or even considerably control them. His ambition active, not soaring. Its natural height to hold the Great Seal thrice: but when the King in 1836 had it conveyed to him that he might be called upon to take the first place, and would he be ready, he exclaimed 'Why, I am a lawyer, not a statesman' and seemed disconcerted: but when he had talked over the matter with a friend,[1] he not only arrived at the result that he was a statesman, but let his Master be assured that he was prepared to do his bidding, though it was one unusually difficult and perilous. His cultivation was considerable: far more than he was given credit for. His reading had been various and extensive, though he never sought to display it; and his scientific acquirements notable. He retained and digested everything; supported by a powerful and well-ordered memory.

A pleader rather than an orator, and never a debater. Unsuccessful in the House of Commons, he rose at once in the House of Lords to a position of unapproached supremacy; the times were favourable to him there. His stately and luminous expositions, in a voice of thrilling music, were adapted to a senate of which he caught the tone with facility. His taste almost amounted to austerity, yet he did not appreciate Demosthenes, and was a strong Ciceronian.

He had a sweet disposition, with a temper that nothing could ruffle; indulgent, placable, free from prejudice and utterly devoid of vanity. His feelings perhaps were not very strong, but they were always lucid. He was wonderfully fond of the society of women, and this not merely from his susceptibility to the sex, which was notorious, but because he was fond of them in every relation of life. He loved to be surrounded by his family, who were all females: a mother of 90, a sister nearly his own age, and who survived him in possession of all her faculties, indulged and devoted daughters. He was happy in two marriages, though his wives in every respect were very different.

His mind was playful, but not witty, and he had little humor though he could sympathise with it. His knowledge of mankind was great, but not consummate, for in their management there was this error, he was willing to give them credit for being influenced by amiable, but not elevated feelings.

His person was highly prepossessing. Far above the middle height, his figure was symmetrical and distinguished, and though powerfully formed, he never became stout. His

[1] There is here an interlineal gloss—'*i.e.*, D.—1873.'

Lord Lyndhurst.

from the Picture by Count D'Orsay assisted by Sir E. Landseer R.A.
In the possession of Mr. Coningsby Disraeli at Hughenden Manor

countenance was that of a high-bred falcon. Indeed, nothing could be finer than the upper part of his countenance. His deep-set eye gleamed with penetrating fire, and his brow was majestic. Nothing could be more beautiful. It was that of the Olympian Jove. The lower part of his countenance betrayed the deficiencies of his character; a want of high purpose, and some sensual attributes.

To Sarah Disraeli.

June 15, 1836.

Chandos is going to give a grand fish dinner on the 18th to the leaders of both Houses, and has asked me. . . . I have dined with Baring Wall in a house the most beautiful I ever entered, built by Kent; domed staircases, landing-places supported by Corinthian columns, and a grand salon, which, for its height, carving, gilding, and richly-painted ceiling, exceeded anything I ever saw in a private house. Our dinner was worthy of the 'veritable Amphitryon' of London, and was served off a set of Dresden china of the most marvellous beauty; the candelabra in the middle of immense size, and covered with groups of shepherds and shepherdesses, the whole mounted on green velvet; even the salt-cellars and handles of knives and forks were china, most charming in this weather; our party eight.

[*Undated.*]

Chandos's dinner was a banquet. I was the only person there not an M.P. Peel and Sir James Graham were there; the first came up to me and resumed our acquaintance most flatteringly. Chandos introduced me to Graham. They went down by water, but I accompanied Lyndhurst. We came home in two omnibuses hired for the owner. . . . What do you think of Spain? Trelawny, who is a Republican, is in raptures with the prospects. 'The Spaniards,' he says, 'are in advance of all countries; they have got their constitution of 1812!' Says James Smith, 'I wish I had got mine.'

Aug. 20.

I suppose you have recognised four bolts of veritable Olympian thunder in *The Times*. It is considered worthy of Jove, and nobody can discover behind what cloud the god is shrouded.[1]

The thunderbolts in *The Times* were in the form of leading articles; but, as is the way with leading articles,

[1] *Letters*, pp. 105, 107.

their lightning has ceased to flash and their thunder to reverberate.

When he comes in the autumn to his now customary review in the diary of the leading events of the year the entries are :

> Establish my character as a great political writer by the *Letters of Runnymede*. Resume my acquaintance with Sir Robert Peel. My influence greatly increases from the perfect confidence of L[yndhurst] and my success as a political writer. Stayed a week with Bulwer this spring and introduced him to L., against whom he was bitterly prejudiced. They became warm friends. I must not forget the singular fate of my friend old Lady Salisbury—burnt to death at Hatfield.

And then follow lists of names, new acquaintances of recent date, or merely mnemonic hints to recall some incident of the year—Francis Baring and Lord Ashburton, Croker, Baring Wall, Duke of Beaufort, 'an amusing character—Major Fancourt,' Lord Mahon, Lord Lincoln, 'Trelawny—a strange character,' 'Maclise—a painter,' Lord Ashley [afterwards the philanthropic Earl of Shaftesbury], Mackworth Praed, Barnes, and Sterling—but whether Edward Sterling of *The Times* or John, his son, the subject of Carlyle's biography, we are left to conjecture.

'It is a very remarkable thing,' said Disraeli to Sir Philip Rose, on some occasion when the *Star Chamber* myth had been revived,

> that whatever may have been ascribed to me I suppose there are few men who ever led a literary and political life as I have done who have written so little for the periodical Press ; and what is remarkable is that I can positively assert that I never in my life either required or received any remuneration for anything I have ever written except for the books published under my name. Of course, I have written at various times for the Press. I wrote a great deal at one time for Lord Lyndhurst, but I never either received or would have accepted any payment. My object was to connect myself with a man who had already been a Minister, and who

was destined to take a conspicuous part in public affairs, and to establish a claim upon him which might some day be useful, but I never held any engagement on the Press or accepted any remuneration ; not that I should have been the least ashamed of it if I had done so, but it is not the fact.

His journalistic activity in these years was great. In the course of the winter of 1836 he contributed to *The Times* a long-drawn series of articles under the title of 'A New Voyage of Sindbad the Sailor, recently discovered,' in which, as the title suggests, he recurred to the method of allegory adopted in *Popanilla*. 'I do not,' said Barnes, 'see much object in allegorising a subject or set of subjects which have been and are daily discussed in the plainest and most intelligible terms' ; and certainly Runnymede had suffered from no restraint of reticence that could be removed by disguising Melbourne as 'Shrugshoulders the Grand Vizier,' or Palmerston as 'the Vizier for Foreign Affairs' of 'His Majesty King Mihrage.' Sindbad, accordingly, had none of the success of Runnymede. Disraeli also tried his hand at political satires in verse. There is 'An Heroic Epistle to Lord Viscount Mel....e' in *The Times* of March 20, 1837 ; but the day of such things was past, and when somewhat later he proposed to renew his poetical declamation, on this occasion in blank verse instead of the heroic couplet, Barnes was not encouraging :—'Your verses have a stately march and the sentiments are just, but they want variety. The tone is a high one, but the sound is monotonous.'

It is the spoken word, however, and not the written, as Lord Salisbury once remarked, that in the end governs England. Disraeli's activity in *The Times* may have brought him no pecuniary reward, but it brought him something else that he valued a great deal more. In December, 1836, there was a Conservative banquet at Aylesbury, and Disraeli, to whom was entrusted the toast of the House of Lords, delighted his hearers with a speech full of wit and vigour. But he delighted not only his hearers. Through the favour of Barnes, *The Times* sent down a special staff of reporters and regaled its readers with a long account of the demonstration, Disraeli's speech, but no other, being given in the first person. 'Now,' wrote his sister, 'you must be satisfied, that you have succeeded in doing that which you so much desired, viz., to make a speech that would be talked of all over England.'

To Sarah Disraeli.

Dec. 15.

The *Spectator* said of the Bucks meeting that the 'speaking, on the whole, was as stupid as usual, except Mr. Disraeli, who, after a little of his usual rhodomontade about the Peers being the founders of liberty, grew abusive and amusing,' and then quoted the Shakespearean passage.

The Shakespearean passage is worth quoting again.

It may be said that the Prime Minister of the Sovereign rather winks approbation at this assault upon the House of Lords than leads on the assailants. It may be so : discretion may be the better part of valour even in Downing Street. The gay Epicurean leader may summon his forces and yet may refuse to march through Coventry with them. . . . He has placed a Justice Shallow in the Cabinet, assigned the seals of one office to Master Silence, and entrusted the management of our foreign affairs to Master Slender. But the rank and file who, after all, are the men to fight at Shrewsbury—he turns up his nose at these—at Mouldy and Wart, and Shadow and Forcible Feeble, and Bull Calf bellowing out 'Down with the House of Lords,' and who must surely have been a member for one of the metropolitan districts ; our Falstaff of the Treasury will not lead these fellows to the field. If we add to these the Milesian Pistol and his ragamuffin tail of cut-purse Nyms and drunken Bardolphs the political picture is complete ; and these—these are our rulers.

More to the taste of his audience, probably, was the following attack on O'Connell.

A denunciation has gone forth against the House of Lords, and from whom ? From the paid agent of the Papacy. I am not surprised at this. It is as natural for Mr. O'Connell to cry out 'Down with the House of Lords' as for a robber to cry out 'Down with the gallows.' Both are national institutions very inconvenient in their respective careers. . . . 'Down with the House of Lords,' cries Mr. O'Connell. Ay, down with the only barrier between him and his disastrous machinations. The House of Lords is a great breakwater of sedition that his waves of commotion will beat against in vain. . . . When I listen to him I am reminded of what the great Dean Swift said of a gentleman who was almost as anxious to plunder the people of Ireland as Mr. O'Connell himself, though not quite so successful—I mean William Wood, who tried to impose on them with brass farthings, 'These are the last howls of a dog dissected alive.'[1]

This sally was greeted with 'loud and continued cheers,' and made a tremendous noise.

To Sarah Disraeli.

Dec. 15.

O'Connell makes no reply; all the Irish papers taunt him. The *Warder* says 'he can find time to attack Fraser, O'Connor, and D. W. Harvey, and to call Mr. Lascelles a blockhead, but why does he not answer Disraeli? "Will not the dog dissected alive give another howl?"' All the country papers are full of it. Lord Strangford, who came up from Strathfieldsaye last night, began, 'You have no idea of the sensation your speech has produced at Strathfieldsaye.' I said, 'Oh, my lord, you always say agreeable things.' He took me aside and said, 'I give you my honour as a gentleman that the Duke said at the dinner-table, "It was the most manly thing done yet; when will he come into Parliament?"'[2]

After this pronouncement by the greatest Englishman of the day there is nothing more to be said.

From Lord Lyndhurst.

PARIS,
[*Dec.*, 1836.]

MY DEAR DISRAELI,

Sindbad tells me you are in London and active in the great cause—able and active as usual. The Bucks dinner was a grand demonstration, and has placed you in an admirable

[1] *The Times*, Dec. 10, 1836. [2] *Letters*, p. 107.

position as far as character and reputation are concerned. It will be infamous if not followed up by some effort to place you in a position which may give the party the full benefit of your talents and of your activity and untiring zeal. . . . It is hard indeed if we don't get you into the House. The Duke, you may depend upon it, is your friend. . . .

They are beginning here to hate us, and they invent all sorts of lies as a ground for abuse. As to Palmerston and the Ministers in general, they are never named in society without expressions of ridicule and contempt. . . .

Suppose (which I think not improbable) there should be a break-up of our Government, how are the parts to be cast in the Tory Administration? This is a difficult affair. I find they talk of me as Home Secretary. I could not afford it. What will they do with Chandos: he is become a very important person. His hold of the country is most powerful and extensive. Will Peel have many of his own click? Give me all the information you can, and as often as you can. . . .

I am now reading the love of Henrietta. I only got the book this morning. Mrs. Gore lent it me. She says it is the best thing you have written since *Vivian Grey*. . . . What I have read of it is light and brilliant and sparkling and impassioned, and all that such a work ought to be.

Ever yours,

L.

CHAPTER XV.

Henrietta Temple and Venetia.

1834-1837.

> Difficile est longum subito deponere amorem :
> difficile est, verum hoc qua lubet efficias.

As we see from Lyndhurst's letter at the end of the last chapter *Henrietta Temple* had been published shortly before the close of 1836 ; and a few months later it was followed by *Venetia*.

Henrietta Temple and *Venetia* are not political works, but they would commemorate feelings more enduring than public passions, and they were written with care, and some delight. They were inscribed to two friends, the best I ever had, and not the least gifted. One was the inimitable D'Orsay, the most accomplished and the most engaging character that has figured in this century, who, with the form and universal genius of an Alcibiades, combined a brilliant wit and a heart of quick affection, and who, placed in a public position, would have displayed a courage, a judgment, and a commanding intelligence which would have ranked him with the leaders of mankind. The other was one who had enjoyed that public opportunity which had been denied to Comte D'Orsay. The world has recognised the political courage, the versatile ability, and the masculine eloquence of Lord Lyndhurst ; but his intimates only were acquainted with the tenderness of his disposition, the sweetness of his temper, his ripe scholarship, and the playfulness of his bright and airy spirit.[1]

Since the failure of the *Revolutionary Epick* in 1834 Disraeli seemed, save for a few slight contributions to *Heath's Book of Beauty*, of which his friend Lady Blessington was editor, to have abandoned the field of imaginative literature; but he had begun *Henrietta Temple* in the summer of 1834, and written a volume before he threw the novel aside. Politics, social engagements, and the worry and burden of his debts sufficiently occupied both his time and energy for the next couple of years, but eventually the urgent need of money compelled him to pick up the discarded manuscript. 'I have agreed to let Colburn have a novel . . . for a greater sum than I have ever yet received,' he writes to Bradenham in June, 1836. The announcement brought no pleasure to his father. 'How,' he anxiously inquires, 'will the fictionist assort with the politician? Most deeply am I regretting that you find it necessary to return to drink of the old waters.' Isaac D'Israeli, however, knew little of his son's embarrassments, and the need for money was far more pressing than he realised. And there was another and a deeper reason that prompted a resumption of the unfinished story, or, at all events, made a resumption no longer impossible. When the first volume was composed Disraeli himself was in the grip of a strong and vehement passion, and the love story could no more have been carried to any fitting conclusion then than could *Vivian Grey* or *Contarini Fleming* or any of the other novels which are chapters in an autobiography and reflexions of an uncompleted personal experience. But in the years that had since elapsed the experience had passed into another phase. Love after its first rapture was over had come into conflict with the harder side of Disraeli's character, with his masterful will and dæmonic ambition; and in the clash

[1] General Preface to the Novels, 1870.

between will and passion will had triumphed. The connexion between his own Henrietta and the novel is indicated by a laconic entry in the Mutilated Diary.

Autumn of 1836.—Parted for ever from Henrietta. Returned to Bradenham at the latter end of August; concluded *Henrietta Temple*, of which one volume had been written three years. It was published early in December, and was very successful.

"Henrietta Temple: a Love Story," was the full title of the book. Ferdinand Armine, the heir of an ancient but impoverished Catholic family, heir also as he fancies to a great estate on his mother's side of the house, is with his regiment at Malta, and living the life of a spendthrift, when he learns that he is disinherited, and that the estate has gone to another, his cousin, Katherine Grandison. Overwhelmed with debt, he returns to England, and finds in the heiress a beautiful girl unversed in the ways of the world, whom, as the easiest mode of escape from his embarrassments, he at once determines to marry. Handsome and brilliant, he easily captivates her and they become engaged, though on his side, at all events, there is no spark of love. But soon afterwards he meets Henrietta Temple, and love, instant and overwhelming, takes possession of his soul.

There is no love but love at first sight. This is the transcendent and surpassing offspring of sheer and unpolluted sympathy. All other is the illegitimate result of observation, of reflection, of compromise, of comparison, of expediency. The passions that endure flash like the lightning: they scorch the soul, but it is warmed for ever.[1]

Henrietta returns his passion and they exchange vows, Ferdinand persuading her into secrecy for a time and concealing from her his engagement to Katherine, which he determines, however, to break at once. But the pressure of his debts and the fear of bringing ruin and disgrace

[1] Bk. II. ch. 4.

upon his father and mother counsel delay and he becomes involved in a course of double-dealing which soon ends in catastrophe. Henrietta and her father discover the prior engagement and draw the worst conclusions; and the rupture that follows is nearly fatal to both the lovers. After some interval they meet again and love is not yet dead though it has fallen on evil days. Chance has made Henrietta one of the greatest heiresses in England and under pressure from her father she has become the affianced bride of Lord Montfort the heir to a dukedom. The knot gets more and more entangled till we find Ferdinand in a sponging house under arrest for debt, his engagement with his cousin, which was the mainstay of his credit, openly terminated, and his heart nearly broken by the loss of Henrietta; but when things are at their worst everything is set right by the skilful diplomacy of Count Alcibiades de Mirabel who is D'Orsay drawn to the life and with very little pretence of concealment or disguise. Ferdinand is reunited to Henrietta and Lord Montfort and Miss Grandison find consolation for their disappointment in an interchange of their more tranquil and accommodating affections.

The interest of the novel as a love story lies mainly in that first volume[1] which takes its inspiration from a vivid personal experience. Some of Disraeli's critics after reading *Henrietta Temple* have contrived to pronounce the love in it affected and unreal; but it would be hard in the annals of criticism to find a more notable instance of the perverse human tendency to ignore obvious facts when they refuse to fit a theory. In the second book of the novel we have a picture of first love at the height of its spiritual ardour and intensity which only a man who had really loved himself could ever have produced. Disraeli indeed had not the simplicity of touch which achieves the supreme lyric effect. That is the privilege of the greatest masters and of them alone; but

[1] Including Books I. and II. of the ordinary editions.

of the essential truth and sincerity of his picture no unbiased reader can really feel a doubt.

Amid the gloom and travail of existence suddenly to behold a beautiful being, and as instantaneously to feel an overwhelming conviction that with that fair form for ever our destiny must be entwined; that there is no more joy but in her joy, no sorrow but when she grieves; that in her sigh of love, in her smile of fondness, hereafter is all bliss; to feel our flaunty ambition fade away like a shrivelled gourd before her vision; to feel fame a juggle and posterity a lie; and to be prepared at once, for this great object, to forfeit and fling away all former hopes, ties, schemes, views; to violate in her favour every duty of society; this is a lover, and this is love! Magnificent, sublime, divine sentiment! An immortal flame burns in the breast of that man who adores and is adored. He is an ethereal being. The accidents of earth touch him not. Revolutions of Empire, changes of creed, mutations of opinion, are to him but the clouds and meteors of a stormy sky. The schemes and struggles of mankind are, in his thinking, but the anxieties of pigmies and the fantastical achievements of apes. Nothing can subdue him. He laughs alike at loss of fortune, loss of friends, loss of character. The deeds and thoughts of men are to him equally indifferent. He does not mingle in their paths of callous bustle, or hold himself responsible to the airy impostures before which they bow down. He is a mariner, who, in the sea of life, keeps his gaze fixedly on a single star; and if that do not shine, he lets go the rudder, and glories when his bark descends into the bottomless gulf.[1]

When that passage was written Disraeli, we may believe, sincerely felt for the moment that the world could be well lost for love; but with a nature such as his the mood could hardly last. We find it succeeded by another, which, if less heroic, is more serene, as we advance into the later volumes of the novel.

Love is inspiration; it encourages to great deeds, and develops the creative faculty of our nature. . . . It is woman whose prescient admiration strings the lyre of the desponding poet, whose genius is afterwards to be recognised by his race, and which often embalms the memory of the gentle

[1] Bk. II. ch. 4.

mistress whose kindness solaced him in less glorious hours. How many an official portfolio would never have been carried, had it not been for her sanguine spirit and assiduous love! How many a depressed and despairing advocate has clutched the Great Seal and taken his precedence before princes, borne onward by the breeze of her inspiring hope, and illumined by the sunshine of her prophetic smile! A female friend, amiable, clever, and devoted, is a possession more valuable than parks and palaces; and, without such a muse, few men can succeed in life, none be content.[1]

The temperature has now fallen and all the uncalculating vehemence of love is gone. In its earlier presentment the passion of Ferdinand and Henrietta is strangely free from all admixture of sense: from the artistic point of view it might indeed be better if there were more, for the sensuous element refined and sublimated in the furnace of the imagination is a necessary ingredient in the poetry of love; but if the sensuous element is absent there is no lack of spiritual warmth and fire. In the later volumes of the novel, however, this is changed: even the spiritual glow of passion has now died away, and love has passed into a sentiment which though pure and tender and reverent is of the intellect rather than of the soul.

The portion of the novel which was written in the autumn of 1836 betrays many signs of crudity in conception and haste in execution. The images of Ferdinand and Henrietta are both in some degree defaced. Ferdinand shows himself such a selfish and deceitful egoist in his love that our sympathy is to a great extent estranged; and in spite of the tact and skill with which the author prepares us for the defection of Henrietta her fickleness cannot be wholly disguised. In the conditions of their genesis there is some resemblance between *Henrietta Temple* and the first part of *Vivian Grey*, in either case a discarded manuscript having been picked up again after the original creative impulse had lost its force. But since the days of *Vivian*

[1] Bk. III. ch. 4.

Grey Disraeli had gained immensely in experience both as an artist and as a man, and with all its imperfections the supplementary work in *Henrietta Temple* is far different in literary value from the concluding chapters of his first novel. If the lyric rapture of first love is partly lost we are given a good deal of delightful comedy in recompense, and many of the secondary characters now introduced are admirable. Lady Bellair is an amusing portrait of Disraeli's eccentric friend and ally, of whom we have heard more than once—old Lady Cork. The unimpassioned Montfort, with whom 'life was the romance of reason' as with Ferdinand it was 'the romance of imagination,' may seem at the first view artificial, but he is of the Disraelian line of Beckendorff and Winter, and interesting as the immediate precursor of Sidonia. Then there is Mr. Bond Sharpe, apparently drawn from Crockford; the little waiter in the sponging house from some unknown model who allowed Disraeli to catch his likeness and was lost in obscurity again; and Mirabel's companions, Mr. Bevil, who 'never permitted himself to smile except in the society of intimate friends,' Lord Catchimwhocan, 'that dear Catch who was always repeating nonsense which he heard from somebody else,' and Charles Doricourt, whom the world called Charley, 'from which it will be inferred that he was a privileged person, and was applauded for a thousand actions which in any one else would have been met with decided reprobation.' But by far the most attractive character of all, perhaps the most attractive that Disraeli ever created or drew, is de Mirabel himself, in whom the wit, the gaiety, the charm, the generosity, and the insouciance of D'Orsay are enshrined for the benefit of future generations.

There was something in Count Mirabel's very presence which put everybody in good spirits. His lightheartedness was caught by all. Melancholy was a farce in the presence of his smile; and there was no possible combination of scrapes that could withstand his kind and brilliant raillery.[1]

His radiant figure lights up all the concluding scenes and makes the last book, with its reconciliation of the lovers, the most readable in the novel.

To Sarah Disraeli.

Dec. 15, 1836.

Strangford [fresh from Strathfieldsaye] said he had not yet seen my novel, and there was only one person at the Duke's who had read it—Lady Wilton. She said she had cried so much that she had excited all their curiosity. Bulwer tells me that at Lady Charlotte Bury's the other night he only heard one report, 'Tears, tears, tears!' so he supposes I am right and he is wrong. Colburn is in high spirits about *H. T.* He says he shall not be content unless he works it up like *Pelham.* There were many reviews yesterday. You have of course seen the *Athenæum*; they were all in that vein, but highly calculated to make people read, if they were wanted, but it is not.[2]

'This vexatious, high-flown, foolish, clever work,' the *Athenæum* called it. Colburn had not lost his skill in working up a novel. 'I hope,' he writes while the book is in the stocks, 'you will have a dozen more originals to draw from besides old Lady C.; an exhibition of two or three leading political characters would not be amiss'; and in another letter he 'wants to know all he can that he may say something about it in the papers to excite curiosity and expectation without in the least gratifying it.' With Colburn's arts to aid its intrinsic merits *Henrietta Temple* was more successful than any of Disraeli's novels that had appeared since *Vivian Grey*. Some of his friends, however, were disappointed. Bulwer 'thinks my speech the finest in the world and my novel the worst,' he writes to his sister; and D'Orsay and Lady Blessington apparently agree with Bulwer. There has

[1] Bk. VI. ch. 14.

[2] *Letters*, p. 108.

been a curious divergence of view among the critics ever since. Those to whom Disraeli is primarily a politician and his distinctive work in literature the creation of the political novel despise *Henrietta Temple* because of the absence of political motive. To Froude, for instance, it is a 'clever story, but without the merit or the interest which would have given it a permanent place in English literature.'[1] Tennyson, on the other hand, 'told Disraeli that the "silly sooth" of love was given perfectly there'[2]; and Leslie Stephen[3] speaks of *Henrietta* and *Contarini* as 'Disraeli's most satisfactory performances,' because in these 'he has worked without any secondary political purpose, and has, therefore, produced more harmonious results.'

From Count D'Orsay.

MON CHER DIS,

J'ai reçu votre lettre avec plaisir, et votre dédicace avec fierté. Le mot d'affectionné ami s'applique tout aussi bien à mes sentiments pour vous que les vôtres envers moi. Je regrette seulement que Mirabel ait fait connaissance avec Armine dans un Hell. C'était probablement pour chauffer leurs sentiments au premier abord que vous avez eu recours à ce moyen qui était inutile. J'espère bientôt vous revoir, pour vous répéter combien votre dédicace est vraie.

Votre affectionné ami,

ALFRED D'ORSAY.

From Alfred Tennyson

CLAPHAM COMMON,
April 28, 1868.

DEAR MR. DISRAELI,

Pray accept my best thanks for the instant attention you have paid to this small matter of mine. . . . Though the result appears to be nil, I do not the less feel an obligation to you; and am quite as much pleased to know that it is

[1] Lord *Beaconsfield*, p. 215. [2] *Life*, II., p. 371.
[3] *Hours in a Library*, II., p. 130.

owing to the author of that charming love story, *Henrietta Temple*, as to the Prime Minister of England.

Believe me, ever yours truly,

A. TENNYSON.

One of Disraeli's critics disputed the truth and accuracy of the scenes in the sponging house in *Henrietta Temple* and of Ferdinand's interview with Levison, of the money-lending firm of Messrs. Morris and Levison ; and congratulated the author on having escaped the 'usurious experience' himself. It is to be feared that the author's knowledge of these things was far greater than his critic's. Since his return from the East, Disraeli's pecuniary embarrassments had multiplied and increased. In the debtor's career it is the first step that is decisive.

> If youth but knew the fatal misery that they are entailing on themselves the moment they accept a pecuniary credit to which they are not entitled, how they would start in their career! How pale they would turn! How they would tremble, and clasp their hands in agony at the precipice on which they are disporting! Debt . . . hath a small beginning, but a giant's growth and strength. When we make the monster we make our master, who haunts us at all hours, and shakes his whip of scorpions for ever in our sight. Faustus, when he signed the bond with blood, did not secure a doom more terrific.[1]

Disraeli had committed the first fatal blunder while he was still young, and had never succeeded in retrieving it. Since his return from the East four contested elections, extravagant companions, and an expensive social environment had increased his liabilities and led him deeper into the mire. He was by nature generous and open-handed, caring only for money as he loved to spend it freely, and with no gift of acquisitiveness or power of accumulation. Debt soon makes a man improvident, if it does not find him so ; his financial vision ceases to extend beyond the date at which the next bill matures, and if, like Disraeli, he be of a sanguine temperament,

[1] *Henrietta Temple*, Bk. II. ch. 1.

he readily convinces himself that a respite is the equivalent of a reprieve, and that if only time can be secured everything will settle itself. During a great part of his life, and in these years especially, Disraeli was in the grip of the moneylenders, never escaping from an atmosphere of bills, writs, annuities, renewals, discountings, assignments, and all the other processes which are the implements and appurtenances of usury. Amid the worries and vexations of such a life most men would have found serious work or even serious enjoyment utterly impossible, but Disraeli contrived to pursue his pleasures, his labours and his ambitions with a wonderful serenity through all. 'As from fear of the Philistines I cannot come and dine with you, you must come and dine with me,' he writes to Austen one day in 1833. 'I am overwhelmed with difficulties,' he tells him in another letter of the same year, though 'all that is necessary to settle my affairs is six months of quiet.' A couple of years later the situation is much the same. 'My affairs have been so involved,' he says in answer to a complaint that he is neglecting his friends, 'that seclusion, absolute seclusion from society and severe daily labour have been to me as much a matter of necessity as choice.' But he has now 'more than a prospect of almost immediately emancipating himself from sufferings not easy to describe.' 'Circumstances have placed him behind the curtain of financial politics,' and he reckons among his assets £1,000 which he is shortly to receive, 'the result of a piece of business which has engaged my attention during the last five months, and respecting which I have twice visited The Hague.' This was written at the beginning of 1836, and in the Mutilated Diary about the same time there is a laconic entry, 'Haber again,' which points to some connexion between the financial politics in question and the Baron de Haber,[1] with whom Disraeli had

[1] Haber was at this time the head of a financial house with a branch at The Hague among other places on the Continent, and Disraeli was no doubt acting for the moment, or aspiring to act, as his London agent.

collaborated in the *Gallomania* several years before. The business seems to have been some affair of a Swedish loan, and it was carried to a stage where, in the sanguine view of Disraeli, only formal difficulties stood between him and his reward. Apparently, however, the reward never came, and when 'from the strange aspect of the money market any immediate prospect of a favourable nature grew desperate,' he was compelled to 'engage in an intellectual effort, painful at all times, under such circumstances a very terrible exertion,' in order, if possible, to meet the demands of his creditors; the intellectual effort being the completion of *Henrietta Temple*.

In these early years his liabilities probably amounted to no more than a few thousand pounds, a sum which would not have been beyond the competence of his father to provide, but throughout he showed the greatest reluctance to seek assistance from his father. 'In the most important step of a man's life,' he writes on one occasion to Austen, who had advised such an application, 'I have opposed his earnest wishes, and have based my dutiful opposition upon my independence. I do not wish by extraordinary money applications to one who is always very generous to me, to revive a most painful subject.' On another occasion when the stress was even greater Austen repeated his advice, urging that this objection should yield to force of circumstances lest character should be compromised; but Disraeli still clung to his precarious independence and persisted in his policy of faith in the future and temporary expedients for the present. An undated letter of these years, which might well have been signed Alcibiades de Mirabel, will give the atmosphere better than pages of accounts or disquisition.

From Count D'Orsay.

I swear before God that I have not six pence at my banker now, having lost the night before last £325. You may judge how disappointed I am not to be able to assist you, but if you find that I could be of any use to you in the way of security I will do for you what I would not do for any other.

Yours affectionately,

D'ORSAY.

Such was the school of finance in which our future Chancellor of the Exchequer graduated. Let it be said at once, however, that though Disraeli ran through the whole gamut of the debtor's customary experience, was guilty of all the improvidence to which embarrassment surely leads, submitted perforce to all the humiliations which it carries in its train, was skilled in all the subterfuges by which debtors commonly evade the importunity of greedy and exacting creditors, and too often caused annoyance to obliging friends by reluctant but unavoidable disappointment of their hopes, nothing that seriously touches his character is to be deduced from the records as they have been preserved; and in the matter of records Disraeli showed himself splendidly indifferent to posterity or splendidly confident as to its verdict. In his career from beginning to end there is no trace of any money transaction that will not bear investigation, and if we waive the inevitably squalid details of a life of embarrassment, nothing that infringes the code of 'the man of honour' or 'the gentleman.' It might even be urged that his debts themselves had a certain disciplinary value. A well-known passage in *Tancred*, if we allow for some whimsical exaggeration, reflects undoubtedly a personal feeling of Disraeli's.

Fakredeen was fond of his debts; they were the source indeed of his only real excitement, and he was grateful to them for their stirring powers. The usurers of Syria are as adroit and callous as those of all other countries, and possess no doubt all those repulsive qualities which are the consequence of an habitual control over every generous emotion. But, instead of viewing them with feelings of vengeance or abhorrence, Fakredeen studied them unceasingly with a fine and profound investigation, and found in their society a deep psychological interest. . . . 'What should I be without my debts?'

he would sometimes exclaim; 'dear companions of my life that never desert me! All my knowledge of human nature is owing to them: it is in managing my affairs that I have sounded the depths of the human heart, recognised all the combinations of human character, developed my own powers, and mastered the resources of others. What expedient in negotiation is unknown to me? What degree of endurance have I not calculated? What play of the countenance have I not observed? Yes, among my creditors, I have disciplined that diplomatic ability, that shall some day confound and control cabinets. Oh, my debts, I feel your presence like that of guardian angels! If I be lazy, you prick me to action; if elate, you subdue me to reflection; and thus it is that you alone can secure that continuous yet controlled energy which conquers mankind.'[1]

No doubt like Fakredeen Disraeli grew 'sometimes a little wearied even of the choice excitement of pecuniary embarrassment. It was too often the same story, the adventures monotonous, the characters identical.' The characters, however, were not always sordid. From those early days in which he took Evans, his fellow clerk, for partner in a speculation in South American shares he showed a notable capacity for enlisting the good offices of friends, for inspiring them with confidence in his future, and winning and retaining their affection. 'The singular good services of Pyne to me' is an entry in the Mutilated Diary for 1836. Pyne was a prosperous solicitor who had succeeded Austen as the repository of Disraeli's confidence in these unsavoury matters, and Disraeli's letters to him, luckily preserved, tell a tale of which one hardly knows whether it calls more often for tears or laughter. By May, 1836, Disraeli, through Pyne's good offices, has been relieved of some of his most pressing claims, and elate with his temporary freedom is ready for any fresh enterprise that presents itself. A 'new weekly journal under the highest patronage' is about to be started and he has been 'offered and has provisionally accepted half the proprietorship which however will

[1] *Tancred*, Bk. V. ch. 3.

require £500.' 'I have little resources except the £200, which are in fact yours, but I think I could scrape enough together. The object is considerable. This speculation, if there be any virtue in calculation, may turn out, and quickly, a considerable property.' How Pyne regarded the speculation there is nothing to show, but by July his client is in trouble again. 'Peel has asked me to dine with a party to-day of the late Government at the Carlton. Is it safe? I fear not.'

To William Pyne.

BRADENHAM,
Sept. 25, 1836.

Your letter rather alarms me; I scarcely think it safe to remain here as any proceedings of the kind here would be confusion. I have not left this house except for County business[1] occasionally, working unceasingly at my forthcoming book. I have no pecuniary cares for the next three months, and I wish if possible to reap a great harvest in this serene interval, and finish, or nearly so, a second novel for January, getting the forthcoming one out in the very early part of November.

BRADENHAM,
Sunday. [*Nov.*, 1836.]

MY DEAR PYNE,

The letter which I received from you to-day fills me with great disquietude. The idea that I am involving Count D'Orsay and yourself, my two best friends, and especially hampering you, is so insupportable, that there seems to me hardly any explanations and crisis which I would not encounter sooner than the present state of affairs. My situation is simply this. I have taken advantage of the temporary repose for which I am indebted to you and with the exception of County business I have not quitted my room for the last ten weeks. I have now written five octavo volumes, *i.e.*, the novel about to be published, and two more of another, which I calculate finishing by the end of the year. If affairs can be carried on, I then purpose commencing a third, but, as you can easily comprehend, such almost superhuman labors, though practicable with a serene mind and unbroken time, are impossible under opposite circumstances. A serene mind I never

[1] He had been sworn in as a Justice of the Peace in the preceding month.

expect to have, but hitherto my time has been little disturbed. If the results are what my publisher anticipates, and I am able to complete this engagement, I think between £3,000 and £4,000 might be poured into my coffers by May : but the ships, though built and building, are not yet launched, and as I have some difficulties with which you are not mixed up, still to contend with, I doubt whether on our present system I can hope effectively to assist you before the Spring. Do you think the present system can be maintained ? That you will 'do your best' I want no assurance, but I am loth to strain a generous steed to whom I am indebted for such great services. I am always afraid that a feeling of false delicacy may prevent you being as frank with me as your interests may require, and that you may imagine that you are in some degree cancelling your unparalleled services to me, by reminding me that they must necessarily have a limit. This never can be the case, and I hope, therefore, you will write to me your wishes, for however disagreeable at this moment may be a family *exposé*, I should prefer it infinitely to your injury.

Ever yours,

D.

BRADENHAM,
Dec. 5 [1836].

Our county Conservative Dinner, which will be the most important assembly of the kind yet held, takes place on Friday the 9th inst. I have been requested to move the principal toast 'The House of Lords.' I trust there is no danger of my being nabbed, as this would be a fatal *contretemps*, inasmuch as, in all probability, I am addressing my future constituents.

BRADENHAM,
Dec. 26.

This is really Xmas. I arrived just in time, for what with the fall and the snow drifting from the hills, our road is really blocked up, in some parts as high as a man's breast, and I doubt almost whether this may reach our post, which is two miles distant. I assure you when I reached the old hall, and found the beech blocks crackling and blazing, I felt no common sentiments of gratitude to that kind friend whose never tired zeal allowed me to reach my house, and is some consolation for the plague of women, the wear and tear of politics, and the dunning of creditors.

We are now, however, comparatively in still waters, thanks to your pilotage, and I am at work again animated by success and by the greatness of future results.

Sunday. [*Jan.* 8, 1837.]

My dear Pyne,

How goes on the damned coin? I am ashamed to bore you, but am beset with as great duns as myself.

I am in good health, considering I have never left my rooms, and have been in worse spirits. But the quantity I have written, and am pouring forth, is something monstrous. I find it a relief, and now that I have nothing else to distract my thoughts, I am resolved to ruin Colburn.

I suppose I shall be in town about the 15th. I am in treaty for Lord Althorp's rooms in the Albany, once Byron's, and now Bulwer's; a curious coincidence of successive scribblers; the spell I suppose growing weaker every degree, and the inspiration less genuine; but I may flare up yet, and surprise you all. I find they won't be dearer than wretched lodgings and infinitely cheaper than the worst hotel; and then I shall be lodged in a way that suits me; gloomy and spacious, with room to stroll and smoke, and able to spout occasionally without being overheard by any damned fellow who steals all your jokes and sublimities.

I am on the whole savagely gay, and sincerely glad that I am freer of encumbrances, in every sense of the word, than I was this time last year.

Ever thine,

D.

A few days later he has heard that the well-known estate of Chequers Court is to be sold and 'we here wish to purchase.' 'I should suppose,' he adds in his usual airy way, 'not under £40,000, perhaps £10,000 more, as there is timber; but at any rate I should like to leave half the purchase money on mortgage, if practicable; if not, we must manage some other way.' 'Be of good cheer,' he concludes, 'the Spring is coming and will bring us all good fortune. I am "bobbish," as Horace says, or someone else, and my fellow is putting on my spurs preliminary to an inspiring canter'; and then follows a cheerful postscript, 'I enclose the blasted bills.'

To Lady Blessington.

BRADENHAM,
Thursday. [*Jan.* 12, 1837.]

MY DEAR LADY,

We have all here been dying of an epidemic; Tita and myself being the only persons who have escaped. I trust that it has not reached K[ensington] G[ore]. All this district are prostrate. I fear for you; D'Orsay I know—immortal youth—is never indisposed. I ascribe my exemption to a sort of low, gentleman-like fever that has had hold of me ever since I came down here, and which is not very inconvenient. I have in consequence never left the house, scarcely my room, and it has not incapacitated me from a little gentle scribbling. I am about something in a higher vein than the last; what you and E. L. B. would call 'worthy of me,' alias unpopular.

I am sorry about B's play[1]; I would not write to him as I detest sympathy save with good fortune; but I am sorry, very, and for several reasons: 1st, because he is my friend; 2ndly, because he is the only literary man whom I do not abominate and despise; 3rdly, because I have no jealousy on principle (not from feeling) since I think always the more the merrier, and his success would probably have assisted mine; 4thly, because it proves the public taste lower even than I imagined it, if indeed there can be a deeper still than my estimate; 5thly, because, from the extracts which have met my eye, the play seems excellent, and far the best poeshie that he has yet relieved himself of; 6thly, because there seems to have been a vast deal of disgusting cant upon the occasion; 7thly, because he is a good fellow; and 8thly,—I forget the 8th argument, but it was a very strong one. However, the actors of the present day are worse even than the authors; that I knew before, but E. L. B. would not believe it and I could pardon his scepticism. As for myself I have locked up my *mélodrame* in the same strong box with my love letters; both lots being productions only interesting to the writer.

I have received several letters from Ld. L., who has sent me H. T. from Paris price 4s. & 2d.; an agreeable present

[1] *The Lady of Lyons.*

'THE AUTHOR OF VIVIAN GREY.'
From a drawing by D. MACLISE, R.A.

[To face page 354.

proving the value of our copyrights to London publishers. It is a vile trade, but what is better? Not politics. I look forward to the coming campaign with unmitigated disgust; and should certainly sell out, only one's enemies would say one had failed, to say nothing of one's friends. The fact is, I am too much committed to the fray to retire at present—but oh! that I had the wings of a dove, &c.

Ld. L. will be with us in a week. I feel interested in his career, more than in my own; for he is indeed the most amiable of men, though that is not very high praise, you will say. Ah! *méchante*! I see the epigram on your lips!

I really grieve if I said anything which deserved the lecture[1] you gave me, though I am almost glad I merited it if only for its kindness. I was rather harassed when I was last in town as you know and have a disagreeable habit of saying everything I feel; but I love my friends and am not naturally suspicious or on the alert to quarrel about straws. I am here pretty well and have my rooms and my time to myself, but still there *is* a family, though an amiable and engaging one; and the more I feel, the more I am convinced that man is not a social animal. Remember me to D'O. and E. L. B.; to nobody else and believe me

Yours,

DIS.

By the middle of January he is in London, the guest of D'Orsay in Kensington. Lady Blessington had left Seamore Place in the previous year and moved to Gore House, once the home of William Wilberforce; and D'Orsay, as Disraeli puts it, had taken 'an elegant residence adjoining her magnificent mansion.'

To Sarah Disraeli.

Wednesday. [*Feb.*, 1837.]

MY DEAREST,

The Whigs and Tories watch each other like a cat and a dog, and neither will make the first move. The Duke is for the tactics of last Session, and I think under the circumstances he is right; Melbourne is pledged to bring the Irish question immediately forward, and if again defeated, as is certain, he will dissolve or resign. This is exactly the state

[1] 'Be more just to yourself and to your friends, than to listen to those pests of society who desire nothing so much as to make mischief'—that is the pith of the lecture.

of affairs. But there is not the slightest doubt that when L. wrote to me from Paris that M. had resigned, &c., it was true. His informant was Ellice, and I have since learnt from an unquestionable quarter that the information was authentic. Through the whole recess there has scarcely been a single Cabinet Council, in consequence of the dissensions in the Cabinet, but Melbourne saw bodies of the Ministers at his own office. He yielded to the representations of Lord John in maintaining his post, as Lord J. is of opinion that if the Whigs go out of office, they should contrive to go out with a claptrap and not quietly resign from difficulties during the prorogation. This will show you on what a frail tenure the whole hinges, and what may be expected.

I am very well, indeed, but with the exception of seeing L. occasionally, I shall devote myself to the fair Venetia. I write well here, as the life suits me, and am at hand if wanted. As we dine late there is a long morning, and the air bath, which is wonderful, renders exercise unnecessary, and does my head much good. It certainly baffled the influenza, of which poor Lady Combermere has died, surviving her father, old Greville, but a few days.

When D'Orsay does not dine out, which is generally every other day, there is usually one or two persons at dinner here. On Monday Ossulston dined *en famille* here and gave us a very agreeable account of the Gramonts, whom he had been visiting at Versailles. The Duc de Gram is D'Orsay's brother-in-law and Oss's uncle. Since the glorious days they have retired from Court and keep themselves aloof, the Duke devoting himself entirely to the education of his three sons. The first, Agenor, the Duc de Guiche, is quiet, with great talents, and at fourteen has just passed the examination of the *école polytechnique*, one of the severest in the world; the second, Augustus, the Marquis de Gramont, is a complete soldier; the third, Alfred, the Count de Gramont, is only eight years of age, but, though brought up in so domestic and even severe a style, is as great a *roué* as his illustrious ancestor; he does nothing but laugh, shrug his shoulders and run after the maids, who complain bitterly of his rudeness. . . .

Miladi here writes ten hours a day; and makes £2,000 per ann. This is true, for she showed me her agreements. Her novels do not sell very much. She only gets £400 for one; copyright and all. But she has a guinea a line for her poetry, of which she is very proud, and receives from Heath altogether £1,000 per ann. She is not entirely free from the irritability of genius, but what can be expected from such severe labor? But she is a good-hearted woman and a warm friend. I could tell you much of her that would amuse and interest you. She allows her father £200 a year, and has twice paid his debts, and has three or four nephews, young Powers, at school, and at very expensive ones, who are no favorites with her and not very engaging, but she acts from principle. One is here, just come over from New Brunswick, where his father has an appointment. This lad is to be sent out to India, a cadet, all by Lady B. Lady Canterbury will do nothing, and turns up her nose at old days of which her sister is not ashamed. D.

If Disraeli escaped the influenza, his general health, as the result of over-work and monetary worries, was by no means robust. Before February was far advanced the death of one of the members for Bucks sent him back post haste to Bradenham, and he performed prodigies of exertion for the Conservative candidate in the bye-election that followed; but on the first day of the polling an incident occurred that greatly alarmed his friends. After canvassing far and wide, he had travelled all through the night to Aylesbury, and, as he stood in front of the George Inn talking to his friends, he fell in a fit, which the doctors, according to his father, explained as a slight attack of epilepsy, but which was, perhaps, sufficiently accounted for by the recording journalist[1] as the result of great fatigue and excitement, acting on a frame already enfeebled. According to the practice of the times, the patient was bled and put to bed, but the following day he was sufficiently recovered to be taken back to Bradenham. This incident seems to have led to an explanation with his father on the state of his affairs and so afforded a great economist an opportunity for lecturing the future Chancellor of the Exchequer on the first principles of finance.

From Count D'Orsay.

Je suis bien aise pour votre intérêt présent et futur que vous vous soyez décidé à avouer à votre père, l'étendue

[1] In *The Times* of Feb. 17, 1837.

de votre scrape. Car les plasterings-over se démolissent toujours et vous en auriez été victime continuellement. Votre imagination vive et brillante, vous fait bâtir des chateaux en Espagne. Tout cela est bel et bon pour les Wonderful Tales of Alroy, mais pour la matérielle vie de l'Angleterre le positif bât l'imaginaire.

In spite of D'Orsay's wise exhortations, Disraeli seems to have given only a half confidence to his father, and the two months that followed were perhaps the most distracting of his life.

To William Pyne.

Sunday. [*Feb.* 19, 1837.]

MY DEAR P.,

I enclose the bill, which I hope will be all right. Your letter is gloomy, but yesterday was Spring and to-day is Winter, and Tuesday may therefore bring sunshine, both moral and physical.

I assure you the trouble, the harass and anxiety, which you must experience in all this, is not the least part of my afflictions: and, indeed, I know not how I can repay you.

I have only 150 pages, or less, of my book to finish, which I ought to canter through in the remainder of the month with ease, but I find it difficult to command the Muse amid all these vexations. The form of Davis, or the unknown visage of Green, mix themselves up, by some damnable process, with the radiant countenance of my heroine, and though visions of spunging houses might have been in keeping with the last vol. of *Henrietta Temple*, they do not accord quite so well with the more ethereal scenes of the fair *Venetia*. Nevertheless I have contrived to write, and I hope my inspiration has not been much diluted by their distractions, but I am a little nervous.

I long to be in town for many reasons. I have a letter from Ld. L. this morning from Paris where he has been detained by the dangerous state of his daughter, now happily ceased, and he writes to me, as if he half thought he should be Lord Chancellor before he reached Dover. I think there is something in the wind.

Vale!

D.

He is soon in town again and again with D'Orsay in Kensington; but early in March he is back at Bradenham once more, still in quest of the peace which ever eludes him. 'Of all things in the world preserve me from a Sheriff's officer in my own county,' he writes to Pyne immediately on his arrival. A fortnight later the Sheriff's officer is at Wycombe, and he fears 'it is no longer possible to prevent a disgraceful catastrophe.' 'Seged King of Ethiopia who was resolved to have a day of happiness was not more unfortunate than I have been with my month of quiet. The blows have been rapid and violent.' This early in April; and a few days later to Austen, 'Every possible claim that could be made upon me has poured in during the last two months. . . . I never have been so distressed.'

To William Pyne.

BRADENHAM,
April 23, 1837.

I conclude from your interview, that the game is up, and that our system has failed. I assure you that the only feelings that I have at this moment are regret for your unavailing exertions, which I feel *no professional remuneration can compensate*, and gratitude for the generous zeal with which you have served me for the now not inconsiderable period of our acquaintance, and of which I believe few men were capable, and certainly no other lawyer. I am sure that your kind feelings and your matchless energy have effected all that was possible, and that you have been baffled only by circumstances which could not be foreseen, and over which you had no control.

Eventually, with the assistance of his father, some *modus vivendi* was discovered; but he shrank from revealing to his father, who was 'one of the old school,' the full complexity of a situation which 'he has long taught me to look upon with the greatest apprehension and mortification'; and the arrangement now effected, though it procured the distracted author a certain breathing space, was uneasy and precarious enough.

Such were the unpromising conditions under which *Venetia* was conceived and written. The agreement with Colburn is dated December 20, and a little earlier, as we have seen, Disraeli expected to have the novel finished by the end of the year: but again and again in those disturbed months his hopes were disappointed and the spring was far advanced before his task was completed.

To Lady Blessington.

BRADENHAM,
March 21. [1837.]

In spite of every obstacle in the shape of harassed feelings and other disagreeable accidents of life, I have not forgotten the fair *Venetia*, who has grown under my paternal care, and as much in grace, I hope, as in stature, or rather dimensions. She is truly like her prototype——

'The child of love, though born in bitterness,
And nurtured in convulsion'; [1]

but I hope she will prove a source of consolation to her parent, and also to her godmother, for I consider you to stand in that relation to her. I do not think that you will find any golden hint of our musing strolls has been thrown away upon me; and I should not be surprised if, in six weeks, she may ring the bell at your hall door, and request admittance, where I know she will find at least one sympathising friend. . . .

I have, of course, no news from this extreme solitude. My father advances valiantly with his great enterprise, but works of that calibre are hewn out of the granite with slow and elaborate strokes. Mine are but plaster-of-Paris casts, or rather statues of snow that melt as soon as they are fashioned.[2]

The novel appeared in May, its full title being 'Venetia or the Poet's daughter,' and its parentage being assigned to 'The Author of *Vivian Grey* and *Henrietta Temple*,' a variant on the previous formula that may be interpreted as Colburn's tribute to the success of *Henrietta*. There is a dedication to Lyndhurst in which the author tells him that 'In happier hours when I first mentioned to you the idea of this work, it was my

[1] These words from the third canto of *Childe Harold* appeared on the title page.
[2] From Mr. Alfred Morrison's collection.

intention, while inscribing it with your name, to have entered into some details as to the principles which had guided me in its composition, and the feelings with which I had attempted to shadow forth, though as "in a glass darkly," two of the most renowned and refined spirits that have adorned these our latter days.' This explanation, which might have been so illuminating, was unluckily never given, and we can only conjecture the motives that prompted Disraeli at this time to turn to the two 'renowned and refined spirits,' Byron and Shelley, in his quest for the material for a new work of fiction. But it would almost appear as if now that he had become a good Conservative something in the depths of his passionate and romantic nature revolted against the dominion of a prosaic political creed and an uninspiring leader ; so that he felt impelled to demonstrate that, though he had submitted himself to the yoke of a definite political allegiance, his thoughts were not therefore to be bounded by the Tamworth manifesto. By choosing as his heroes the two greatest revolutionary figures that England had produced he made proclamation in no uncertain tones that as an artist at all events he was determined to retain his freedom and not to bow down before the idols of the Philistines. As one[1] of the best and most appreciative critics of the book has said, 'a waft of liberty flutters through its pages.'

In the complete absence of direct political motive *Venetia* resembles *Henrietta Temple*, and it is peculiar, among Disraeli's novels, in the comparative absence also of reflexions of his own personality or drafts from his own personal experience ; unless indeed we are to see in Cadurcis, who stands in the book for Byron, something of Disraeli himself. The idea is by no means fanciful. Disraeli had grown to manhood, as we have seen, in an atmosphere where reverence for Byron was almost a religion, and to

[1] Dr. Georg Brandes in his *Study of Lord Beaconsfield*, p. 152.

him, even more than to most of the aspiring youth of the day, Byron had been an inspiration and a model. Many also as are the obvious differences between the two men they had a certain natural affinity of character and genius, alike in their strength and in their weakness. There is something in both of the same dæmonic force, the same devouring ambition, the same self-idolatry, the same disposition to coxcombry and affectation; and in the wayward childhood and tempestuous career of Cadurcis we are not infrequently reminded of Disraeli himself, though there is nothing to suggest that the resemblance was intended. Yet in spite of the author's sympathy, latent or avowed, it can hardly be maintained that Byron's personality as presented in Cadurcis is really attractive; though in that perhaps the picture was only true to life. Far more pleasing is the presentation of Shelley in the person of Marmion Herbert. Disraeli had less in common with Shelley than with Byron; but in strange combination with Byron's ambitious egoism he had also something of Shelley's power of seeing visions of the future, and he had studied Shelley's poetry as closely as he had studied Byron's. Meredith's diary gives us a glimpse of him, during their enforced stay at Falmouth on the way to the East, deep in the *Cenci*, and he had pursued his studies later, as the *Revolutionary Epick* shows. In the matter of personal details Tita[1] served him as an authority for Shelley as well as for Byron; and in the year in which *Venetia* was begun, Disraeli, it will be remembered, had also made the acquaintance of that 'strange character' Trelawny, the friend of Byron and Shelley, who in company with Byron had burnt Shelley's body on the Tuscan shore. Whether Tita or Trelawny was the source, the accuracy of the personal touches is attested by high authority.[2] Herbert, we are assured, 'is drawn in conformity with the most orthodox Shelleyan

[1] See Appendix A.

[2] The late Dr. Garnett in a privately printed essay, *Lord Beaconsfield and Shelley*.

tradition'; the picture of his appearance in youth is the picture also of Shelley's, and the details of the final catastrophe are in strict accordance with the fact. Even the colloquy between Herbert and Cadurcis, in which Cadurcis by comparison is so flippant and unsatisfying, is derived almost word for word as regards Herbert's portion from Shelley's *Discourse on the Manners of the Ancients*, a work then known to few. In one respect, indeed, the portrait is hardly faithful. It ignores too much perhaps the element in Shelley's character which made him describe himself as 'sudden and swift and proud'; but Herbert, it may be urged, is an older man than Shelley, and allowance must be made for the mellowing effect of age. At the time *Venetia* was written Shelley was still something of a bugbear to the narrow and self-sufficient English world of the day; his fame as a poet had not yet won him forgiveness for his transgressions as a man, and still less for the crude and aggressive opinions which had brought him into such violent collision with orthodoxy as established in Church and State. To Disraeli's credit be it remembered that he was one of the first who had the courage to attempt to do him justice or, in defiance of popular prejudice, to present his personality in a sympathetic light.

The division of parts between the two poets is very curious and complex. The genius and personality of Byron are assigned to Cadurcis; but the external circumstances of Byron's life are apportioned almost equally between Cadurcis and Herbert. To Cadurcis are given the wilful childhood, the foolish mother, the sudden poetic success, the relations to Lady Caroline Lamb, who appears in the book as Lady Monteagle, and the outburst of popular hostility which closed Byron's career in England; but his unhappy marriage and subsequent relations to his wife and 'Ada, sole daughter of my house and heart,' are transferred to Herbert, who has the genius and personality of Shelley. Both poets are involved in a common end—the end, in fact, of Shelley. The link between the two in life is Venetia, herself a beautiful figure, though, as befits a daughter of Shelley's, almost too ethereal. Long before the world at large was disposed to be just to Disraeli either as a novelist or as a man, some forgotten critic[1] noted that he was almost the first writer 'who resolutely set himself to picture the child life,' and accounted this to his credit 'as proving a greater depth of character and more freshness of feeling' than were commonly attributed to him. Of this phase of his art we saw something in *Contarini*, and we shall see more in *Coningsby*; but it is in *Venetia* that we find it in its perfect expression. Disraeli has written nothing more pleasing than those early chapters, in which the child Venetia is growing up by her mother's side, in happy ignorance of her father, and with the strangely contrasted but ever affectionate Plantagenet as her constant companion; and the story of the subsequent awakening, in spite of all her mother's precautions, of love and admiration for the unknown and banished father, and of the development of these sentiments into an intense and overmastering passion, is told with power and pathos. Even when Disraeli, greatly daring, tries to write verses for both Byron and Shelley, he is happiest when his subject is a father's love; for nowhere perhaps has he come nearer to real poetry than in the lines written by Herbert 'On the night our daughter was born.'

Of the secondary characters the most interesting and attractive are George Cadurcis, the cousin of the poet, in whom is well exemplified the truth of a maxim that comes strangely from Disraeli, 'Though we are most of us the creatures of affectation, simplicity has a great charm'; and the good Dr. Masham, in whom we have a first-rate picture of the 'regular orthodox divine of the eighteenth century'—

With a large cauliflower wig, shovel hat, and huge knee-buckles, barely covered by his top-boots; learned, jovial,

[1] His words are preserved in a letter of Sarah Disraeli's, who was ever ready to seize on any morsel of praise bestowed on her beloved brother.

humorous, and somewhat courtly; truly pious, but not enthusiastic; not forgetful of his tithes, but generous and charitable when they were once paid; never neglecting the sick, yet occasionally following a fox; a fine scholar, an active magistrate, and a good shot; dreading the Pope, and hating the Presbyterians.[1]

'I fear,' Disraeli wrote to Pyne on the eve of publication, 'my book bears marks of the turbulence of the last two months.' Many signs of hasty and imperfect workmanship there are. The introduction of Herbert's mistress is a serious æsthetic blunder. Lady Annabel Herbert in the earlier portion of the book is a stately though severe, if not awe-inspiring, figure; but her behaviour towards the end is hardly consistent with her character, and her reconciliation with Herbert strikes us as somewhat forced. Probably also the conditions under which the book was written supply the best explanation of a curious plagiarism from Macaulay which has often been discussed. The well-known passage in the essay on Moore's *Life of Byron* beginning 'We know no spectacle so ridiculous as the British public in one of its periodical fits of morality' is appropriated bodily with no better acknowledgment in the original text of the novel than the introductory phrase, 'It has been well observed'; though in subsequent editions to fence in the borrowed passage the words 'These observations of a celebrated writer' are introduced into the sentence with which the narrative is resumed.

Venetia had not the popular success of *Henrietta Temple*, though it pleased the critics more. Even the *Athenæum* hailed it as exhibiting 'much less of affectation and disordered ardour' than that 'incoherent love-story'; and its appearance was made the occasion for an article in the *Edinburgh Review*[2] which was written in no captious spirit, but endeavoured, though not sparing Disraeli's faults, to do justice to his merits as a novelist. The reviewer, however, upbraided him

1 Bk. I. ch. 4. 2 For Oct., 1837.

severely for 'intruding into the domestic life of a poet and his relations and extracting the materials of fiction out of events so recent and so melancholy'; and the introduction of Lady Caroline Lamb was especially condemned both then and later. Though Lady Caroline Lamb had been in the grave many years, her husband was still alive and—a fact that is not irrelevant—the Whig Prime Minister; but it may probably have been some feeling of the delicacy of the experiment that prompted Disraeli to throw the whole story back by nearly a generation. If the story was to be told at all, it has been told with admirable tact; 'a masterpiece of tact' is the judgment of an eminent critic [1] on the novel as a whole.

[1] Dr. Brandes.

CHAPTER XVI.

PARLIAMENT AT LAST

1837.

An entry in the Mutilated Diary resumes the narrative.

Returned to London on the first of May; entered much into society: invited by Lord Francis Egerton[1] personally to a magnificent entertainment, which I attended—Sir J. Tyrrell, Q. Dick, Lord Walpole, Exmouth, Fector, Grimston. Distinguished myself very much in the election of Burdett for Westminster; the success mainly attributable to myself: proposed and organized the youth of the Carlton, including all the nobility, fashion, and influence of our party to canvass ——Lord Forester and his brother, Codrington, H. Baring, Pigot, Sir H. Campbell, &c., &c.

To Sarah Disraeli.

May, 1837.

Town is quite full, and the only thing talked of is the Westminster election. I am on Burdett's committee and obliged to canvass. My district, which is Bolton Street, Clarges, &c., is all right, though, curious enough, Leader[2] is one of my list.

P. is the most wonderful person in the world. He lives in one of the most expensive houses in Portland Place, many servants in livery, a handsome wife ornately dressed, children in fancy dresses tumbling on ottomans, one swearing he is a Tory, the other a Radical, &c. An expenditure not under £5,000 per annum, and no one is the least aware of his

[1] Second son of the 1st Duke of Sutherland, and himself subsequently 1st Earl of Ellesmere.

[2] Burdett's opponent.

means. The party was very stupid. A few Carlton men, mixed up with some Marylebone and Bloomsbury slip-slop; but I like to go to a house for the first time.

I suppose the King has really rallied, as I met Tom Young, who affected that he had never even been in danger. I met Sir J. Hanmer, the youthful M.P. for Shrewsbury, and his pretty wife, and was glad to make his acquaintance, for he is full of talent and literature, and so enthusiastic an admirer of mine that he had absolutely read the *Revolutionary Epick*.

The party at Bridgewater House last night turned out to be a grand concert, and the best assembly that has been given this season. There were about one thousand persons, and the suite of apartments, including the picture gallery, all thrown open and illuminated, and I enjoyed myself excessively.[1]

Among Disraeli's papers there is an account [2] of Burdett which is interesting, if for no other reason, because there was a certain analogy between Burdett's political vicissitudes and his own; both of them having been Radicals and Reformers while Toryism was unregenerate; both becoming Tories when Toryism had recovered its vitality.

Sir Francis Burdett was a very high-bred man, very tall, and with a distinguished countenance. He was a complete Norman. As an orator, in his best days, he had no equal. It was all grace and music; never was a more commanding manner or a finer voice. The range of his subjects was limited, referring mainly to the character of the constitution; the rights and grievances of the people, &c., &c.; but of these he was master. His declamation was fiery and thrilling, but always natural. He was one of the most natural speakers I recollect; never betrayed into bombast, either in matter or manner. He had considerable power of sarcasm, and his hits always told. His quotations were, I think, generally from Shakespeare.

In politics he was a Jacobite. He was sprung from a Jacobite family, and entered life with the hereditary opinions of his class. He was against the Boromongers, that is to say, the new capitalist classes which William the Third and the House of Hanover had introduced: he was for annual Parliaments and universal suffrage, as Sir William Wyndham and Sir

[1] *Letters*, p. 112.

[2] Written about 1863.

John Hinde Cotton had been before him, in order to curb and control these classes. The latter (Sir J. Cotton) also was for the ballot. It so happened, that the French Revolution was coincident with Burdett's appearance in public life, and so, in the confusion of circumstances it turned out that he was looked upon as a Jacobin, when in reality he was a Jacobite. The English public, which is particularly ignorant of history, joined in the taunts of his inconsistency when, late in life, the Boromongers having been got rid of, Burdett turned out to be what he started, a high aristocratic English politician.

He was extremely vain, but not offensively so; his high breeding prevented that: and under all circumstances, he was distinguished by simplicity. I think he was the greatest gentleman I ever knew. For many years after he entered Parliament he rode up to Westminster from his seat in Wiltshire on horseback. The country, especially in that part of England, was then very open, and abounded in downs and commons. In one of his best speeches in Parliament (then reformed, and full of quiet middle-class people) on the expenses of elections, he greatly denounced them, and observed that he had a right to give an opinion on the subject, as there was a period in his life when Parliamentary contests had reduced him to a state of absolute beggary. There was a murmur of admiring incredulity. 'I assure you, Sir,' he continued, 'I am indulging in no exaggeration. Honorable gentlemen may not believe it, but I can assure them there was a time when Lady Burdett had only one pair of horses to her carriage.' The effect of this remark in one of the early reformed Parliaments, full of retired tradesmen, many of whom had amassed wealth, but had never plucked up courage to keep a carriage, may be conceived. It was the most patrician definition of poverty ever made.

He was very good-natured, especially to young members, but rather absent and thoughtless in domestic arrangements. He would say to me (1838 and so on) 'Will you take your mutton with me to-day? We are quite alone. Come in boots. You won't be wanted for an hour.' And I often went. He lived in St. James's Place. His dinners were most agreeable. Lady Burdett, a clever woman, but a great invalid, appeared after dinner: and there were several agreeable daughters. One day he asked me to take mutton, and so on, and, when I arrived in frock, I was ushered into illumined saloons, full of grand guests in full *tenue*!

When he was taunted at the beginning of 1837 (I think) with changing his opinions, he gallantly resigned the seat for

Westminster, and declared himself at the same time a candidate for the vacancy. It was a crisis in the Conservative cause, and it was generally felt on both sides that his fate would decide the future course of politics. The Tories worked hard. The Carlton Club mapped the City into districts and divided these among the ardent youth of the party. May Fair fell to me and Sir Robert Pigot, and very great fun we had. There was one street in our district entirely filled with cooks, chiefly foreigners. Ten years afterwards, writing *Tancred*, I availed myself of the experience then obtained, and it formed my first chapter. Burdett won his election: and no one ever enjoyed a triumph more. Perhaps he found the contest still more exciting. He was 'at home' every evening during it, in his dining room, and all might come who cared. There he delivered every evening one of his constitutional harangues, or invectives, against O'Connell, then in the Liberal ascendant. They were very fiery and created great enthusiasm when he denounced the manner of the famous agitator 'half bully, and half blarney.'[1]

To Sarah Disraeli.

June 19, 1837.

There was an agreeable party at Madame Montalembert's; but whether la Comtesse had taken an extra glass of champagne, or what might be the cause, she lionised me so dreadfully that I was actually forced to run for my life. She even produced *Venetia* and was going to read a passage out loud, when I seized my hat and rushed downstairs, leaving the graceful society of Lady Egerton, much to my vexation. . . .

I have just seen a very interesting letter from Munster dated 11 last night. The King dies like an old lion. He said yesterday to his physicians, 'Only let me live through this glorious day!' This suggested to Munster to bring the tricolor flag which had just arrived from the Duke of Wellington, and show it to the King. William IV. said, 'Right, right,' and afterwards, 'Unfurl it and let me feel it,' then he pressed the eagle and said, 'Glorious day.' This may be depended on. He still lives.

D.[2]

The King died in the course of the night, and Queen Victoria began that long reign in which Disraeli himself

[1] Burdett reappears, with many of the features of this sketch reproduced, as Sir Fraunceys Scrope in *Endymion*, ch. 76.

[2] *Letters*, p. 113.

was to be so conspicuous a figure. By eleven o'clock the following morning her first council was assembled.

I accompanied Lord Lyndhurst to Kensington Palace. when, on the accession of the Queen, the peers and privy councillors and chief personages of the realm pledged their fealty to their new Sovereign. He was greatly affected by the unusual scene: a youthful maiden receiving the homage of her subjects, most of them illustrious, in a palace in a garden, and all with a sweet and natural dignity. He gave me, as we drove home, an animated picture of what had occurred in the presence chamber, marked by all that penetrating observation, and happy terseness of description, which distinguished him. Eight years afterwards, with my memory still under the influence of his effective narrative, I reproduced the scene in *Sybil*, and I feel sure it may be referred to for its historical accuracy.[1]

Throughout the session the Whig Government had been tottering to its fall, but a political struggle was now precipitated, as in those days the death of the Sovereign rendered a dissolution necessary.

To Sarah Disraeli.

CARLTON CLUB.

[*June* 20.]

DEAREST,

I write in the midst of three or four hundred persons and in a scene of great excitement.

The battle now approaches; what will be my fate I pretend not to foresee. They tell me Ashburton is safe and it has been offered me, but I have refused it, as I should have had to leave town to-night. I suppose in the course of two or three days I shall be able to speak more definitely.

Lord Lyndhurst attended the Privy Council at Kensington and kissed the young Queen's hand, which all agreed was remarkably sweet and soft. She read her address well and was perfectly composed though alone in the council chamber and attended by no women.

As yet there are not even rumours; all is tumult and like a camp.

Ever,

D.

[1] General Preface to the Novels, 1870.

In a speech in the course of the election campaign which followed, Disraeli declared that no one probably during the few preceding months had received more requisitions to become a candidate for Parliament than himself. Not only was Ashburton offered, but proposals came from Derby, Chichester, and Dartmouth, and also from his former friends in Marylebone and Taunton. It was all but arranged that he should stand for Barnstaple; but eventually an opening presented itself that proved more attractive than any of the others. The borough of Maidstone, then with two members, had been represented in the expiring Parliament by a Conservative and a Liberal, the Conservative being Wyndham Lewis, husband of the 'pretty little flirt and rattle' whom Disraeli had met at Bulwer's five years before. It was at first the intention of the local Conservatives to nominate Lewis only, but when they had completed the first day's canvass they found their position so much stronger than they had supposed that they despatched a deputation to the Carlton Club in quest of a second candidate, and the choice fell upon Disraeli.

To Sarah Disraeli.

Friday. [*June* 30.]

The clouds have at length dispelled, and my prospects seem as bright as the day. At six o'clock this evening I start for Maidstone with Wyndham Lewis, and I suppose by Wednesday I shall have completed my canvass. I doubt whether there will be a contest.[1]

His address to the electors of Maidstone is worth preserving as a model of vigour in thought and terseness in expression.

I solicit your suffrages as an uncompromising adherent of that ancient constitution which once was the boast of our fathers, and is still the blessing of their children. I wish to see the Crown enjoy its prerogative, both Houses of Parliament their equal privileges, and the great body of the nation

[1] *Letters*, p. 114.

that unrivalled and hereditary freedom which has been the noble consequence of our finely-balanced scheme of legislative power. Convinced that the reformed religion as by law established in this country is, at the same time, the best guarantee for religious toleration and orthodox purity, I feel it my duty to uphold the rights of our national Church, that illustrious institution to which we are not less indebted for our civil than for our spiritual liberties. Resident in an agricultural county, and deeply interested in the land, I will on all occasions watch with vigilant solicitude over the fortunes of the British farmer, because I sincerely believe that his welfare is the surest and most permanent basis of general prosperity.

To Sarah Disraeli.

MAIDSTONE,
Tuesday. [*July* 4.]

Last night there was a full meeting, and I think I made the best speech I ever made yet—as well maintained as the Aylesbury one, and more than an hour in length ; so to-day I canvassed on *my own* influence. I do not see how we can be defeated, but I have said little about the affair generally, as when one feels assured it is best to be quiet.[1]

Of the speech on this occasion Wyndham Lewis wrote to his wife, 'Disraeli was on his legs more than an hour : he is a splendid orator and astonished the people.' In the matter of political doctrine the speech followed the lines that have become so familiar to us, and with the exception of an impassioned attack on that 'flagitious statute,' the new Poor Law, there is nothing in it now that calls for attention. The new Poor Law had been passed by the Whigs in 1834 with the full approval of Peel and Wellington, but though it corrected flagrant abuses, its harshness made it unpopular, and the cruelties that attended its enforcement had for some time been denounced daily in the columns of *The Times* and by John Walter, the chief proprietor of *The Times*, from his place in the House of Commons.

It is not to elicit an electioneering cheer [said Disraeli], it is not to gain a single vote that I tell you I have long since

[1] *Ibid.*, p. 115.

registered myself among the sternest opponents of that measure. I can appeal to a career which, though private, is not altogether obscure, in proof of my sincerity and consistency. I have the proud consolation to know that, with the exception of the honorable member for Berkshire [John Walter], I was the first county magistrate who raised his voice against that odious Bill. I had the honor of calling the first meeting in my own county against it, and it was this right hand inscribed one of the first petitions to both Houses of Parliament. I hope, therefore, my sincerity cannot for a moment be doubted. That Bill bears fearful tidings for the poor. Its primary object is founded not only on a political blunder, but a moral error—it went on the principle that relief to the poor is a *charity*. I maintain that it is a *right*! . . . I would not have the poor man deprived of the small consolation of witnessing the games of his grandchildren—I would not deny him the mournful satisfaction of viewing the tombs of his forefathers. One of our poets has beautifully said—'Sweet is the music of the Sabbath bells,' but of this music the Whigs have deprived the poor and the aged. For him the Sabbath bells sound no more. Immured in a prison, no spiritual consolation can he derive in the hallowed temple of his ancestors; but, at length, broken-hearted, he quits a world with which he is disgusted. To sum up my feelings in a sentence—I consider that this Act has disgraced the country more than any other upon record. Both a moral crime and a political blunder, it announces to the world that in England poverty is a crime.

'I was glad,' he remarks to Pyne in praying him to guard against the descent of writs during the election, 'to find the Sheriff's officer here among my staunch supporters: I suppose gratitude.' He was sanguine from the first, and when the Liberal candidate, Wyndham Lewis's colleague in the late Parliament, retired from the contest it looked for a moment as if he would be returned unopposed.

To Sarah Disraeli.

July 22.

The accounts from Maidstone continue as favorable as ever. Several of Robarts' supporters have come over to me since his secession. I believe I am the only *new* candidate of our side who has not an opposition. . . . So much for the 'maddest of all mad acts,' my uncle G.'s[1] prescience, and B.E.L.'s unrivalled powers of encouragement! The nomination day is fixed for the 25th.[2]

On the 25th, however, Colonel Perronet Thompson, editor of the *Westminster Review*, and a well-known figure among the Radicals of the day, more adventurous than Robarts, allowed himself to be nominated. 'I hope,' said his proposer when he found occasion to mention Disraeli, 'that I pronounce his name aright.' 'Colonel Perronet Thompson,' retorted Disraeli in the opening sentences of his speech, 'I hope, as Mr. Ellis said, that I pronounce his name aright.' Disraeli's ready wit and eloquence had made him a favourite with his side, though, as his popularity grew, the animosity of his opponents increased in like proportion. On this occasion a hostile paper tells us, 'the Blues opened the floodgates of their recriminating eloquence on the degraded Disraeli, who winced beneath the cries of "Old clothes!" "Shylock!" and various other complimentary epithets for nearly an hour.' Such are the amenities of electioneering.

To Sarah Disraeli.

MAIDSTONE,
July 27, 1837. 11 o'clock.

DEAREST,

Lewis 707
Disraeli 616
Colonel Thompson 412

The constituency nearly exhausted.

In haste, DIZZY.[2]

When the final figures were declared they were not far different: he had reached the goal at last.

[1] George Basevi, a brother of Disraeli's mother. Another Miss Basevi, their sister, had married a Mr. Lindo, and 'B.E.L.' was her son, and therefore Disraeli's cousin.

[2] *Letters*, p. 115. It is about this time that the familiar appellation which is here used as signature, and which was subsequently to become so famous, begins to make its appearance.

Mrs. Wyndham Lewis to Major Viney Evans.[1]

July 29, 1837.

Mark what I say—mark what I prophesy: Mr. Disraeli will in a very few years be one of the greatest men of his day. His great talents, backed by his friends Lord Lyndhurst and Lord Chandos, with Wyndham's power to keep him in Parliament, will insure his success. They call him my Parliamentary *protégé*.

To Mrs. Wyndham Lewis.

BRADENHAM, SUNDAY.
[*July* 30, 1837.]

MY DEAR MRS. WYNDHAM,

You may conceive my astonishment yesterday on entering the County of Bucks to find the walls of every town plastered over with pink (my colour at Wycombe) placards 'Maidstone Election; State of the Poll; Lewis and Disraeli!' &c., &c. It was curious to meet our united names thus unexpectedly, and as I had been dozing in the postchaise, I really thought, on waking, that I had been dreaming all the while of home and Buckinghamshire, and that I was still by the waters of the Medway and among the men of Kent. All doubt, however, was dispelled on my arrival at Wycombe, where I found that on the previous day there had been a great festival spontaneously and suddenly celebrated by my neighbours in honour of our victory. Friday was market day at Wycombe, which is the greatest corn market in England, and the news arrived there about noon. Immediately all the bells were set a-ringing, a subscription made at the market tables to illuminate the town in the evening, and the band called out, parading long after midnight. At Aylesbury, twelve miles further on, the news was known earlier, and was announced from the hustings by Lord Chandos, whereupon the multitude gave three times three for Lewis and Disraeli, and cards were printed by Praed's committee, circulating the intelligence. I thought all this would amuse you, and indeed I was rather gratified by finding that those among whom I lived, and who, after all, in this world, must know me best, felt such genuine satisfaction in my success.

We all here wish very much that Mr. Wyndham and yourself would come and pay us a visit among our beechen groves. We have nothing to offer you but simple pleasures, a sylvan scene and an affectionate hearth. I hope to get to

[1] Her brother.

town on Tuesday evening after polling. I am rather nervous about our county election ; our third man lost the show of hands on Saturday, which they are pleased to say would not have occurred had I spoken. I suppose my colleague is in Glamorganshire. My kind regards are his and yours.

DIS.

To Sarah Disraeli.

[*Aug.* 5.]

DEAREST,

The Government talks of breaking up! Lord Melbourne really said that he could not carry on the thing with 'Irish boroughs against English counties.' The Whigs now confess that they are beaten to pieces. . .

I dined with Munster, Strangford, Shaftesbury, Exmouth, and Loftus at the Carlton the day that Hume was thrown out. It is a fact that the little Queen clapped her hands when she was told that Hume was out. Yesterday I dined at the W. L.'s. The Clarendons, Prince and Princess Poniatowski, Mrs. C. Gore, Lady Floyd; Mrs. Dawson, Parnther, Beauclerk, and myself; a fine dinner well cooked and gorgeous service; very friendly, more friendly every day; certainly W. L. is one of the oddest men that ever lived, but I like him very much.

What do you think of Lyndhurst's marriage? I had long heard, but never credited it. . . . I am very well and begin to enjoy my new career. I find that it makes a sensible difference in the opinion of one's friends; I can scarcely keep my countenance.

I received my father's letter, for which I send my love, and to all.

DIS.[1]

[*Aug.* 12.]

DEAREST,

I did not see the *Herald*[2]; but I find my advent canvassed in many papers; among them the *Spectator*, who puts Holmes, Sugden, and myself as men whom the Whigs would anxiously have kept out; but says they have no doubt I fancy I shall be the terror of the Treasury bench, but they shall be 'agreeably disappointed if I turn out anything better than a

[1] Brit. Mus. Addit. MSS.

[2] His sister had written :—'A few days back the *Morning Herald* said something of two men being returned to this Parliament of whom great things were expected. Who is the second?'

buffoon.' This must come from Col. Thompson & Co., who did not particularly relish my nomination jokes. Clear your head of all nonsense about scrutinies, petitions, &c., &c. There is not a safer seat in England than mine. They have not a shadow to work upon. . . .

I franked your letter. . . .

From the prospects of the undecided elections there is no doubt there must be 318 Tories in the House . . . and I shall be rather surprised if we don't pick up a few more. In short, the Government is done, and I doubt whether they will meet Parliament. . . . The Whigs are more than low-spirited; they are *in extremis*; they give the affair up. Peel says he can carry on the Government with the present Parliament, not the slightest doubt, so I hope we are sitting for seven years. What fun! And how lucky after all I should esteem myself!

My love to all,

D.

To Mrs. Bulwer Lytton.

[*Undated.*]

It was odd that my electioneering struggle should terminate in being M.P. for Maidstone. As I am already a believer in destiny, it required not this strange occurrence, and doubly strange from the manner in which it took place, to confirm me in my Oriental creed. . . . We are the children of the gods, and are never more the slaves of circumstances than when we deem ourselves their masters. What may next happen in the dazzling farce of life the Fates only know.[1]

To Mrs. Wyndham Lewis.

BRADENHAM,
Sept. 1, 1837.

After you went, everything and everybody were most dull and *triste*. The truth is the visit was too short. Yesterday I 'executed justice and maintained truth' at West Wycombe, where they kept me so late that I missed the post. Here everything remains the same, save that it is now the memorable first of September and the boys are out shooting.

[1] From a letter in Mr. Alfred Morrison's collection.

They went out at six this morning and have not yet made their reappearance.

We must ask you for news: you cannot expect it from this sylvan solitude. Not an incident ever occurs here; one day is as like another as fruit on a tree. The weather has been more favorable, which made us all still more deplore the absence of our recent guests.

All unite here in love and affection and compliments to you and Wyndham: I send my quota.

DIS.

Mrs. Wyndham Lewis to Major Evans.

Sept. 8, 1837.

I have been paying a visit to Mr. Disraeli's family. They reside near High Wycombe—a large family house, most of the rooms 30 and 40 feet long, and plenty of servants, horses, dogs, and a library full of the rarest books. But how shall I describe his father; the most lovable, perfect old gentleman I ever met with? A sort of modern Dominie Sampson—and his manners are so high-bred and natural. Miss Disraeli is handsome and talented, and two brothers. Our political pet, the eldest, commonly called Dizzy, you will see a great deal of; you know Wyndham brought him in for Maidstone with himself.

To Sarah Disraeli.

WOOLBEDING.
[*Oct.* 24 (?), 1837.]

MY DEAREST,

I arrived here yesterday at 3 o'clock, having travelled through a fine country, Esher, Guildford, Godalming, until leaving at that point the high road, I entered a region of picturesque and sylvan beauty I have never seen equalled, in the midst of which, after a hilly drive of 20 miles, I found Woolbeding on the banks of the Rother. This is a house rather old-fashioned than antiquated, but very convenient and compact, covered with ivy, with the Church joining it in the same green garb, and a very fine conservatory. The grounds and gardens are as remarkable for their beautiful forms and rich shrubs as you can conceive, with the river winding all about. The place belongs to Lord Robert Spencer's heirs, who are doubtful, and is only used by Maxse[1]

[1] Mr. James Maxse, his host. Lady Caroline Maxse, his hostess, was a daughter of the 5th Earl of Berkeley.

as a shooting box. His principal residence is in the West of England and he only lives here in the sporting season. . . .

It rains to-day without ceasing. Here are at present nothing but shooting dandies ; Lord Rokeby, Henry Berkeley, and Whyte Melville. . . . We dine at half past six and there is a constant breakfast—the only rule, as Maxse says, being that it is expected that his guests will endeavour to breakfast before he dines : there is no end of horses, guns, and dogs and a very large company of London servants. All you have to do is to give your orders without delicacy. Lady Caroline is amiable, and has four beautiful and interesting children, to whom she is devoted. . . .

I see by the *Globe* of last night that the forthcoming *Edinburgh* has an article on 'Disraeli's Novels'—I suppose to assist my parliamentary *début*. Very kind of the Whigs. I am, however, perfectly callous.

I will write when there is matter for a letter ; but if it rains I doubt whether there will be. At any rate I shall not stay here longer than I can help. In the course of my travelling down I passed many famous places, Ockham (Lord King's), Loseley House, and Sutton Place, but the latter was so embosomed in trees I could not distinguish it : all this on the high road.

Your affectionate,

D.[1]

WOOLBEDING,

[*Oct.* 26 (?).]

MY DEAREST,

. . . . .

Yesterday Lady Caroline drove me to Cowdray, Mr. Poyntz's, in one of the most brilliant equipages I ever witnessed. Her poneys, for such they are styled though they are 15 hands high, are thoroughbred, and worthy of George the Fourth, as well as her carriage, which is of cane on a frame of a peculiarly brilliant and rich green ; she has two outriders, and the moment there is the slightest elevation the poneys break into a gallop of their own accord to the fear and astonishment of all passengers. She is, however, a good whip and knows her cattle and country. . . . .

Cowdray is one of the most magnificent demesnes in England. Poyntz has about 25,000 acres. The old Tudor Hall which you approach from Midhurst by an avenue was

[1] Brit. Mus. Addit. MSS.

burnt down many years ago and is now only a picturesque ruin; but in the most favored spot of the park, surrounded by the most poetic timber in the world, with a fine view of the South Downs through their tall stems, is the modern residence, an irregular cluster of great extent and presenting no lack of tall chimneys built at different times and added as occasion prompted. . . . .

I doubt whether I shall stay here beyond Saturday; but I find it difficult to get away, being very popular with the women, who are charmed I do not shoot. I like my friends; they are very good, warm-hearted people indeed. I am going to Petersfield to see the Jolliffes to-day. . . . .

Your affectionate,

D.[1]

To Mrs. Wyndham Lewis.

WOOLBEDING, MIDHURST,
Oct. 29.

Your letter of the 18th did not reach me until yesterday, as I have been rambling about. I date this from the Maxses, where I have been staying three or four days and which I leave to-morrow. The house is full of shooting dandies, not much in my way. Until the last fortnight, I have been in Bucks, but on the wing. I stayed a week at Lord Chandos' at Wotton, a few days with Sir Gore Ouseley, and a few days at Newport Pagnell in the extreme north of the county, where we had a great Conservative dinner. We have indeed had a brisk campaign in this respect in our county, and I am quite wearied with after-dinner spouting. I have heard nothing directly from Maidstone, but indirectly I am sorry to say I learnt yesterday that they are still very eager about their dinner, which they intend shall take place in November, though I should think this were impossible. Tell my colleague he must be in his place by the 15th. There is a pressing circular out. What is to happen no one knows, but there is a very active whip. Lord John had the impudence to write to Peel, enquiring whether there would be a division on the Speakership; Sir Robert gave him a caustic reply and now the Whigs protest there will certainly be a struggle, though I doubt it myself. My health is excellent. . . .

An extraordinary season is expected; at present the only topic of interest is the Queen's visit to the City, and all the triumphal arches through which she is to pass before she

[1] Brit. Mus. Addit. MSS.

tastes the orthodox turtle cooked in the sound of Bow Bells; as there are to be no toasts given the affair must be very dull. The Duke of Wellington dines there, and I hope Sir Robert Peel. The Queen and Lord Melbourne are having their portraits taken by Hayter at the same time and under the same roof. Melbourne lives only at Brighton, the other Ministers work, except Palmerston, who is Leporello to our Don Juan.

My kind regards to Wyndham.

D.

The last entry in the Mutilated Diary carries us on to the eve of the meeting of Parliament.

BRADENHAM,
Nov. 12, 1837.

To-morrow I leave Bradenham to take my seat in Parliament, *i.e.*, on the 15th. I have passed these three months since my election chiefly in Bucks, and in a run of desultory political reading, though chiefly on Ireland. Attended several political dinners in my County, to which I limit myself: spoke often and well—at Newport Pagnell, where there was great enthusiasm, and Great Marlow. After the Quarter Sessions, the 17th of October, went to Woolbeding, Lady Caroline Maxse's, where I passed a week. Returned to Bradenham that I might pass ten quiet days.

My health wonderfully renovated: were it not for the anxiety the state of my affairs occasionally causes me I should laugh at illness. My life for the past year has been very temperate; my nervous system consequently much stronger. I am now as one leaving a secure haven for an unknown sea. What will the next twelve months produce?

APPENDIX A.

TITA.

This interesting personage, one of the many links between Byron and Disraeli, was a Venetian whose full name was Giovanni Battista Falcieri, and who, entering Byron's service as gondolier, had become his devoted personal servant and was with him at Missolonghi when he died. He is introduced in *Don Juan* (II. 56),

> 'Battista, though' (a name call'd shortly Tita),
> 'Was lost by getting at some aqua-vita,'

and is mentioned by Shelley in a letter written from Ravenna, Aug. 15, 1821:—'Tita, the Venetian, is here, and operates as my valet—a fine fellow with a prodigious black beard who has stabbed two or three people, and is the most good-natured looking fellow I ever saw.'[1] After Byron's death Tita fought for the Greek cause at the head of a regiment of Albanians; but at the close of the war he fell into distress, and in this condition was picked up by Clay at Malta in the summer of 1830, and accompanied Clay and Disraeli in their subsequent wanderings in the Levant. On their return to England, when Clay had no further occasion for Tita's services, Disraeli sent him down to Bradenham, where at first he startled the inhabitants of the quiet Buckinghamshire village by his dress, appearance, and habits, and where he remained a privileged favourite till Isaac D'Israeli's death in 1848. The rest of the story can

[1] Moore's *Life of Byron*, III., p. 237.

be given in the words in which Disraeli himself told it to Sir Philip Rose.

One of the chief anxieties of my sister and myself was, what was to be done with Tita. Our embarrassment was increased by the announcement of his marriage to 'Hughes,' my mother's former maid, who remained on as housekeeper—an event which we suspected had taken place some years previously. It was dreadful to think that a man who had been in Byron's service, and soothed his last moments, who had been the faithful attendant and almost the companion and friend of my father, for so many years, who had actually died in his arms, should end his days in the usual refuge for domestic servants, by keeping a public-house, or a greengrocer's shop; but, happily, just at that moment I accidentally met Sir John Cam Hobhouse, in a country house, and asked him if he remembered Tita in Byron's service. He replied, 'Perfectly.' Then I said, 'He now wants a friend, and he has an hereditary claim on you as Byron's executor.' I told him his subsequent history and my anxiety to provide for him, and asked him for an appointment as messenger in some department of the Government. Hobhouse gave me little hope at the time, but, within a week of our meeting, I received a letter that a messengership at the Board of Control had fallen vacant, to which he should be happy to appoint Tita, and so we landed him. Another crisis occurred when the Board of Control was abolished, and Tita was liable to be dismissed, on a small pension; but fortunately we were then in power, and Stanley was head of the India Office, to whom I related Tita's history, and appealed to him to look after his interests. The result was that Tita was appointed chief messenger at the new India Office, then temporarily located in Victoria St., but without the liability of having to carry messages.

Tita died in 1874 at the age of 76; and the following letter well illustrates Disraeli's habit of pertinacious kindness for those whom he had once admitted to his friendship or taken under his protection:—

To Queen Victoria.

10, DOWNING STREET, WHITEHALL,
Jan. 13, 1875.

Mr. Disraeli with his humble duty to your Majesty. He earnestly recommends to your Majesty, for a pension of £50,

Sarah Falcieri, the widow, after thirty years of much devotion, of Giovanni Battista Falcieri, the faithful servant of Lord Byron.

In Mr. Disraeli's youth, 45 years ago, Falcieri travelled with him for two years, in Egypt, Syria, and other parts of the East : a most faithful and gifted man. Then he served your Majesty, as a Messenger in the India Office ; and retired pensioned and universally beloved. His widow is an Englishwoman.

APPENDIX B.

LORD LYNDHURST'S RECOLLECTIONS.

1826-1832.

The accounts of the sessions of 1835 and 1836 on pp. 301, 327, are taken from a memorandum headed 'Summary of Events—mainly Lord Lyndhurst's career from 1826 to 1836; written at Bradenham, Sept. 17, 1836,' and inscribed with the motto, 'Those who anticipate their century are persecuted when they live and pilfered when they are dead!'[1] The earlier portion of the memorandum, though it has no connexion with Disraeli's own political career, is interesting as a contribution to Lyndhurst's biography and perhaps to the history of the time:—

Copley [1826] at Duke of Montrose's, which he joined from the circuit: very dull: intended to go abroad, but detained a week by waiting for remittance from London. On his way up found at Manchester a communication from the Minister offering him the Mastership of the Rolls. Had he been abroad perhaps it would not have been offered. Lord Gifford had died suddenly, killed by his wife: a cold and fever—wished not to travel to Dover; she insisted upon it, and he died from inflammation on his arrival.

Canning, aware of the impending fate of Liverpool, had long been maturing a party of his own; had sounded Copley. Canning aware that the Duke of Wn. meditated the premiership. There had long been two parties in the Cabinet, Canning's and Wellington's; but Lord Liverpool supported Canning. A breeze in the H. of C. between Canning and Copley, a little before the death of Liverpool, on

[1] *Vivian Grey*, Bk. VI. ch. 4; 'He who anticipates his century is generally persecuted when living and is always pilfered when dead.'

the Catholic question. Canning irritated by Copley's rechauffing in a speech Phillpotts' (afterwards Bishop of Exeter) pamphlet. When Canning wrote to him to offer the great seal added at the end 'Phillpotts *non obstante*.' Canning wished to get Brougham out of the H. of C., and offered him the Chief Barony of the Exchequer. B. took time to consider, and was to report to the Lord Chancellor : declined to Lyndhurst, saying that he had consulted his brother (the one who died), who recommended him not to leave the H of C.

Lyndhurst, not very sanguine as to the success of the Canning Cabinet ; but the great seal and a peerage ! 'Who would refuse it ? I thought I would not baulk fortune, and that a seat in the H. of L. would always keep me a career.' Canning had resolved not only not to press the Catholic Question, but had promised the King that he would prevent it being carried in the Commons. Difficulty in forming a Cabinet unrivalled. Now the difficulty is to satisfy so many, then to find Ministers. The seals of the Home Office actually begging, as Canning wanted a Protestant Secretary. At last Sturges Bourne took them out of mere friendship. Canning elated at obtaining the adhesion of Lansdowne : Holland very eager to take office.

Nothing annoyed Canning more than the denunciation of Lord Grey. Said to Lyndhurst, 'I feel I must remain in the Commons, but I am half tempted to ask for a peerage merely to let fly at him.' Nothing could exceed the virulence of the party of defection. There was a dinner, I think, at Bathurst's. It had been an invitation of a month. The Copleys had been asked before the break-up. L. hesitated about going, but thought it was shabby and spiritless to decline. Went and sat next to Mrs. Arbuthnot : nothing could be more bitter. The only person who was civil and good-humoured was old Eldon. Lady L. sat next to him.

Canning had been long ailing. Eat voraciously. There was a Cabinet dinner at Lord L.'s at Wimbledon. A beautiful day with a clear blue sky, but a cutting easterly wind. Canning rode down. They were tempted by the fine weather to hold the Cabinet in the garden. Soon Canning complained of the cold and shivered. Went in to dinner, but even the dinner, though he eat voraciously, did not remove it. Went home, was taken ill, and died very shortly.

Nothing can give an idea of the scene under Goderich. No order at the Cabinet. A most ludicrous scene. Nothing ever done. Anglesea sitting with a napkin round his head from the tic, but the only one who seemed to exert himself. As they went home L. said to a colleague, 'This can never last.' In a few days Goderich sent for L. to Downing Street—walking up and down the room in great agitation, wringing his hands, and even shedding tears. Told L. that he must resign. L. tried to reason with him, but no avail. Resigned the next day. Geo. IV. sent for L. and asked what he was to do. L. said there was only one thing. 'Send for the Duke of Wellington.'

Knighton had arranged the Canning Cabinet, and was C.'s friend. That appointment had been long maturing—much intrigue. Knighton very able—the real king of this country—did everything—wrote all the King's letters. When a weak or indolent person in a high situation once admits the assistance of an inferior, soon becomes a slave. What is occasional becomes a habit. The Wellington Cabinet broke up on the Catholic question, and were out for four and twenty hours. The King was firm. The Duke, Peel, L., &c., went down to Windsor and resigned the seals. The King kissed each of them. George IV. was much distressed—acted in spite of Knighton. They went back to London and dined at Bathurst's, and were in high spirits at being free of office. In the middle of the night letters came to the Duke and Lynd. giving up. Knighton had worked upon his distress after their departure.

The Catholic Bill.—Lord Grey wanted office, and it was known that he would have taken the viceroyalty of Ireland (*e.g.*). Once the intention of the Duke to admit the Grey party. Took a sudden prejudice to Grey. Something happened on a coal committee. Told L. afterwards he had seen enough of Grey that morning to have nothing to do with him.

1832.—L.'s motion that enfranchisement should precede disfranchisement threw out the Whigs. It was the intention of the Tories to make the Speaker Premier. A weak man, but a stalking-horse. Peel would have been the virtual Premier. L. was deputed to make the offer. I must do Manners Sutton the justice to say that he at first burst out laughing and said, 'Why, it will be the Doctor over again.' But after some conversation he entertained the idea, seemed very complacent, and asked until to-morrow to decide. Thence L. went to offer Baring the Chancellorship of the Exchequer. He sent for Holmes out of the H. of C. and told him to find Baring and send him to him. Baring hesitated and asked for twelve hours. The next morning M. S. and

B. both refused in consequence of the vote of the H. of C. It was the original intention not to have given the House time to come to this vote, but to have prorogued it that morning. The hesitation of M. S. and B., and the unwillingness of Peel to act without their adhesion, lost everything. Had the Tories formed their Government it would have had the power of modifying the Reform Bill.

Among some of my papers will be found an account[1] of the secret political movements of 1834, and the formation of the Peel Government, in which preceding movements I was engaged. Four places in the Cabinet offered to Lord Stanley: one reason of his declining, unwillingness to act with the Duke of Wellington.

A few undated political notes, written in Disraeli's hand apparently about the same time, and relating to the same period, may conveniently be added.

Committee on the Reform Bill, Sir James Graham, Lord J. Russell, Lord Durham, Lord Duncannon, divided on the ballot, three to one in favour. The one was Duncannon: not known—Graham always insinuating it was himself. Had Lord Durham lived would have made a communication in the House of Lords, he was so indignant.

On leave to bring in the Reform Bill, Peel was anxious to meet it at once with a direct negative—it would have been thrown out by a very considerable majority, and the question would have been finished. Lord Granville Somerset was the person who dissuaded Peel. The consequence of the delay was the agitation of the country, &c.

Lord Duncannon twice offered O'Connell office—once under the Government of Lord Grey with the Premier's sanction. It was the Mastership of the Rolls.

[1] See pp. 262-265.

APPENDIX C.

D'ORSAY'S PORTRAIT OF LYNDHURST.

The portrait of Lyndhurst by D'Orsay, which is reproduced in this volume, has an interesting history. It some how came into the possession of Mr. Gladstone, and was by him despatched to Christie's with other pictures and his collection of china when he left Carlton House Terrace in 1875. Disraeli, hearing that the picture was to be sold, sent Mr. Montagu Corry, his private secretary, to buy it; but in the meantime it had occurred to Mr. Cecil Raikes to invite a number of Conservative members of Parliament to join him in securing it with a view to a presentation. The rival bidders reached the auction room about the same time, but only to find that the picture had been already sold at an extremely low price. By the offer of a very handsome profit, Mr. Corry tried to obtain it, but his offer was rejected; and eventually, after some amusing manœuvres by the purchaser, which are related in the *Life of Raikes*,[1] it was secured by Mr. Raikes for a sum nearly ten times as great as the original auction price. The picture was sent to the Prime Minister accompanied by the following letter:—

House of Commons Library,
July 2, 1875.

Dear Mr. Disraeli,

Knowing the friendship that united you both to the late Lord Lyndhurst and to Count D'Orsay, we beg to express the

[1] Pp. 100-102. The story as given there differs in some small particulars from the version here adopted, this latter being based on a contemporary memorandum written by Lord Barrington.

hope that you will accept from us the portrait of the one painted by the other as a mark of our sincere admiration and respect.

Barrington, Robert Bourke, Henry Chaplin, W. Romaine Callender, George Cubitt, W. Hart Dyke, Henry W. Eaton, Alex. Staveley Hill, Henry G. Lennox, John Manners, Charles H. Mills, Mahon, Henry W. Peek, Henry Cecil Raikes, Sandon, W. H. Smith, Newport, Fred. Stanley, Gerard Sturt, C. Sykes, Richard Wallace, Row. Winn, H. Drummond Wolff.

Disraeli addressed his acknowledgment to Lord Barrington.

2, WHITEHALL GARDENS,
July 12, 1875.

MY DEAR BARRINGTON,

Do me the favour of expressing to those members of the House of Commons who, with yourself, have made me an offering, which I infinitely value, the gratitude and the gratification which I feel at this graceful act of friendship, and my sense of the refined manner in which it has been conveyed.

Yours ever,

B. DISRAELI.

INDEX

END OF VOL. I.

Printed by JOHN PARKINSON BLAND, at The Times Office, Printing House Square, E.C.